Commentary on

Galatians
Ephesians
Philippians
Colossians

by

JAMES BURTON COFFMAN,
Minister of the Gospel
Houston, Texas

Volume VIII

A·C·U PRESS
Abilene, Texas

ISBN 0-915547-10-4

DEDICATION

Almost concurrently with the publication of this volume, the 50th Anniversary of the 1927 Class of Abilene Christian University was held; and on May 1, 1977, this author was privileged to give the Anniversary Address at Abilene, Texas. This volume is lovingly dedicated to those members who attended the reunion of the Class of 1927:

Henry T. Hogg, President, El Dorado, Arkansas
Verda Crabtree Banowsky, Houston, Texas
Mary Louise McCurley Belcher, Abilene, Texas
Alma Floy Richardson Bradley, Roswell, New Mexico
Nadine Martin Callan, Rotan, Texas
Gladys Agnew Carter, Rising Star, Texas
Odelle Chrane Cody, Austin, Texas
James Burton Coffman, Houston, Texas
Mable Fuchs Colby, Abilene, Texas
Madge Lewis Etter, Abilene, Texas
Joyce Elizabeth Woods Garrett, Brownwood, Texas
Esther Stagner Gibson, Abilene, Texas
Gorman Kenley, Abilene, Texas
Dr. Eugene Kraner, Lampasas, Texas
Clarence Nelson, Big Spring, Texas
Lorene Parker, Abilene, Texas
Eva Grace Ewing Porter, San Angelo, Texas
Clover Virginia Peters Shore, Lott, Texas
Bess Ellen Scruggs, Abilene, Texas
Guy Scruggs, Abilene, Texas
Rita Foster Stocking, Arlington, Virginia

PREFACE

With deep thanksgiving to Almighty God for his blessing, this eighth volume is released for publication; and grateful acknowledgment is also expressed for the encouraging reception which has been accorded the entire series. Most of the NT is included in these first eight volumes, leaving only four more projected volumes for the completion of the whole project. Prayers are solicited that the Father will provide the time and strength required for its completion.

CONTENTS

LIST OF ABBREVIATIONS

AV	—	Authorized Version
RV	—	Revised Version
RSV	—	Revised Standard Version
NEB	—	New English Bible
NT	—	New Testament
OT	—	Old Testament
ISBE	—	International Standard Bible Encyclopedia
H.S.	—	Holy Spirit
*CM	—	Commentary on Matthew
*CMK	—	Commentary on Mark
*CL	—	Commentary on Luke
*CJ	—	Commentary on John
*CA	—	Commentary on Acts
*CR	—	Commentary on Romans
*CC	—	Commentary on 1 & 2 Corinthians
*CH	—	Commentary on Hebrews
*CMY	—	Mystery of Redemption
*CD	—	Commentary on the Ten Commandments

*Books by James Burton Coffman

Galatians

INTRODUCTION

Concerning the authorship: That the apostle Paul is indeed the author of this epistle is a fact so certain and so universally accepted that little needs to be said about it. "No breath of suspicion as to the authorship, integrity or apostolical authority of the Epistle to the Galatians has reached us from ancient times."[1] The radical anti-Christian enemies of the NT, in the very few instances where any of them have dared to question it, have succeeded invariably only in achieving the discredit of themselves. The names of such offenders do not deserve to be repeated or remembered, any more than the names of the Judaizers against whom so large a part of Galatians was directed. Now and again in Christian history, some who have been called "great scholars" have attacked the word of God, but in such attacks they have inevitably forfeited any right to any such acclaim. Cunning, skillful and clever they may have been, but "scholars" in any true sense they were not.

Regarding the identity of "the Galatians": Before moving to assign an approximate date of this epistle, the question of the persons to whom it was written has priority; because with the determination of that, the problem of the date when it was written is clearly linked. The very term "Galatia" had two meanings. The Roman province of Galatia embraced a very large section of Asia Minor, including in its northern latitudes a relatively small subsection also called "Galatia." It had originally been populated by Gauls from western Europe; and its stormy population constituted in a technical sense "the Galatians," a designation that also quite properly belonged to all citizens of the much larger Roman province of Galatia. Paul's missionary tour was spent in the establishment of churches in the south part of the greater Galatian province, Pisidian Antioch, Iconium, Lystra and Derbe being among them. Those cities were not all in the same subdivision of greater Galatia, but some were in Pisidia, others in Lycaonia; and, if Paul had addressed those Christians converted on the first tour, there would have been no single term including them all except "Galatians." It is the opinion of this writer that it was precisely those churches which

---

[1]*ISBE*, p. 1156.

1

are addressed in Galatians, i.e., the South Galatians. It does not lie within the scope of this work to enter into the volumes of controversy arrayed on opposite sides, some maintaining the viewpoint accepted here, and others dogmatically certain that the original "Galatians" of the north were meant. For those interested, perhaps the work of William M. Ramsay is as thorough and convincing as any that may be consulted.

In addition to the necessity of addressing the recipients in terminology that would include them all, and which alone could have induced Paul to use "Galatians" in a different sense than the ordinary, there are internal considerations within the text of the letter itself (and of the book of Acts) which appear to determine the matter in favor of the South Galatians as recipients.

There are the repeated references to Barnabas in a manner suggesting that he was fully known to the persons receiving this letter; and, of course, those churches of South Galatia were the only ones, as far as either secular history or the NT is concerned, in which Barnabas was a companion and helper of Paul. This is not denied by the fact that Paul did not recognize Barnabas as co-founder of those churches in this letter, nor share with him the spiritual fatherhood of them which Paul claimed for himself (4:19); but the reasons for that are not far to seek. See notes under 4:19.

The great crest of the Jewish Christian confrontation reached its flood at the so-called Jerusalem Council (Acts 15); and the vehement and passionate teaching on that question in Galatians makes that very time to be the historical occasion for Galatians to have been written; and, at that time, the first missionary journey had just been concluded, making it exceedingly likely that the churches of that tour of South Galatia were the ones addressed. The book of Acts also places large numbers of Jews and proselytes among those very churches (Acts 13-14).

Nor is the identity of the Galatians with those southern provinces of Pisidia and Lycaonia denied by Paul's mention of two journeys having been made to them prior to writing this letter. In the first place, the Greek NT barely supports the allegation that two journeys have been made, some able scholars emphatically denying that it does so at all. The conviction here is that the Greek does not even mention two tours (see notes on 4:13), and that, even if it did, there were "two journeys" to those

South Galatian congregations recorded in Acts 14:21ff. The arbitrary manner of classifying all of Paul's many journeys on the first extended tour of indefinite length, lasting one or two or three years, as Journey I is mere pedantry. Paul himself referred to his labors of that period as being composed of "journeyings often" (2 Cor. 11:26). The statement that Paul in 4:13 was distinguishing between the return journey of Acts 14:21 and the previous one when the gospel was first preached there is just as reasonable as the notion that it refers to the scholars' major classification such as Journey II, or Journey III. Why should Paul have used "journeys" in any such school-boy fashion? The blunt rejection of this explanation as "one that cannot be accepted,"[2] itself cannot be accepted. Again, reference is made to the notes under 4:13.

The seeking of other "Galatians" than those of the South as recipients of this letter, with the corollary of a much later date, based upon the premise of the theology of Galatians representing "a later development" of Paul's teaching is worthless; because such arguments are founded on the false notion that Paul "developed" his understanding of the gospel, rather than having received it directly from the Lord, as emphatically taught in the NT.

All of the above reasons for accepting the South Galatian identity of "the Galatians" are supplemented by the numerous subtle, but convincing, allusions in the body of the epistle to events which definitely occurred in the very cities of the first journey, of which allusions there are many, an example of which is 6:17. See notes under that verse.

Date: From the above, it is clear that the date of Galatians coincides very closely with that of the Jerusalem Council, which must be very near that of the year 50 A.D. See complete discussion of this in CA chapter 15. That it was written shortly after the so-called Council, and not before it, is evident from his reference to the Council as an event already held. The refusal to allow this on the basis that Paul would have included the "findings of the council" in the Galatian letter, if it had been written afterward, is based upon a misconception of what that gathering in Jerusalem actually was. It certainly had no

---

[2]*ISBE*, p. 1159.

authority whatever regarding Paul and his preaching. In this very epistle he said, "They imparted nothing to me" (2:6). Paul's function in Jerusalem was that of straightening out the apostles and elders there and of *correcting them.* That Galatians was written very soon after the Council appears in Paul's mention of Barnabas' dissimulation (2:13), with no mention of his having corrected it, a correction that certainly occurred within a short time, as evidenced by Paul's willingness to undertake a second missionary journey with him so soon afterward (Acts 15:36).

Thus it is apparent that, when Paul went up to the Council, he learned of the deplorable conditions threatening his beloved converts of South Galatia; whereupon, he sat down and poured out the impassioned words of this glorious epistle.

Theme: The vital and all-pervading theme of Galatians is that of the Law of Moses vs. the Law of Christ, with its corollary of Justification by the Faith of Christ. The Christian freedom proclaimed in the name of this epistle is true to the extent that it is understood as "freedom from the burdens, ceremonies and all other externals of the Law of Moses"; but the false doctrine which makes Galatians a charter of "salvation by faith alone" is nowhere visible in it, but on the other hand is thwarted and denied by every line of it.

JUSTIFICATION BY THE FAITH OF CHRIST

Galatians, more than any other book in the NT, makes it clear that sinners are not saved by sinner's faith in any frame of reference whatever, except in the limited sense of believing in Christ being invariably a prerequisite of being assimilated "into Christ," and being in fact not even the sole condition of that assimilation. In the body of the notes, reference to the scientific work of Professor George Howard of the University of Georgia is made because of the significant strengthening derived from his work, in support of the thesis set forth in this series of commentaries in the publication of Romans. It is a source of joyful gratification that current scholarly studies of the highest level corroborate the glaring truth which is plainly evident in the context of various NT texts, namely, that it is the "faith of Christ," not "faith in Christ" which Paul presented as the grounds of justification. The true ground of justification is the perfect faith and obedience of the Son of God and never in a million years the mere subjective faith of sinners. Serious students of God's word should more and more concern themselves with this incredibly important truth. The faith and obedience of Christ achieved during his earthly ministry are "the righteousness of God in Christ" (Rom. 3:22, RV margin); and men are saved through being "in Christ," fully identified with Christ, and "as Christ."

CHAPTER 1

This chapter contains Paul's salutation (1-5), the dramatic introduction of his reason for writing the epistle, which was the developing apostasy of the Galatians (6-10), a bold defense of his apostleship (11-17), and the additional evidence of his independence and authority as an apostle (18-24).

Verse 1, *Paul, an apostle (not from men, neither through man, but through Jesus Christ and God the Father, who raised him from the dead).*

"Paul, an apostle . . ." The great apostle to the Gentiles did not always stress his apostleship in the same manner as here; but he did so in letters to churches where he was unknown or where his authority was being questioned, as in the first verse of each of his letters to the Romans, Corinthians, Ephesians and Colossians. "In cases where the churches were thoroughly devoted to him, he dropped it altogether, as in the salutations in Philippians, 1 Thessalonians and 2 Thessalonians."[1] Of course, false teachers who were stealing the Galatians away from the truth were challenging Paul's apostleship, making it most appropriate that he should have so vigorously stressed it here. *"An apostle* is a minister plenipotentiary."[2]

Regarding the identity of those who were denying Paul's apostolical authority among the Galatians, it is clear enough that they were Judaizers, "who were saying that Paul was not an original apostle, and that he derived his teaching from the Twelve."[3]

"Not from men, neither through man . . ." This does not deny that human agency was involved in Paul's conversion, for he was baptized by Ananias (Acts 22:12ff). Sanday observed that:

The part of Ananias was too subordinate to introduce a human element into it; and the subsequent "separation" of Paul

---

[1]J. R. Dummelow, *Commentary on the Holy Bible* (Old Tappan, N.J.: Fleming H. Revell Co., 1937), p. 946.

[2]Herman N. Ridderbos, *The Epistle of Paul to the Churches of Galatia* (Grand Rapids: Wm. B. Eerdmans Publishing Company, 1953), p. 40.

[3]Henry H. Halley, *Halley's Bible Handbook* (Grand Rapids: Zondervan Publishing House, 1927), p. 559.

and Barnabas for their mission to the Gentiles, through the act of the church at Antioch, was dictated by the Holy Spirit, and did not confer a new office or new powers.[4]

Furthermore, "The commission itself had first of all been uttered by Christ, not by Ananias."[5]

It should be noted that Paul was not here making a distinction between himself and the other true apostles in Jerusalem. "For they did not owe their commission to man any more than he did."[6] The truth affirmed here was two-fold, (a) Paul's apostleship was on a full equality with that of the Twelve, and (b) it was genuine, as contrasted with that of the false teachers who were operating among the Galatians. Macknight believed that there is also in view here a denial that Paul had been appointed to the apostleship by the Twelve, as had been the case with Matthias. "He seems to have Peter and James in his eye, whom alone he saw at his first coming to Jerusalem after his conversion, and denies that he was appointed an apostle by them."[7]

"Who raised him from the dead . . ." McGarvey was surely correct in pointing out that by this reference to the resurrection of Christ, "Paul paved the way"[8] for the principal theme of the epistle, which is *justification through the faith of Jesus Christ, rather than by the Law of Moses.*

One very hurtful interpretation of this verse is the following:

Paul's commission came neither from a human source nor through man, but directly from and through God . . . Paul's gospel rested on his personal relationship with God through Christ, and he was working it out in his own creative way.[9]

Such a view would make Paul, not Christ, the author of Christianity, a proposition that Paul vehemently denied. Paul

---

[4]William Sanday, *Ellicott's Commentary on the Whole Bible* (Grand Rapids: Zondervan Publishing House, 1959), p. 426.

[5]William Hendriksen, *New Testament Commentary on Galatians* (Grand Rapids: Baker Book House, 1968), p. 31.

[6]R. A. Cole, *Tyndale New Testament Commentaries, Galatians* (Grand Rapids: Wm. B. Eerdmans Publishing Company, 1965), p. 32.

[7]James Macknight, *Apostolical Epistles with Commentary and Notes* (Grand Rapids: Baker Book House, 1969), p. 107.

[8]J. W. McGarvey, *The Standard Bible Commentary, Galatians* (Cincinnati: The Standard Publishing Company, 1916), p. 249.

[9]Raymond T. Stamm, *Interpreter's Bible* (New York: Abingdon Press, 1953), Vol. X, p. 243.

"received" a body of truth from the Lord Jesus Christ; and the gospel he preached is not anything that Paul "worked out" for himself. Not going beyond the things which were written (1 Cor. 4:6) was a caution which Paul faithfully honored. Paul did not "evolve" his gospel, despite the insinuations to that effect. His gospel was revealed to him from on high. Furthermore, it was in no manner whatever any different from the gospel already being preached by the Twelve, except in the single particular of extending it to Gentiles. See under verse 23, below.

Verse 2-3, *And all the brethren that are with me, unto the churches of Galatia: Grace to you and peace from God the Father, and our Lord Jesus Christ.*

"All the brethren . . ." does not imply that Paul had discussed the situation in Galatia with his associates and that they concurred in his admonitions; on the contrary, as Wesley put it, "This phrase must be regarded as belonging exclusively to the greeting, and not to the exhortations which follow it."[10] It is pointless to speculate on the identity of these "brethren." We simply do not know.

"Churches of Galatia . . ." It is remarkable that Paul did not address them as churches "of God" or "of Christ," possibly "because they did not deserve such honorable appellations because of their great defection."[11] However, Paul's omission of this usual designation does not deny it in their case but merely avoids emphasis of it. For the identity of these congregations, see the introduction. The view being followed in these studies is that they were the churches of southern Galatia, i.e., the ones founded on Paul's first missionary tour.

Of deep significance are the titles of God and Christ in the third verse. Paul spoke of "the Father" when he had in mind the unique relationship between God and the Lord Jesus Christ, who alone in the the NT referred to God as "my" Father, but who also taught his followers to pray "our" Father. Paul often used "our Father" in his epistles (Rom. 1:7; 1 Cor. 1:3; 2 Cor. 1:2; Phil. 1:3; Philem.3).

---

[10]John Wesley, *One Volume New Testament Commentary* (Grand Rapids: Baker Book House, 1972), *in loco.*

[11]James Macknight, *op. cit.,* p. 108.

"Jesus" is the transliteration of the Hebrew name Joshua, meaning Jehovah is salvation, or Jehovah is Saviour; and "Christ" is the Greek rendition of the Hebrew word Messiah, meaning anointed.[12]

"Lord" is the translation of a Greek term *Kurios*, and it had at first a number of secondary meanings; but the Christians, from the very first, applied the term to Christ in the sense of absolute Diety. Thus Thomas said of Christ, "My Lord and my God" (John 20:28); Peter on Pentecost preached of Jesus that God had made him "Lord" (Acts 2:36); and again, in the home of Cornelius, said, "He is Lord of all" (Acts 10:36). Paul's use of "Lord" in the exalted sense in this epistle a bare twenty years after the resurrection of Christ shows that from the very first and reaching far back into the Lord's personal ministry, the exalted meaning prevailed. Jesus, from the very first, used the title of himself in the sense of the All-Powerful One. Thus, "Many shall say to me in that day (that is, the judgment day), Lord, Lord, etc." (Matt. 7:22). For more extensive commentary on this title, see CL, introduction.

Verse 4, *Who gave himself for our sins, that he might deliver us out of this present evil world, according to the will of our God and Father.*

"Who gave himself . . ." The essential Christian doctrine of Christ's vicarious sacrifice of himself to save men from sin is here emphasized in order to contrast the true source of salvation in Christ with the false premise of the Judaizers which made redemption to depend upon observing forms and ceremonies of the Law of Moses. In the last clause of this verse, Paul noted that Christ's giving himself was according to the will of God. For seven centers of initiative in the crucifixion of Christ see CR 3:25-26. The word "ransom" is used of this sacrifice of Christ in Matthew 28:28, Mark 10:45, and in I Timothy 2:6. As Sanday observed, "It was a sacrifice for sinners, wrought in their behalf for their benefit, a sacrifice wrought in their stead. He suffered in order that they might not suffer."[13] Paul's stressing this here was for the purpose of "convincing the Galatians that the

---

[12]W. E. Vine, *An Expository Dictionary of New Testament Words* (Old Tappan, N.J.: Fleming H. Revell Co., 1940), ii, p. 274, i, p. 190.

[13]William Sanday, *op. cit.,* p. 427.

pardon of sin was not to be obtained by the Levitical atonements, nor by any service prescribed in the Law."[14]

"Deliver . . ." suggests rescue from a state of utter helplessness. However, the deliverance made possible in Christ is not universally applicable to sinners apart from their response to the gospel. As Howard put it, "Such a rescue is not the universal and automatic consequence of the cross, but is a provided possibility."[15]

"This present evil world . . ." The world is evil in the sense of its populations being largely dominated by the influence of Satan. As an apostle said, "The whole world lieth in the evil one" (1 John 5:19). This has always been true, but there was a special sense in which the world of Paul's day was "evil." The pagan culture of the ancient Roman empire represented the culmination of long centuries of mankind's turning away from God and walking in darkness.

Verse 5, *To whom be the glory for ever and ever. Amen.*

The paramount function of all created things is to glorify God. It is true of the material universe. "The heavens declare the glory of God" (Ps. 19:1). It is true of the angels; for when they appeared at the birth of Christ, their song was "Glory to God in the highest" (Luke 2:14). It is even true of all the lower forms of life.

> And every creature which is in heaven and on earth and under the earth, and such as are in the sea, and all that are in them, heard I saying, Blessing and honor and glory and power be to him that sitteth upon the throne, and unto the Lamb forever and ever (Rev. 5:13).

EVERYWHERE
Where myriad waterfowl with thunderous wings
  Ascend to climb dawn's flaming stair,
The oratorio of all created things
  Is heard upon the morning air.
Where velvet footsteps march beneath the shade
  Of mammoth trees and move along
The resinous forest's colonade,
  God hears the thrilling Glory Song.

---

[14]James Macknight, *op. cit.,* p. 109.
[15]R. E. Howard, *Beacon Bible Commentary* (Kansas City: Beacon Hill Press, 1965), Vol. IX, p.40.

> Where countless life-forms teem the ocean floor,
>   Is sung God's glory in the sea,
> A mighty chorus shore to shore
>   To justify their right to be.
> Where Pleiades and Morning Star adorn
>   The arch of heaven, even there,
> From Creation's birthday morn,
>   God's glory sings, and EVERYWHERE!
>
>   JBC, 1962

Since the very purpose of man's existence is to glorify God, it follows that when man circumvents or countermands this purpose, he forfeits his right to live. Man cannot rise in his own strength alone, but must place his hand in the hand of his Creator, and like Enoch of old, learn to walk with God. How profound is the thought that man at last may attain eternal fellowship with the Father. What joys unspeakable are implied in this!

"Amen . . ." As Cole observed:

> *Amen*, like *Hosanna, Hallelujah, Maranatha* and *Abba*, is one of the "fossilized survivals" of Hebrew and Aramaic language of worship, transmitted through the NT Greek-speaking church to the later Latin-speaking church, and ultimately to most languages of earth.[16]

For further comment on "Amen," see CH 13:25.

Verse 6, *I marvel that ye are so quickly removing from him that called you in the grace of Christ unto a different gospel.*

Hendriksen pointed out that it was Paul's manner to commend before he began to condemn";[17] but there is nothing like that here. In the very place where commendation was usually written, Paul thundered his indignant astonishment at a fully developed and continuing apostasy of his beloved converts among the Galatians. As Wesley said, "The Greek word here rendered *marvel* usually expressed surprise at something blameworthy."[18]

"Ye are so quickly removing . . ." The present tense indicates that the defection of the Galatians was well under way and still going on. There are several possible meanings of this clause:

---

[16]R. A. Cole, *op. cit.,* p. 37.
[17]William Hendriksen, *op. cit.,* p. 37.
[18]John Wesley, *op. cit., in loco.*

(a) "It refers to moral speed,"[19] that is, they were more quickly accepting the false teaching than they had accepted the gospel at first; (b) it means, "So soon after Paul's visit to them";[20] or (c) it means, "So soon after their conversion." There is no certain way to know exactly what shade of meaning Paul had in mind; and, for this reason, it is precarious to build a theory regarding the date of this epistle on any alleged meaning of this clause.

The reason why Paul speedily moved to attack and destroy the rampant heresy involved a number of facts, the details of which he would set forth in the bulk of the epistle. As Coad said, "The new teaching was retrograde, a return to bondage (5:1)."[21] To surrender to the Judaizers was to negate the glory of the cross of Christ and to make the death of Christ on Calvary of no effect. It should be constantly borne in mind that the error Galatians was designed to correct was that of grafting Judaism into Christianity. There is absolutely nothing in this letter which may legitimately be construed as the stressing of "faith only" as opposed to "faith and obedience" as proclaimed in the Christian gospel from the beginning. Paul was not here giving a revised Christian doctrine, but defending the true doctrine already known and preached, from the encroachments of Judaism. Some of the comment one encounters regarding Galatians misses this very important point.

Verse 7, *Which is not another gospel; only there are some that trouble you, and would pervert the gospel of Christ.*

This verse should be read in close connection with the previous one. Regarding the exact meaning, Ramsay preferred as the simplest and best, "that which the RV gives in the margin,"[22] giving the thought thus: "A different gospel which is nothing else save that there are some that trouble you and would pervert the gospel of Christ." There is no hint in this passage that Paul actually considered Judaism "another gospel" in any

---

[19]J. W. McGarvey, *op. cit.,* p. 250.

[20]John Wesley, *op. cit., in loco.*

[21]F. Roy Coad, *A New Testament Commentary* (Grand Rapids: Zondervan Publishing House, 1969), p. 446.

[22]William M. Ramsay, *A Historical Commentary on St. Paul's Epistle to the Galatians* (Grand Rapids: Baker Book House, 1965), p. 264.

genuine sense. See note regarding "Another Gospel" at end of this chapter.

A sample of the erroneous and irresponsible comment foisted upon this passage is the following:

> (The false teaching) was surely a teaching according to which men are saved through *faith plus law-works,* a perversion of the true gospel which proclaims the glad tidings of salvation (by grace) *through faith alone.*[23]

Such a view is untrue, misleading, and anti-scriptural. A NT writer flatly declared that men are not justified "by faith alone" (James 2:24); and no scholar has a right to contradict the NT. Note the expression "law-works," used to make it appear that Paul belittled the Christian ordinances; but it is not *Christian* ordinances and commands which Paul was denouncing, but works of the Law of Moses. We have reason to be thankful for brilliant scholars like R. E. Howard who spoke out against the heresy that men attempted to import into this passage, saying:

> The logical implication of justification by *faith alone* is antinomianism, against which Paul vehemently objected . . . His repeated warning that wrong living excluded men from God's kingdom should leave no doubt as to his attitude . . . The new faith provided the only adequate means for ethical conduct, rather than absolving men from that responsibility.[24]

Any person familiar with the meaning of ordinary words must know that salvation "by faith alone" means salvation without obeying the Christian ordinances, without holiness, without moral conduct, without respect for any Christian duty, without the church and without the new birth or anything else. Such is the meaning of the word "alone" or its equivalent "only." The only religious error ever known which rivals that of so-called salvation "by faith only" is the Christian Science proposition that there is no pain, sickness or death!

"Them that trouble you . . ." Vine stated that the word thus rendered by this verse means "subverting the souls of believers by evil doctrine."[25] The exact chacteristics of the evil teaching

[23]William Hendriksen, *op. cit.,* p. 40.

[24]R. E. Howard, *op. cit.,* p. 23.

[25]W. E. Vine, *op. cit.,* iv, p. 157.

going on among the Galatians were gleaned from this epistle by
David Lipscomb thus:

> It puts in bondage (2:4), causes entanglement (5:1), could not
> bring justification (2:16), or freedom (5:1); it made Christ of no
> profit (5:2), and it made the death of Christ, which is the very
> essence of the gospel, a superfluous thing of no account (2:21);
> and in addition to providing no blessing whatever, it puts men
> under a curse (3:10); and all who accepted it fell from grace
> (5:4).[26]

Verse 8, *But though we or an angel from heaven, should
preach unto you any gospel, other than that which we preached
unto you, let him be anathema.*

Paul's indignation here stood upon the very highest ground.
"It is not on account of antagonism to himself, but antagonism
to the truth. Though he himself should fall away from it, the
truth must still be supreme."[27] In fact, supposing that he himself should defect from the truth, Paul invoked upon his own
head the curse of God.

"An angel from heaven . . ." McGarvey pointed out that the
word of Christ was superior to that of angels who had ministered
the old covenant, and "The sayings of Jesus were weightier than
the words of angels in this very respect."[28] This probably
accounts for Paul injecting the thought of angels into this passage. Also, as Cole said, "Paul may be using this word to show
them the possibility of Satan himself appearing as an angel of
light to deceive them."[29] It will be remembered that when Peter
proposed to Christ the elimination of the cross, our Lord said,
"Get thee behind me, Satan" (Mark 8:33).

"Anathema . . ." Some have sought to soften the meaning of
this word, but there can be no doubt that it is the strongest curse
that can be uttered, having the meaning of "yielded up to the
wrath of God, surrendered to the curse of God."[30]

"The gospel which we preached . . ." It is a gross error to
suppose that Paul's gospel was different from that proclaimed

[26]David Lipscomb, *A Commentary on the New Testament Epistles* (Nashville:
Gospel Advocate Company, Vol. III, p. 190.

[27]John Wesley, *op. cit., in loco.*

[28]J. W. McGarvey, *op. cit.,* p. 251.

[29]R. A. Cole, *op. cit.,* p. 42.

[30]Herman N. Ridderbos, *op. cit.,* p. 50.

by all the Twelve, although it is true that Paul had a more accurate understanding of its being for Gentiles and not restricted to Jews only. Paul wrote, "According to my gospel" (Rom. 2:16); but he meant it was his in the sense of "my God" (Phil. 4:9) and "my Lord" (Phil. 3:8). Of the same gospel, he wrote that it is "our gospel"; (2 Thess. 2:14). In verse 23, below, Paul's gospel was exactly the same gospel that was being preached by others while he was yet a persecutor. Thus, "Paul was referring to his gospel in opposition to all counterfeits,"[31] especially persistent Judaism. Even here, Paul did not say, "the gospel I preach," but "the gospel we preach." Dummelow affirmed that the "we," both here and in the following verse, is epistolary;[32] but it seems mandatory to read it as Paul's conscious intention of including the other apostles as also being preachers of the true gospel.

In later historical times, "anathema" came to refer to excommunication by ecclesiastical authority; but "this curse may not be thought of as anything like that; after all, an angel too is hypothetically involved."[33] No angel was ever subject to ecclesiastical descipline.

Verse 9, *As we have said before, so say I now again, If any man preacheth unto you any gospel other than that which ye received, let him be anathema.*

In this verse Paul applied the curse concretely to the false teachers operating among the Galatians at that very moment. This verse is not a curse upon some hypothetical violator, but upon the guilty perverters preaching error at that very moment. This progression from the general to the specific dramatically emphasized the fatal danger of surrendering to Judaism.

Verse 10, *For am I now seeking the favor of men, or of God? or am I striving to please men? if I were still pleasing men, I should not be a servant of Christ.*

"Seeking the favor of men . . ." Paul brought into view in these words the bitter human opposition that accompanied his

---

[31]Arthur W. Pink, *Gleanings from Paul* (Cicago: Moody Press, 1967), p. 49.
[32]J. R. Dummelow, *op. cit.*, p. 947.
[33]Herman N. Ridderbos, *op. cit.*, p. 50.

preaching everywhere he went. "His patient endurance made manifest that he was a genuine minister of Christ."[34] "Paul here showed the utter inconsistency of service of men (in sense of trying to curry favor)."[35]

"If I were still pleasing men . . ." The adverb here "marks the contrast between his position before and since conversion."[36] Yes, when Paul was a Pharisee, he attempted to serve God and please men at the same time, but no such thing was possible for the Christian apostle.

"Servant of Christ . . ." The word actually means "bondservant" or "slave"; and with Paul it was no pious pretense. He truly served the Lord.

Verses 11-12, *For I make known unto you, brethren, as touching the gospel which was preached by me, that it is not after man. For neither did I receive it from man, nor was I taught it, but it came to me through revelation of Jesus Christ.*

Paul's affirmation that he possessed a personal revelation from the Lord of glory which had endowed him with full and complete knowledge of the gospel was indeed bold and astonishing. It cannot be wondered that some of his contemporaries were concerned about whether or not he could be trusted in this; but it should always be borne in mind that the great miracles which the apostle Paul performed all over the Roman Empire confirmed and authenticated his message. There has not arisen another like him since NT times. None of the so-called "inspired" leaders of current times is worthy to be compared with Paul. As Howard expressed it:

> The revelation of the written word is unique. It is terminal and not continuous. Paul's audacious claims were fully substantiated by the Holy Spirit. Our task is not to add to the written revelation, but to understand it and explain it.[37]

Of course, Paul would at once offer proof to substantiate so bold a declaration; and, first of all, he appealed to the record

---

[34]Arthur W. Pink, *op. cit.,* p. 74.

[35]R. A. Cole, *op. cit.,* p. 45.

[36]W. J. Conybeare, *The Life and Epistles of St. Paul* (Grand Rapids: Wm. B. Eerdmans Publishing Company, 1966), p. 480.

[37]R. E. Howard, *op. cit.,* p. 34.

which was open and to be read of all men concerning what the gospel had wrought in his own amazing life.

Verses 13-14, *For ye have heard of my manner of life in times past in the Jews' religion, how that beyond measure I persecuted the church of God, and made havoc of it: and I advanced in the Jews' religion beyond many of mine own age among my country-men, being more exceedingly zealous for the traditions of my fathers.*

In these two verses, "Paul was saying that no *human* persuasion could ever have been able to impart the gospel to such a confirmed and ferocious persecutor."[38] Only the power of God could have done such a thing. And what was that power? It was noted above that the Spirit of God through the enabling of power to work miracles had confirmed the fact of Paul's having the *revelation from Christ* (v.12); but it should be carefully noted that the Holy Spirit did not convey the revelation, for that was done personally *by Christ.* The function of the Holy Spirit, even in the Twelve, was not that of conveying God's truth to them, but that of helping them remember the truth Christ conveyed; and the same fact is in evidence with reference to the revelation Paul had received from Christ, not from the Holy Spirit. See extensive comment on this exceedingly important truth in CJ 16:13. The Lord revealed that the Holy Spirit "shall not speak of himself" (John 16:13), meaning that power to convey gospel truth did not reside in the Third Person of the Godhead. There were limitations upon the Second Person during his incarnation (Matt. 24:36); and, similarly, there were limitations upon the Spirit's power in men.

The proposition that the Holy Spirit operated upon Paul directly, independently of the word which Christ delivered to humanity, is a contradiction of everything in the NT. If the Spirit *could have* done such a thing, it would not have been necessary at all for Christ to come into this world in the first place, nor would it have been necessary for him to appear *personally* to Saul of Tarsus. Paul received a full knowledge of the gospel in exactly the same manner as the Twelve received it, i.e., from Christ *himself,* as Paul affirmed in verse 12; and the function

---

[38]William Hendriksen, *op. cit.,* p. 52.

of the Holy Spirit in Paul was to enable Paul to remember all that Jesus said, exactly as in the case of the Twelve (John 14:26). Since the personal appearance of Christ to Saul of Tarsus, and later to John the apostle, in all ages since, the Holy Spirit has never conveyed a single new truth to any person whomsoever; and, as always, the Spirit's function even in those instances was to enable truth to be remembered and not to convey it. So-called "spirituals" in our own times have nothing except the sacred scripture; because, if they did have truth to convey to others, the Spirit of God would confirm it with the power to do "signs and wonders and mighty deeds," as he did in the case of Paul and the Twelve. They were guided into "all truth" (John 16:13).

"I persecuted the church . . ." This went even further than many Pharisees were willing to go. "The ravening wolf of Benjamin"[39] was "laying waste the church." Paul here declared "ye have heard" of this, indicating the notorious nature of his conduct, and also, perhaps, that "He brought his own career and experience into his preaching (as in this epistle), so that they may have heard it from his own lips."[40] Paul's persecution of the church was totally the equivalent of persecuting Christ personally (Acts 22:8). Cole elaborated on this thus:

> Opposition to the church is not only opposition to Jesus the Messiah . . . It is opposition to God, who in the OT had chosen Israel as his "company," and who now has chosen the Christian church, whether Jew or Gentile.[41]

"The Jews' religion . . ." "The Judaism," as it is in the Greek, includes both the divine original as conveyed through Moses and the prophets and also that incredibly large body of traditions and elaborations of it which had been added by the religious hierarchy of Israel, the latter coming in time to surpass (in their eyes) the importance of the God-given law itself, making it "of no effect" (Mark 7:13; Matt. 15:6). Paul's here speaking of Judaism as something apart from Christianity shows that within two decades after the resurrection of Christ the term had become synonymous with opposition to Christianity. However, since Jews were the first Christians and have always been welcome

---

[39]Everett F. Harrison, *Wycliffe Bible Commentary* (Chicago Moody Press, 1971), p. 695.

[40]William Sanday, *op. cit.,* p. 430.

[41]R. A. Cole, *op. cit.,* p. 49.

to accept Christ, the term "Jews," as used here and extensively in John, has religious rather than racial overtones. The blunder of the Medieval church in blurring this distinction is one of the great tragedies of all time. Some scholars, including Lipscomb, believed that Paul here referred exclusively to the Pharisaical additions to God's law; but it is an obvious truth that he exceeded his countrymen in knowledge of the divine law itself, as evidenced by his writings.

"Church of God . . ." Paul also referred to the community of believers as the church of Christ; and apparently the reason for making it "church of God" in this place was to emphasize that the church was not merely of Christ but also, in view of Christ's oneness and equality with God (a fact the Judaizers at work among the Galatians would deny), the Christians were "the congregation of God,"[42] no less than being the church of Christ.

"Exceedingly zealous . . ." Acts 9:1 and 22:4 reveal the murderous and fanatical persecution Paul mounted against Christianity, resulting in the death of "both men and women." Paul's hatred of the church sprang from the vivid accuracy with which he saw the true nature of Judaism, the typical forms and ceremonies of which are simply unreconcilable with Christianity. The very heart of the sacred Law itself was typical and preparatory by nature; and Paul's favorite words regarding it were: "abrogated, done away, taken away, annulled, etc." It was this aspect of Christianity, truly understood, which so antagonized and enraged Saul of Tarsus. As soon as he accepted Christ, he accepted the very first corollary of the faith, i.e., that as far as worshiping Almighty God is concerned, it is all over and done with for Judaism.

Verses 15-17, *But when it was the good pleasure of God, who separated me, even from my mother's womb, and called me through his grace, to reveal his Son in me, that I might preach him among the Gentiles; straightway I conferred not with flesh and blood; neither went I up to Jerusalem to them that were apostles before me: but I went away into Arabia; and again I returned unto Damascus.*

---

[42]*The Emphatic Diaglott* (Brooklyn: Watchtower Bible and Tract Society), *in loco.*

The whole burden of Paul's defense of his apostleship in this and in chapter 2 was summarized thus by Hayes:

> I was an apostle before I ever saw an apostle; I was recognized as an equal by the apostles the first time they ever met me or heard what gospel I preached. . . . I have preached it with the official sanction of the apostles, and I have preached it in defiance of the apostles (Gal. 2:14). I am an apostle of God, and my gospel is the gospel of God![43]

The revelation which Jesus Christ gave personally to Paul was exactly the same as that given to the Twelve. Paul did not claim superiority to them but equality with them, and that implies the equality of the revelation to himself with that of the Twelve. Since the three verses above concern the *source* of Paul's revelation, there is a strong inference that Arabia was the place where Christ met him to expound the truth of the gospel. It could also have been there that Paul experienced the visit (whether in the body or out of it being unknown) to the third heaven and to Paradise. It should be carefully noted that the revelation did not "flash into Paul's mind," as some claim; but it was conveyed personally by Jesus Christ our Lord.

"Called me through his grace . . ." It was not the Holy Spirit which called Paul, for Paul himself taught that the Spirit was an endowment only of those *already* sons of God; and, as always in the NT, the call of God means God's invitation accepted. Paul became a Son of God in the same manner as all Christians, by believing, repenting, confessing Christ and being baptized into him (Acts 22:16).

"I conferred not with flesh and blood . . ." Tenney noted that this is a figure of speech, called synecdoche, in which some significant and essential part is used to identify the whole.[44] The meaning is, "I did not confer with any human being." Sanday also detected a special meaning in "conferred," as used here. "The Greek word contains the idea of taking counsel in a personal interview, much as we now use the word *apply* in the phrase to *apply to a person.*"[45] Paul did not apply to the Twelve for permission to accept his call from Christ to the apostleship.

---

[43]D. A. Hayes, *Paul and His Epistles* (Grand Rapids: Baker Book House, 1915, reprint 1969), p. 293.

[44]Merrill C. Tenney, *Galatians the Charter of Christian Liberty* (Grand Rapids: Wm. B. Eerdmans Publishing Company, 1950), p. 138.

[45]William Sanday, *op. cit.*, p. 431.

Nothing of the length of time Paul spent in Arabia is known except that from the time of his conversion at Damascus and his preaching in that city for an undetermined length of time, till his escape from the plot under Aretas, was three years, including the sojourn in Arabia.

Verse 18, *Then after three years I went up to Jerusalem to visit Cephas, and tarried with him fifteen days.*

This and the following verses were added by Paul as an explanation of what he had just said and to checkmate any denial of it by any one who might have known about the trip in view here. He noted that it was three whole years after he had become a preaching apostle and that even then he saw only Peter and James, the purpose being in no sense whatever to apply to them or to complete his knowledge of the gospel, but just in order to become acquainted. Ramsay says the word "visit" here was "used by those who go to see great and famous cities."[46] He also quoted Lightfoot and Chrysostom as maintaining the same thing. So Paul went to see two of the most distinguished persons in the early church in the same way one would go to see any celebrity. John Wesley also insisted that the word "implied the desire to see a celebrity."[47] That so busy and distinguished a person as Peter would have devoted an entire fifteen days to Paul shows that he received and entertained him as an equal, and not merely as some appellant seeking a favor.

Verses 19-20, *But other of the apostles saw I none, save James the Lord's brother. Now touching the things which I write unto you, behold, before God, I lie not.*

"Save James . . ." The frequent persecutions might have caused the other apostles to be absent from the city; or they might have been engaged in various preaching missions in Judaea. Later, even Peter was forced to flee the city.

"The Lord's brother . . ." This was one of the persons mentioned as brothers and sister of Jesus, i.e., children born to Mary and Joseph subsequent to the birth of Christ (Matt. 13:55). For detailed comment see CM 1:24. He became the official leader of the congregation in Jerusalem; nevertheless, his being

---

[46]William M. Ramsay, *op. cit.*, p. 283.
[47]John Wesley, *op. cit., in loco.*

called an apostle here must be understood (a) either as a complimentary title bestowed upon him by the early church due to his close personal relation to Jesus, or (b) because he was an apostle in the secondary sense, like Barnabas. James was not a plenary apostle like the Twelve and Paul.

"Before God, I lie not . . ." Paul considered the information he conveyed here as paramount in importance and appealed to God who knows the hearts of all men, indicating the absolute truth and sincerity of his words.

Verse 21, *Then I came into the regions of Syria and Cilicia.*

It is hard to be patient with commentators who find some big "difficulty" in equating what is said here with the Lucan account in Acts, where it is related that the brethren, fearing for Paul's life, "brought him down to Caesarea and sent him forth to Tarsus" (Acts 9:30). There is no difficulty. Tarsus is the chief city of Cilicia; and that was exactly where Luke says Barnabas found Paul and brought him to Antioch, the capital of Syria; and the fact of the order of Paul's going to those places (in Acts) was Cilicia and Syria, whereas here, it is Syria and Cilicia, is nothing but a quibble. Since it had been at Antioch in Syria where Paul had bestowed the new name on the followers of Christ (Acts 11:26), and as Antioch was the sponsoring congregation who sent him forth on his mission to the Gentiles, it was only natural that Syria should have been mentioned ahead of Cilicia in this place.

Verse 22, *And I was still unknown by face unto the churches of Judaea which were in Christ.*

There is a distinction between Judaea and Jerusalem. In all probability, Paul would not have been in that city some two or three Lord's days without visiting the church there; but, as the Jews were trying to kill him, it could be that he had attended worship as inconspicuously as possible. No matter how one reads it, what Paul said here was true.

"In Christ . . ." As often pointed out in this series of commentaries, this is one of the most meaningful phrases in the NT. Stamm noted that "It is Paul's most unique phrase, being used 164 times in Paul's letters."[48] John Mackay placed the number

---

[48]Raymond T. Stamm, *op. cit.,* p. 464.

at 169.[49] Most commentators either ignore it altogether or, after noting it, give no adequate evaluation of it. Therefore, the following from Ridderbos is especially welcome:

> As a matter of fact, this *in Christ* represents, in a remarkable and comprehensive way, the whole profound view which Paul unfolds in his letters concerning the significance for believers of the salvation that has appeared in Christ.[50]

Without exception, all Christians are those, and those only, who have been "baptized into Christ." For extensive discussions of this exceedingly important premise, see CR 3:22

Verse 23, *But they only heard say, He that once persecuted us now preacheth the faith of which he once made havoc.*

Nothing in the NT more emphatically nails down the fact that Paul did not "bring a brand-new way of salvation." The gospel he preached was exactly the truth he persecuted. The conflict which underlies Paul's extensive writings on faith vs. law is not a conflict between two ways of understanding the gospel; but it is a conflict between the one faith vs. the *Law of Moses* as interpreted by the Judaizers who made keeping it necessary and essential unto salvation (Acts 15:1).

If one might be permitted to speculate upon the reason why Almighty God moved to supplement the personnel of the original Twelve by the addition of Paul, the reason must be sought in the fact that in one essential particular the Twelve did not fully comprehend the absolute freedom (a term Paul himself used to describe the break in Romans 7:1ff) of Christianity from the totality of Judaism. *That* God Almighty could not allow, no matter what miracles were involved in order to prevent it. Paul was surely one of those miracles. Paul never went beyond Jesus' revelation to the Twelve, except in the application of the gospel to all men, and to Gentiles in particular, instead of merely to the Jews. The reason Paul was able to do that did not derive from any difference in Christ's revelation to himself and to the Twelve; for they had all received the same revelation Paul was given. Peter, for example, on Pentecost had plainly declared that the gospel was for "them that are afar off," obviously meaning

---

[49]John Mackay, *God's Order* (New York: The Macmillan Company, 1953), p. 97.

[50]Herman N. Ridderbos, *op. cit.,* p. 72.

Gentiles. The thing that enabled Paul more readily and effectively to apply this truth (although all of the apostles eventually succeeded in doing so) was his greater knowledge of the OT, and in addition, many elements in the personality of the man himself.

Dummelow's comment on this verse is illustrative of the type of thinking that often clutters the minds of scholars on this question. He wrote: *"Preacheth the faith* proclaims the necessity of trust in Christ as the sole essential to salvation!"[51] Indeed, indeed! Paul was preaching the same gospel Peter preached, and Peter commanded believers to "repent and be baptized" in order to receive the remission of sins (Acts 2:38); and this verse is an affirmation that Paul preached exactly the same gospel.

Verse 24, *And they glorified God in me.*

For thoughts regarding the glory of God, see under verse 5, above. As Pink said, "To honor that blessed One whose we are and whom we serve, to so conduct myself that fellow saints glorify God in me, *that* is to adorn the doctrine of God our Saviour in all things (Titus 2:10)."[52] Ridderbos commented on the fact that the churches of Judaea glorified God in Paul, despite their having suffered so much at his hands "How different the attitude among the Galatians who had received only good from him."[53] Such is the mystery of human behavior. Cole accurately pointed out the reason why those in Judaea glorified God in Paul.

They recognized his gospel at once as *that which they had preached.*"[54]

THOUGHTS REGARDING ANOTHER GOSPEL

Paul's times were not unique in producing advocates of "another gospel," which in reality is "no gospel," but falsehood.

Some advocate the gospel of salvation by morality, supposing that the only requirement for eternal life is to live respectably before one's contemporaries. Others advocate the gospel of an infallible church, whereas no church was ever infallible, not even any that were founded, or planted, by the apostles them-

---

[51]J. R. Dummelow, *op. cit.,* p. 948.
[52]Arthur W. Pink, *op. cit.,* p. 231.
[53]Herman N. Ridderbos, *op. cit.,* p. 74.
[54]R. A. Cole, *op. cit.,* p. 59.

selves, as detailed in the first chapters of Revelation. Still others preach the gospel of salvation by faith only, notwithstanding the fact that such a so-called gospel is anti-scriptural, delusive, deceitful and contrary to everything in the NT. The great fad of our own times is the gospel of humanism, which deifies man himself, leaves the Son of God completely out of consideration, and equates humanitarian and charitable works with God's unqualified approval, despite the truth that no present-day humanitarian may lay claim to any better service than that rendered by Cornelius, who was a lost man till he obeyed the gospel.

Contrasting with all such false gospels is the only one true and eternal gospel of Jesus Christ revealed in the NT; and if one desires to know what it is and receive its blessings, he must find it here, and having found it: (a) believe the great facts it reveals, (b) obey its commandments, and (c) receive its glorious promises! Amen!

CHAPTER 2

Two major divisions of this chapter are (1) Paul's appeal to the fact that fourteen years after his conversion (long after he had been successfully preaching the gospel), the leading apostles in Jerusalem fully endorsed his preaching and extended to him the right hand of fellowship (1-10), and (2) that in one very important particular he had withstood the apostle Peter face to face, exposing his sin and hypocrisy, the obvious conclusion from such an incident being that (in one particular at least) he was superior to the apostles in Jerusalem (11-21).

Around these two major themes of the chapter, however, Paul wove some of the most important theological principles revealed in the NT, introducing the main theme of Galatians in 2:16, which is "Justification by the Faith of Christ, and not by the Law of Moses."

Verse 1, *Then after fourteen years I went up again to Jerusalem with Barnabas, taking Titus with me.*

Paul's intention here was to justify his apostleship, as not having been received through men; and, since that apostleship began with his conversion, the "fourteen years" here means fourteen years after his conversion. It is remarkable how religious fads can blind the eyes of expositors, and a startling example of it is seen in the usual treatment of this visit, making it fourteen years after his last visit to Jerusalem. This is based on the mistaken view that Paul in this letter had set out to name every trip he had ever made to the capital of Judaism. He obviously had no such intention. He left out of consideration altogether a trip to Jerusalem which he and Barnabas had made to deliver famine relief "to the elders" in Jerusalem (Acts 11:30); but, as that trip came about the time when Peter was imprisoned, James had been martyred, and all of the apostles were in hiding, it could have had no bearing whatever on what Paul was emphasizing here.

"I went up again to Jerusalem . . ." has the simple meaning of "upon another occasion I went up to Jerusalem." It is totally wrong to read this as if it said, "the second time I went up to Jerusalem." The NT merely states that he went up "again." As Ridderbos said, "Once one has rid himself of the idea that Paul

wants to give a summary here of all his trips to Jerusalem,"[1] it
is easy to see that the meeting described in these verses is the
so-called Jerusalem Council (Acts 15:1ff), and that there is no
need to identify it as the famine visit of Acts 11:30. McGarvey
was in perfect agreement with this view;[2] and, as Harrison
asked, "If the question of the admission of Gentiles into the
church had been settled on the famine visit,"[3] why was another
conference necessary to settle the same question?

"Titus . . ." For full discussion of this man, see under 2 Corinthians 7:6.

"Barnabas . . ." It should be noted that Paul, in order to avoid
assuming any domination over Barnabas, stated that he went
"with" him; whereas, in the case of Titus, one of his faithful
followers, he referred to "taking him."

One of Paul's purposes, in addition to that of defending his
apostleship by making this journey, was to prove that he
properly respected and honored those who were apostles before
him; and, as Barclay noted, "To prove that his independence was
not anarchy, nor schismatic and sectarian, but that his gospel
was indeed no other than the faith delivered to the church."[4]

Another important sidelight here is that Paul spoke of Barnabas here with the necessary implication that he was already
known to the Christians in Galatia, "a further indication that
they were the churches of the first missionary journey,"[5] in
which Barnabas shared.

Verse 2, *And I went up by revelation; and I laid before them
the gospel which I preach among the Gentiles but privately before
them who were of repute, lest by any means I should be running,
or had run, in vain.*

"By revelation . . ." From Luke (Acts 15:2), it is clear that the
church in Antioch commissioned Paul and Barnabas to go to

[1]H. N. Ridderbos, *The Epistles of Paul to the Churches of Galatia* (Grand
Rapids: Wm. B. Eerdmans Publishing Company, 1953), p. 78.

[2]J. W. McGarvey, *The Standard Bible Commentary, Galatians* (Cincinnati:
The Standard Publishing Company, 1916), p. 256.

[3]Everett F. Harrison, *Wycliffe Bible Commentary* (Chicago: Moody Press,
1971), p. 698.

[4]William Barclay, *The Letters to the Galatians and Ephesians* (Philadelphia:
The Westminster Press, 1964), p. 16.

[5]F. Roy Coad, *A New Testament Commentary* (Grand Rapids: Zondervan
Publishing House, 1969), p. 449.

Jerusalem; but from this it is learned that Paul went by "revelation." As Macknight said, "If the church at Antioch were directed by divine revelation to send Paul and Barnabas on this mission, he could justly say that he went by revelation."[6] There is also the possibility that Paul, at first, would not go, until specifically commanded by Christ to do so. It is a fact that Christ personally stood by Paul on occasions (Acts 22:18). Furthermore, Paul's reasons for going were not for the purpose of receiving instruction or of getting the apostles in Jerusalem to decide anything. He went there for the purpose of straightening out the error that, for the moment, was rampant in the church in that city. There is nothing in this whole episode that reveals "the Mother Church settling important matters of doctrine." See comment on this so-called council in CA chapter 15.

"And I laid before them . . ." Paul's efforts here were directed to the purpose of correcting false views prevalent in the church in Jerusalem; therefore, he laid the pure gospel before them. This does not mean "that Paul had begun to feel insecure about his gospel."[7] It was an effort to unify the church.

"Who were of repute . . ." seems somewhat ironical. Ridderbos said, "It positively is not that."[8] However, Paul's mention of this, using similar and somewhat more emphatic terms, no less than four times in this passage would definitely suggest that very possibility.

"But privately . . ." Some scholars dogmatically assert that Paul's account of the "council" here cannot be harmonized with Acts 15:1ff; but that is only because they fail to see that there were private discussions which took place before the public and more formal meeting later on. Huxtable noted that Luke mentions no less than three separate meetings[9] in verses 4, 6 and 12 of Acts 15. Even today large public meetings are usually preceded by private discussions of those in charge of them. Lipscomb said:

> These private consultations were a wise precaution to avoid misunderstanding. Such private conferences are usually held

[6]James Macknight, *Apostolical Epistles with Commentary and Notes* (Grand Rapids: Baker Book House, 1969), p. 122.

[7]Herman N. Ridderbos, *op. cit.,* p. 81.

[8]*Ibid.*

[9]E. Huxtable, *Pulpit Commentary* (Grand Rapids: Wm. B. Eerdmans Publishing Company, 1950), Vol. 20, p. 70.

in connection with public assemblies for the purpose of preparing and maturing business for final action.[10]

"Lest by any means I should be running . . . in vain . . ." If the Twelve had repudiated Paul's gospel, it would, in a sense, have nullified his whole life's work, making it to be largely "in vain." Paul definitely did not mean here that he had any question regarding his own redemption.

Verses 3-5, *But not even Titus who was with me, being a Greek, was compelled to be circumcised: And that because of the false brethren brought in, who came in privily to spy out our liberty which we have in Christ Jesus, that they might bring us into bondage: to whom we gave place in the way of subjection, no, not for an hour; that the truth of the gospel might continue with you.*

"The apostle's language here is somewhat ambiguous,"[11] as Bruce said, making the interpretation to be: The first time I took Titus to Jerusalem the question was not even raised; but, at a later time, the false brethren spied on us and demanded that he be circumcised; but we refused to do so, etc. Sanday, Bruce and others make verses 2-5 a parenthetical statement. However, it appears to this writer that the parenthesis is to explain the fact that, even under pressure from the demands initiated by the false brethren, Titus was not circumcised, the mention of the false brethren being for the purpose of showing how the question came up. In any case, the big point is that Paul absolutely refused to have Titus circumcised; and that, even if pressure was applied to Titus personally, he also refused to accommodate the Judaizers.

"To spy out our liberty . . ." "The notion of hostile intent is strongly suggested by this."[12] The Judaizing party in the church was prepared to go to any lengths to enforce law-keeping and circumcision upon all who became Christians, whether Jew or Gentile.

"Liberty which we have in Christ Jesus . . ." "Being *in Christ* is primal in all Pauline teaching; once grasped, the secret to Paul

---

[10]David Lipscomb, *A Commentary on the New Testament Epistles* (Nashville: Gospel Advocate Company, n.d.), p. 203.
    [11]F. F. Bruce, *Answers to Questions* (Grand Rapids: Zondervan Publishing House, 1972), p. 103.
    [12]E. Huxtable, *op. cit.,* p. 73.

is discovered."[13] "If any man be in Christ, he is a new creature" (2 Cor. 5:17). The liberty which Paul had in view here was primarily freedom from the ceremonials of Judaism; but there is a notable and extensive freedom "in Christ" from all encumbering religious devices. Even the grand ordinances of Christianity are only two in number, i.e., baptism and the Lord's Supper; and one of these is observed only once at the beginning of the Christian life. How antagonistic to the true teachings of the NT are the declamations of those who attempt to make Paul's words here to mean that Christians are free from *those* ordinances! It was not freedom from Christ's commandments that Paul taught, but freedom from the forms and ceremonies of Judaism. Jesus himself declared that "Whosoever therefore shall break one of these least commandments, and shall teach men so, shall be called least in the kingdom of heaven" (Matt. 5:19). The contrast between the teaching of Paul and the teaching of men here is observable in the following:

PAUL: The binding of circumcision and Jewish ceremonial upon Christians violates the truth that the Christian religion is all that is needed for salvation. . . . TRUE.

MEN: The binding of circumcision, etc., nullified the truth that faith in Christ is the *sole* and sufficient ground of justification.[14] . . . FALSE.

Such audacious perversions of sacred truth should be detected and rejected by all true believers in Christ.

Verse 6, *But from those who were reputed to be somewhat (whatsoever they were, it maketh no matter to me: God accepteth not man's person) — they, I say, who were of repute imparted nothing to me.*

"Who were reputed to be somewhat . . . who were of repute . . ." Paul does not here question the legitimate reputation and prominence of the Twelve, but he is careful not to admit any lack of equality with them on his own behalf. As Howard said it: "He did not want to imply total submission to their judgment, or deny his own unique and divinely given authority."[15]

---

[13]Raymond T. Stamm, *Interpreter's Bible* (New York: Abingdon Press, 1953), Vol. X, p. 472.

[14]E. Huxtable, *op. cit.,* p. 74.

[15]R. E. Howard, *Beacon Bible Commentary* (Kansas City: Beacon Hill Press, 1965), Vol. IX, p. 41.

"God accepteth not man's person . . ." No man's opinion
should be received merely upon the basis of who he is, his
position in life or any office that he holds. Even Jesus our Lord
did not require men to believe him upon the basis of his status
as a human being, but upon the basis that God had given him
a message, and that *that* message of God was what he taught.
Paul's reference here is addressed exactly to that very principle.
Not even an apostle should be believed *as a man,* but *as a true
messenger of God.* See more on this in CJ 12:49. How differently
are the sayings of men urged upon us today. Lo! a bishop has
spoken, a pope has circulated an encyclical, the head of a church
has spoken, or a general conference has decided it, etc. The
human failing in relying upon such things predisposes men to
find a similar thing at Jerusalem in the events related in this
chapter. Indeed this has been called the First Ecumenical
Council of the Church, but it was no such thing.

"They imparted nothing to me . . ." Paul was the one who
imparted the truth on that occasion, not the so-called council.
How amazing is a comment like this:

"Added nothing to me . . ." Paul does not mean that he
received from them nothing essential for his gospel![16]

Despite such allegations, if language has any meaning at all,
that is exactly what Paul did mean, namely, that the council
made no contribution of any kind whatever to the gospel he
preached, to the revelation of Christ which he had received, or
to anything whatever that concerned Paul.

Scholars are critical of Paul for not delivering the "findings
of the council" to the Galatians in this letter, and for not any
time or anywhere even mentioning them in his epistles. Some
even presume to date Galatians at a time far removed from this
council in order to account for his not delivering the decisions
of it; but the reason for such omission is clear enough in this
dynamic clause. The council made no contribution whatever to
the gospel, the great result of the meeting being that they
received Paul's views in their entirety and began to preach as
they should have been doing already, in full consonance with the
gospel Christ had given them, exactly as he had to Paul. Stamm
asserted that "Acts says that this conference was called to decide

---

[16]Raymond T. Stamm, *op. cit.,* p. 474.

whether Gentile converts must be circumcised";[17] but this is due to misreading Acts 15:1ff. Stamm's very next line is, "But (Acts) in reporting the action of the council says nothing about circumcision."[18] Of course it didn't! No such purpose is discernible anywhere. The question of whether Gentiles were to be circumcised had long ago been revealed to the Twelve, as well as to Paul. Peter himself had received into full fellowship the uncircumcised Cornelius, baptizing him into Christ, and defending the action against some who questioned it (Acts 10 and 11). Not only had the question already been determined, all of the apostles on earth, in conference assembled, did not have the authority to alter that decision in any manner. To be sure, the councils of men held today are even more incompetent and unauthorized to meet and determine Christian doctrine; and their presuming to do so is the prime scandal that has perverted Christianity in so many particulars through the ages.

Verse 7-8, *But contrariwise, when they saw that I had been intrusted with the gospel of the uncircumcision, even as Peter with the gospel of the circumcision (for he that wrought for Peter unto the apostleship of the circumcision wrought for me also unto the Gentiles).*

"Gospel of the circumcision . . . of the uncircumcision . . ." Huxtable was correct in the observation that:

This does not indicate any diversity in the doctrine communicated to the uncircumcision from that communicated to the Jews, but simply a diversity in the sphere of its proclamation.[19]

The marvelous tenderness and forebearance of the heavenly Father are fully in view in all of these remarkable events. The failure of the apostleship in Jerusalem to get on with preaching the gospel "to the whole creation" as Christ had commanded them to do (Mark 16:15, 16) was the most deplorable sin they ever committed. For God to have permitted the Judaizing of Christianity would have been, in its final result, the restriction of salvation to Jews alone; and the entire premise of God's loving all men and desiring their salvation would have been countermanded and nullified. That was the acute and fatal nature of the

[17]*Ibid.*, p. 477.
[18]*Ibid.*
[19]E. Huxtable, *op. cit.*, p. 75.

problem. The intervention of God himself at such a juncture was
the only way to correct it. This accounts for the conversion of
Saul of Tarsus who had the power to cut the umbilical cord that
strapped the infant church to Judaism, threatening to strangle
Christianity to death.

The weakness of the Twelve, springing from their environment, and their failure (at first) to understand the world-wide,
independent nature of Christianity, was contained by Almighty
God in those events clustered around the name of Paul; and with
infinite mercy and tenderness, the Father did not remove or
punish the Twelve, but on the other hand, committed the preaching to the Gentiles to one more able than themselves to do it.
Later on, of course, the Twelve took up and discharged fully their
total responsibility. Would they ever have been able to do so
without Paul? It seems unlikely; therefore the miracle of Paul!

Verse 9, *And when they perceived the grace that was given unto
me, James and Cephas and John, they who were reputed to be
pillars, gave to me and Barnabas the right hands of fellowship, that
we should go unto the Gentiles and they unto the circumcision.*

"James and Cephas and John . . ." James the brother of John
had already been slain by Herod (Acts 12), and this James was
the oldest brother of Jesus (Matt 13:55f), which probably
accounts for his influence in the Jerusalem church at this time.
Here he was named even ahead of Peter and John; and his
position seems to have been that of a "leading elder" in the
church there.

"Were reputed to be pillars . . ." Paul does not deny with this
the high office belonging to the Twelve, not the deserved reputation and esteem they enjoyed in Jerusalem; but there is a hint
here that their specific behavior with regard to the Gentiles was
unbecoming. The "reputed pillars" had caved in in this glaring
particular. The words are therefore spoken in love and pity,
rather than reproachfully.

"Right hands of fellowship . . ." This was the big point of
Paul's relating this incident. Despite their own defection (in that
sense), they nevertheless unhesitatingly agreed that Paul was
preaching the pure and unadulterated gospel, a thing which
they, through timidity, at the moment were not doing; and some
little time would elapse before they would.

Verse 10, *Only they would that we should remember the poor; which very thing I was also zealous to do.*

Paul mentioned this as a practical matter and with a view to alerting the Galatian churches that they might expect him to raise money from them to be distributed among the poor, as soon as he should have the opportunity. On Paul's final visit to Jerusalem, he delivered such a contribution to James and the elders in Jerusalem (Acts 21:17).

THE CONFRONTATION WITH PETER

The next eleven verses (11-21) were written, it seems, to emphasize, not merely that Paul's gospel had been approved by the Twelve, but that in one grave particular, he preached the true gospel even when it was opposed by such men as Peter and even Barnabas. The chronology of the incident described here is difficult, if not impossible, to determine. Dummelow noted that:

> Some hold that St. Paul in this passage is not mentioning a later instance of his independence, but merely another instance of it which was earlier in time than that mentioned in verses 1-10.[20]

Favoring that understanding are the indefinite "when Cephas came to Antioch" (v. 11), and the "before that" of verse 12, which may be Paul's way of saying that the episode he was about to relate happened "before" the one just recorded. This would make Peter's conduct appear to be a little less flagrant than when it is understood as coming immediately after the events just narrated. However, if it was an earlier action, it still came after the experience he had in the home of Cornelius (Acts 10), being totally reprehensible, no matter when it occurred. Ramsay also held that is is not mandatory to interpret the last half of this chapter as coming after the first part, quoting Turner and Zahn as having the same view.[21]

McGarvey wrote that "It was probably very soon after the council in Jerusalem."[22] Lipscomb declared that "I am confident that it could not have come before";[23] and Ridderbos said, "It

---

[20]J. R. Dummelow, *Commentary on the Holy Bible* (New York: The Macmillan Company, 1937), p. 949.

[21]William M. Ramsay, *A Historical Commentary on St. Paul's Epistles to the Galatians* (Grand Rapids: Baker Book House, 1965), p. 304.

[22]J. W. McGarvey, *op. cit.,* p. 260.

[23]David Lipscomb, *op. cit.,* p. 208.

seems to lie in the whole bearing of the context that Peter came to Antioch after the apostolic council."[24] John William Russell thought, "This was previous to the visit of Paul to Jerusalem."[25] Not a great deal hinges on the point, either way.

Verse 11, *But when Peter came to Antioch, I resisted him to the face, because he stood condemned.*

"He stood condemned . . ." Far from being infallible in matters of doctrine, the apostle Peter, who is alleged to have been the first pope, here committed the most fundamental doctrinal error imaginable, upsetting completely the false teaching of Peter's supremacy. Peter was not merely condemned by a fellow-apostle, he was self-condemned, his own conscience reproving and repudiating his actions. Paul stated in Romans (2:1) the principle that holds a man self-condemned if he practices what he condemns in others. This Peter did, for he advocated eating with Gentiles in Acts 10; but here he refused to do so.

Before going any further with this said failure of the beloved Peter, it should be brought to mind that this was only a momentary thing. As Halley put it:

> It took a few years for the apostles to get adjusted to the new teaching; and Paul adjusted more quickly than Peter did. The Galatian incident happened after Paul had come all the way out of Judaism, and while Peter was coming out. But Peter did come all the way out before any of the books of the NT were written, and there is not an iota of difference between the teaching of Paul and Peter in the NT.[26]

Paul was compelled to relate this for reasons which were no doubt providential. The utter condemnation of all the arrogant claims of the historical church regarding the supremacy of Peter, his infallibility, and their own alleged succession to such prerogatives is accomplished by this narrative, as well as the practical thing at hand, in which Paul used it to defend his own apostleship.

Verses 12-13, *For before that certain came from James, he ate with the Gentiles; but when they came, he drew back and*

---

[24]Herman N. Ridderbos, *op. cit.,* p. 95.

[25]John William Russell, *Compact Commentary on the New Testament* (Grand Rapids: Baker Book House, 1964), *in loco.*

[26]Henry H. Halley, *Halley's Bible Handbook* (Grand Rapids: Zondervan Publishing House, 1927), p. 561.

separated himself, fearing them that were of the circumcision. And the rest of the Jews dissembled likewise with him; insomuch that even Barnabas was carried away with their dissimulation.

"From James . . ." In Acts 15, it is learned that these Judaizers actually had no commission whatever from James (Acts 15:24), yet they were sinfully and deceitfully operating in his name.

The identity of these Judaizers is provided in Acts 6:7, 15:5, where it is made clear that they were priests of the sect of the Pharisees who had accepted the gospel, but were unwilling to give up the customs and ceremonies of Judaism. They were a powerful and very influential group, and Paul here made extenuating remarks regarding the conduct of both Peter and Barnabas, Peter's mistake being due to fear of the powerful Pharisaical party, and Barnabas' being that he was just "carried away" with it in a moment of weakness.

Verse 14, *But when I saw that they walked not uprightly according to the truth of the gospel, I said unto Cephas before them all, If thou, being a Jew, livest as do the Gentiles, and not as do the Jews, how compellest thou the Gentiles to live as do the Jews?*

"I said unto Cephas . . . before them all . . ." This bold rebuke administered by Paul to Peter may not be taken as a relaxation of Jesus' rule that the brother having sinned should first be approached privately (see CM 5:24). The situation was not one which pertains to any persons today, for both Paul and Peter were inspired apostles of the highest rank; and the near-unique situation demanded exactly what Paul did here. We therefore disagree with Hendriksen that here is established the principle of "rebuking publicly those who have sinned publicly,"[27] unless and until the three steps commanded by Jesus in Matthew 18: 15-17 have been taken. Church leaders, as recommended by Calvin, taking upon them to imitate Paul's action here, are presuming far too much. Besides, it is not certainly known that Paul had not already, in this case, taken the steps of the first and second admonitions, as he had instructed Titus to do (3:10); but no matter what Paul did, it is the instruction to Titus that more correctly fits the analogy with church leaders today. See much more on this in CM 18:15.

---

[27]William Hendriksen, *New Testament Commentary on Galatians* (Grand Rapids: Baker Book House, 1968), p. 96.

Verses 15-16, *But we being Jews by nature, and not sinners of the Gentiles, yet knowing that a man is not justified by the works of the law but through* FAITH OF JESUS CHRIST *even we believed on Christ Jesus, that we might be justified by the* FAITH OF JESUS CHRIST, *and not by the works of law; because by the works of the law shall no flesh be justified.* (AV)

This passage announces the great theme of Galatians, which is *Justification by the Faith of Christ*; and the key words in it have been properly rendered, in the light of the best scholarship on earth, and capitalized to emphasize the truth.

RE: THE TRANSLATION ACCEPTED HERE

The teaching set forth in this series of commentaries with regard to justification is advocated fully in CR 3:22; and the student is referred to that for a great deal of material that cannot be repeated here. Since the publication of that volume in 1973, further scholarly studies by distinguished theologians have fully confirmed the undeniable accuracy of translating "faith of Christ" instead of "faith in Christ" in this place and a number of other places in the NT. Of course, the AV is correct in most of these places, though not in all; and strong voices have for years been crying out against the perversion inherent in changing God's word to read otherwise than the way it is handed down to men in the Greek NT. Foy E. Wallace, Jr., decried the butchering of the passage at hand thus:

> In this verse (Galatians 2:16), "by the faith of Christ" is changed to "only through faith in Christ"; but " the faith of Christ" refers to the gospel system of faith, and they have manipulated this passage to teach justification by faith only, going so far as to change "the works of the law" (the law of Moses) to "deeds dictated by law"; yet faith itself is a law (Rom. 3:27). . . . A committee of text-makers who will artfully twist such a specific gospel passage to implement the false doctrine of faith alone will do anything in the name of translation.[28]

As recently as April, 1974, Professor George Howard, University of Georgia, published a study of "The Faith of Christ" in *Expositor Times*, pointing out that James Macknight in the 19th century, Gabriel Hebert in 1955, and other great scholars have demanded that this passage be translated correctly as "the

---

[28]Foy. E. Wallace, Jr., *A Review of the New Versions* (Fort Worth: The Foy E. Wallace, Jr., Publications, 1973), p. 509.

faith of Christ."[29] After citing dozens of scientific studies by distinguished linguists, he gave as his conclusion that:

We may conclude then that grammatically speaking *pistis Christou* should be rendered "faith of Christ."[30]

He even went further and affirmed that the usual definition of faith as the word is used in the NT is not trust/faith as usually thought, but "faithfulness," in the sense of "obedience," "reliability," or "fidelity."[31] That this is the truth appears from Paul's references to "obedient faith" at both ends of the book of Romans (1:5; 16:26).

Thus the "faith of Christ" includes both his own trust/faith in the heavenly Father, and his perfect obedience and fidelity in the discharge of his mission of redemption. The doctrine of salvation through faith only is wrong on many counts. It is wrong in misunderstanding the sinner's trust/faith as the ground of justification, whereas it is actually the obedient faith of the Son of God; and even in the Lord's case, it was not faith *only*, but faith and perfect obedience. It is totally wrong to regard "faith in Christ" (as used in the NT) as reference to the theological concept trust/faith, or subjective faith of the sinner; because as noted by Howard, the usual *definition in the NT* is not that at all, but fidelity. There are other instances in which "faith in Christ" means "the Christian religion," a definition Wallace applied in this verse, but which this writer feels is incorrect in this context. Over and beyond all this, let the key expression "in Christ" be given its proper emphasis, and it is at once clear that no man who ever breathed has "faith in Christ" when he himself has refused to be baptized into Christ, in which case he might have faith out of Christ," but not "in him." Another legitimate meaning of "faith in Christ" is faith exercised by one who is "in Christ," having been baptized into him, made partakers of the Holy Spirit, and fully identified as a member of Christ's spiritual body, the church.

"The faith of Christ . . . ." meaning his perfect fidelity and obedience, is actually the ground of man's redemption. Absolute perfection is required of all who would be saved (Matt. 5:48), a

---

[29]George Howard, Article: "The Faith of Christ," in *Expositor Times,* Vol. 7, pp. 212-214, April, 1974.
[30]*Ibid.*
[31]*Ibid.*

state that is not attainable by any man who ever lived, save only Jesus Christ our Lord, Immanuel. Perfection being the *sine qua non* without which none shall enter eternal life, how may it be procured and in a sense achieved by man? God's device of making one perfect, in the sense of being absolutely justified, is that of transferring him into Christ, identifying him with Christ and as Christ, a transferrence and identity achieved on behalf of the Christian when he is in the spiritual body of Christ. Thus Paul could say, "That we may present every man perfect in Christ" (Col. 1:28). See article on "Jesus Christ, Inc.," in CR. As Paul would say a little later in this chapter, the life which the Christian lives is not his own, but Christ's (v.20).

"Even we believed on Christ Jesus . . ." This is sinners' faith, introduced into the passage after the "faith of Christ" was mentioned just ahead of it; and if "faith of Christ" meant a sinner's believing in Christ, this clause would not have been added. Paul develops this great theme throughout the following passages in the epistle.

"Works of the law . . ." refers to Jewish ceremonial in the Law of Moses and has no reference whatever to the ordinances of the Christian religion and to moral obligations and duties of Christians.

Verse 17, *But if, while we sought to be justified in Christ, we ourselves also were found sinners, is Christ a minister of sin? God forbid.*

This is somewhat parenthetical to clear up any possible misunderstanding. Paul had just laid down the gospel that we are justified by the faith of Christ; and, in order to prevent any man from thinking that his own fidelity and compliance with Christ's teaching were not needed, Paul effectively denied such a thought with this verse. Christians are not saved in their sins but from their sins. And holiness is an attainment without which no man shall see the Lord. This does not imply that one has to be perfect, an impossibility anyway, but it does teach that a man must do his best to serve God. God will supply whatever is lacking on the Christian's part, so that at last every man shall be accounted "saved by grace" and not by any merit whatever.

Verse 18, *For if I build up again those things which I destroyed, I prove myself a transgressor.*

Hendriksen paraphrased the meaning of this as, "If I start to rebuild the very things I have torn down, it is then that I prove myself a transgressor."[32]

"The things I have torn down" would be the ceremonial regulations of Judaism; and Paul here stated that it would be sinful if again he reverted to their observance.

Verse 19, *For I through the law died unto the law, that I might live unto God.*

"To live unto God" is to be in Christ who lives at God's right hand; where Christ is, there the Christian is; for because of his membership in Christ's spiritual body, there is a sense in which he "is Christ." Christ died, therefore we have died in his person on Calvary as our substitute. That is what Paul meant by saying, "We are baptized into his death." Through the Christian's being "in Christ," and identified with Christ, he has already perished upon the cross in the person of his substitute. "Being dead to sin but alive unto God in Christ" (Rom. 6:11) has a meaning parallel with this verse. The Romans passage does not mean that "in Christ" the Christian is no longer tempted; but that "in Christ" the penalty of sin, which is death, is already paid upon behalf of the Christians by Christ who died on the cross. Here the thought is that "in Christ" Christians have already fulfilled all of the law, since that is what Christ did; and we are "in him " and "of him." Also, there is here the thought that men are dead to the law through the body of Christ.

Verse 20, *I have been crucified with Christ; and it is no longer I that live, but Christ liveth in me: and that life which I now live in the flesh I live by the* FAITH OF THE SON OF GOD *who loved me, and gave himself for me.* (AV)

Here we have followed the AV, because of the accurate rendition of "FAITH OF THE SON OF GOD."

"It is no longer I that live . . ." This touches the incredibly important truth that no man is ever saved in his own personal identity as possessing any true righteousness. All of the righteousness of God is in Christ (Eph. 1:3); and no mortal may be saved as John Doe. He must renounce self and become identified with Christ who *is righteous.* "As Christ," therefore, he is

---

[32]William Hendriksen, *op. cit.,* p. 101.

dead to sin, has fulfilled the law, is alive unto God, and the heir
of eternal glory "in Christ." "This doctrine, one of the fundamen-
tals of Pauline theology, is one of the concepts which gives meaning to and ties together in a coherent whole the various aspects
of Paul's gospel."[33] This forsaking of one's identity to be "Christ,
in a sense, *in Christ*" was announced by Christ himself, who
said, "If any man would come after me, let him deny himself,
and take up his cross, and follow me" (Matt. 16:24). Also he said,
"He that abideth in me, and I in him, the same beareth much
fruit . . . If a man abide not in me, he is cast forth as a branch,
etc." (John 15:4-6). Therefore, if a man is able to answer two
questions affirmatively, there is no way he can be lost. (1) Is he
"in Christ"? (The only way one can be "in Christ" is to be
baptized into him.) (2) Will he be "found in him"? (Phil 3:9). This
means, will he still be "in Christ" when life ends, or the Lord
comes? The person described by affirmative answers to these
questions is of them concerning whom the voice from heaven
said, "Blessed are the dead who die in the Lord" (Rev. 14:13).

Verse 21, *I do not make void the grace of God: for if righteousness is through the law, then Christ died for naught.*

The great problem existing from the day man first committed
sin is, "How can even God justly declare a human being to be
righteous?" That the Law of Moses could not do it is an axiom.
If true righteousness could have been procured by any man who
ever lived on earth through means of the Mosaic Law, Christ's
death would not have been necessary. The corollary of that is
that for one to rely upon law-keeping for justification is to
repudiate and reject Christ' sacrifice.

And *how* does God justly account a man to be righteous? It
is not by shooting righteousness into him gratuitously because
he believed, but by transfering the sinner into Christ who IS
righteous, the sinner first of all renouncing his own identity, in
the sense of having any merit (as Jesus said, "denying himself"),
being baptized into Christ and remaining "in him" till the final
summons. It is the perfect faith and righteousness of Jesus
Christ which constitute "the righteousness of God through the
FAITH OF CHRIST" (Rom. 3:22-26). Please see CR, chapter 3, for
extensive discussion of this.

---

[33]George Howard, *op. cit.,* p. 214.

CHAPTER 3

In this great chapter, Paul proceeded, after relating his confrontation with the apostle Peter, to expound the central theme of Galatians, which is Justification by the Faith of Jesus Christ. This chapter is considered by many commentators and theologians to be the stronghold of their doctrine that the *subjective faith only* of Christians is the ground for justification, notwithstanding the truth that not a single word in the chapter may legitimately be construed as teaching such a proposition.

Some prior knowledge of Almighty God and the nature of his dealings with mankind will help to understand this chapter. From the days of Cain and Abel, one of whom was cursed and the other blessed, for the simple reason that the deeds of one were righteous and the deeds of the other were evil (1 John 3:12), and throughout the history of the patriarchs, and continuing down through the Jewish monarchy, where of various kings it is said that some "did that which was right and good in the eyes of the Lord" (2 Chron. 14:2), and of others, that they "did that which was evil in the sight of the Lord" (2 Chron. 33:2), with the result that some received God's blessing and others did not, men's obedience or disobedience to God's commandments has been the primary and invariable determinator of their destiny. Not even the perfect salvation which Christians have received "in Christ" nullifies this basic law of God's dealings with mankind. As Paul wrote the Corinthian church:

> For we must all be manifest before the judgment seat of Christ; that each one may receive the things done in the body, according to what he hath done, whether it be good or bad (2 Cor. 5:10).

Any notion that Paul relaxed or countermanded this truth is erroneous. The relationship between the Jews and the Law of Moses, as contrasted with the relationship between the Christian and the "law of the Spirit of life in Christ Jesus" (Rom. 8:2), lies only in this: (1) if the Jew did his best to live up to the law (and failed, as all must fail), he nevertheless stood condemned anyway; (2) but if the Christian does his best to keep all of the commandments of the gospel (failing in particulars, as all must fail), he is nevertheless justified and remains uncondemned, because through his identity with Christ "in Christ" and "as Christ," the righteousness of Christ, with whom the true Christian is fully identified, stands in the stead of his own failure, saving his soul anyway. But in such a conception there is no relaxation whatever of the eternal rule that obedience to God is the *sine qua non* of salvation. In Christ, the obedience is provided by Christ, but certainly not on behalf of those who refused to obey, believed that they were not required to obey, or who through indifference and neglect never got around to obeying. The great fallacy of salvation by "faith only" is that it utterly removes from human hearts all concern whatever with regard to keeping the commandments of the Lord. Paul thunders the refutation of that fallacy throughout his writings, as in this example:

> Rest with us at the revelation of the Lord Jesus from heaven with the angels of his power in flaming fire, rendering vengeance to them that know not God, and to them that obey not the gospel of our Lord Jesus (2 Thess. 1:7, 8).

Furthermore, the necessity of obedience (to the fullest extent of human ability) in order to be saved, does not make man his own Savior; because the Christian, no more effectual than the Jew, is simply not able to give perfect compliance to God's teachings. Thus, all salvation is by grace, without human merit, unearned and incapable of being earned. Despite this, how can any man be saved who has consciously rejected for himself any requirement whatever that God has enjoined upon men? On the basis that he *merely believed*? Even devils believe (James 2:19).

Another fundamental truth regarding this chapter was enunciated by Halley, thus:

> Those Galatians had swallowed the Judaizers' message so completely that they had instituted Jewish festival days and ceremonies (4:8-11), evidently trying to combine the gospel with the Mosaic Law. Paul plainly tells them the two systems do not combine.[1]

The *works* vs. *faith* contrast in this epistle regards the incompatibility of Judaism and Christianity, and absolutely nothing else. The separation of subjective faith from Christian obedience with regard to the ground of justification is not under consider-

---

[1]Henry H. Halley, *Halley's Bible Handbook* (Grand Rapids: Zondervan Publishing House, 1927), p. 561.

ation at all, nor may a single line in the whole epistle be rightfully applied to such a proposition.

Verse 1, *O foolish Galatians, who did bewitch you, before
whose eyes Jesus Christ was openly set forth crucified?*

"Jesus Christ and him crucified" was the burden of Paul's
preaching throughout every moment of his apostleship. The
scholarly conceit that Paul only came to this method after failing with a different method at Athens is refuted by the fact that
in Galatia, long before Paul came to Corinth, his message was
the same.

"Foolish Galatians . . ." By such an adjective, Paul did not
violate the Saviour's injunction in Matthew 5:22. It is the same
word Jesus used in Luke 24:25."[2] Phillips' translation renders
this "You dear idiots," and the NEB has "You stupid Galatians."

"Who did bewitch you . . . ?" Barclay declares that the word
here means "the evil eye," rendering it, "Who has put the evil
eye on you?"[3] Still, it is wrong to suppose that Paul absolved the
Galatians themselves from the blame. It was their stupidity that
lay at the base of it.

"Jesus Christ was openly set forth . . ." This is "from the
Greek word *prographein*, used for putting up a poster."[4] This
means that the dramatic story of Jesus' crucifixion, burial and
resurrection had been emphatically and publicly proclaimed.

Verse 2, *This only would I learn from you, Received ye the
Spirit by the works of the Law, or by the hearing of faith?*

It will be noted that "Law" has been capitalized throughout
this chapter to indicate the one and only law Paul referred to
throughout, meaning the Law of Moses. The commentators are
less than candid when they use terminology that confuses this,
as Dummelow, who said: "The apostle upbraids their speedy
change from faith to legal observances," [5] leaving room for the
allegation that something other than the Mosaic Law is meant.

---

[2]William Sanday, *Ellicott's Commentary on the Whole Bible* (Grand Rapids:
Zondervan Publishing House, 1959), p. 440.

[3]William Barclay, *The Letters to the Galatians and Ephesians* (Philadelphia:
The Westminster Press, 1954), p. 24.

[4]*Ibid.*, p. 26.

[5]J. R. Dummelow, *Commentary on the Holy Bible* (New York: The Macmillan Company, 1937), p. 950.

"The hearing of faith . . ." This is a shameful rendition of a phrase which actually means "the obedience of faith."[6] As so frequently in the NT, faith must be understood as an obedient faith, as in Romans 1:5; 16:26. "The hearing of faith" in this verse means exactly the same thing, as Macknight pointed out:

> Here, as in verse 5, it means "the obedience of faith," as also in 1 Samuel 15:22 (LXX), "behold, obedience is better than sacrifice." In like manner, the compound word means "disobedience," as translated in Romans 5:19.[7]

Cole is therefore absolutely wrong in rendering this "hearing and believing."[8] Foy E. Wallace decried the butchering of this text, saying flatly that it has "been bungled."[9] Of course, it was bungled on purpose to support a theory. Riddebos spoke of this passage as being "not easy to manage";[10] and indeed it is *impossible* to manage it in such a manner as to make it support the "faith only" thesis, except by mis-translating it. The "obedience of faith" mentioned here at the head of the chapter makes it certain that Paul was dealing with a contrast between Judaism and Christianity, and not between two ways of understanding the gospel.

Verse 3, *Are ye so foolish? having begun in the Spirit, are ye now perfected in the flesh?*

"In the Spirit . . . in the flesh . . ." is another way of contrasting Judaism and Christianity, "the Spirit" being the endowment of all Christians, and "fleshly descent" being the total basis of Jewish confidence. But the constant manipulation of every text in the NT to fit the "faith only" notion must be maintained: "They received the Spirit by faith,"[11] as one declared, despite the fact that faith is not mentioned in this verse, and despite the further fact that nobody ever received the Spirit except in conse-

---

[6]James Macknight, *Apostolical Epistles with Commentary and Notes* (Grand Rapids: Baker Book House, 1969), p. 139.

[7]*Ibid.*

[8]R. A. Cole, *The Epistle of Paul to the Galatians* (Grand Rapids: Wm. B. Eerdmans Publishing Company, 1965), p. 89.

[9]Foy E. Wallace, Jr., *A Review of the New Versions* (Fort Worth: The Foy E. Wallace, Jr., Publications, 1973), p. 442.

[10]H. N. Ridderbos, *The Epistles of Paul to the Churches of Galatia* (Grand Rapids: Wm. B. Eerdmans Publishing Company, 1953), p. 113.

[11]R. E. Howard, *Beacon Bible Commentary* (Kansas City: Beacon Hill Press, 1965), Vol. IX, p. 55.

quence of his believing, repenting and being baptized into Christ (Acts 2:38), or as Paul said a little later in this epistle, "Because ye are sons God has sent forth the Spirit of his Son into our hearts" (4:6). The full meaning is: "Are you so foolish, after receiving the Spirit in consequence of your faithful obedience of the gospel, to think that Judaism can bless you in any manner?"

Verse 4, *Did ye suffer so many things in vain? if it be indeed in vain?*

Some translate "suffer" here as "experience" (NEB); but even if this is allowable, their experience would have included their sufferings. This writer agrees with Howard that this refers to the persecutions brought against them from the very first by the Judaizers. The whole passage, as Ramsay thought, points squarely at Pisidian Antioch, Iconium, Lystra and Derbe of the first missionary journey.[12]

Verse 5, *He therefore that supplieth to you the Spirit and worketh miracles among you, doeth he it by the works of the Law, or by the hearing of faith?*

"Worketh miracles among you . . ." "This is exactly the same phrase as in 1 Corinthians 12:10,"[13] and logically refers to the miracles which Paul himself had performed among them, notable examples of which, as Ramsay pointed out, were (1) the healing of the lame man at Lystra (Acts 14:9), and (2) the signs and wonders done at Iconium (Acts 14:3). Of course, Ramsay identified "the Galatians" as those churches of Paul's first missionary journey.[14]

"Works of law . . . hearing of faith . . ." See under verse 2.

Verse 6, *Even as Abraham believed God, and it was reckoned unto him for righteousness.*

By the introduction of this great truth, Paul refuted the notion that the Law of Moses had had anything to do with the salvation of Abraham. Since Abraham was justified, or reckoned righteous in God's sight, without regard to the Law of Moses,

---

[12]William M. Ramsay, *A Historical Commentary on St. Paul's Epistles to the Galatians* (Grand Rapids: Baker Book House, 1965), p. 327.

[13]W. J. Conybeare, *The Life and Epistles of St. Paul* (Grand Rapids: Wm. B. Eerdmans Publishing Company, 1966), p. 484.

[14]William M. Ramsay, *op. cit.*, p. 327.

Abraham being the ancestor of every Jew on earth, why should any of his remote descendants, much less the Gentile Galatians, think to gain anything at all from it? The argument is profound and beautiful.

"Abraham believed God . . ." Abraham's faith, not his faith only but his *obedient faith*, was the basis of God's reckoning him to be righteous. Of course, Abraham did not obey perfectly; but the whole compass of his life was lived out in a frame of obedience to God's commands. The ridiculous postulations of the "faith only" advocates to the effect that, since Abraham was justified without obeying the Law of Moses (which never even existed till centuries after Abraham) and without circumcision (which also came long after God's justification of him), therefore he was justified by "faith only" and without any obedience whatever, is just as illogical as it is ridiculous. The NT plainly reveals the *time* of God's justifying Abraham in such places as the following:

Was not Abraham our father justified by works, *when* he had offered Isaac his son upon the altar? (James 2:21 AV).

Was not Abraham our father justified by works, in that he offered up Isaac his son upon the altar? (James 2:21 RV).

Despite the obvious attempt to soften this in the RV (to accommodate a theory?), the meaning shines through anyway; for it was not Abraham's "mere faith" which resulted in justification, but justification was "by works." It did not occur as soon as Abraham believed, but "in that he offered" Isaac. Both the Emphatic Diaglott and the Nestle Greek retain the "when."

And if these references should be thought of as insufficient, go back to Genesis. It is revealed that God "did test" Abraham's faith (Gen. 22:1). There were many tests; but the great one was the command to offer up Isaac; and Abraham did so. He actually offered him and would have slain his son had not God interposed. And upon that occasion, God said:

Now I know that thou fearest God, seeing that thou hast not withheld thy son, thine only son from me (Gen. 22:12).

By such a declaration, God implied that until then, the issue of Abraham's faith had not been settled. When Abraham met the test, God said, "*Now* I know."

Now the absurdity of supposing that today God saves men without any test whatever of their faith, and merely upon their supposition that they have had some kind of subjective experience of "faith," is clearly evident. Exactly the same kind of divinely imposed test of every man's faith in Christ was announced by none other than the Christ himself who declared, "He that believeth and is baptized shall be saved" (Mark 16:15, 16); furthermore, in that passage, Jesus gave that as his own personal definition of the gospel. Let men scream about it if they will, the truth shines in the word of God; and may God protect all of us from the stupidity of the Galatians in turning away from it.

"Works" as advocated in the NT as entering into Abraham's justification should not be understood in the sense of any perfect obedience by Abraham to everything God commanded, for he palmed off his wife as his sister, and was doubtless guilty of other sins; but, in the all-important matter of meeting the final test of doing what God commanded instead of obeying his own human will, Abraham passed the test. Among Christians, it may be supposed, perfect obedience is not considered to be possible; but in basic tests such as complying with the divinely imposed preconditions of redemption, such tests must be passed by those who hope to enter eternal life. Also, Christians will not merit, earn, or deserve salvation any more than did Abraham.

Verse 7, *Know therefore that they that are of faith, the same are sons of Abraham.*

The grand argument is that Abraham was justified upon the exhibition of an obedient faith; and persons today who manifest an obedient faith through their acceptance of the gospel message and obedience to it are true children of Abraham "in Christ." See under verses 16, 27.

Verses 8-9, *And the scripture, foreseeing that God would justify the Gentiles by faith, preached the gospel beforehand unto Abraham, saying, In thee shall all the nations be blessed. So then they that are of faith are blessed with the faithful Abraham.*

"Justify the Gentiles by faith . . ." The NT meaning of the word "faith" has been grossly distorted by post-Reformation theologians. "Its meaning in the NT is most often *faithfulness*,"[15] which is the normal meaning of the word in the LXX, where the word never means *trust/faith* in the sense of the current usage

---

[15]George Howard, Article: "The Faith of Christ," in *Expositor Times,* Vol. 7, pp. 212-214, April, 1974.

of it."[16] "The normal meaning of *faith* in the Greek language is not *trust/faith*, but *reliability*, or *fidelity*."[17] Of course, anyone with a knowledge of Pauline teaching could not possibly believe that Paul here meant that the Gentiles were saved by *trust/faith only*. In the language in which Paul was writing, such a thought did not normally belong to the word at all.

"The gospel unto Abraham . . ." The words "In thee shall all the nations be blessed," immediately following, identify what Paul meant by the gospel preached to Abraham. The word *nations* in the promise to Abraham means "Gentiles," who would be saved in exactly the same manner as Abraham, namely, by the "obedience of faith." Paul elaborated that in verse 16, below.

Verse 10, *For as many as are of the works of the law are under a curse: for it is written, Cursed is every one who continueth not in all things that are written in the book of the law, to do them.*

The human impossibility of any man's doing "All the things of the law" rendered every man attempting to do so subject to the curse, here quoted from Deuteronomy 27:26. The Galatians, by fooling around with circumcision and Jewish festival, had inadvertently obligated themselves, under penalty of God's curse, to keep the whole law, every jot and tittle of it, an achievement which only Jesus Christ accomplished.

Verses 11-12, *Now that no man is justified by the Law before God, is evident: for, The righteous shall live by faith; and the Law is not of faith; but, He that doeth them shall live in them.*

"No man is justified by the Law . . ." The reason this is true is cited in verse 10. There was another important indication of the same truth, which Paul then quoted from Habakkuk 2:4, i.e., "The righteous shall live by faith"; thus the prophets had borne testimony to the fact that the purpose of God, even in the OT, was looking for an "obedient faith" in his children, and not merely for the legalistic type of rule-keeping which was the essence of the Law. The Law did not even require faith, as seen in the quotation Paul gave here from Leviticus 18:5, the meaning of which may be paraphrased, "No matter about faith;

---

[16]*Ibid.*
[17]*Ibid.*

do the Law and live." This was the essence of Judaism. See note 2, at end of chapter.

Now regarding the conceit that would make Habakkuk say, "The righteous shall live by FAITH ONLY!" such a meaning was never in any OT usage of *faith*. As we have already observed, *trust/faith* or *faith only* simply did not pertain to the word in the OT. Paul was here merely pointing out that, from the beginning, God had been interested in receiving "faithful obedience" from his followers, and not a mere faithless rule-keeping. We might add that the meaning of *trust/faith* or *faith only* is also foreign to the meaning of the word in the NT, or even in the Greek language, as Professor Howard has so effectively demonstrated.

There was still another sense in which the Law was a curse, and Paul quickly pointed that out.

Verse 13, *Christ redeemed us from the curse of the Law, having become a curse for us: for it is written, Cursed is every one that hangeth on a tree.*

The quotation is from Deuteronomy 21:23; and, since Christ was crucified on "the tree," the curse of the Law rested upon the Saviour and Redeemer of all mankind, and this in spite of the fact that Jesus our Lord was the unique and only person of all time who ever kept the totality of the Law in perfection. Cole was doubtless correct in seeing in this verse a rough parallel with 2 Corinthians 5:21, where it is declared that "God made him who knew no sin to be sin on our behalf." Only by his crucifixion and suffering "without the camp" could the holy prophecies have been fulfilled by the Lord.

Verse 14, *That upon the Gentiles might come the blessing of Abraham in Christ Jesus; that we might receive the promise of the Spirit through faith.*

"In Christ Jesus . . ." This is the cornerstone and foundation of the gospel Paul (and all the apostles) preached. The Gentiles will be blessed, along with Abraham, "in Christ," thus becoming technically part of Christ's spiritual body, therefore truly of "the seed singular" of Abraham, which is Christ. See under verse 16, where Paul elaborated this.

"Through faith . . ." Every scholar on earth knows that the article precedes "faith" in this place in the Greek NT, and that the only honest translation is "through the faith," meaning through the Christian religion. See Emphatic Diaglott, Nestle

Greek Text, or any dependable Greek-English rendition of the
NT. Foy E. Wallace also pointed this out. The attempted
perversion of the meaning of this chapter is so extensive as to be
phenomenal. The last thing on earth that this passage could mean
is that the Gentiles shall be saved through *trust/faith alone*, which
by any definition can be nothing but a subjective personal
experience without any merit or trustworthiness whatever.

Verse 15, *Brethren, I speak after the manner of men: though
it be but a man's covenant, yet when it hath been confirmed, no
man maketh it void, or addeth thereto.*

Paul is here still exposing the sinful arguments of the
Judaizers, who despite the fact of Abraham's being accounted
righteous by God, long before the giving of the Law, were insisting that God, in a sense, had amended the requirements of
righteousness by the addition of the Mosaic Law. This Paul
denied on the basis that, even in the case of a human covenant,
it could not be altered by one of the parties after it had been
ratified and confirmed, thus demonstrating the proof that God's
covenant with Abraham was founded, not upon his keeping the
Law (which never existed till centuries afterward), but upon
God's promise made long before the Law came into being. The
application of this is the same as that Paul pointed out in verses
6ff, namely, that if the ancestor of all Jews was redeemed without the Law, there could be no earthly use of anyone's keeping it.

"Covenant . . ." For extended remarks on the use of this word
in the NT, see CH 9:16-17.

Verse 16, *Now to Abraham were the promises spoken, and to
his seed. He saith not, And to seeds as of many; but as of one, And
to thy seed which is Christ.*

"There is in this verse a sense of the corporate meaning of
Christ, as in 1 Corinthians 12:12,"[18] where is mentioned "the
body of Christ" inclusively of all the redeemed. Christ is again
called the "seed singular" in 3:19. This is the verse that tells
"how" the Gentiles, and even the saints of the OT, are saved.
They are saved "in Christ," there being this correspondence
between the manner of their salvation and our own, namely, that

---

[18]Everett F. Harrison, *Wycliffe Bible Commentary* (Chicago: Moody Press,
1971), p. 707.

both for them and for us, the basis of it was "the obedience of faith," notwithstanding the tests for them were not the same as the test which those under the New Covenant must meet. For us, the manner of our being "in Christ" is dogmatically declared to be the baptism of believers "into Christ," as Paul would forcefully show a moment later (3:27).

Howard thought this verse was "an afterthought";[19] Hendriksen spoke of "its being a bit of rabbinical casuistry (equivocal reasoning), ingenious perhaps, but unconvincing";[20] Coad labeled it a "parenthesis";[21] and on, and on. Clearly there is no help from the majority of commentators on this verse. Nevertheless it is the key verse of the entire third chapter. This eliminates completely the nonsense about being saved "by faith only," by making it clear that all salvation is "in Christ," a principle which Paul repeated 169 times in his writings! It is tragic that men would prefer to label the apostle Paul as "an equivocator" rather than face the unwelcome truth of this passage.

Verse 17, *Now this I say: a covenant confirmed beforehand by God, the Law, which came four hundred and thirty years after, doth not disannul, so as to make the promise of none effect.*

This was Paul's repetition for the sake of emphasis of the argument already delivered above.

"Four hundred and thirty years . . ." For comment on the variation in this figure from that given by Stephen in Acts 7:6, see CA 7:5-8. Paul used the figure also found in the LXX, and Stephen used a round number.

Verse 18, *For if the inheritance is of the Law, it is no more of promise: but God hath granted it to Abraham by promise.*

This is based on the profound truth that "all the nations" shall be blessed in the "seed singular" which is Christ. Any salvation allegedly derived from keeping the Law of Moses would, of course, nullify and countermand this promise.

Verse 19, *What then is the Law? It was added because of transgressions, till the seed should come to whom the promise*

---

[19]R. E. Howard, *op. cit.,* p. 62.

[20]William Hendriksen, *New Testament Commentary on Galatians* (Grand Rapids: Baker Book House, 1968), p. 134.

[21]F. Roy Coad, *A New Testament Commentary* (Grand Rapids: Zondervan Publishing House, 1969), p. 134.

hath been made; and it was ordained by angels through the hand of a mediator.

The Law of Moses expired by limitation when Christ came, because it was given only "until" that event.

"Because of transgressions . . ." Paul elaborated the fuller meaning of this in Romans 3:19ff; and for discussion of the utility of the Law see CR. The great service of the Law was to demonstrate that all men are sinners (even the Jews), a fact many of them were loath to admit.

Verse 20, *Now a mediator is not a mediator of one; but God is one.*

This writer will spare the reader any exegesis of this verse. The full or even approximate meaning of it is unknown; and as proof of *that*, it must be pointed out that Huxtable said there are literally hundreds of interpretations;[22] McGarvey said, "This verse has been interpreted in more than three hundred ways;"[23] and Ridderbos declared that "There are four hundred and thirty interpretations of verse 20."[24] It only remains to be added that this writer has never seen an interpretation of it that is wholly satisfactory.

Verse 21, *Is the Law then against the promises of God? God forbid: for if there could have been a Law given which could make alive, verily righteousness would have been of the Law.*

The impossibility of even God's Law making men righteous derived from the weakness and frailty of men. The helplessness of mankind is implicit in this, that man alone unaided, is simply incapable of fully measuring up to God's perfect and holy standard. Glorious is the thought, therefore, that Christ did it for all men who will receive and obey him. Christ fulfilled all of God's Law perfectly; and then, through the device of setting up an extra-literal "body," called in the NT "the body of Christ," into which men upon believing, repenting and being baptized are enrolled, thus becoming in a true sense "Christ," and therefore "in him," achieving saving righteousness. That is what is meant by "the righteousness of God in Christ." This is a genuine

---

[22]E. Huxtable, *Pulpit Commentary* (Grand Rapids: Wm. B. Eerdmans Publishing Company, 1950), Vol. 20, p. 138.

[23]J. W. McGarvey, *The Standard Bible Commentary* (Cincinnati: The Standard Publishing Company, 1916), p. 268.

[24]Herman N. Ridderbos, *op. cit.,* p. 139.

righteousness, not an imputed thing at all, except by the device of the corporate body of Christ. The present-day notion of God in some manner "injecting righteousness," or imputing righteousness to sinners upon the basis of mere faith is incorrect, because "faith only" bypasses the corporate body of Christ, which is his church. This means that it bypasses the "seed singular" who is Christ!

Verse 22, *But the scripture shut up all things under sin, that the promise by faith in Jesus Christ might be given to them that believe.*

As rendered here, this verse makes no sense whatever, for the paraphrase of the latter part of it is, "that the promise by faith in Jesus Christ might be given to them that have faith! What then, is the true rendition? The Authorized Version gave the correct translation thus: "That the promise by the faith of Jesus Christ might be given to them that believe." Even without the authority of the AV, however, it is absolutely clear that sinner's faith is in *the last clause* of this verse, and it has to be the "faith of Christ" in the preceding clause. The faith that saves is never that of the sinner, but that of Christ. Only his faith was perfect, and only his faith was perfectly obedient. In the ultimate sense, there is nothing that any sinner can either believe or perform that is capable of justifying him in the eyes of Almighty God, except in the limited and secondary sense of his "obedience of faith" upon his believing and being baptized, these being prerequisites of his salvation, and thus, in that lower sense, justifying him. See note 3, at the end of this chapter.

Thus the full meaning of verse 22 is that the "promise of sharing in the perfect faith and obedience of Christ (called the faith of Christ) might be given to them that believe." Thus, the *faith only* concept is wrong on two counts, (1) the notion that it is the sinner's imperfect faith that saves, and (2) the proposition that faith should be understood as meaning "faith only." Not even Christ's faith was "faith only," for he was obedient in all things, becoming "unto all them that obey him, the author of eternal salvation" (Heb. 5:9).

"Shut up all things under sin . . ." One great purpose of the Law of Moses was to convict Israel of sin and make the nation conscious of their need of salvation from it. As used by them, however, it became a source of greater pride than ever on their part. The Law's holy commandments were nullified, expanded, contradicted and perverted in countless ways; as Jesus himself revealed to them, "(You) make void the word of God by your tradition, which ye have delivered: and many such like things ye do" (Mark 7:13). If Israel had properly responded to the Law by realizing and confessing their inability to keep it, and the crying need of their souls for redemption from sin, there would have been a far different attitude on their part when the true Messiah came. That favorable attitude looking to the coming of the Redeemer, however, did not develop in Israel to any great extent, thus frustrating the purpose of the Law to prepare men for Christ.

Verse 23, *But before faith came, we were kept in ward under the Law, shut up unto faith which should afterwards be revealed.*

The figure of speech here is that of a jailer keeping his prisoners shut up. The Law could not save men, and the hope of deliverance from the sin which the Law could not forgive could be realized only by the coming of the Holy One.

Verse 24, *So the Law is become our tutor to bring us unto Christ, that we might be justified by faith.*

This verse should be read with careful attention to preceding verse 23, where Paul mentioned "the faith that should afterward be revealed." As Howard said, "The coming of faith (v. 23) here relates to the objective and historical coming of Christ on his redemptive mission and not to the repeated and subjective experience of believers."[25] Furthermore, what "faith" certainly means in verse 23, it means exactly the same thing in verse 24.

"The Law is become our tutor . . ." This rendition is unfortunate, for "The Law was our schoolmaster (tutor) to bring us unto Christ" (AV) is far better. The Law of Moses is not in this dispensation, in any sense whatever, "our tutor." Although the Greek will bear the translation "has become our tutor,"[26] it is clear from verse 25, below, that Christians are not under it.

The translators need to do a little further work on this verse, for neither "schoolmaster" nor "tutor" conveys the thought of

[25]R. E. Howard, *op. cit.,* p. 66.

[26]Alfred Marshall, *The Interlinear Greek-English New Testament (The Nestle Greek Text)* (Grand Rapids: Zondervan Publishing House, 1958), p. 749.

the Greek, where the word is "pedagogue." "He was not a school-master (nor a tutor), but the servant who had the care of the children to lead them to and bring them back from school, and had care of them out of school hours."[27] Thus it is clear that the character Paul used as a comparison with the Law did not teach anything.

"Justified by faith . . ." Exactly like Paul used "faith" in the preceding verse as a reference to historical Christianity, he used it here. A better rendition of it would be "justified by the faith." As frequently in Paul's writings, "faith" is used extensively as a metaphor (synecdoche) of the religion of Christ, or the primary steps of obedience. As invariably in the NT, "faith" in such a context means "the obedience of faith."

Verse 25, *But now that faith is come, we are no longer under a tutor.*

See under verse 24, above, for discussion of this. Note that "faith" is still being used in the sense of the historical arrival of the Christian religion, having no reference at all to subjective trust/faith of individuals. The total separation of Christianity from the Law is here dramatically stated with the comparison to a "pedagogue" no longer needed.

Verse 26, *For ye are all sons of God through faith in Christ Jesus.*

Note that we have omitted the commas (RSV) which serve no purpose and even hinder the meaning. It has already been noted that Paul in this section is using "faith" in the sense of histori-cal Christianity, the same usage being continued here. Mac-knight translated this verse correctly thus: "For ye are all sons of God through the faith published by Christ Jesus."[28] That this meaning is mandatory is clear enough from the whole context. As Cole remarked with reference to theology itself, "it is noth-ing more than ordinary rules of grammar and logic applied to the text of scripture."[29] It has long been apparent that it is not a knowledge of the Greek, but of the grammar, that leads to an accurate understanding of the New Testament.

---

[27]Adam Clarke, *Commentary on the Holy Bible* (New York: Carlton and Porter, 1829), Vol. VI, p. 401.

[28]James Macknight, *op. cit.,* p. 161.

[29]R. A. Cole, *op. cit.,* p. 87.

Verse 27, *For as many of you as were baptized into Christ did put on Christ.*

"Baptized into Christ . . ." is here used in exactly the same manner that "Faith" was in the preceding verse, that is, as a synecdoche for the primary steps of accepting the gospel and becoming a Christian; and by the use of it, Paul testified to the essentiality of it. It violates the rules of grammar to use in such a synecdoche any non-vital, unnecessary or unessential part to stand for the whole. Yet there is a difference between "faith" and "baptism," for here it is declared that men are baptized "into" Christ, a declaration nowhere existing in the NT with regard to "faith."

"As many of you as were baptized into Christ . . ." is only another way of saying that "all of the Galatians" had been so baptized. Howard was certain "that this refers to the initiatory rite of water baptism."[30] Ramsay correctly read Paul's meaning here as follows: "Beyond all doubt Paul considered that, practically, to become a part of Christ implied membership in the church of Christ."[31] The use of "As many of you . . ." means that any who might not have been baptized were *not* in Christ. Ridderbos was correct in seeing this verse "as a limitation on the preceding verse,"[32] making the "ye all" of verse 26, to be modified and restricted to those who had received Christian baptism, thus clearly denying that any persons whomsoever had believed themselves into Christ without being baptized as Jesus commanded.

Of course, there are trainloads of books coming off the presses every month denying the obvious truth of this verse; and among the countless objections alleged against the truth, perhaps the most common is that "Well, not everyone who is baptized is saved." Such an error is due to a misunderstanding of the prerequirements of baptism, i.e., faith and repentance. Now, any person being immersed without those vital prerequisites to baptism is not baptized at all, but merely wet. It must be confessed that perhaps there are those who have thus been immersed without being saved; but nobody was ever saved without being immersed. See note 1, at end of chapter.

---

[30]R. E. Howard, *op. cit.*, p. 67.
[31]William M. Ramsay, *op. cit.*, p. 386.
[32]Herman N. Ridderbos, *op. cit.*, p. 147.

Verse 28, *There can be neither Jew nor Greek, there can be neither bond nor free, there can be no male and female; for all are one man in Christ Jesus.*

Every possible kind of racial, economic and sex distinction finds its great equalizer "in Christ." The bond of love and fellowship in the Lord is sufficiently strong to contain all outward differences among God's children.

Verse 29, *And if ye are Christ's then are ye Abraham's seed, heirs according to the promise.*

This is not merely a continuation of the argument Paul has been making, but it is continued into chapter 4. The true seed of Abraham (in the plural sense) are all of those who, believing the gospel, have been baptized into Christ, comprising in their corporate totality the seed singular which is Christ, in the sense of his spiritual body. This enabled the Gentiles to be accounted the true seed of Abraham, bypassing the Law of Moses altogether, thus inheriting through the promise to Abraham (Gen. 12:3; 18:18; 22:18).

Huxtable has this pertinent observation on this final verse of the chapter.

> Those who believe in Christ and are baptized in him are to be understood as here being affirmed to be "Abraham's seed," because, being clothed with Christ, they share his position. "Heirs . . ." They are heirs, not of Abraham, but of God; for the idea connects to that of the sonship to God (v. 26), of believers in Christ.[33]

NOTE 1: ON COMMENTS REGARDING VERSE 27

Observations under verse 27 are not intended as a presumption that any mortal knows the *mind of God* (1 Cor. 2:16), or the ultimate judgment of the Almighty regarding any man's destiny; for God is too wise to make a mistake and too good to do wrong. The whole province of judging is denied to Christians (Matt. 7:1); on the other hand, the observations under verse 27, and throughout this series, are merely a conscientious effort to read what seems to be the clear and unequivocal meaning of the sacred NT itself. It was Christ who said, "He that believeth and is baptized shall be saved" (Mark 16:16), and the antithesis of that bold

---

[33]E. Huxtable, *op. cit.*, p. 147.

promise justifies the deductions offered under verse 27. The NT is all that men have as the basis of eternal hope; and it is in that frame of reference alone that men have any right to express opinions or form judgments of what is truth. The Lord has promised eternal life *conditionally*, and only God could change the conditions.

Upon behalf of many precious souls, apparently devoted, spiritual and praiseworthy in so many ways, who have decided to trust God for salvation regardless of their refusal to comply with the conditions, and in many cases, even admit that there are any conditions, let it be said that *only God knows* if he will or will not find a way for them to whom he has made no promise in the NT. The clear and, in a sense, dogmatic interpretations which have been attempted in this series regard only what has been revealed in the NT and do not presume to judge the eternal destiny of any fellow-mortal whomsoever, the sole purpose being that of persuading men to accept the salvation of God in Christ upon the condition of their exhibiting "the obedience of faith" (to the best of their intention and ability), the same being the only condition upon which God has *promised* (in this dispensation) to give any man eternal life. The presumption to affirm what the one true and Almighty God will do for us sinners-all, over and beyond what he has *promised* to do, simply does not lie within the boundaries of the purpose of these studies.

Note 2: Justification Not Possible by Law

The term "Law" was capitalized throughout this chapter to indicate that the Law of Moses was the opposite of Christianity which Paul was discussing. In two or three places in this chapter, however, Paul used "law" in a sense that many scholars interpret to be more extensive than the Law of Moses *only*, the logic of such interpretations being clear enough. No doubt Paul's using the "law" in that wider application was for the purpose of including any *human* law, code of ethics, or system of rules as also being powerless to give justification. Certainly, it is a necessary deduction that if the sacred and divine Law of Moses could not do it, then no lesser system of law whatever could do so.

However, the deduction of theologians to the effect that grace abolishes "all law" is sinful and presumptuous as any religious error ever advocated among men. Paul flatly declared: "Do we then make law of none effect through faith? God forbid: nay, we establish law!" (Rom. 3:30). It should be observed that in this quotation the RV margin has been followed, giving "law" the wider sense of meaning, being in no way a reference to the Law of Moses. So there is a law which faith establishes; and the nature of it is revealed in the NT, as follows:

> The law of faith (Rom. 3:27).
> The law of the Spirit of life in Christ Jesus (Rom. 8:2).
> The perfect law (James 1:25).
> The royal law (James 2:8).
> The law of liberty (James 2:12).
> So fulfill the law of Christ (Gal. 6:2).

In the light of the above passages, it is futile to think of being "under grace and not under law," unless the meaning excludes the law of Christ which every Christian is under. See "The Law of Christ" under 6:18.

Furthermore, when the author of Hebrews spoke of the abolition of the Law of Moses, he did not say that all law had been abolished, but that "there was of necessity a *change* of the law"! (Heb. 7:12). It is that change which Paul discussed in the above chapter, the change from the Law of Moses to the Law of Christ.

One other extremely important consideration is due in this context. If grace has abolished law, then there is no such thing as sin! "Sin is not imputed where there is no law" (Rom. 5:13). "Where there is no law, neither is there transgression" (Rom. 4:14). "For sin is the transgression of the law" (1 John 3:4). It is clear then that the interpretation of Romans 6:14, "For ye are not under the law, but under grace," if applied to the higher law of the Saviour, becomes the Magna Carta of antinomianism.

Note 3: The Faith of Christ

This chapter states no less than three times that it is the faith of Christ which saves and justifies, as utterly distinguished from the false notion that it is the sinner's faith which does this. This is in perfect consonance with an extensive body of NT teaching to the same effect, as witness the following: (Most of the following is from the AV.)

•Even the righteousness of God through faith of Jesus Christ unto all them that believe; for there is no distinction (Rom. 3:22).

That he might be just and the justifier of him that is of the faith of Jesus (Rom. 3:26)

*A man is justified not by the works of the law but through faith of Jesus Christ, even we who believed on Christ, that we might be justified by the faith of Christ and not by the works of the law (Gal. 2:16).

It is no longer I that live, but Christ liveth in me: and that life which I now live in the flesh I live by the faith of the Son of God who loved me, and gave himself for me (Gal. 2:20).

*But the scripture hath concluded all under sin, that the promise by faith of Jesus Christ might be given to them that believe (Gal. 3:22).

In whom we have boldness and access with confidence by the faith of him (Christ) (Eph. 3:12).

And be found in him, not having mine own righteousness, which is of the law, but that which is through the faith of Christ, the righteousness which is of God by faith (Phil. 3:9).

The failure of the RV to render these passages according to their true meaning is one of the most deplorable errors in any translation ever distributed. Not only do the AV and the best modern scholarship testify to the true rendition; but in those instances marked with an asterisk (above), the context itself reveals the meaning to be certainly not that of the sinner's faith in Christ, since the sinner's faith is specifically mentioned in the succeeding clauses. A full dissertation on this exceedingly important truth is given in CR 3:22ff.

CHAPTER 4

The argument of this whole chapter is a continuation of Paul's teaching on the abolition of the Law of Moses and the replacement of the entire system by Christianity. First, he compared the Law to the conditions governing a person not yet come of age, as something sure to be replaced by another arrangement later on (1-7). Secondly, he pointed out the restrictive and onerous nature of the Law itself, comparing it to slavery or bondage (8-11). Next, he reminded them of the circumstances of their conversion, their love for him, and warned them against the evil men who were seducing them away from the faith (12-20); and finally, he appealed to an allegory based upon the life of Abraham, which was climaxed by "Cast out the handmaiden and her son," meaning, in the analogy, "Christianity and Judaism are not compatible, or reconcilable; and it is the Law of Moses that has to go!" (21-31).

Verses 1-2, *But I say that so long as the heir is a child, he differeth nothing from a bondservant though he is lord of all; but is under guardians and stewards until the day appointed by the father.*

It is plain, as Ridderbos suggested, that Paul's language here is not technical. "He is not thinking of a special legal procedure,"[1] but using an illustration that would be appropriate in any society. No child of whatever culture is to be trusted with an inheritance until the age of responsibility. The word here rendered "child" really "means babe,"[2] as Paul used the same word in 1 Corinthians 3:1 for a child needing a milk diet; but the evident meaning here is simply that of "a minor." As McGarvey noted, "In this paragraph Paul resumes the metaphor of 3:24ff, but from a slightly different point of view."[3] There it is the pedagogue which is stressed; here it is the child himself.

---

[1] Herman N. Ridderbos, *The Epistle of Paul to the Churches of Galatia* (Grand Rapids: Wm. B. Eerdmans Publishing Company, 1953), p. 152.

[2] R. Alan Cole, *Tyndale NT Commentaries, Galatians* (Grand Rapids: Wm. B. Eerdmans Publishing Company, 1965), p.112.

[3] J. W. McGarvey, *The Standard Bible Commentary, Galatians* (Cincinnati: The Standard Publishing Company, 1916), p. 271.

Verse 3, *So we also, when we were children, were held in bondage under the rudiments of the world.*

"We. . ." The word here means all men, Jews and Gentiles alike, the world itself being in bondage to all kinds of rudimentary and imperfect conceptions until Christ came.

"Bondage . . ." Peter himself described the Law of Moses in this same terminology (Acts 15:10); and when one considers the incredible number of rules and regulations which were enforced by it, it becomes clear enough that it was indeed slavery.

Some commentators have expressed surprise that Paul did not restrict the "bondage" to primitive religions, making a distinction between the Mosaic Law and the pagan religions; but, while it is true enough that Judaism was magnificently superior to the pagan systems, there were many particulars in which it rose above them scarcely at all. It was purely legalistic; it subjected every violator to death without mercy, and as Macknight said:

> It prescribed no better sacrifices than the heathen religions . . . could not cleanse the conscience of the sinner from the guilt of sin, afforded no assistance to enable men to obey it, and was utterly unable to procure pardon and eternal life for its adherents, being precisely the same (in all these categories) as the heathen religions.[4]

"Under the rudiments of the world . . ." The simple meaning of this place is, "The letters of the alphabet, i.e., elementary education in any branch of knowledge."[5] The meaning of "world" is that of the "world of men," not that of the "cosmos" or "universe." The RSV rendition of this is absurd: "We were slaves to the elemental spirits of the universe"! As Foy E. Wallace, Jr. said, "Besides its obscurity, not a word of it is in either the Greek or any (previous) English translation of it."[6] Of course, this perversion of the sacred text was done to accommodate some rather wild speculations regarding the religion of the Galatians prior to their acceptance of Christianity.

---

[4]James Macknight, *Apostolical Epistles and Commentary* (Grand Rapids: Baker Book House, 1969), p. 169.

[5]Raymond T. Stamm, *Interpreter's Bible* (New York: Abingdon Press, 1950), Vol. IX, p. 521.

[6]Foy E. Wallace, Jr., *A Review of the New Versions* (Fort Worth: The Foy E. Wallace, Jr., Publications, 1973), p. 443.

Verses 4-5, *But when the fullness of time came, God sent forth his Son, born of a woman, born under the law, that he might redeem them that were under the law, that we might receive the adoption of sons.*

"The fullness of time . . ." has the meaning of "At God's appointed time." All of the grand events of God's plan for the redemption of mankind were scheduled in advance, and from the beginning, even the final judgment itself being a planned and scheduled event. "God has appointed a day, etc." (Acts 17:31).

"God sent forth his Son . . ." This is a dogmatic statement of the Incarnation, being a clear reference to the pre-existence of Christ with God before the world was (John 1:1). This clause teaches: (1) the deity of the Son of God, (2) "the going forth of the Son from a place where he was before, and (3) his being invested with divine authority."[7] We agree with Ramsay who said that it was simply "incredible that some unbelievers find here the statement that Christ was only a man."[8]

"Born of a woman . . ." In view of the clear meaning of the preceding clause, it is impossible to accommodate the opinion so often expressed by otherwise reputable and dependable scholars that "this is not a reference to the virgin birth."[9] Since the father of Jesus Christ is clearly set forth as the heavenly Father, pray tell how the Lord could have been born, or entered our earth life, in any other way, except by virgin birth? Are all the commentators ignorant of the fact that if there was cohabitation, in the usual sense, involved in the birth here mentioned it *could not have produced* one who had previously existed with God before the world was, but would invariably and certainly have produced a brand new individual? To be sure, Paul did not here stress the virgin birth, but there is no way that these words could have been spoken by the blessed apostle unless he truly believed it and so arranged his teaching here as to bear an eloquent witness of it.

Furthermore, it is highly questionable if "born of a woman" is the proper translation of the Greek expression "becoming of

---

[7]H. N. Ridderbos, *op. cit.,* p. 155.

[8]Wm. R. Ramsay, *A Historical Commentary on St. Paul's Epistle to the Galatians* (Grand Rapids: Baker Book House, 1965), p. 396.

[9]Everett F. Harrison, *Wycliffe Bible Commentary* (Chicago: Moody Press, 1971), p. 709.

a woman." While true enough that Christ was born of a woman, that is not the word Paul used. Huxtable believed a better translation is *made to be of a woman,* preferring it because "Such a translation would imply a previous state of existence (a thought most certainly in the context), whereas *born* does not."[10] To say the least, Huxtable's translation more accurately reflects the thought of the whole passage.

"Born under the law . . ." "Made to be under the law" is better in this place also, where the same word is used. There is a genuine sense in which Christ was not "born" under the law, because as the true Temple of God, the Head of the Theocracy, and the divine Son of God, he was *intrinsically* absolutely above the law, as emphatically indicated in Matthew 17:25-27, where it is recorded that Jesus consented to the payment of the temple tax, not because he owed it, but because he did not wish to cause men to stumble. See in CM 17:24ff. In the same manner as indicated there, Christ consented to "be made" under the Mosaic obligations for the purpose of fulfilling them, obligations that did not derive in any sense whatever from his birth, but from his joint-purpose with God even before the Incarnation was begun.

"The adoption of sons . . ." Adam was the "son of God" by creation (Luke 3:38), a status that does not pertain to any of Adam's posterity due to the disastrous behavior of the great progenitor which involved the entire human race in ruin. God's purpose of redemption is that of adopting all of us "Adamites" into the status of sonship with the Father, the same having been the purpose of the Incarnation, the virgin birth, the making of Christ to be under the law, and, in fact, the total family of events clustered around the sacred name of Jesus Christ our Lord.

Verses 6-7, *And because ye are sons, God sent forth the Spirit of his Son into our hearts, crying, Abba, Father. So that thou art no longer a bondservant, but a son; and if a son, then an heir through God.*

---

[10]E. Huxtable, *Pulpit Commentary* (Grand Rapids: Wm. B. Eerdmans Publishing Company, 1950), Vol. 20, p. 183.

Some scholars read the first clause, "as proof that ye are sons";[11] but Sanday believed it is better to retain it as in the RV,[12] showing that the time of receiving the gift-ordinary of the Holy Spirit is subsequent to achieving the status of sonship and a consequence of it. This is without doubt the true meaning, for it coincides with the promise of the apostle Peter (Acts 2:38) that the reception of the Holy Spirit is to be expected *after* faith, repentance and baptism into the name of Christ, and as a *promise* to be fulfilled subsequently to such faith and obedience. That is why Paul also referred to the same gift as "the Holy Spirit of promise" (Eph. 1:13).

"Whereby we cry, Abba, Father . . . (AV)" indicates that one of the fruits of the Holy Spirit in Christian hearts is the sense of nearness to God, indicated by the prayers addressed to God in such terms of intimacy, "Abba" being the ordinary word used by Hebrew children in addressing their father. However, it is ridiculous to equate this word with the English word "Daddy," which in current usage has lost a lot of the reverential respect which pertained to the Aramaic word, "Abba."

"No longer a bond servant, but a son . . ." The world, at least that portion of it which accepts Christianity, has come of age in Christ. The idols, liturgical externals, pageantry, regalia and all other visible external spectacularism of pagan worship are not merely unnecessary, but destructive of genuine worship and service of Christ.

"If a son, then an heir through God . . ." A Christian is not an heir of Abraham, but an heir with him, by virtue of sonship and union with Christ. The reason Paul stressed God's Fathership of the Lord Jesus Christ in verse 4 was correctly discerned by Pink who declared that "God must be the Father of the Lord Jesus Christ, in order to be the God and Father of his people whom he chose in Christ."[13] The Christian's sonship to God is derived from his unity with Christ, identity with Christ, as being "in Christ," and thus a part of that spiritual body which "is Christ," who is truly and actually the sinless and perfect Son of God.

---

[11]William Barclay, *The Letters to the Galatians and Ephesians* (Philadelphia: The Westminster Press, 1954), p. 38.

[12]William Sanday, *Ellicott's Commentary on the Whole Bible* (Grand Rapids: Zondervan Publishing House, 1959), p. 450.

[13]Arthur W. Pink, *Gleanings from Paul* (Chicago: Moody Press, 1967), p. 93.

Verse 8, *Howbeit at that time, not knowing God, ye were in bondage to them that by nature are no gods.*

This is a reference to the idolatry of the Galatians before they accepted Christ. "Bondage" is an apt term to describe the merciless, unfeeling subjection of the pre-Christian pagan world to the devices of idolatrous priests. True, the same word was used of Judaism, but there was a marked difference, due to the sensuality and immorality which were the stock in trade of the idol worshipers.

"No gods . . ." Paul wrote the Corinthians that, "No idol is anything in the world, and there is no God but one" (I Cor. 8:4). See CC, under that verse, for further comment.

Verse 9, *But now that ye have come to know God, or rather to be known by God, how turn ye back again to the weak and beggarly rudiments, whereunto ye desire to be in bondage over again?*

"To know God, rather to be known by God . . ." There is a distinction in this that Paul always observed, as in 1 Corinthians 8:3; because, as Leon Morris noted, "The really important thing is not that we know God, but that he knows us!"[14] All true knowledge of God comes from God, and even that conveyed by the blessed Saviour himself came from the Father. See Matthew 16:17, where Peter's confession of Christ as the Son of God was said by Jesus not to have been revealed by "flesh and blood," but by "the Father in heaven."

"Weak and beggarly rudiments . . ." In that Paul declared that the Galatians were again coming into "bondage" to such things, it is clear enough that the RSV translation of verse 3 is erroneous. Whatever the word means here, it means there; and there cannot be any doubt of what it means here, namely, that they were on the verge of becoming entangled again with observing the regulations, sabbaths, etc., of the Jewish law.

Why were these things called "weak and beggarly"? See Macknight's lucid comment under verse 3, above. They were also beggarly in the sense of being "poor" in contrast to the unsearchable riches of Christ. Dummelow thought that such a defection

---

[14]Leon Morris, *Tyndale Commentary, 1 Corinthians* (Grand Rapids: Wm. B. Eerdmans Publishing Company, 1958), p. 93.

by the Galatians into Judaism "was a return, not, indeed, into idolatry, but into an imperfect and rudimentary religion."[15] Of course, such a view of Judaism's superiority over paganism is true of it *before* the First Advent of the Son of God and the Jewish rejection of him; but in this dispensation, such a superiority no longer pertains. As Russell put it:

> Jewish laws and ceremonies were but symbols of Christ, through which they were to know God as Father, and be known by him as sons. Turning back to exalt mere forms was idolatry.[16]

Verses 10-11, *Ye observe days and months and seasons and years. I am afraid of you, lest by any means I have bestowed labor upon you in vain.*

Sabbatarians have done their best to eliminate the meaning of this passage, but as Huxtable tells us, the words used here "were used by Josephus for the keeping of sabbath days";[17] and when read in conjunction with Colossians 2:16 there cannot be any doubt that the sin of the Galatians was simply that of keeping, after the Jewish manner, the sabbaths, festivals and special days of the Old Covenant, which if persisted in, would mean their total loss to Christianity. The whole thesis of this epistle is that "Judaism and Christianity do not mix."

Verse 12-13, *I beseech you, brethren, become as I am, for I also am become as ye are. Ye did me no wrong: but ye know that because of an infirmity of the flesh I preached the gospel unto you the first time.*

Paul has given up all ceremonies of Judaism, the few times he observed any of them after becoming a Christian always having some special purpose in mind, like that of avoiding unnecessary persecution or looking to the purpose of preventing disunity in the church. The statement here shows Paul's utter repugnance for such things. It is in this that he wishes the Galatians to become like himself.

---

[15]J. R. Dummelow, *Commentary on the Holy Bible* (New York: The Macmillan Company, 1937), p. 953.

[16] John William Russell, *Compact Commentary on the NT* (Grand Rapids: Baker Book House, 1964), p. 468.

[17]E. Huxtable, *op. cit.,* p. 190.

"Ye did me no wrong . . ." As Howard said, "The Galatians would certainly have known what Paul means by this, but it is not clear to modern readers."[18] Perhaps, as Phillips translated this place, we should read it, "I have nothing against you personally."

"Because of an infirmity of the flesh . . ." Endless specula- tions concerning the illness (that is the way it must be under- stood) that caused Paul to preach to the Galatians have found no general agreement among scholars; but the most reasonable explanation of it would seem to be that advocated by William M. Ramsay and accepted by Dummelow, Barclay and many others to the effect that when Paul came to Perga in Pamphylia on the first missionary journey (Acts 13:13ff), he did not preach there (at Perga), due to a sudden onset of malaria, taking ref- uge in the highlands of Pisidian Antioch (and later going to the other cities of the first tour). The question is not really important.

"Preached the gospel unto you the first time . . ." The last two words of this clause are important with regard to the problem of dating Galatians, some scholars reading these words as a declaration that Paul had made "two missionary tours" to the Galatians before writing this epistle, which, if allowed, would make it considerably later than if only one tour is men- tioned here. See introduction. Dummelow, Sanday, Huxtable and many others insist that the words imply two tours had been made when this was written; but, as Howard observed, "From a lexical point of view, it is not possible to prove that Paul wished here to differentiate between a later visit and an earlier one."[19] The simple truth is that the words merely mean "formerly" or "on the first occasion" of Paul's seeing them; and William Hendriksen, who accepted the implication of two tours previous to this letter, translated the place "on the former occasion,"[20] which certainly allows that Paul's writing this letter was the occasion present, to be distinguished from the other. It seems to this student that all of the arguments about this are futile,

---

[18]R. E. Howard, *Beacon Bible Commentary* (Kansas City: Beacon Hill Press, 1965), Vol. IX, p. 74.

[19]*Ibid.*

[20]William Hendriksen, *New Testament Commentary on Galatians* (Grand Rapids: Baker Book House, 1968), p. 170.

because on the first tour, Paul made *two visits* to every one of the cities of south Galatia, with the lone exception of Derbe, the second visit being the occasion when Paul appointed elders in each of the churches he had established (Acts 14:23). Therefore, if *two visits* are a mandatory understanding of this verse, one has to look no further than the first missionary journey of Paul to find both of them!

Of course, it is declared that "The explanation that the apostle intended to distinguish his first arrival at the several South Galatian churches from his return in the course of the same journey cannot be accepted!"[21] Such an opinion, however, is unsupported by any hard evidence, being quite arbitrary and unreasonable. *Why* could not Paul have made such a distinction? Especially in view of the fact that at Perga he did not preach on the first of those two occasions, whereas on the other he did. It is ridiculous to suppose that Paul counted his journeys in exactly the same manner as the latest Sunday school lesson, and the fact of the evangelist Luke having distinguished the two we have cited is more than sufficient authority for our doing the same thing. Scholars get carried away. They neatly classify Paul's labors as Tour I, II and III, then suppose that when Paul is speaking of "journeys" he is using their terminology!

Verse 14, *And that which was a temptation to you in my flesh ye despised not, nor rejected; but ye received me as an angel of God, even as Christ Jesus.*

There is always a temptation to belittle a sick man, especially one seeking to change one's whole manner of life, but the Galatians did not yield to it. It seems that all speculations about how repulsive and repugnant Paul's disease was are merely morbid imagination. He was sick. That is all that is said here.

"As an angel of God . . ." As a matter of fact, some of the Galatians tried to worship him, before they understood his message (Acts 14:11ff).

Verse 15, *Where then is that gratulation of yourselves? for I bear you witness, that if possible, ye would have plucked out your eyes and given them to me.*

---

[21]*ISBE,* p. 1159.

Of course, here is the ground of the speculation that Paul's infirmity was temporary blindness, which of course is a possibility; but such an expression as Paul used here is proverbial, and there can be no certainty that any such thing is meant. Ridderbos said, "Verse 15 has nothing to do with Paul's infirmity."[22] Whatever lay behind such a statement, Paul here appealed to the love which the Galatians manifested toward him from the very first time he ever saw them.

Verse 16, *So then am I become your enemy by telling you the truth?*

In context, the thought is, "Surely one whom you have loved so much cannot become your enemy merely by telling you the truth about people who are now trying to exploit you."

Verse 17, *They zealously seek you in no good way: nay, they desire to shut you out, that ye may seek them.*

This was spoken with reference to the Judaizers, whose purpose was to control and exploit the Galatians by using them to support Jewish religious enterprises. "They seek you in no good way" is a figure of speech, called *litotes*, which is "the affirmation of a truth by denying its opposite,"[23] the meaning being that the Judaizers were hypocritical, and that their motives in cultivating the Galatians were impure.

Verse 18, *But it is good to be zealously sought in a good manner at all times, and not only when I am present with you.*

By this, Paul meant that he was not merely jealous of the attention others were giving the Galatians, a thing he was diligent to give himself when present with them, but that in the case of these particular ardent cultivators of their friendship, they were up to no good whatever.

Verse 19, *My little children, of whom I am again in travail until Christ be formed in you —* .

"My little children . . ." This claiming on Paul's part of the Galatians as his spiritual children has also entered into scholarly efforts to determine the date of Galatians and also the

---

[22]H. N. Ridderbos, *op. cit.,* p. 167.

[23]Merrill C. Tenney, *Galatians the Charter of Christian Liberty* (Grand Rapids: Wm. B. Eerdmans Publishing Company, 1950), p. 148.

identity of the churches to whom it is addressed, the questions, of course, being related to each other. It is said that "The churches of south Galatia had two founders (Paul and Barnabas), and owed allegiance to Barnabas along with Paul." This is true, of course, but Paul had just written to them of Barnabas' being "drawn away" into accepting the position of the Judaizers (2:13), and until that had been resolved, it would have been improper for Paul to have associated himself with Barnabas in this appeal. Over and beyond that, it is not true that Barnabas was the co-founder of those churches, his status in all of Galatia being more that of Paul's assistant than that of a co-leader. The dramatic change had come at Paphos. Furthermore, the pagans calling Barnabas, *Jupiter*, the king of pagan dieties, and Paul only *Mercury*, the chief speaker, was merely pagan lack of discernment, basing their judgment upon external appearance only. The Jews of south Galatia, who knew the real power of both Paul and Barnabas, as regards the founding of those churches, tried to kill Paul, not Barnabas. It was therefore altogether all right and proper for Paul to have claimed spiritual fatherhood of those churches, even if the defection of Barnabas had been corrected.

"Again in travail . . ." Two things appear in this: (1) there had been an agony of travail (like that of a woman in childbirth) on Paul's part at the founding of those churches, Acts 13 and 14 giving many of the details of his sorrows and bitter sufferings, and (2) he was going through the same deep anxieties again upon their behalf.

"Until Christ be formed in you . . ." The drifting into Judaism had blurred and distorted the image of Christ in their hearts, and Paul wishes it to be perfectly formed.

Verse 20, *But I could wish to be present with you now, and to change my tone; for I am perplexed about you.*

This is an inverted manner of Paul's saying that he regretted the necessity of reprimanding in order to correct those whom he loved so much.

ALLEGORY OF ISAAC AND ISHMAEL

Verse 21, *Tell me, ye that desire to be under the law, do ye not hear the law?*

"Desire to be under the law . . ." There has always been a basic natural appeal in visible, ceremonial, liturgical, external and spectacular religion, as witnessed continually by the churches of all ages in the persistent drifting into those very things. To the Galatians, so soon out of paganism, they were simply hypnotized and seduced into receiving the allegations of the Judaizers. Paul's argument, however, here seems to say, "Do not merely look at it, listen to what it teaches!" There is a lot in religion today that needs to be analyzed in the same way.

The Judaizers were talking about being "sons of Abraham," which in a sense (carnal) they were; and the thunderbolt in the next verse is that "Abraham had *two* sons; which kind were the Judaizers?"

Verse 22, *For it is written that Abraham had two sons, one by the handmaid, and one by the freewoman.*

Ishmael was the son of Hagar, Sarah's maid, whom she gave to Abraham, in order to claim a son (by such a device) for herself. Abraham had many sons by concubines, but they were his property, not Sarah's. Isaac was the actual son born to Sarah, born as a result of the promise of God long after the time when either Abraham or Sarah might have expected to have children. Sarah of course was free, the lawful wife of the mighty patriarch. The full account of all this is in Genesis, much of the entire book being given over to the recounting of it. A summary of the allegory Paul was about to give is the following:

JUDAISM	CHRISTIANITY
The bondwoman, Hagar	The freewoman, Sarah
Son of the bondwoman, Ishmael	Son of the freewoman, Isaac
Natural birth	Supernatural birth by promise
Mount Sinai, the Law	Mt. Zion, the Law of Christ
The earthly Jerusalem	The heavenly Jerusalem
Enslaved	Free
Fruitful	Barren (at first)
Small offspring	Large offspring
Persecuting	Persecuted
Expulsion	Inheritance
Judaism a bondage	Christians free

These analogies will clarify many of the points Paul made in the next few verses.

Verse 23, *Howbeit the son by the handmaid is born after the flesh; but the son of the freewoman is born through promise.*

Ishmael was born as a result of the selfishness of Sarah and the natural cohabitation of Abraham with her slave girl. God was simply not in the arrangement; but Isaac, the son of promise, was born through the enabling promise of God himself, contrary to all natural expectations.

These two sons, as Paul would promptly point out, typified the two types of "sons of Abraham," as represented after Ishmael in the persons of the unspiritual Sadducees and Pharisees, with Isaac typifying the true spiritual seed of Abraham, as elaborated by Jesus in John 8, and by Paul throughout the book of Romans, where the distinction is often made between the fleshly Israel and the spiritual Israel, which is the church.

Verses 24-25, *Which things contain an allegory: for these women are two covenants; one from mount Sinai, bearing children unto bondage, which is Hagar. Now this Hagar is mount Sinai in Arabia and answereth to the Jerusalem that now is: for she is in bondage with her children.*

"Hagar is mount Sinai . . ." Chrysostom stated that "Hagar is the word for mount Sinai, in the language of that country";[24] but scholars question this on the basis that they do not know where he got his information! As he lived more than a millenium before any of us, it would appear to be a little late to inquire. As Dummelow pointed out, Sinai and Jerusalem mean the same thing, law and bondage; and Hagar typified both."[25]

"Bearing children unto bondage . . ." This was, first of all, true literally, as Jerusalem itself was subjected to Rome at the time of this writing; and it was also true spiritually. As McGarvey said, "The Jews themselves universally recognized the law as a practical bondage (Acts 15:10; Matt. 23:4)."[26]

Verse 26, *But the Jerusalem that is above is free, which is our mother.*

---

[24]E. Huxtable, *op. cit.*, p. 203.
[25]J. R. Dummelow, *op. cit.*, p. 954.
[26]J. W. McGarvey, *op. cit.*, p. 278.

Abraham was a recognized type of God in the OT, a type recognized by Christ himself in the parable of the rich man and Lazarus; and Sarah herself therefore bore a certain analogy as the holy bride, the church (the unity of God and Christ being pertinent to the analogy). As the sons of Sarah, Christians are upon a much higher level than the sons of the bondwoman.

"Which is our mother . . ." There also seems to be more than a hint here that Paul was rejecting any notion whatever that the Jerusalem church was in any sense "the Mother church" in the earthly sense of that word. The "Mother Church" virus has afflicted all generations of Christians, notwithstanding the truth in evidence here that nothing "on earth" may in any sense be understood as "the Mother Church." It is likely here that one needs to look for the reason for Paul's refusal to deliver the findings of that church in Jerusalem to these very Galatians.

Verse 27, *For it is written,*
> *Rejoice thou barren that bearest not;*
> *Break forth and cry, thou that travailest not:*
> *For more are the children of the desolate than of*
>   *her that hath the husband.*

This is quoted from Isaiah 54:1, the application being to Sarah and Hagar, as follows: Sarah at first had no child, but when the promise of Isaac was fulfilled, her posterity exceeded that of Hagar; but in the instance of the spiritual fulfillment of this, the numberless "Sons of Sarah" in the church of the living God even more overwhelmingly outnumber those of Hagar.

Verse 28-29, *Now we, brethren, as Isaac was, are children of promise. But as then he that was born after the flesh persecuted him that was born after the Spirit, so also it is now.*

Here the reference is to the event of Genesis 21:9ff. The enmity between these two branches of Abraham's family has continued till the present day; and there has also been a corresponding hatred of the secular, carnal, fleshly and unspiritual against the holy teachings of Christ also. Paul intends for the Galatians to see that the Judaizers are actually their enemies, having no good thing for them, at all, in their purposes.

Verse 30, *Howbeit what saith the scripture? Cast out the hand-maid and her son: for the son of the handmaid shall not inherit with the son of the freewoman.*

This is the dramatic and blunt conclusion Paul enforced by his appeal to this allegory. "When the Judaizers pride themselves on the fact that they are 'sons of Abraham,' let it be remembered that Abraham had two sons."[27] In Paul's times, and until now, there are still two classes of "sons of Abraham"; and the significant question is, "Who is a *real* son of Abraham?" Paul had already given the answer in 3:26-29. The reason why all natural religious systems are bound to come in conflict with Christianity is that Christianity is supernatural, and the natural systems cannot coexist as parallel paths to the same goal."[28] The law of Moses and the gospel of Christ cannot be blended, and as Wesley said "It is the Law which must go, and the gospel which must enjoy an unshared supremacy."[29]

Macknight was surely correct in the thought that "In this allegory, Paul prophesied the rejection of secular Israel, the natural seed, from being the church and people of God."[30] Paul never pointed that analogy out, but it is surely there; and "Lightfoot remarked that Paul's confident application of verse 30 is a striking tribute to his prophetic insight."[31] This is true, because when Paul wrote, it was to human eyes far from certain that the old Jewish system would be cast out of its inheritance, an event, however, that was dramatically and violently fulfilled in the total destruction of Jerusalem about twenty years after this letter was written.

Verse 31, *Wherefore, brethren, we are not children of a hand-maid, but of the freewoman.*

This was Paul's summary of the allegory just related.

---

[27]William Hendriksen, *op. cit.,* p. 189.

[28]R. Alan Cole, *op. cit.,* p. 135.

[29]John Wesley, *One Volume NT Commentary* (Grand Rapids: Baker Book House, 1972), *in loco.*

[30]James Macknight, *op. cit.,* p. 186.

[31]F. Roy Coad, *A New Testament Commentary* (Grand Rapids: Zondervan Publishing House, 1969), p. 453.

CHAPTER 5

Paul in this summarized his teaching of the last three chapters preceding this (1-5), and then distinguished between the works of the flesh and the works of the Spirit, appealing to the Galatians to live by the Spirit (6-26).

Verse 1, *For freedom did Christ set us free: stand fast therefore, and be not entangled again in a yoke of bondage.*

The second clause here makes the identity of the freedom in the first clause easy to ascertain. "There can be no doubt that it refers to freedom from the slavery of the Law of Moses."[1] As a summary statement, this also shows the meaning of "freedom from law" as taught in the previous chapters. That it never had any reference to Christian obligations, whether in the realm of obedience to the primary ordinances of God, or adherence to the ethical commandments of our holy faith, is absolutely certain.

"Stand . . . therefore . . ." Paul, by this admonished the Galatians to hold their ground, resist the Judaizers and reject the persuasions of those who would entangle them in such things as sabbath days, feast days, circumcision and all other Jewish regulations.

Verse 2, *Behold, I Paul say unto you that, if ye receive circumcision, Christ will profit you nothing.*

"Behold, I Paul say unto you . . ." Intensely personal and dramatic, this appeal was intended to affirm in the most dogmatic and positive way possible the truth which he was uttering.

"Circumcision, Christ will profit you nothing . . ." There were exceptions to this rule, for Paul himself had been circumcised; and what is meant is "that circumcision with any view to its aiding or leading to one's justification would be a denial of Christ, a repudiation of the Christian gospel and the forsaking of Christianity." As Macknight said, "This general expression must be limited; because we cannot suppose that the circumcision of the

---

[1]R. E. Howard, *Beacon Bible Commentary, Galatians* (Kansas City: Beacon Hill Press, 1968), Vol. IX, p. 82.

[2]James Macknight, *Apostolical Epistles and Commentary* (Grand Rapids: Baker Book House, 1969), p. 190.

Jewish believers incapacitated them from being profited by Christ."[2]

The deduction is mandatory that the purpose of the Judaizers among the Galatians had made this their purpose, to circumcise the Galatians, no doubt representing to them that it was no great thing and did not involve them in the more onerous and expensive obligations of Judaism. Paul would expose the fraud in such a proposition in the very next verse.

Verse 3, *Yea, I testify again to every man that receiveth circumcision, that he is a debtor to do the whole law.*

So it was no small thing at all the Judaizers had in mind. They would impose the whole corpus of Jewish law-keeping on the Christian converts of Galatia; and in the process, the gospel of Christ would be totally neglected and replaced.

Verse 4, *Ye are severed from Christ, ye that would be justified by the law; ye are fallen from grace.*

Howard observed that "This, in capsule form, is his contention throughout the entire argument. All the other points climax in this."[3] Of course, this is true; and the allegation that Paul was, in these chapters, displaying a brand new conception of being saved "by faith only" is absolutely foreign to the entire Galatian letter, and the whole NT.

The present tense in this verse must be read as indicating that some of the Galatians had actually defected from Christianity in the manner indicated, with the result that they had "fallen from grace." Apparently, Paul was no Calvinist.

Verse 5, *For we through the Spirit by faith wait for the hope of righteousness.*

"Through the Spirit . . ." The Holy Spirit is conferred upon all baptized believers, according to the promise of Acts 2:38, thus identifying those who "by faith" were waiting for the hope of righteousness.

"By faith . . ." has the meaning here of "by the Christian religion." "Faith" as used in the popular theology of this current era, meaning the subjective experience of sinners and the sole ground of their justification, is merely the jargon of religious cultism, utterly different from the NT meaning of the word.

---

[3]R. E. Howard, *op. cit.,* p. 83.

Cole's opinion that "The gift of faith is the first gift of the Spirit"[4] cannot be correct; because only those who have already believed, repented and have been baptized into Christ are promised the Holy Spirit (Acts 2:38).

Verse 6, *For in Christ Jesus neither circumcision availeth anything, nor uncircumcision; but faith working through love.*

This means "neither circumcision nor uncircumcision is relevant to Christianity." The question of true justification does not regard such a thing in any manner whatever. Some have wondered why Paul included "uncircumcision" in this declaration; but, as many of the Galatian converts had been won from the Jewish synagogues (where Paul always went first with the gospel), it was mandatory that none of them should be concerned with the fact that they had been circumcised long ago, nor concern themselves with trying to undo it. Some indeed had, through surgery, attempted to become "uncircumcised." Although there is no evidence that any of the Galatians had done that, it may be inferred from 1 Corinthians 7:18, 19 that some at Corinth had gone that far; and as Macknight said, "Apostate Jews fancied that by such actions they could free themselves of their obligation to keep the Law of Moses."[5] There was also another consideration: "From Paul's speaking so much against circumcision, some might have believed that there was something meritorious in uncircumcision."[6] As Howard correctly summarized it, "For salvation, circumcision had no value; and for salvation, uncircumcision had no value."[7]

"But faith working through love . . ." Contrasted with things of no value, here is the essence of justification; and sure enough, it is not "faith alone," but "faith working through love," thus presenting the emphatic apostolic denial of the favorite heresy of our age. To be sure, men do not like this verse, rendering it "faith inspired by love" (NEB margin), or otherwise avoiding the word "working" as they would strive to avoid the plague! It

[4]R. A. Cole, *Tyndale NT Commentaries, Galatians* (Grand Rapids: Wm. B. Eerdmans Publishing Company, 1965), p. 143.

[5]James Macknight, *Apostolical Epistles and Commentary, Corinthians* (Grand Rapids: Baker Book House, 1969), p. 108.

[6]James Macknight (on *Galatians*), *op. cit.,* p. 192.

[7]R. E. Howard, *op. cit.,* p. 83.

happens that Paul used the expression "circumcision nor uncircumcision, etc." three different times thus:

Neither circumcision nor uncircumcision . . . but faith working through love (Gal. 5:6).

Neither circumcision nor uncircumcision . . . but a new creature (Gal. 6:15).

Neither circumcision nor uncircumcision . . . but the keeping of the commandments of God (1 Cor. 7:19).

From the above comparison, it can be seen that "faith working by love" means the same thing as being baptized into Christ in order to become "a new creature" (2 Cor. 5:17); nor is it limited to that, for it also means "keeping the commandments of God." This threefold summary of what *does avail*, as contrasted with circumcision or uncircumcision which *do not avail*, should be pondered by all who seek to be known of the Lord and to stand with Christ "in that day." It is a source of thanksgiving that a scholar of the stature of Huxtable also testified to the truth thus:

"Faith operative through love" must be identical with, or involve "the keeping of God's commandments," and "a new creature." A close examination of the first of these three sentences will show that this is so. (Huxtable attached an extensive exegesis of the Greek text here, proving that passive renditions such as "faith wrought in us," etc., are absolutely "inadmissible and preposterous.")[8]

Of all the preposterous interpretations insinuated into this passage, however, none of them is as incredibly evil as that of William M. Greathouse, who wrote: "All Paul had to say about circumcision he would say equally about baptism!"[9] Nevertheless, Greathouse must be commended in this, namely, that he bluntly stated the *conviction* of the entire "faith only" family of interpreters, who by their writings attempt to lead the reader to that same conclusion, yet lack the courage to say what they mean as Greathouse did. See under verse 12 for comment on "in Christ."

Verse 7, *Ye were running well; who hindered you that ye should not obey the truth?*

---

[8]E. Huxtable, *Pulpit Commentary* (Grand Rapids: Wm. B. Eerdmans Publishing Company, 1950), Vol. 20, p. 242.

[9]William M. Greathouse, *Beacon Bible Commentary, Romans* (Kansas City: Beacon Hill Press, 1969), p. 103.

In all Paul's writings, he sought to lead men into "the obedience of faith"; and his writings in Galatians do not deviate from that invariable purpose.

"Who did hinder you . . . ?" "The original meaning of the word translated *hinder* is *to break up a road,* as an army before the advance of hostile forces."[10] A paraphase of this metaphor, is "Who tore up the race track in front of you?"

"That ye should not obey the truth . . . " Some of the Galatians had stopped obeying the truth, as taught by Paul and the other apostles, perhaps neglecting to observe the Lord's supper and failing to do other things which have been distinctive of the Christian life in all ages. The clause here shows that this disobedience was a prime concern of the apostle's. Note, particularly, that it is not said that they had stopped "believing in Christ," for there is no evidence that such was the case. "Faith only" for them was as impotent as it is today. By their falling into Jewish observances, they were neglecting and had stopped obeying the teachings of Christ.

Verse 8, *This persuasion came not of him that calleth you.*

This simply has the meaning that "their disobedience of Christ's teachings, due to fooling around with Judaism, did not come of anything that Christ, who had called them through the gospel, had taught them."

Verse 9, *A little leaven leaveneth the whole lump.*

It is believed here that Dummelow read this correctly as meaning "that only a few of the Galatian converts were affected by the false teachings."[11] The danger of the situation, however, was not to be judged by the small size of the defecting group. As Lipscomb said: "Just as one plague-infected person may bring devastation to a city, so may one teacher of doctrine subversive of the gospel corrupt a whole community of believers."[12]

---

[10]William Sanday, *Ellicott's Commentary on the Whole Bible, Galatians* (Grand Rapids: Zondervan Publishing House, 1959), p. 456.

[11]J. R. Dummelow, *Commentary on the Holy Bible* (New York: The Macmillan Company, 1937), p. 956.

[12]David Lipscomb, *A Commentary on the NT Epistles, Galatians* (Nashville: The Gospel Advocate Company, n.d.), p. 260.

Verse 10, *I have confidence to you-ward in the Lord, that ye will be none otherwise minded: but he that troubleth you shall bear his judgment, whosoever he be.*

"I have confidence . . ." Paul did not believe that the Judaizers would succeed in Galatia, and they did not succeed. All efforts to meld Judaism with Christianity were thwarted and checkmated by this very epistle and other NT writings. See under verse 12, below, for comment on "in the Lord."

"Shall bear his judgment . . ." The Judaizer (whether one or more) would bear the judgment Paul had written a moment earlier, that of being "severed from Christ," "fallen from grace," etc.

Verse 11, *But I, brethren, if I still preach circumcision, why am I still persecuted? then hath the stumbling-block of the cross been done away.*

"If I still preach circumcision . . ." This evidently refers to the allegations of the false teachers to the effect that Paul himself taught circumcision, an argument they reinforced, no doubt, by appealing to the known instance of Paul's circumcising Timothy, whose mother was a Jewess (Acts 16:3). Paul's reason for doing that, however, had nothing whatever to do with Timothy's salvation, but was for the purpose of avoiding and frustrating Jewish persecution. Any allegation that Paul considered circumcision as related in any manner to salvation was effectively denied by the fact that "if Paul indeed honored circumcision in any such way, the Jews would have stopped persecuting him."

"The stumbling-block of the cross . . ." The cross of Christ was preeminently above everything else the center and citadel of Christian hope; and if Paul trusted circumcision for anything, reliance upon the Great Atonement would have been forfeited. But is is not forfeited. The cross remains!

Verse 12, *I would that they that unsettle you would even go beyond circumcision.*

"The priests of Cybele, whom the Galatians had formerly worshiped,"[13] made themselves eunuchs. Also, "The cult of Attis, whose famous temples were at Rome and in Phrygia of Asia

---

[13]J. R. Dummelow, *op. cit.,* p. 956.

Minor, practiced sacral castration."[14] None of the Galatians, therefore, could misunderstand Paul's ironic, and perhaps humorous, remarks here. Paul was so disgusted with all the argument demanding circumcision that he uttered this outburst, which may be paraphrased, "It would be good if you fellows, always wanting to circumcise somebody, would just circumcise yourselves like those priests of Cybele!" Criticism of Paul's remark here is unbecoming, for the remark is a protest, not any sort of recommendation.

Before moving to a study of the next paragraph, the student should observe the double reference "in Christ" (v. 6) and "in the Lord" (v. 10), indicating the ever-present consciouness on his part of the dominating concept which pervades all of his writings, i.e., that salvation is always a matter of one's being "in Christ," who alone is righteous, and whose perfect faith and perfect obedience are the only true ground of redemption for any man. When one is "baptized into Christ" be *becomes Christ*, in the sense of being part of his spiritual body, being saved, not in his own identity, but "as Christ." This expression, "in Christ," or its equivalent, is found 169 times in Paul's writings.

Verse 13, *For ye brethren, were called for freedom; only use not your freedom for an occasion to the flesh, but through love be servants one to another.*

Freedom from Jewish observances did not mean freedom to indulge in things forbidden, which Paul would promptly enumerate. No relaxation of the commandments of Christ was for one moment intended by anything Paul had written about being "under grace" and not "under law." Here he cited the great motivator of Christian morality, namely love of the brethren.

Verse 14, *For the whole law is fulfilled in one word, even this: Thou shalt love thy neighbor as thyself.*

The "law" in view here is the "law of Christ," mentioned again in 6:2. True, this was a commandment of the Law of Moses (Lev. 19:18), but that is not the frame of reference applicable here. Christ himself had made the "first and great commandment" to be the "love of God, and love of one's neighbor" (Mark

---

[14]Herman N. Ridderbos, *op. cit.,* p. 195.

12:29-31), nor has there ever been, from the morning of creation, the slightest relaxation of this primary obligation of all who were ever born on earth. In Romans 13:8-10, Paul outlined this principle more fully, specifying as specific components of this law of Christ such commandments as "Thou shalt not commit adultery . . . nor steal . . . nor kill . . . nor covet, etc." There also, Paul indicated that love of the brethren is the heart condition that makes the honoring of such commandments possible for the Christian. As Huxtable said, "This passage in Romans is a lengthened paraphrase of the one before us."[15] For further exegesis on all of this, see CR 13:9-10.

Verse 15, *But if ye bite and devour one another, take heed that ye be not consumed one of another.*

Christian faith and behavior are never more frustrated and disgraced than by spiteful criticisms, derogatory remarks, snide observations and poison-tongue fulminations of Christians against each other. The fate of any group permitting such a development issues inevitably in that of "The Gingham Dog and the Calico Cat":

> The truth about the cat and the pup
> Is this: they ate each other up!

The apostle said as much in this very passage.

Verses 16-17, *But I say, Walk by the Spirit and ye shall not fulfill the lust of the flesh. For the flesh lusteth against the Spirit and the Spirit against the flesh; for these are contrary the one to the other; that ye may not do the things that ye would.*

In this passage is the key to righteous living, Everyone is familiar with the seductive force of carnal, or fleshly desire, a force that operates subjectively within the minds of men, aided, of course, by all kinds of external suggestions and allurements. This "lusting against the Spirit" by that force has its stronghold in the mind, in the imagination particularly. Even in the OT, the climax and pinnacle of the so-called "seven deadly sins" (Prov. 6:18) was revealed as "a heart that deviseth wicked imaginations." The total corruption of the antediluvian world

---

[15]E. Huxtable, *op. cit.,* p. 250.

had been achieved by the evil one when the "imagination of men's hearts" had become evil, and only evil, without intermission (Gen. 6:5). This was the essence of pre-Christian debauchery of the Gentiles (Rom. 1:21); and it was "imaginations" which Paul identified as being "exalted against the knowledge of God" (2 Cor. 10:5), the Christian warfare being simply that of "casting down," i.e., eliminating, reducing and controlling the imaginations of the heart.

Now the contrary force to evil imaginations is exerted in the mind, the same being the battlefield where the warfare is decided. The pursuit of sacred studies, the thinking of loving and generous thoughts and the soul's welcome of the thoughts and attitudes of the Saviour, all of these things coming from the indwelling Spirit but remaining only if they are desired and welcomed — all of these things "lust against the flesh." This means that such Spirit-induced thoughts, if permitted to dwell within, will actively dissipate and destroy their opposites, namely, the fleshly lusts. These two verses are the summary of the thoughts in mind in the following verses, where Paul described the two kinds of life, that of the flesh and that of the Spirit.

Verse 18, *But if ye are led by the Spirit, ye are not under the law.*

Judaism was almost totally concerned with external, liturgical, spectacular, material and physical things; and the filling of men's minds with that type of observances would add nothing at all, and even detract from the energies needed in the true spiritual warfare. Paul did not hate Judaism, as such; but it simply *could not* do any good in the kind of warfare that must be won by the soul if men are to please God. The moral commandments of the Mosaic Law are to be fulfilled by Christians, no less than under the law of Christ (see under v. 14); and Paul's stress here is laid not upon the relaxation of such obligations, but upon the only manner of their fulfillment.

Verses 19-21, *Now the works of the flesh are manifest, which are these: fornication, uncleanness, lasciviousness, idolatry, sorcery, enmities, strife, jealousies, wraths, factions, divisions, parties, envyings, drunkenness, revellings, and such like; of which I forewarn you even as I did forewarn you, that they who practise such things shall not inherit the kingdom of God.*

This is another of Paul's lists of evil works, similar but longer than the one in 1 Corinthians 6:9, 10, and also resembling those given in Romans 1:27-32 and 2 Timothy 3:1-8. Extensive comments on various items in this list have already been made in CR and CC in this series.

There are fifteen evils listed here by Paul, and Ramsay identified them all as characteristic of "the kinds of influence likely to affect the South Galatians recently converted from paganism."[16] Any thoughtful person could today make up his own list of the sins, perversions and gross wickedness characteristic of the current culture.

"Sorcery . . ." has been cited by some as proof that Paul believed in the reality of witchcraft; and, in the sense of believing that it was a gross work of the devil being practiced in the culture of those times, of course he did believe. But from this, it is not inferred that Paul believed that so-called witches or sorcerers could actually do the things they claimed and pretended to do. This writer believes in witchcraft in exactly the same way, as being a work of the devil advocated and practiced in the city of Houston at the present time, and being just as sinful now as it was in the days of the apostles; however, it is also believed that the claims and devices of such practitioners are fraudulent, untruthful, deceitful and powerless to do anything either good or evil, except in the sense of causing evil in the people who resort to such things.

Verses 22-23, *But the fruit of the Spirit is love, joy, peace, longsuffering, kindness, goodness, faithfulness, meekness, self-control; against such there is no law.*

Most of these wonderful virtues are subjective, lying within the hearts of Christians, but kindness, goodness and faithfulness are, at least in their manifestation, objective qualities.

"Faithfulness . . ." includes not merely the inward qualities of "keeping on believing in Christ," but it also means remain-

---

[16]William M. Ramsay, *A Historical Commentary on St. Paul's Epistles to the Galatians* (Grand Rapids: Baker Book House, 1965), p. 447.

ing loyal and faithful to the church. Goodness and kindness are likewise determined by actions involving others outside the person of the believer.

Significant especially in this list are the things left out of it. The apostle Paul did not list tongue-speaking, charismatic experiences, visions, premonitions, and things like that as being connected in any manner with the "fruit of the Spirit." Strangely enough, some who believe that those omitted things are the fruit of the Spirit very frequently stop being faithful to the church.

There is more misunderstanding in current times over the meaning of the Spirit's indwelling of Christian hearts than of any other doctrine of the NT. As frequently pointed out in this series, there are no less than *eight designations* in the NT of a single condition (see summary below). Note:

> Ye are the temple of the living God (1 Cor. 3:16; 6:16).
> For it is God that worketh in you (Phil. 2:13).
> God abideth in us . . . we abide in him and he in us . . . God abideth in him and he in God . . . he that abideth in love abideth in God and God abideth in him (1 John 4:11-16).
> The entire Thessalonian church was said to be "in God" (1:1).

From the above citations, there can be no way to avoid the truth that *Christians are in God, and God is in them.*

But note also the following:

> If any man is in Christ, he is a new creature (2 Cor. 5:17).
> Paul's writings alone contain 169 references to being "in Christ, in him, in the Lord, in the beloved, etc."
> If Christ is in you . . . the spirit is life (Rom. 8:10).
> It is Christ that liveth in me (Gal. 2:20).
> That Christ may dwell in your hearts by faith (Eph. 3:17).

From the above citations, there can be no way to avoid the truth that *Christians are in Christ, and Christ is in Christians.*

Note likewise these references:

> The Spirit of God dwelleth in you (1 Cor. 3:16).
> The Spirit . . . dwelleth in you (Rom. 8:11).
> God sent the Spirit of his Son into our hearts (Gal. 4:6).
> I was in the Spirit on the Lord's Day (Rev. 1:10).
> Walk in the Spirit (AV, Gal. 5:16). If we live in the Spirit (AV), let us also walk in the Spirit (AV, Gal. 5:25).

The obvious and undeniable teaching of the NT is that *the Spirit is in Christians and that Christians are in the Spirit.*

In addition to the above, it should also be observed that Christians are commanded to "have this mind in you, which was also in Christ Jesus" (Phil. 2:5), Paul declaring that he himself had "the mind of Christ" (1 Cor. 2:16). Also, it is a commandment to the church of all ages that they shall "let the word of Christ dwell in you richly" (Col. 3:16). Thus the *mind of Christ dwells in Christians, and the word of Christ dwells in Christians.*

SUMMARY

God is in Christians.
Christians are in God.
Christ is in Christians.
Christians are in Christ.
The Holy Spirit is in Christians.
Christians are in the Holy Spirit.
The mind of Christ is in Christians.
The word of Christ is in Christians.

These are descriptions of ONE CONDITION, the saved condition; and there is no stretch of philosophical doodling that can find one iota's difference in the true meaning of the above descriptions of the state of enjoying the salvation of God through Jesus Christ. A full understanding of this, with all of the implications of it, will eliminate the mystical nonsense which has been advocated in this connection. The perfect identity of all of the above as various expressions meaning the same thing is perfectly and glaringly obvious; but, in addition, all of the above expressions are used *interchangeably* in the NT.

"Joy . . ." This may be taken typically of all the various "fruits" here mentioned. This is by no means an experience attributable to the Holy Spirit as separated in any manner from the other persons in the godhead, or even apart from the mind of Christ and the word of Christ dwelling in men's hearts. To be filled with the word of God is to have this same joy. To have the mind of Christ is to have it. To have Christ in us is to have it, etc., etc.

Verse 24, *And they that are of Christ Jesus have crucified the flesh with the passions and lusts thereof.*

Continuing to walk in the Spirit, centering and continuing the thoughts and meditations of the heart upon the teachings of the Lord, actively seeking to maintain identity with the mind

of Christ, consciousness of the indwelling Father, Son, and Holy
Spirit — these things wiil indeed "crucify" the lusts and evil
imaginations which feed them. This is possible only in the
spiritual religion of Christ Jesus, free from the externals and
attractive allurements of spectacular Judaism, the same being
the blessed "freedom in Christ."

Verse 25, *If we live by the Spirit, by the Spirit let us also walk.*

"In the Spirit . . ." instead of "by the Spirit" is far better, the
same being the rendition in the AV. The current conception is
so obsessed with "Spirit in us" that they are reluctant to admit
that it is also true the other way around, we being "in the
Spirit." See notes under verse 23.

Verse 26, *Let us not become vainglorious, provoking one
another, envying one another.*

Vainglory and jealousy are two of the fundamental fleshly
lusts, especially degrading and unbecoming in the church of
Jesus Christ. Nothing that anyone is or has is of himself, but
of God. As Russell said: "Even Jesus said, 'The Son can do
nothing of himself' (John 5:19)."[17] All of the miracles of our Lord
were done as a result of prayer to the Father. See John 11:42
and comment in CJ.

---

[17]John William Russell, *Compact Commentary on the NT* (Grand Rapids:
Baker Book House, 1964), p. 471.

CHAPTER 6

In this final chapter of the epistle, Paul reached the glorious climax of the whole letter dealing with the contrast between the Law of Moses and the Law of Christ, with SO FULFILL THE LAW OF CHRIST standing as the essence of the total admonition. Without the understanding of this final chapter, much that Paul has written earlier might have appeared incomplete and inconclusive. This writer's interpretation of this chapter is at variance with the traditional views concerning it which dominate so much of the current literature on Galatians, but it is presented in the conviction that the sheer logic of the view here advocated will commend itself to the discerning student.

Verse 1, *Brethren, even if a man be overtaken in a trespass, ye who are spiritual restore such a one in a spirit of meekness; looking to thyself, lest thou also be tempted.*

"Overtaken in a trespass . . ." The situation here envisioned is not that of some Christian overtaking trespass, but that of the trespass overtaking him! Sin committed impetuously through the sudden and unexpected onset of temptation, actual sin, not a mere "fault," is to be understood here. The term "trespass" does not entail any "absolution of responsibility";[1] "Of the guilt, there is no palliation indicated by the word *fault* or *trespass*."[2] Despite this certainty regarding the NT usage of this word, men still cling to the phantom supposition that there is less blame in it than accrues to "sin." As Childers said, regarding the Lucan form of the Lord's prayer, where "sin" is used for "trespass," "We who believe that Christians do not commit sins and remain Christians sometimes avoid this form of the prayer."[3] A comparison of the two NT accounts of the Lord's prayer, however, shows that Christ used "sin" and "trespass" interchangeably. Thus the simple meaning here is, "If a Christian brother unexpectedly commits some sin, etc."

---

[1]Herman N. Ridderbos, *The Epistle of Paul to the Churches of Galatia* (Grand Rapids: Wm. B. Eerdmans Publishing Company, 1953), p. 212.

[2]E. Huxtable, *Pulpit Commentary* (Grand Rapids: Wm. B. Eerdmans Publishing Company, 1950), Vol. 20, p. 294.

[3]Charles L. Childers, *Beacon Bible Commentary* (Kansas City: Beacon Hill Press, 1964), Vol. *Romans*, p. 508.

"Ye who are spiritual . . ." is not restricted to ministers, elders, or other special workers in the church but is applicable to all who love the body of the Lord and are zealous for building it up. Obviously, those persons in whom the spiritual life is not dominant would be useless in the endeavor proposed, hence the admonition that "ye who are spiritual" should do it.

"Restore such a one in a spirit of meekness . . ." Amazingly, the commentators have almost invariably described this verse as "a command to love thy neighbor as thyself"; and of course the Christian love of the brethren is an implied necessity, but *it is not here mentioned.* This is a flat, unequivocal commandment to go out and restore the sinful, the same being one part, and only one part of the Law of Christ, mentioned a moment later in connection with another part of that same Law of Christ.

"Looking to thyself, lest thou also be tempted . . ." The thought here echoes that of 5:26, showing the coherence and unity of Paul's continuing message. The deceitful and seductive nature of sin being what it is, the child of the Lord should tread fearfully in the presence of any who have broken the sacred Law, being constantly aware that the same lure of the forbidden which has already trapped a brother might also entangle himself in disobedience.

Verse 2, *Bear ye one another's burdens, and so fulfill the Law of Christ.*

It will be observed that "Law" has been capitalized here, the great pity being that it was not done in the common versions. There is no excuse whatever for writing this word with a capital "L" where the Law of Moses is concerned, as throughout this epistle, and then writing it with a little "l" where the superior and glorious Law of Christ is involved. Of course, there is a rebellious and sinful design in such an unjustifiable discrimination, that being the unbelievable theological proposition that there is no "Law of Christ"! We are under grace! This verse deals the *coup de grace* to any such fallacy. See summary of THE LAW OF CHRIST at the end of this chapter. In the verse before us, two essential elements of that Law have already been mentioned in this chapter, and others will be enumerated in a moment. No. 1 is: "Restore the Backsliders" (v. 1). No. 2 is "Bear Ye One Another's Burdens" (v. 2).

Of course, in verse 5, Paul said, "Each man shall bear his own burden"; but it is still surprising that even a Christian scholar should read this as a "contradiction," even Ridderbos saying, "It is not necessary to eliminate contradiction."[4] The Greek words from which the translation comes are diverse; one is *baros*, denotes a *weight*, and is applicable to a *spiritual burden*; whereas the other is *phortion*, which means *load*, being used in Acts 27:20 of the cargo of a ship, thus something that relates to the purpose of being.[5] Thus in verse 2, Paul speaks of Christians bearing each other's sorrows, due to sins or misfortunes; and in verse 5, he speaks of every man bearing his own responsibility, fulfilling the purpose of his own responsibility, fulling the purpose of his own life. See article, "What To Do with Burdens," under verse 5.

"So fulfill the Law of Christ . . ." It is almost unbelievable that Christian scholarship has so nearly unanimously ignored or misinterpreted LAW OF CHRIST. That Paul meant the Christian duty of helping fellow Christians to be understood as the totality of the Law of Christ is a preposterous error. Of course, such a view is so patently wrong and unreasonable that the rule on burden-sharing is interpreted in a wider frame of reference to mean "Love thy neighbor as thyself"; and that *misinterpretation* is hailed and saluted as the law of Christ (little "l")! Note what is alleged:

> The meaning is that by showing sympathy to others . . . the Christian will best fulfill that "new commandment" . . . "the law of love" (John 13:34, 1 John 3:23).[6]
> In such a statement Christ is not being set up over against Moses as a new lawgiver![7]
> There is a law to which they owe obedience and devotion — the new commandment of Christ . . . the royal law of love.[8]
> "The law of Christ," an uncommon expression, is the law of love.[9]

---

[4]H. N. Ridderbos, *op. cit.,* p. 215.

[5]*Vine's Greek Dictionary,* on "burdens."

[6]William Sanday, *Ellicott's Commentary on the Whole Bible* (Grand Rapids: Zondervan Publishing House, 1959), p. 460.

[7]H. N. Ridderbos, *op. cit.,* p. 213.

[8]J. R. Dummelow, *Commentary on the Holy Bible* (New York: The Macmillan Company, 1937), p. 957.

[9]John Wesley, *One Volume NT Commentary* (Grand Rapids: Baker Book House, 1973), *in loco.*

It seems better to take it of the whole moral institution of
Christus.[10] (This restriction eliminates the ordinances Christ
commanded).

(It is) Christ's law of love.[11]

The law of Christ (little "l") is not a law in the legal sense
of the word.[12]

To fulfill the law of Christ is to love thy neighbor as thyself.[13]

The law of Christ which bids us to love one another.[14]

With all due deference to the learning, scholarship and
devotion of the advocates of such interpretations, all of them
utterly fail to get the point which is that Christians are to obey
the Law of Christ (all of it) as distinguished from the Law of
Moses. As for the allegation that the "law of Christ is not a law
in the legal sense," there is no way to read "Law of Christ"
except in the sense of "God's Law"; and how could divine law
be defined as not being in a legal sense? The very term *legal*
means "pertinent to or conformity to law." So the proposition
means "Christ's law is not pertinent to law!" Such a notion must
be rejected. Moses was the type of Christ, and Christ surpassed
Moses, being the Lawgiver for all mankind.

Thus Paul's true meaning in this place must be, "Fulfill the
Law of Christ," in this particular also, that of bearing each
other's burdens! All of the interpretations cited above make bearing burdens to be inclusive of the larger principle of "love thy
neighbor"; but the interpretation here makes Law of Christ to
mean just what it says: the totality of our blessed Saviour's
teachings. See article, "Law of Christ," at end of chapter.

The total disbelief of many scholars that there is really any
such thing as "the Law of Christ" is as incredible as it is unreasonable. That holy Law is mentioned in that terminology in this
verse; and the context cites a number of its components such as
No. 1 and No. 2, above, and others to be noted below.

Verse 3, *For if a man thinketh himself to be something when
he is nothing, he deceiveth himself.*

---

[10]E. Huxtable, *op. cit.*, p. 296.

[11]James Macknight, *Apostolical Epistles with Commentary and Notes* (Grand
Rapids: Baker Book House, 1969), p. 201.

[12]David Lipscomb, *A Commentary on the NT Epistles, Galatians* (Nashville:
The Gospel Advocate Company, n.d.), p. 277.

[13]J. W. McGarvey, *The Standard Bible Commentary, Galatians* (Cincinnati:
The Standard Publishing Company, 1916), p. 285.

[14]William Hendriksen, *op. cit.*, p. 235.

This appears to be addressed to any of the "spiritual" in verse 1 who might consider themselves above "sinners" and thus under no obligation to restore them.

Verse 4-5, *But let each man prove his own work, and then shall he have his glorying in regard of himself alone, and not of his neighbor. For each man shall bear his own burden.*

"Work . . ." here means "practical behavior contrasted with profession."[15] Such a work is here set forth as the basis of one's "glorying," a Pauline expression meaning "rejoicing in the hope of salvation." This is a companion statement to "Work out your own salvation with fear and trembling" (Phil. 2:12). Standing, as it does, here at the end of Galatians it is the effective and irrefutable denial of the slander that would make Paul's rejection of the "works" of the Law of Moses as having any connection with salvation, to be in any sense inclusive of the "work of faith" which is required of every Christian (1 Thess. 1:3). Henriksen revealed a shade of meaning accurately in his rendition thus: "Let each one test his own work; then his reason to boast will be in himself alone, and not in (comparing himself) with someone else."[16]

What to Do with Burdens

Every man, rich or poor, old or young, wise or foolish, weak or strong, has some burden to bear. One's neighbors may not always see it, for some burdens are hidden; and there must be many like the ancient Jewish king who wore sackcloth beneath his royal robes. Some smiling faces mask a burdened heart.

The word of God reveals that burdens may be handled in three ways. Some may be shared with others; other burdens must be borne by every man himself (see under verse 1); and of a third class, the scriptures command, "Cast thy burden upon the Lord" (Ps. 55:22, RV margin).

A. Burdens that may be shared with others. There is many a load of life that grows infinitely lighter under the touch of a friendly hand or the sound of an encouraging word. When the storms of life's deepest emotions have been unloosed by over-

---

[15]E. Huxtable, *op. cit.,* p. 296.

[16]William Hendriksen, *New Testament Commentary on Galatians* (Grand Rapids: Baker Book House, 1968), p. 234.

whelming experiences, it is the glory of Christians to "rejoice with those that do rejoice, and to weep with those who weep." Love and toleration for the weak, and loving compassion for the needy, as well as love and appreciation for every soul's unique and eternal value "in Christ" can ease the burdens of the weary and bless the giver and the receiver alike.

B. The burdens one must bear himself. No one may share another's responsibility. "Every man shall bear his own burden." "Every one of us must give an account of himself to God" (2 Cor. 5:10; Rom. 14:12). Every man must bear the burden of ordering his life after "the sayings of Jesus Christ" (Matt. 7:24-27), upon pain of being either a wise or a foolish builder; and no commentator or preacher ever had the right to bear that burden for him. See Law of Christ at end of chapter.

C. The burdens that are too heavy to be borne. Of a third class of burdens, it is said, "Cast thy burdens upon the Lord." Our sins are such a burden. Our sins we cannot ignore, deny or make restitution for them; only "in Christ" may they be forgiven. Our anxieties are too frustrating and depressing to be borne by mortals. All of them should be cast upon the Lord (Phil. 4:6). Great natural calamities, wars, pestilence, revolutions and countless other things are burdens no mortal can bear. Cast them upon the Lord.

Verse 6, *But let him that is taught in the word communicate unto him that teacheth in all good things.*

Huxtable noted that this exhortation to "liberality toward our teachers is perfectly germane to the preceding topics of sharing one another's loads, and so carrying our own pack."[17] However, it is germane in another very important relationship. Paul here was enumerating a number of things included in the Law of Christ, not a total summary, of course, but a list of particulars in which he felt the Galatians might need special exhortation. This is No. 3 of a group of things Paul stressed. It means financially support your teachers. Conybeare made the meaning clearer by capitalizing Word,[18] showing that not all teachers are indicated but that teachers of the Word of God are meant.

---

[17]E. Huxtable, *op. cit.,* p. 297.

[18]Conybeare and Howson, *The Life and Epistles of St. Paul* (Grand Rapids: Wm. B. Eerdmans Publishing Company, 1966), p. 492.

Howard observed that the word here rendered "communicate" is *koinoneo*, meaning to share, or participate, even as a partner.[19] Failure to understand this reference to the Christian duty of giving support of the gospel as pertaining to the Law of Christ led to the somewhat humorous exclamation of Ridderbos that "It is difficult to find the right connection between verse 6 and what precedes . . . "[20] Of course, it connects with that Law of Christ which none of the commentators can see!

Verses 7-8, *Be not deceived; God is not mocked: for whatsoever a man soweth, that shall he also reap. For he that soweth unto his flesh shall of the flesh reap corruption; but he that soweth unto the Spirit shall of the Spirit reap eternal life.*

"Soweth unto his flesh . . ." is a reference to living after the lusts of the flesh as Paul had just outlined in 5:18-21; and sowing to the Spirit is the equivalent of living the kind of life that exhibits the fruit of the Spirit (5:22-24).

SOWING AND REAPING

A. The principle of sowing and reaping is handed down from the throne of God himself. None can deny it; no skeptic can scoff at it; it was true in the garden of Eden that Adam reaped what he sowed, and it has been true ever since. It is true of every individual, of every saint and sinner, or every hypocrite who thinks he is a saint; it is true of every race, society and nation. It was true of Babylon, Persia, Greece, Rome, France and Germany, and it will be true of the United States of America.

It is true in both physical and spiritual creations. Both the OT and the NT teach it. "Whoever perished being innocent?" (Job 4:8); "they have sown the wind and shall reap the whirlwind" (Hosea 8:7); "he who sows injustice will reap calamity" (Prov. 22:8, RSV).

In the NT, Paul used this principle to teach Christian giving (2 Cor. 8, 9). "No planting, no harvest" is the law of life. The mandate to the church is "preach the gospel." It is the executive order of God for every individual. There are no small and big opportunities; all opportunities are BIG with eternal potential.

---

[19]R. E. Howard, *Beacon Bible Commentary, Galatians* (Kansas City: Beacon Hill Press, 1965), Vol. IX, p. 116.

[20]H. N. Ridderbos, *op. cit.,* p. 216.

B. Extensions of this principle. The reaping is always more than the sowing. It is inevitably in kind. No man ever sowed to the flesh and reaped eternal life, or the other way around. It is inevitable. There is no art or device of man that can countermand, avoid, or checkmate this eternal law of God. The sons of Jacob sold their brother; and all of them became slaves in the same land. America sowed the wind (of slavery) and reaped the whirlwind of civil war. Germany sowed the wind when they listened to the Pied Piper of Munich and reaped the devastation of World War II. Wherever men or nations today obey their own foolish philosophies instead of the word of God they are sowing to the wind; and already the whirlwind gathers dark and threatening upon the horizons of all the troubled earth. It might be almost time to reap the whirlwind.

C. There is a good side to this also. Sowing to the Spirit promises certain, inevitable, increased reward in kind. They who have loved and sought the fellowship of Christ in God shall at last enter the eternal fellowship above, where all the problems of earth are solved in the light and bliss of heaven.

Verse 9, *And let us not be weary in well-doing: for in due season we shall reap, if we faint not.*

"Be not weary in well doing . . ." This is No. 4, being an undeniable component of the Law of Christ who went about doing good (Matt. 21:15). How could any man imitate Paul as he imitated Christ without doing good? This touches the principal practical business of Christians on earth. It is amazing how little regard some seem to have for it.

"In due season we shall reap if we faint not . . ." For discussion of fainting, see CH 12:3. Many things can cause Christians to faint, among them being the evil doctrines which undermine and destroy their faith.

Verse 10, *So then, as we have opportunity, let us work that which is good toward all men, and especially toward them that are of the household of the faith.*

The badge of Christian behavior is that of positive good toward all on earth. "Work that which is good . . ." Strange that Paul should have mentioned this, especially if he had been advocating for five chapters that "works" do not have anything to do with salvation! Of course, the meaning in those previous chapters refers to the works of the *Law of Moses* and not to that class of works which Christians *must* do. Yes, the word is *must!* Christ equated salvation with this very principle Paul had in view here, there being the same distinction between "everybody" and "the household of faith" in the great passage from Matthew 25:31-46. Although the Christian must do good and not do evil to all men, there is a special and prior obligation to Christian brothers, as elaborated by Jesus in the passage cited. "Inasmuch as ye have done it unto one of the least of these MY BRETHREN ..." was the test of receiving or losing eternal life. The savage humanism of the current era which would tie the full resources of the church of God to every social scheme that comes along cannot be justified by a proper respect to what Jesus said there and what Paul said here.

Verse 11, *See with how large letters I write unto you with mine own hand.*

Scholars advocate opposing views on what is meant by this; for certainly, it may be translated otherwise than in RV. Macknight rendered it thus:

> The phrase is rightly translated *how large a letter.* The first word properly signifies *of what size*; and the second denotes *an epistle*, as well as the letters of the alphabet.[21]

As in all cases where two translations are possible, the context and other overall consideration must be resorted to. Of pertinence here, it seems, is the opinion of Ramsay, who said, "Those who suppose that a trifling detail, such as the size or shape of Paul's handwriting, could find room in his mind as he wrote this letter are mistaking his character."[22]

"I write ..." is also better rendered as "have written," thus having, as Dummelow thought, "a reference to the foregoing letter of Galatians."[23]

Scholarly objections to this on the basis that after all, Galatians is not as large as Romans, are not valid, as Romans had not been written, nor, for that matter, any of the other Pauline letters. We have followed the opinion of Hendriksen who wrote: "If, of all Paul's letters that have been preserved, Galatians was

---

[21]James Macknight, *op. cit.,* p. 206.
[22]Wm. M. Ramsay, *A Historical Commentary on St. Paul's Epistle to the Galatians* (Grand Rapids: Baker Book House, 1965), p. 466.
[23]J. R. Dummelow, *op. cit.,* p. 957.

the very first one that he wrote, as we have assumed, he could perhaps have written, 'See what a big letter I wrote you'."[24]

Most current scholars go the other way, however, taking an alternate rendition and interpreting it to mean Paul's eyesight was bad, or his handwriting was characteristically large, thus forming a kind of signature, or even that he was somewhat illiterate! It seems to this student that such guesses have little in their favor.

Verse 12, *As many as desire to make a fair show in the flesh, they compel you to be circumcised; only that they may not be persecuted for the cross of Christ.*

This verse is valuable as showing that this whole chapter still deals with the Moses vs. Christ theme; and that it is not "looking quite away from the Judaic controversy,"[25] as alleged by Ramsay and many others. No, Paul is still on the same subject; and that Judaism vs. Christianity is still his primary concern surfaces again in verse 15.

"Only that they may not be persecuted for the cross of Christ . . ." This is Paul's charge that the Judaizers were insincere hypocrites who cared nothing at all for the Law of Moses (see next verse), but that they were merely striving to accommodate to Jewish opinion for the sake of self-promotion. This was a devastating charge. Even the errors of sincere men may be tolerated and understood, but the pretensions of self-seeking hypocrites can receive nothing except utter contempt.

Verse 13, *For not even they who receive circumcision do themselves keep the law; but they desire to have you circumcised, that they may glory in your flesh.*

Something of the strategy of the Jerusalem hierarchy is detected in these two verses. They evidently had persuaded certain Christians who had become Judaizers to procure, by any practical means, the circumcision of as many of the Gentile converts as possible, leaving out of sight the ultimate amalgamation of all of them as proselytes to Judaism, which they doubtless envisioned as coming at a later phase of the effort. This accounts for the fact that the Judaizers neither kept the Law

---

[24]William Hendriksen, *op. cit.,* p. 241.
[25]Wm. M. Ramsay, *op. cit.,* p. 454.

themselves nor sought to bind any of its more objectionable features upon their followers. The hypocrisy of such a device Paul exposed in this verse.

Thus, as Huxtable discerned, those Judaizers were courting favor with the Jewish hierarchy. He said: "Paul meant, It is from no zeal for the Law that they do what they do, for they are at no pains to keep the Law; but only with the object of currying favor with the Jews."[26]

Verse 14, *But far be it from me to glory, save in the cross of our Lord Jesus Christ, through which the world hath been crucified unto me, and I unto the world.*

"Glory, save in the cross . . ." The cross of the Son of God, by the love for men exhibited upon it by the Saviour, by the atonement for sins provided upon its crude beams, by all the hope of the gospel which it symbolizes, is indeed the only grounds of rejoicing and glorying on the part of Christians.

"Through which . . ." This should not be "through whom"; for Christ does not crucify Christians, nor the world; it is the cross which does so.

"The world hath been crucified unto me . . ." The cross has crucified the world to Christians in the sense that the hope of the gospel achieved and symbolized thereupon has made the world to be, in the eyes of Christians, crucified by the cross of Christ.

"And I unto the world . . ." Macknight has this comment:

The cross of Christ crucifies Christians to the world, by inspiring them with such principles and leading them to a course of life which renders them in the eyes of the world as contemptible, and as unfit for their purposes as if they were crucified and dead.[27]

Verse 15, *For neither is circumcision anything, nor uncircumcision, but a new creature.*

For full discussion of this thought, see under 5:6, above. The significance of its recurrence here is that of focusing upon Paul's main theme continuing right through this chapter and to the very end of it, namely, that of the Law of Moses vs. the Law of Christ, forcing the conclusion that "Law of Christ" in

---

[26]E. Huxtable, *op. cit.,* p. 308.
[27]James Macknight, *op. cit.,* p. 210.

verse 2, is not a mere afterthought with regard to the general rule of "love thy neighbor," but an emphasis upon that glorious entity, the Law of Jesus Christ, which is antithetical to the Law of Moses, abrogating and replacing it altogether.

Verse 16, *And as many as shall walk by this rule, peace be upon them, and mercy, and upon the Israel of God.*

"As many as shall walk by this rule . . ." that is, the Law of Christ, not regarding merely the portions of it stressed in this final chapter, but all of it.

"Peace . . . and mercy . . ." The apostolical blessing is invoked upon those who will walk under the Law of Christ, as distinguished from them that desire to cling to the Law of Moses.

"And upon the Israel of God . . ." It is surprising that any could misunderstand this, as if Paul were, in any manner, invoking a blessing upon racial Jews. "Israel of God," in the true sense, with Paul, was never racial Israel, but the spiritual Israel. See Romans 2:28, 29; 4:13-16 and 9:6-8. This meaning of "spiritual Israel," of course, included all of every race, including Jews, who accepted Christ. "Israel of God," according to Wesley, means "the church of God, which consists of all those, and only those, of every nation and kindred, who walk by this rule."[28]

This benediction is not addressed to two distinct sets of persons (those who walk by this rule, and upon the Israel of God) but upon the same set of persons addressed in two ways, as if he had said, "Yea, upon the Israel of God."[29]

Verse 17, *Henceforth let no man trouble me; for I bear branded on my body the marks of Jesus.*

This is doubtless a reference to the scars of such suffering as Paul's stoning at Lystra, among these very Galatians, on the first tour; and he considered such "marks" as positive and undeniable evidence of the genuiness of his apostleship. Any interpretation of this passage as a statement that nailprints had appeared in Paul's hand and feet in some supernatural manifestations of the *Stigmata* belongs to the Dark Ages. Nothing like that is in the passage.

There might be, however, some comparison intended with certain practices among the heathen. "The mark of the pagan

[28]John Wesley, *op. cit., in loco.*
[29]William Sanday, *op. cit.,* p. 463.

god Dyonysus was that of an ivy leaf burned into the flesh with a branding iron,"[30] and such a practice widely known to the Galatians might have suggested Paul's using the term "branded" here; but beyond that, there could have been no connection. As Ramsay eloquently declared, "The marks that branded Paul as a slave of Jesus were the deep cuts of the lictor's rods of Pisidian Antioch and the stones of Lystra!"[31]

Verse 18, *The grace of our Lord Jesus Christ be with your spirit, brethren. Amen.*

Paul gave no commendation at the beginning of Galatians, and the tone of the whole letter is one of hurt surprise, sorrow and indignation; but in this final word "brethren," one finds the loving heart of Paul yearning for his beloved converts in Galatia. It is a final word of love and hope for all of them. He had not given them up; they were still brethren. History gives no clue to the manner of their receiving this letter, nor to the continued success or failure of the Galatians; but as McGarvey said:

> We have no word of history which reveals to us the immediate effect of Paul's epistle; but the fact that it was preserved argues well that it was favorably received. Due to its vigor and power, it could not have been otherwise than effective.[32]

This epistle, along with the Corinthians and Romans, staggered Judaism and restrained it till, smitten by the hand of the Almighty at the destruction of Jerusalem in A.D. 70, it ceased to trouble the church any more until the times of the apostasy, when its forms and systems were revived, and in modern times when sabbatarians still attempt to bind such things as the sabbath day.

THE LAW OF CHRIST

1. He that heareth and doeth Christ's "sayings" shall be saved; he that does not do so shall be lost (Matt. 7:24-29).
2. "He that believeth and is baptized shall be saved, and he that disbelieves shall be condemned" (Mark 16:15, 16).
3. "Except a man be born again he cannot see the kingdom of God" (John 3:5).

---

[30] E. Huxtable, *op. cit.,* p. 314.
[31] Wm. M. Ramsay, *op. cit.,* p. 472.
[32] J. W. McGarvey, *op. cit.,* p. 288.

4. Regarding the Lord's supper: "This do ye until I come" (1 Cor. 11:24ff). "Except ye eat the flesh and drink the blood of the Son of man ye have no life in you" (John 6:54ff).

5. Observe all things whatsoever I have commanded you" (Matt. 18:18-20).

6. Whosoever shall break one of the least of these commandments and teach men so, shall be called least in the kingdom of heaven" (Matt. 5:19).

7. "Abide in me . . . apart from me ye can do nothing." "If a man abide not in me, he is cast forth as a branch and is withered; and they gather them and cast them into the fire" (John 15:4-6).

8. "Be ye therefore perfect, as your heavenly Father is perfect" (Matt. 5:48). The manner of keeping this is discussed under Colossians 1:28, which see.

9. What is done to the church, the spiritual body of Christ, is also done to Christ (Acts 9:4ff).

10. "Be thou faithful unto death, and I will give thee the crown of life" (Rev. 2:10).

Etc.

This is no more than a few suggestions; but they do not represent human opinion at all, but what Christ said. Let every man ponder this Law. The notion that the apostle Paul set aside all of the words of Christ and substituted a "faith only" way of attaining salvation fails to take account of the fact that Christ is the head of his church, not Paul. Apostle though he was, he was a mortal, the eloquent and holy apostle and most distinguished preacher of all times; but he was the bond-slave of Jesus Christ who gave men the teachings of the NT. Those who believe that Paul would have said or done anything to pervert or change the teaching of Christ understand neither Paul nor Christ.

A popular superstition is that "The Law of Christ is a positive law, not a negative law." In the sense of stressing many positive values, of course, it is; but the Law of Christ has many negatives also. Notice just a few of them from the Sermon on the Mount:

Swear not at all (Matt. 5:34).
Judge not that ye be not judged (Matt. 7:1).
Ye cannot serve God and mammon (Matt. 6:24).
Be not therefore anxious (Matt. 6:31).
Give not that which is holy unto the dogs (Matt. 7:6).
In praying use not vain repetitions (Matt. 6:7).
And ye shall not be as the hypocrites (Matt. 6:5).
Lay not up for yourselves treasures on earth (Matt. 6:19).

If ye forgive not . . . neither will your Father forgive you (Matt. 6:15).

Everyone that heareth these words of mine and doeth them not . . . like the foolish man who built his house on the sand . . . great was the fall thereof (Matt. 7:26-27).

The above are merely representative of a vast body of similar teaching in the Magna Carta of the Christian religion, called the Sermon on the Mount.

But, is not the Law of Christ a "law of liberty" in comparison with the Law of Moses? To be sure it is. All of the vast ceremonial, with its physical sacrifices, presentations upon certain days, and intricate, elaborate procedures for every conceivable kind of violation — all that is gone. The subjection to priestcraft, which was an inevitable accompaniment of the Old, has been taken away. There is forgiveness of violations under the New, but there was none under the Old. The indwelling of the Spirit of God aids the Christian, but did not aid the worshiper under Judaism. Not any of the morality, integrity, honesty, truthfulness, sobriety, chastity, etc., that were required under Moses have been abrogated or relaxed under Christ. The notion that Christianity has a looser moral code than Judaism is ridiculous; and yet that is precisely the understanding some have regarding the wonderful "freedom in Christ." Such is a fatal delusion. It will be apparent to any who will contemplate it, that if Christ came into the world in order merely to relax the will of God regarding what is or is not righteousness, such an alteration could in no case have required the death of the Son of God. As a matter of truth, the morality of Christ is a higher, stricter and tighter code than Judaism ever was, as specifically elaborated in the Sermon on the Mount. This undeniable truth sends shudders of apprehension through those who see it and draw back and cry, "Impossible! Who can be *perfect?* Where is any possible ground of confidence?"

THE CONFIDENCE IN CHRIST

Despite the higher level of morality required of Christians, and despite the specific commandments of both a positive and negative nature which abound in Christian doctrine, and despite the fact that no salvation of any kind is promised to them who "obey not the gospel," there is, nevertheless, the solid ground of absolute trust and confidence "in Christ." The forgiveness provided in the love of Christ in the New Dispensation is operative on a constant and continual basis, "cleansing us of all unrighteousness"; and two questions only, if they may be honestly answered affirmatively by the human conscience, bestow full and mighty confidence in the Christian. "Am I in Christ?" and "Shall I be found in him?" All of our confidence is not in our own success as to meeting God's standards, but it is in Jesus Christ our Lord. Amen.

BIBLIOGRAPHY . . . GALATIANS

The following authors and sources were quoted in the text of the commentary on Galatians:

Barclay, William, *The Letters to the Galatians and Ephesians* (Philadelphia: The Westminster Press, 1954).

Coad, F. Roy, *A New Testament Commentary* (Grand Rapids: Zondervan Publishing House, 1969).

Cole, R. A., *Tyndale NT Commentaries, Galatians* (Grand Rapids: Wm. B. Eerdmans Publishing Company, 1965).

Conybeare, W. J., *The Life and Epistles of St. Paul* (Grand Rapids: Wm. B. Eerdmans Publishing Company, 1966).

Dummelow, J. R., *Commentary on the Holy Bible* (New York: The Macmillan Company, 1937).

Emphatic Diaglott, The (Brooklyn: Watchtower Bible and Tract Society).

Greathouse, William M., *Beacon Bible Commentary, Romans* (Kansas City: Beacon Hill Press, 1968).

Halley, Henry H., *Halley's Bible Handbook* (Grand Rapids: Zondervan Publishing House, 1927).

Harrison, Everett F., *Wycliffe Bible Commentary* (Chicago: Moody Press, 1971).

Hayes D. A., *Paul and His Epistles* (Grand Rapids: Baker Book House, 1969).

Hendriksen, William, *NT Commentary on Galatians* (Grand Rapids: Baker Book House, 1968).

Howard, George, article: "The Faith of Christ" in *Expository Times,* Vol. 7, pp. 212-214, April, 1974.

Howard, R. E., *Beacon Bible Commentary,* Vol. IX (Kansas City: Beacon Hill Press, 1965).

Huxtable, E., *Pulpit Commentary,* Vol. 20 (Grand Rapids: Wm. B. Eerdmans Publishing Company, 1950).

Lipscomb, David, *Commentary on the NT Epistles* (Nashville: Gospel Advocate Company, 1939).

McGarvey, J. W., *The Standard Bible Commentary* (Cincinnati: The Standard Publishing Company, 1916).

Mackay, John, *God's Order* (Old Tappan, N.J.: Fleming H. Revell Co., 1953).

Macknight, James, *Apostolical Epistles with Commentary and Notes* (Grand Rapids: Baker Book House 1969).

Morris, Leon, *Tyndale Commentary, 1 Corinthians* (Grand Rapids: Wm. B. Eerdmans Publishing Company, 1958).

Pink, Arthur W., *Gleanings from Paul* (Chicago: Moody Press, 1967).

Ramsay, William M., *Historical Commentary on St. Paul's Epistle to the Galatians* (Grand Rapids: Baker Book House, 1965).

Ridderbos, Herman N., *The Epistle of Paul to the Churches of Galatia* (Grand Rapids: Wm. B. Eerdmans Publishing Company, 1953).

Russell, John William, *Compact Commentary on the NT* (Grand Rapids: Baker Book House, 1964).

Sanday, William, *Ellicott's Commentary on the NT* (Grand Rapids: Baker Book House, 1964).

Stamm, Raymond T., *Interpreter's Bible,* Vol. X (New York: Abingdon Press, 1953).

Tenney, Merrill C., *Galatians, Charter of Christian Liberty* (Grand Rapids: Wm. B. Eerdmans Publishing Company, 1950).

Vine, W. E., *An Expository Dictionary of NT Words* (Old Tappan, N.J.: Fleming H. Revell Co., 1940).

Wallace, Foy E., Jr., *A Review of the New Versions* (Fort Worth: The Foy E. Wallace, Jr., Publications, 1973).

Wesley, John, *One Volume NT Commentary* (Grand Rapids: Baker Book House, 1972).

Ephesians

INTRODUCTION TO EPHESIANS

Authenticity. "None of the epistles which are ascribed to Paul have a stronger chain of evidence to their early and continued use than that which we know as the Epistle to the Ephesians."[1] Clement of Rome evidently quoted from this epistle prior to 95 A.D.; and there are many evidences that Ephesians was known from the earliest years of the second century.[2] Internally, the epistle carries the affirmation throughout that Paul is the author of it; the general style and form of it are absolutely Pauline; and all objections to Paul's authorship are based upon very tenuous and insufficient ground, there being nothing of any substance whatever to cast any reflection against it. All of the arguments about the question are summed up thus:

> The attack on the epistle fails, whether it is made from the point of teaching or language; and there is no ground whatever for questioning the truth of Christian tradition that St. Paul wrote the letter which we know as the Epistle to the Ephesians.[3]

Place and Date of Writing: There are many good reasons for holding that Ephesians was written from Rome, during Paul's imprisonment there the first time (the one recorded in Acts 28:30), and that Philippians, Colossians and Philemon were also written about the same time. The year 58, or thereabouts, may be assigned as a likely date.

To Whom Written: The words "at Ephesus" are missing from certain old manuscripts (see under 1:1, below); but the very fact of Tychicus being chosen by Paul to convey this letter to the addressees would suggest that it was surely addressed to some congregation in Asia (Tychicus was a citizen of Asia); and, as Ephesus was the principal congregation of the entire province, there was no way that the Ephesians would not have received it, either as addressed directly to them, or along with other congregations as fellow-recipients of a kind of circular letter intended for Christians throughout the area, and in fact everywhere. Certainly no harm is done by calling it the letter to the Ephesians.

---

[1]*ISBE* p. 956.
[2]*Ibid.*.
[3]*Ibid.* p. 957.

Some have objected that if Paul had written to the Ephesians, he would have mentioned a number of Christians personally; but such an objection has no value for two reasons: (1) If the letter had been addressed to the Ephesian congregation, Paul's long residence there and widespread acquaintance would have made it improper for him to single out a lot of people for personal greetings, as he would have been required to leave out far more than he could have included. One can only be amused by many of the scholars who are inclined to make a big thing out of this so-called omission of personal greetings. No scholar objecting to such a thing seems to be aware of the personal relations problem that would have been created by the inclusion of a list of personal names in a letter to a church where Paul knew hundreds of them!

(2) The evidence seems to favor the view that Paul, writing from a Roman prison, and desiring to achieve the widest possible circulation for the epistle, probably caused a number of copies of it to be made, dispatching them all by Tychicus, and with specific names of various congregations inscribed appropriately at the beginning. If such a thing was done, it would explain, how a copy came down through history, without being inscribed to any particular church, a deficiency that would have been supplied by later copyists. This would also explain why Paul did not include personal greetings; but the view here is that he would not have included them even if the epistle had been intended for Ephesus alone.

Character of the Epistle: This letter is one of the most magnificient in the NT, containing the very essence of Christianity and bearing in every line of it the most convincing evidence of its vitality, authenticity and relevance to the Christian faith. The great reciprocal relations spelled out in the last two chapters constitute the Christian ethic which broke the back of the pagan empire. Thirty times, the expression "in Christ," or its equivalent, is used, providing the most definitive and specific statement of the blessings "in Christ" to be found in the NT. It is writing of incredible beauty and charm.

Some scholars have objected that Ephesians is closely parallel to Colossians; but this is not really an objection. Paul wrote both letters, at or very near the same time, and dispatched both of them to their destinations by the same person, Tychicus. Why would they not have been nearly verbatim copies of the same message?

CHAPTER 1

Paul began here in the manner of all writers of his time with a salutation (1-2); and pausing a moment to consider the sublime and heavenly theme upon which he was about to write, penned the noble words of a grand doxology (3-14), and then a fervent and beautiful prayer for those who would receive his letter (15-23).

Verse 1, Paul, *an apostle of Jesus Christ through the will of God, to the saints that are in Ephesus, and the faithful in Christ Jesus.*

"Paul, an apostle . . ." Although the word "apostle" was sometimes used in a secondary sense to include such faithful missionaries as Timothy, Silvanus, (1 Thess. 2:6) and Barnabas (Acts 14:14), Paul's use of the title for himself was always in the highest sense of a plenary representative of Christ who in harmony with the will of God had personally commissioned him; and as in the instance of the Twelve (Luke 6:13) the "Lord named him" an apostle. The title was not one which "developed" in the early church but goes back to Christ himself.

"To the saints . . ." This frequent designation of all Christians in apostolical times regarded what they were called to become more that it did any perfection of their achievement. As Foulkes put it, "The word expresses at once the privilege and the responsibility of the calling of every Christian, not the attainment of a select few."[1]

"That are at Ephesus . . ." Some very ancient authorities omit this phrase (RV margin), including the Chester Beatty Papyrus 46, dated about 200 A.D. Also the phrase as it stands in the Vatican and Sinaitic codices was apparently added by a later copyist.[2] The most widely accepted explanation of this is that some early copies left the words "at Ephesus" out on purpose so that other churches might insert their own names, since the purpose of the writer to include all Christians everywhere is clear enough in

---

[1]Francis Foulkes, *Tyndale Commentary, Ephesians* (Grand Rapids: Wm. B. Eerdmans Publishing Company, 1963), p. 43.

[2]F. F. Bruce, *The Epistle to the Ephesians* (Old Tappan, N.J.: Fleming H. Revell Co., 1961), p. 26.

the very next clause. "Certainly nothing has been advanced to show that the claim of Ephesus as recipient ought to be surrendered in favor of any other."[3] If, as has been widely supposed, Paul had a number of copies of the letter made, dispatching them by hand of Tychicus to a number of churches, the preservation of one of the "blank" copies which has come down to us would be explained, and also the reason why Paul did not send personal greetings to individual Christians in the text of the letter. The early centuries of Christianity found no difficulty in receiving this as Paul's letter to the Ephesians; and certainly there is no logical reason for refusing to do so now.

"And the faithful in Christ Jesus . . ." This clause makes it mandatory to supply the name of a specific group to stand as the coordinate in this sentence; and the very fact of its being addressed, not only to the specific group, but to the "faithful in Christ," shows Paul's purpose of addressing the entire Christian world in this epistle.

"In Christ Jesus . . ." This phrase, or its equivalent, "occurs one hundred seventy-six times in the Pauline writings, thirty-six times in Ephesians alone."[4] Although scholars count these occurrences somewhat differently, depending on the version or translation used, it must be agreed by all that "in Christ" is the cornerstone and foundation of Paul's theology. The NEB approached the meaning of this incredibly important phrase with the rendition "believers incorporate," missing it only in the *identity* of the corporation. It is not *believers* incorporate, but *Christ* incorporate. For additional comment on Jesus Christ, Inc., see CR, chapter 3. Also, there is a summary of the salient features of this incorporation at the end of this chapter.

Verse 2, *Grace to you and peace from God our Father and the Lord Jesus Christ.*

The linking of the Saviour's name with that of the Father as the source of grace and peace indicates the apostolical certainty of our Lord's oneness with deity itself.

"Grace and peace . . ." "Grace" with variations was a typical Greek greeting, and "Peace" was a Hebrew greeting. Paul

---

[3]W. G. Blaikie, *Pulpit Commentary,* Vol. 20, *Ephesians* (Grand Rapids: Wm. B. Eerdmans Publishing Company, 1950), p. v.

[4]D. A. Hayes, *Paul and His Epistles* (Grand Rapids: Baker Book House, 1969), p. 393.

combined the two, with his own genius for improving both of them and expanding their meanings. In the Christian concept, *grace* is not merely "cheerio," but the joy unspeakable flowing outward to men from the fountain of God's gracious and overflowing love, forgiveness and mercy, and that without any merit whatever on the part of men. *Peace* is not merely the tranquility and equilibrium of a soul in harmony with the Creator, but the word also anchors and symbolizes one of the great valuejudgments of Christianity, namely, that peace is better than war. As Martin noted, "This same greeting is found in all of Paul's epistles, though the word *mercy* is added in the Pastorals."[5]

Peace Better Than War

So deeply ingrained in the fabric of Western civilization is the basic Christian concept of peace being better than war, that there are many who are seemingly unaware of its origin and of the Christian roots that sustain it.

Whence came the idea that peace is better than war? The native civilization of North America certainly subscribed to no such principle. Modern tyrants like Hitler and Mussolini both expressed a preference for war, consciously choosing for themselves and their nations what they thought to be the advantages of war. That they were able to do such a thing came about through their rejection of the teachings of the Bible. It is the word of God alone that creates and binds upon men the judgment that peace is better than war. Such a view is absolutely incompatible with unregenerated humanity. The first poem ever written glorified the crime of murder (Gen. 4:23); and humanity, apart from the holy scriptures, has invariably adored and elevated the ruthless mass-murders and spoilers of the human race. Take the Bible away, and men will automatically revert to pillage, plunder, rape and bloodshed in the same manner as the sow returns to her wallowing in the mire. The preference for peace is not a desire that flows out of unregenerated hearts; but it comes from the benign influence of the Prince of Peace, who constantly challenges men and makes them ashamed as they move over grotesque moonlit battlefields at night, covering the

---

[5]Alfred Martin, *Wycliffe Bible Commentary on the New Testament* (Chicago: Moody Press, 1961), p. 725.

faces of the dead as they advance. It is the light that shines in
the Bible that allows men to see the atrocious ugliness of war.
Such a value-judgment is implicit in the glorious words of this
Pauline salutation.

It is not a denial of this truth which is indicated by the extensive and widespread acceptance of the superior blessings of peace
on the part of men, generally, throughout the world; but that
acceptance is evidence that the whole civilized world still
remains, partially, within the perimeter of Christian influence.
Should that influence continue to be abated and eroded, rever-
sion to the old value-judgments will follow.

Verse 3, *Blessed be the God and Father of our Lord Jesus
Christ, who hath blessed us with every spiritual blessing in the
heavenly places in Christ.*

"Every spiritual blessing . . ." There are no spiritual blessings of any kind whatever, other than "in Christ." As Bruce said,
"Paul here struck the keynote of Ephesians at once. The writer
and his readers are 'in Christ,' members of Christ, sharers of his
resurrection life."[6]

"In heavenly places . . ." Macknight gave the meaning here
as "in the Christian church";[7] and, although the blessings "in
Christ" are certainly those in his spiritual body, which is the
church, it seems evident that more is intended here. As Bruce
expressed it, "Christ is exalted to the heavenly realm, and thus
those who are 'in him' belong to that heavenly realm also."[8] This
remarkable expression occurs five times in this epistle (1:3, 20;
2:6; 3:10; 6:12) and nowhere else. The expression was evidently
used by Paul to convey the idea that the totality of all blessings
of a spiritual nature and having eternal value are to be found
exclusively "in Christ."

With this profound verse, Paul began a doxology which runs
through verse 14, composed of one long complicated sentence
"impossible to analyze, in which each successive thought crowds
in on the one before."[9] Some of the grandest and most perplex-
ing words in the vocabulary of Christianity are used in

---

[6]F. F. Bruce, *op. cit.*, p. 27.

[7]James Macknight, *Apostolical Epistles and Commentary, Ephesians* (Grand
Rapids: Baker Book House, 1969), p. 258.

[8]F. F. Bruce, *op. cit.*, p. 27.

[9]Francis Foulkes, *op. cit.*, p. 44.

it, such as *adoption, redemption, foreordained, heritage* and *sealed.*

Verse 4, *Even as he chose us in him before the foundation of the world, that we should be holy and without blemish before him in love.*

Inherent in this is the fact of God's calling and electing men before the foundation of the world; and very few theological questions have demanded more attention and interest than this. Clearly revealed in this is the fact that the coming of Jesus Christ into the world for the purpose of taking out of it a people for himself and redeeming them unto eternal life was no afterthought on God's part. Before the world was ever created, the divine plan of the Son of God's visitation of the human family existed in the eternal purpose of God. That body that Christ would gather from the populations of earth is destined to receive eternal life; because what God purposes is certain of fulfillment. Such a calling and election of those "in Christ" to receive eternal glory, however, is not capricious. Every man may decide if he will or will not become a part of it and receive the intended blessing.

"Before the foundation of the world . . ." All attempts to get rid of the plain meaning of this phrase have been futile; for, as Bruce said:

> Whatever be the interpretation of Genesis 1:2, it is certain that *katabolē* can mean nothing but "laying down" in the sense of "establishing" or "founding"; the phrase used here and in ten other New Testament passages is unambiguous and denotes the creation of the universe.[10]

"In love . . ." standing squarely between verses 4 and 5 may in fact belong to either, scholars being sharply divided as to where, exactly, it belongs. If it goes with verse 4, it would refer to the love of God for those whom he will redeem from sin unto eternal life. Both thoughts are fully in keeping with the scriptures; and, from the involved nature of Paul's sentence here, it might even be inferred that he intended a double meaning, true either way it may be read.

"Holy and without blemish . . ." The thing in view in this is perfection, and it is incorrect to read it otherwise than as

---

[10]F. F. Bruce, *op. cit.,* p. 28.

descriptive of the state of being "in Christ." These words apply to those whom "God chose . . . in him," as stated in the first of the verse. Of course, there is the ethical intention of God to change the moral character of men in order for their lives to conform more and more to the perfect and holy standards of the will of God; but this verse is not an affirmation that Christians *achieve* such holiness and perfection, but a declaration that they are credited with it! How? That is the fundamental question of the ages. See below:

PERFECTION OF CHRISTIANS

The requirement of Almighty God was bluntly stated by the Lord himself in the Sermon on the Mount: "Ye therefore shall be perfect, as your heavenly Father is perfect" (Matt. 5:48). This is the master imperative demanding perfect faith, perfect love, perfect obedience and perfect holiness. This eternal demand of the Father upon the part of those who would be his children has never been repealed. Jesus referred to this when he said to the rich young ruler, "If thou wouldest be perfect, go sell . . . etc." (Matt. 19:21). Significantly, the rich young ruler was unable to "keep" all of the holy commandments; and that failure is the highlight of that episode. Christ found no man upon earth who *could* keep them all. All of the apostles were weak and sinful men; Christ found no perfection in humanity.

The personal ministry of Christ, the writings of the apostle Paul and the universal experience of man reveal the *inability* of any mortal ever born to achieve *perfection* and to stand clothed with his own merit and without blemish before God himself! This being true, how can the perfection God demands be accredited to men?

There are a number of ways in which it may not be accredited. (1) It is not accredited by God's merely scaling down the requirements of holiness and perfection. The ethical and moral requirements of Christianity are higher and stricter than the Law of Moses, because the intention and motivation of men are considered. (2) It may not be accredited through any man's achieving it. (3) It may not be accredited upon the basis of what any mortal man ever believed or did. Man in his own identity, man as himself, is wicked and sinful; and absolutely *nothing* that sinful man can ever believe or do can change that. *In his own identity,* he can never be anything else except sinful and wicked. The most preposterous heresy of all ages is that a wretched sinner can "believe in Christ"; and BINGO God accredits that stinking sinner with RIGHTEOUSNESS AND PERFECTION! The NT does not have even a suggestion of such a doctrine in it.

Before any man can be saved, he must renounce himself, get rid of his own identity in the sense of its ever being perfect. As Jesus put it:

If any man would come after me, let him deny himself, and take up his cross, and follow me. For whosoever would save his life shall lose it: and whosoever shall lose his life for my sake shall find it (Matt. 16:24, 25).

If any man would come after me, let him deny himself, and take up his cross, and follow me. For whosoever would save his life shall lose it; and whosoever shall lose his life for my sake and the gospel's shall save it (Mark 8:34, 35).

If any man would come after me, let him deny himself, and take up his cross daily, and follow me. For whosoever would save his life shall lose it; but whosoever shall lose his life for my sake, the same shall save it (Luke 9:23, 24).

"Deny . . ." This is one of the strongest words in the Greek NT. There is a weaker form, also translated "deny," but it is *arneomai*; this word, translated "deny" in the above passages, is *antilegō*, a much stronger word; and Vine's first definition of it is: "To deny utterly, to adjure, to affirm that one has no connection with a person, as in Peter's denial of Christ."[11] The meaning of our Lord is thus clear enough, a man must not predicate his hope of eternal life upon *anything* connected with himself. The faith that saves is not of sinners but of Christ.

How is the sinner's identity renounced? (1) He confesses, not himself, or how *saved* he is, or how *blessed* he is, or what God has done for him; he confesses *not himself* but *Christ!* A lot of so-called "witnessing for Jesus" in these times is no such thing. It is, on the contrary, a witnessing of the prideful egotism of persons who are obviously glorying in how wicked they *were* and how gloriously they are *now saved*! Is the old identity of the sinner renounced or forsaken in such a "confession"? Indeed no; the last ugly details of the old life are dragged in and made a part of the confession; and the confession itself is not a confession of Christ but a confession that one is already saved!

---

[11] *Vine's Bible Dictionary.*

(2) Identity inevitably involves a name; and a change of identity means a change of name; nor did any man ever deny himself until he had accepted the name of Christ. The Great Commission as recorded by Matthew required that people of all nations be "baptized into the Name," there being revealed no other way by which one may lawfully wear it. In his baptism, the person who would be saved renounces himself to be buried out of sight completely in the water. It is precisely this that makes the God-given ordinance of Christian baptism repulsive to many men and many churches who have no intention whatever of ever *denying themselves!*

(3) Through faith, repentance and baptism "into Christ" the penitent rises to walk in newness of life (a new identity), being no longer himself, but Christ. As Paul stated it: "It is no longer I that live, but Christ liveth in me" (Gal. 2:20). Here then is the secret of that perfection required of all whom God will receive. It is the perfection of Christ, not of Joe Doakes, nor of any other mortal *in his own identity.*

What kind of righteous perfection, then, is in Christ? It is total and complete. Christ's life was sinless, perfect, beautiful, holy, undefiled and glorious. The righteousness of Christ is not relative but absolute like that of God; and that is the only righteousness that could ever save any person. How may sinners acquire it? How may such righteousness be accredited to mortals? Since true righteousness has never been identified with but one single, unique Person in the history of the whole world, salvation is achieved in the only way possible by identifying the sinful mortal with Christ *who is righteous,* and upon the prior condition of the sinner's renunciation of himself. This is accomplished by transferring the sinner "into Christ," not by transferring Christ's righteousness into sinners. The post-Reformation theory that proposes to make sinners righteous through God's transference of the righteousness of Christ *into sinners* is impossible of any intellectual, moral or practical acceptance. To identify the righteousness of God with any person who had not achieved it would be immoral. Calling wicked sinners *righteous* does not make them so (no matter what they believed or did); but the acceptance of Christ (with all members of his spiritual body) as *righteous* is based upon the sinless perfection of the Son of God. Paul summed it all up in one glorious word:

"THAT WE MAY PRESENT EVERY MAN PERFECT IN CHRIST" (Col. 1:28). It is precisely that perfection that Paul had in view in the above verse where he spoke of being "holy and without blemish"!

Verse 5, *Having foreordained us into adoption as sons through Jesus Christ unto himself, according to the good pleasure of his will.*

Under verse 4, it was noted that the phrase "in love" may logically be referred to this verse also, as in the RSV. The AV, RV, and RSV use three different words for the action described in this verse, as follows:

"He predestinated us . . ." (AV).
"Having foreordained us . . ." (RV).
"He destined us in love to be his sons through Christ" (RSV).

Theologians have tried for ages to make something hard out of predestination; but the meaning is not difficult. God designed the whole creation to accomplish the fulfillment of the plan which existed *before* creation. That is a simple definition of it. It applies to men, planets, galaxies, everything God ever made. Regarding men, God's purpose in creating man was that he might become a Son of God through Jesus Christ. That is the destiny God intended for every man ever born on earth. Stars and galaxies may not oppose or thwart their intended destiny; but with men, there is another factor, the freedom of the human will, enabling men to hinder or even prevent the fulfillment of God's purposes in their lives. For further study of this, see CR, 8:29.

The subjects related to this verse are commented upon much more extensively in Romans than will be necessary here; but one primary truth should be reiterated, namely that God in designing the creation of men with the express purpose of making men his sons through Christ would most certainly not have created men in such a manner that the highest happiness of them could be achieved in the service of Satan rather than in the service of himself!

"Adoption . . ." is used here to describe the acceptance of sinners into the family of God. This is thought to refer to a Roman rather than a Jewish legal custom. It is only one of many words that describe the relationship Christians receive when they are converted. Thus, they are "the temple of God, the family of God, the bride of Christ, the vineyard of the Lord, the church of the firstborn, and (as here) the adoption." Each of these different terms describes some special and significant feature of the "new creation." The word *adoption* seems to stress the fact of the Christian's privileges in God's family being totally undeserved and unmerited, just as an abandoned and forsaken child may be taken into a family by adoption, such a legal action bestowing upon the child all of the rights and privileges of that family without regard whatever to any merit of the child. Also, there is another suggestion in the fact of an adopted child's being of a different kind (that is, a different family) from that into which it is adopted. A glimpse of primal truth is here. Adam was created in God's image; but he begat a son "in his own image" at a time after he had become an outright servant of the devil. The contamination that has come down from that disaster is extensive and fundamental. Although any such thing as total hereditary depravity is nothing but a theologian's nightmare, those unregenerated "Adamites" who descended from the great progenitor are essentially bastards with regard to God's family, until they shall be "born again." The term, meaning the same thing, is here "adoption."

Verse 6, *To the praise of the glory of his grace, which he freely bestowed on us in the Beloved.*

The initial triple phrase recurs as in a refrain in verses 12 and 14. The Father is the source of blessing here, the Son in verse 12, and the Holy Spirit in verse 14. It would appear that Paul built up this type of phrase to extol and praise God as the giver of all blessings.

"Freely bestowed on us in the Beloved . . ." In the AV this is "He hath made us accepted in the Beloved." "The verb here is the same verb used in Luke 1:28, and nowhere else in the New Testament."[12] Of the greatest significance is the past tense, not perfect, indicating that God's action in making men accepted is not a continuing operation. Sinners are not acted upon continually and individually as they may believe in Christ; the great enabling charter of all human redemption has already been granted, sealed and delivered. This tremendous reservoir of

---

[12]Alfred Barry, *Ellicott's Commentary on the Whole Bible*, Vol. 8 (Grand Rapids: Zondervan Publishing House, 1959), p. 17.

divine grace has already been given "in the Beloved," that is, "in Christ." Through the gospel, men are called to believe the truth and to be baptized into Christ; and the human response to that invitation determines destiny.

The significance of this same verb being used in the Annunciation to Mary, and nowhere else in the NT, lies in the fact that, as in the case of the blessed Mary, who was "full of grace" in the sense of grace received, not grace to bestow; so it is with God's church, it is the recipient, not the dispenser of God's grace.

"In the Beloved . . ." This was probably an ancient messianic title, corresponding to "Son of his love" (Col. 1:13), and "my Beloved" (Mark 1:11). The great truth here is, as Bruce said, "That all the blessings which are ours by God's grace are *ours in Christ*; there is no way apart from him in which God either decrees or effects the bestowal of his grace on men."[13]

Verse 7, *In whom we have redemption through his blood, the forgiveness of our trespasses, according to the riches of his grace.*

"In whom . . ." that is, "in Christ," carrying the great truth that the blessings enumerated in this epistle belong exclusively to those who have been "baptized into Christ," there being absolutely no other way mentioned in the NT through which any man may dare to fancy that he is "in Christ." If there is any other way to be *in Christ*, someone should cite the NT passage which tells sinful men what it is, because it is clear enough that many are spurning the manner of being united with God "in Christ" through faith, repentance and submission to God's ordinance of baptism (1 Cor. 12:13; Rom. 6:3-5; Gal. 3:27).

"Redemption through his blood . . ." The NT presents the blood of Jesus Christ as the purchase price of the church, the grounds of redemption and the great atonement (Acts 20:28; 1 Cor. 6:20; 1 Peter 1:18-20; Col. 1:14). As Foulkes said, "Such redemption is found *in Christ*, not merely through him, but by men coming to live *in him*."[14] As pointed out earlier, this also means denying one's self and receiving identity with Christ *as Christ*. See under verse 4.

There are two fundamental teachings in regard to the great sacrifice for human transgression paid by Jesus our Lord upon

---

[13]F. F. Bruce, *op. cit.,* p. 30.
[14]Francis Foulkes, *op. cit.,* p. 52.

the cross, which appear in this passage: (1) the concept of a ransom paid in order to deliver, and (2) the idea of sins forgiven, remitted, taken completely away. Jesus Christ himself described his earthly mission in respect of both of these, "giving his life a ransom for many" (Matt. 20:28), and "shedding his blood for the forgiveness of sins" (Matt. 26:28). "The word Paul used here for "forgiveness" is *aphesis,* used by him in only two other passages (Rom. 4:7; Col. 1:14). It means 'letting go,' not 'exacting payment for'."[15]

"According to the riches of his grace . . ." The supply of grace is one of surpassing richness, fullness and over sufficiency. "Abundant entrance" will be granted to the redeemed (2 Peter 1:11).

Verses 8-9, *Which he made to abound toward us in all wisdom and prudence, making known unto us the mystery of his will, according to his good pleasure which he purposed in him.*

"Which he made to abound . . ." This reference is to the "riches" just mentioned, "wisdom and prudence" being among the great blessings "in Christ." The difference in wisdom and prudence is this:

Wisdom: This is knowledge that sees into the heart of things, which knows them as they really are.[16] It is the ability to see the great ultimate truths of eternity.[17] It more nearly approximates our word "insight."[18]

Prudence: The three scholars just cited also defined this word as "the understanding which leads to right action," "the ability to solve the problems of each moment of time," and "wise conduct."

Neither wisdom nor prudence is merely a matter of an IQ. The only true wisdom and prudence are revealed from God through the sacred scriptures. "It is not in man that walketh to direct his steps."

"The mystery of his will . . ." The NT use of the term "mystery" is not very closely related to the modern use of the word,

[15]Willard H. Taylor, *Beacon Bible Commentary,* Vol. 9, (Kansas City: Beacon Hill Press, 1965), p. 154.

[16]J. Armitage Robinson, *St. Paul's Epistle to the Ephesians* (London: Macmillan Company, 1903), p. 30.

[17]William Barclay, *The Letters to the Galatians and Ephesians* (Philadelphia: The Westminster Press, 1954), p. 96.

[18]Willard H. Taylor, *op. cit.,* p. 154.

conveying instead the meaning of "a secret once unknown, now
revealed." Mackay called it "God's unveiled secret."[19] There are
many mysteries referred to in the NT, but that in view here is
the "great mystery" (1 Tim. 3:16), embracing in its fullness the
total sphere of God's dealings with his human creation. Various
phases of this great mystery appear to be in Paul's thought in
the dozen NT passages where he mentioned it. Here the mystery
is God's infinite purpose of summing up all things "in Christ,"
mentioned in the next verse. This writer has published a dissertation on the subject of "The Mystery of Redemption"; and reference is made to that for those who might be interested in a
further pursuit of the subject.[20]

Verse 10, *Unto a dispensation of the fulness of the times, to
sum up all things in Christ, the things in the heavens, and the
things upon the earth;* IN HIM, *I say.*

We have taken the liberty of capitalizing the phrase which
dominates this entire epistle. One may easily imagine that Paul
here made some emphatic gesture, as he dictated these words,
or raised his voice in repeating these dynamic key-words of the
NT. Any failure to get the full meaning of being "in Christ" is
to forfeit all hope of understanding that part of the NT written
by the apostle Paul.

"Dispensation of the fullness of times . . ." Although "dispensation" is a word normally connected with a servant's adminis-
tration of the affairs of another, "Here it is applied to the disposal
of all things by God himself, according to the law which he has
set himself to do all things by."[21]

"Fullness of times . . ." This is a reference to the fact that God
scheduled all of the events of time and history, whether sacred
or profane, *in advance.* The first Advent of Christ (Gal. 4:4), the
events of our Lord's ministry (John 2:4; 17:1), the resurrection
of the dead (John 5:28), the eternal judgment (Acts 17:31), the
rise, growth and subsidence of nations (Acts 17:26), and the
Second Advent of Christ with the summing up of God's total
purpose in him, as glimpsed in this verse — all things move

---

[19]John Mackay, *God's Order* (New York: The Macmillan Company, 1953),
p. 59.
[20]See under *Abbreviations.*
[21]Alfred Barry, *op. cit.,* p. 18.

according to the cosmic schedule of God himself. Colossians 1:16-20 and Philippians 2:9, 10, are similar to this passage.

"Sum up all things in Christ . . ." The view in this letter is nothing less than universal; as Hayes said, "The word *all* occurs in this epistle fifty-one times!"[22] Paul is thinking of the ultimate total and complete victory of God in Christ over all evil. Amazingly, Paul's writings leave no doubt that there are implications and results of that victory which far transcend the affairs of mortals. "Things in heaven and things upon the earth," as well as things "under the earth" (Phil. 2:10) shall finally recognize the authority and dominion of Christ and confess his name to the glory of God.

Foulkes noted that "This verse has been used as the keystone of the doctrine of 'Universalism,' to the effect that all men shall be saved in the end."[23] Nothing in the passage, however, supports such a view. Indeed "all things" shall be compelled to acknowledge the authority and glory of the Son of God; but Jesus himself spoke of certain ones in the final judgment scene who indeed acknowledge him as "Lord," but who shall not enter into life (Matt. 7:21-23).

A practical deduction from this was made by Martin thus:

Since Christ is preeminent in God's purpose in the whole universe as well as in the church, the individual who does not have Christ preeminent in his life is entirely out of harmony with the purpose of the Father.[24]

Verse 11, *In whom also we were made a heritage, having been foreordained according to the purpose of him who worketh all things after the counsel of his will.*

In this Paul seemed to have the calling of the Jews as a chosen people in mind, because the "we" in this place contrasted with "ye also" of verse 13 is usually understood as a distinction between Christians of Jewish origin and those of Gentile origin.

"In whom . . ." Even the purpose of God in the calling of Israel in the OT had respect to the fulfillment of God's purpose in Christ. Evidently Paul intended to bring into view here the fact that even the choice of Israel was not the totality of God's plan, but only a part of it, which from the beginning included also the

---

[22]D. A. Hayes, *op. cit.,* p. 388.
[23]Francis Foulkes, *op. cit.,* p. 53.
[24]Alfred Martin, *op. cit.,* p. 727.

bringing of the Gentiles to receive his mercy and grace and become a part of the same inheritance, or heritage, along with the Jews.

"Foreordained . . ." See discussion of this under verse 5, above.

Verse 12, *To the end that we should be unto the praise of his glory, we who had before hoped in Christ.*

"Unto the praise of his glory . . ." The great purpose for which God created men is that of glorifying God. The catechisms used for ages often begin with this very fact. The Westminster Shorter Catechism has this: (Q) What is the chief end of man? (A) Man's chief end is to glorify God, and to enjoy him forever.[25] See more on this under Galatians 1:5.

"Who had before hoped in Christ . . ." This is generally interpreted to mean that the Jewish dispensation looked to the coming of Christ, hoping for the deliverance that he would bring. Anna and Simeon are representative of those who did this; but, despite the popularity of this explanation, there is also the glaring possibility that the clause might very well be a qualifier of them who shall be "unto the praise of God's glory," the same being limited to those, and only those, who had before that future event, laid hold upon the hope in Christ. Even if we agree with the vast majority of the scholars who interpret it differently, it must be admitted that the alternate understanding suggested here does no violence to the truth.

Verse 13, *In whom ye also, having heard the word of the truth, the gospel of your salvation — in whom, having also believed, ye were sealed with the Holy Spirit of promise.*

> In whom, having believed, ye were sealed with the Holy Spirit . . . (RV).
> In whom also after that ye believed, ye were sealed with that Holy Spirit . . . (AV).

This very interesting discrepancy between the RV and the AV reveals the error in the RV. It is not a mere case of choice of words. The two versions teach different things, and there is no way both of them can be correct. The AV rendition shows that the sealing of the Holy Spirit of promise took place in those "in

---

[25]*Ibid.,* p. 726.

Christ" at some point in time "after" they had become believers in Christ; but the RV muddles the meaning, leaving the possible interpretation that the "sealing" took place coincidentally and at the same time of their believing. In the general sense, of course, if "believing" is understood as the whole complex of actions involved in conversion (faith, repentance, confession, and baptism), no error is implied; however, "believing" or "faith" as used in the limited, technical sense of the theological jargon current today, is alleged to be something apart from being baptized into Christ. That this is a false view is evident since both versions reveal the sealed persons to be those "in Christ"; and since no one was ever "in Christ" except by being baptized into him, the true meaning shines through despite all efforts to hide it.

Bruce made a big point out of the fact that the participle "having believed" here is identical with the same words in Acts 19:2, where the RV rendition is "when ye believed."[26] But, of course, the RV missed it in both places; and the device of proving one false rendition by a second false rendition cannot prove Bruce's notion that the sealing and believing were "coincident in time." Those believing in Acts 19:2 had not only failed to be sealed with the Holy Spirit at the time they became believers, they never were sealed until they were scripturally baptized! (Acts 19:5).

Moreover, it is exceedingly significant that in the case of the Holy Saviour himself, the Spirit did not descend and remain upon him until *after he was baptized*. Why, then, should it be thought strange that the blessed Holy Spirit of promise in view here is exactly that mentioned by Peter on Pentecost, the promise that belongs to all of those in all times whom God shall call unto himself? — why should it be thought strange that *that gift* of the Holy Spirit was promised only to believers who would repent and be baptized?

It is amazing how commentators cite a dozen other NT passages searching for the "Holy Spirit of promise," all of them apparently never having heard of Acts 2:38, 39! It is a positive certainty that if the "promise of the Holy Spirit" in that passage does not connect with Paul's reference to the "Spirit of promise" here, then nothing in the NT does!

---

[26]F. F. Bruce, *op. cit.,* p. 36.

Verse 14, *Which is an earnest of our inheritance, unto the redemption of God's own possession, unto the praise of his glory.*

THOUGHTS REGARDING THE EARNEST

The meaning of "earnest" as used here is exactly the same as that intended by the use of the word today to refer to a partial payment tendered as a guarantee that the full amount promised will be paid in the future. The earnest of the Holy Spirit is given to Christians by the Father in heaven, or by Christ (it is true both ways), as a pledge of the ultimate reception of the redeemed souls into eternal fellowship with the Father in heaven.

The earnest is always merely a token, not any large share of the amount guaranteed. Those receiving the earnest of God's Spirit are not thereby commissioned to throw away their Bibles and start "walking by the Spirit"! Regarding the NT teaching of what this gift is, what it does for Christians, and what it is not, and some of the synonyms by which it is called in the NT, see under Galatians 5:22ff.

The "love, joy and peace, longsuffering, kindness, goodness, etc.," which mark the true Spirit of promise in Christian hearts are here considered to be one in kind with the joys of the redeemed in heaven. The Christian life, faithfully lived, is itself the beginning of the heavenly adventure.

Verse 15, *For this cause I also, having heard of the faith in the Lord Jesus which is among you, and the love which ye show to all the saints.*

"Heard of the faith . . . among you . . ." Beare said this is "fiction, and not specific," and tried to prove it by a distorted quotation, or paraphrase, "The saints who are faithful (v. 1) have faith!"[27] His words are cited here not as any worthy testimony whatever against this letter, but as a clear demonstration of the partial, warped, biased and prejudiced exegesis by which some critical scholars seek to maintain their ridiculous theories. What about the words, "AND THE LOVE YE SHOW TO ALL THE SAINTS"? Is that not a specific? Beare ignored this, but in doing so he discredited his exegesis.

---

[27]Frances W. Beare, *Interpreter's Bible*, Vol. X (New York: Abingdon Press, 1953).

Another critical blow aimed at this verse is this: Almost the exact parallel of this verse is in Colossians 1:4, addressed to a church Paul has never seen. The same words here addressed to the recipients of this letter must therefore mean that Paul had never seen *them*! Which means, of course, that it is not Paul's letter to the Ephesians, where he had spent three whole years! Such a deduction, however, cannot be intelligently supported, because Paul used almost exactly these same words, and certainly the full thought of them, in Philemon 5, to one of his own converts.

Thus, it is clear enough that Paul did not mean in this verse that he had heard "for the first time" of the faith and love of the Ephesians, but that he had heard such things of their members following the time when he had worked among them.

This verse is the beginning of a prayer Paul penned on behalf of his addressees, running through verse 22.

Verse 16, *Cease not to give thanks for you, making mention of you in my prayers.*

Several things about prayer are evident in this specimen. First of all, Paul did not cease to give thanks for his converts. The constant, never-failing supplications of Paul for the beloved in Christ cannot fail to impress any thoughtful person. Paul never forgot to pray for others. In the second place, thanksgiving was a prominent, invariable element in all of Paul's prayers that have come down to us. Whatever the circumstances, he always found something to be thankful for.

Verse 17, *That the God of our Lord Jesus Christ, the Father of glory, may give you a spirit of wisdom and revelation in the knowledge of him.*

David Lipscomb pointed out that just as the God of the ancient Hebrews was "the God of Abraham and the God of Isaac and the God of Jacob; to Christians, God, is the God of our Lord Jesus."[28]

Macknight accurately discerned the meaning of this verse thus:

The apostle did not pray that God would give to all the Ephesians the knowledge of the doctrines of the gospel, by an

---

[28]David Lipscomb, *New Testament Commentaries, Ephesians* (Nashville: The Gospel Advocate Company, 1939), p. 31.

immediate revelation made to themselves; but that he would enable them to understand the revelation of these doctrines which was made to the apostles, and which they preached to the world.[29]

There is still a need for Christians to pray that God will help them to understand the revelation of the sacred scripture, because most of its marvelous teachings require more than a little application and serious study to be clearly understood.

Verse 18, *Having the eyes of your heart enlightened, that ye may know what is the hope of his calling, what the riches of the glory of his inheritance in the saints.*

"The eyes of your heart enlightened . . ." This was a prayer by Paul that God would give true spiritual discernment to the Ephesians. "Both Plato and Aristotle spoke of the 'eye of the soul'."[30]; and it is this human faculty that Paul had in mind.

Nothing can bless men any more than sensitivity to spiritual truth. It is a sad fact that people may hear the glorious news of the salvation in Christ until it no longer arouses any emotion at all in their hearts. The joyful personal news that "my immortal soul has been redeemed from sin and death and that I myself, even I, shall be received into heaven itself by Christ the Redeemer to enjoy through endless eternity the bliss and rapture of everlasting glory" — God grant that our hearts may never be insensitive to such a message. How can this earth which is so much with all of us, but which like ourselves is designed to perish, and which is unable to supply the deep needs of our souls — how can this earth come to be *everything* to men, and the hereafter *nothing*? God help men to tune their hearts to hear the Christ speaking across centuries of time to every soul, "Come unto me . . . I will give you rest."

Verses 19-20, *And what the exceeding greatness of his power to us-ward who believe, according to the working of the strength of his might which he wrought in Christ, when he raised him from the dead, and made him to sit at his right hand in the heavenly places.*

---

[29]James Macknight, *op. cit.,* p. 269.
[30]Francis W. Beare, *op. cit.,* p. 629.

These two verses set forth the power of God, with Paul using a succession of very strong words to describe it. Beare describes these thus:

Dynamis means the ability to accomplish, the cognate verb means "I am able."

Energeia means power to work, not mere potential power but active power.

Kratos means the power that rules, has dominion, especially over rational beings.

Ischys means inherent strength, or might. It has more to do with potential, intrinsic might, whether active or not.[31]

Significantly, the climax, the very ultimate demonstration of God's power, was cited by Paul here as the resurrection of Christ. That is *the act* above all others and beyond all others that shows the unlimited power and ability of God to do all that he has promised to do for his children. Without the resurrection of Christ, the Christian gospel is stripped of all credibility and relevance for men; and that is why Paul never forgot to include it in the very heart of every message and every letter. As Markus Barth said, "If we kept silent about the resurrection, we would not be speaking of God."[32]

This reference to the ascension of Christ "is a declaration by inspiration of the fact recorded in Mark 16:19."[33] While it may be true as Wedel said, that "The modern church makes very little out of the ascension of Christ," [34] there can be no doubt whatever that the early Christians made everything of it, as indicated by Paul's dramatic emphasis of it in the closing lines of this chapter.

Verse 21, *Far above all rule, and authority, and power, and dominion, and every name that is named, not only in this world, but also in that which is to come.*

In Matthew 28:18, Jesus Christ spoke of "all authority" in heaven and upon earth having been given unto him; and exactly the same teaching is here. Besides ten passages of the Greek NT which flatly refer to Jesus Christ as God, there are at least a

---

[31]*Ibid.*, p. 632.

[32]Markus Barth, *The Broken Wall* (London: Collins, 1960), p. 48.

[33]James Macknight, *op. cit.,* p. 270.

[34]Theodore O. Wedel, *Interpreter's Bible* (Nashville: Abingdon Press, 1953), Vol. X, p. 633.

hundred others such as this one which convey exactly the same teaching. Of what mere mortal could it be said the he sits above "all rule and authority and power and dominion . . . not only in this world, but in that which is to come"?

Verses 22-23, *And he put all things in subjection under his feet, and gave him to be the head over. all things to the church, which is his body, the fulness of him that filleth all in all.*

It is not merely the fact of Christ's universal, eternal power which Paul affirmed here; the significant thing is that he is the head of that community of men and women on earth called "the church" who are his body, his spiritual body, having an intimate and eternal connection with the all-powerful One who is actually the "head" of that spiritual body. Thus the apostle Paul glorified and elevated the church of Jesus Christ in a manner that staggers the imagination, even yet. Men who make little of the church on earth know nothing of what Paul taught. The amazing prepositional phrase "in Christ" that so permeates and dominates his NT writings can be nothing at all unless it is the church; and, although the ultimate meaning goes beyond that, for all practical purposes in the present times, it is synonymous with it.

Theologians find it very difficult to accept the implications of Paul's teaching on this subject, Bruce, for example, pointing out that "In those earlier epistles, Christ is not viewed as the head of the body . . . Paul compared an individual believer to the head (1 Cor. 12:21)."[35] However, it was a physical body that Paul used as the basis of comparison in 1 Corinthians 12; and it is a spiritual body of which Paul is speaking here. It is an extra-literal, that is, not literal, body, like that of a legal corporation which is recognized by law in every country on earth as a legal *person*. That is what is meant by "the body of Christ."

JESUS CHRIST, INCORPORATED

The NEB translated "believers incorporate" (v. 1) and "incorporate in Christ" (v. 13), thus recognizing that an extra-literal body, called an *incorporation*, is indeed certainly apparent in the whole chapter; but the NEB is profoundly wrong in making it belong to the believers! No! *The believers belong to it! Christ,* not the believer, is the corporation.

---

[35]F. F. Bruce, *op. cit.,* p. 44.

The Pauline conception of the spiritual body of Christ existing as the heavenly device by which mortals may be "in Christ" was not "evolved" or "developed" by Paul as many allege. It appeared in its totality in one dazzling burst of glory on the Damascus road where Paul suddenly learned that all he was doing to the church he was in fact doing to Christ. The Pauline expression "in Christ" makes no sense at all except as a reference to the spiritual body which is the church; and, although Paul used that expression thirty times in Ephesians, he also used it about one hundred forty times elsewhere. It is extensively used in Galatians, the first of his letters, and extensively used in the letters of his last imprisonment. Take this concept out of Paul's writings and absolutely nothing is left.

Christ is the head of this corporation.

The identity of it is Christ, no sinful mortal being able on his own identity to enter it. He must deny himself.

All of the riches of Christ are in this "body."

All of God's righteousness is in it.

Every spiritual blessing is in it. (This is to be understood superlatively to include salvation, eternal life, forgiveness, etc., absolutely all spiritual blessings.)

Those who are in Christ are perfect, not in their merit, but in the merit and righteousness of Christ.

Christ keeps the books on this corporation, laying down rules of entry, terms of membership, and doing the "adding" to it of any who may qualify. All such regulations and information are in the "little book" of Revelation 10, the NT.

Like all good corporations, Christ's has a seal, that of the promised gift of the Holy Spirit (1:13), promised to all believers upon condition of their repentance and baptism (Acts 2:38, 39).

In the NT, no other means of coming into this corporation, that is, being "in Christ," is revealed except that which is taught by Paul and Jesus alike, namely, by being "baptized into Christ" (Gal. 3:27; Rom. 6:3-5; 1 Cor. 12:13). For all who insist that they can be "in Christ" by some other action, a reminder is in order, that the corporation is not *theirs*, but Christ's.

As being in Christ, of Christ, and in the scriptural sense *actually Christ*, Christians have already died to sin (that is, paid the penalty of sin) in the body of Christ; they are resurrected with him in the new life "in Christ," "risen with him," even exalted to eternal glory "in him," this latter thing, of course, being potential and not actual now, but sure to be actual later.

This is only a little summary of the immense theological implications of the "spiritual body of Christ"; a little fuller discussion has been included in this series in CR, chapter 3. One additional thought, as regards justification, the ultimate and final ground upon which God declared men to be righteous and deserving of no punishment: the Pauline doctrine of "salvation in Christ" places the ground of justification totally in Jesus Christ.

Except in the secondary, limited and lower-level use of "justification" to enumerate steps of primary obedience, as when Peter said, "Save yourselves, etc.," nothing that a sinner can either believe or do "saves" him. He is saved, not by himself, but by Christ. When Paul says he is justified "by faith," it is not the sinner's faith, but Christ's which is meant. Paul reiterated the thought four times in the first letter that he ever wrote that men are saved by "the faith of Christ" (see notes on Galatians). In that other, and secondary sense of what saves men, there are surely things that every man must both believe and do if he would enter into life (see discussion of The Law of Christ, under Galatians 6:18).

CHAPTER 2

Paul's theme in this chapter continues to be the glorious blessings of the saved "in Christ," as contrasted with their former state of being without any hope whatever. Those who were once "dead in sins" are now alive in Christ (1-10); and those who were once "aliens and strangers separated from God" are now members of God's family (11-22).

Verse 1, *And you did he make alive, when ye were dead through your trespasses and sins.*

"To be dead in trespasses and sins does not mean unconsciousness or non-existence"[1] (1 Tim. 5:6; Rev. 3:1). In the scriptural view, sin equals death; and there is no light or casual view of either in the Bible.

"You did he make alive . . ." Beare pointed out that the various pronouns "you" (vv. 1, 2), "we all" (v. 3), and "us . . . we" (v. 4), "refer to the distinction between Jews and Gentiles only to nullify it. Both are shown to have been alike guilty and in need of God's mercy."[2]

"Trespasses and sins . . ." Barry suggested a difference in the meaning of these terms, making "sins" to "denote universal and positive principles of evil doing, and *trespasses*, failure in visible and special acts of those not necessarily out of the right way."[3] However, such a distinction is not corroborated by other NT use of the terms. For example, the Matthew and Luke accounts of the Lord's Prayer use the words interchangeably; and, as Blaikie said, "The distinction cannot be carried out in all other passages."[4] The full thought would seem to be "all kinds of sin."

It is evident in this verse that the deadness of unregenerated men is a derivative, not of their birth, but of their sins. Death always implies a change from the state of being alive. Therefore,

---

[1] John William Russell, *Compact Commentary on the New Testament* (Grand Rapids: Baker Book House, 1964), p. 476.

[2] Francis W. Beare, *Interpreter's Bible* (New York: Abingdon Press, 1953), Vol. X, p. 638.

[3] Alfred Barry, *Ellicott's Commentary on the Whole Bible* (Grand Rapids: Zondervan Publishing House, 1959), Vol. VII, p. 23.

[4] W. G. Blaikie, *Pulpit Commentary* (Grand Rapids: Wm. B. Eerdmans Publishing Company, 1950), Vol. 20, *Ephesians*, p. 61.

the thought of total human depravity as something inherited
must be incorrect. Sinners in their pre-Christian state were
"dead in sins"; but that deadness was not something they
inherited, but came about through the guilt of sins committed.

There is a world of difference in being dead in sins, as here,
and being dead to sin in Christ Jesus. Those in Christ are legally
dead to sin, in the sense of being free of the penalty of it, through
the death of Christ. They are in Christ; Christ died, and therefore *they* died. Neither in that blessed state in Christ, nor in the
wretched condition mentioned here, is there any such thing as
"being dead to sin" in the sense of exemption from the temptations to sin. Even Christ was tempted.

Verses 2-3, *Wherein ye once walked according to the course
of this world, according to the prince of the powers of the air, of
the spirit that now worketh in the sons of disobedience; among
whom we also all once lived in the lusts of our flesh, doing the
desires of the flesh and of the mind, and were by nature children
of wrath, even as the rest.*

"Walked according to the course of this world . . . " This refers
to the behavior which is characteristic of unregenerated men.
Such persons do what men are normally expected to do, from
motives that are common to all, and invariably governed by selfishness. The course of this world is laid out in harmony with self
and selfish desires. The person walking after this manner
regards not the will of God but only the passions, appetites and
ambitions of egocentric self.

"The prince of the powers of the air . . ." The character in view
here is most assuredly Satan, who is called the "god of this
world" in 2 Corinthians 4:4, and who was called the "prince of
this world" (John 14:30; 16:11) by none other than the Christ
himself. Only those who consciously reject the teaching of the
NT can deny the existence of the personal ruler of this world's
darkness. Christ himself taught men to pray, "Deliver us from
the evil one!" Therefore all men should reject the snide
arrogance which says:

> The idea of a personal devil is all but unimaginable to the
> mind of our own times, and is capable of interpretation only as

a personification of the external forces of evil which play upon the human life.[5]

The greatest deception Satan ever perpetrated upon men is that of persuading them that he does not exist. The intelligent organization of complementary and interlocking systems of wickedness all over the world proves the intelligent and personal nature of the evil one. The intellectual snobbery that sets aside the teaching of the Christian scriptures on this subject has already run its course; and, as Wedel said, "Sober theologians are again wrestling openly with the problem of the 'demonic'."[6] Such things as psychology, social pressures, poverty, etc., are simply not an adequate explanation of evil; and the more thoughtful and perceptive scholars are already aware of this; but the great rank and file of mankind have never been deceived for a moment. They invariably accept the terminology of the NT for what it says. Again from Wedel, "Simple folk are often better theologians than the learned of the schools."[7]

It is clearly Satan which Paul referred to in this place; but what is meant by "powers of the air"? In this also, it is necessary to discard many current interpretations. This is not merely "a reference to the prevailing superstitions of those times that the air was full of evil spirits."[8] It is not an accommodation of Christian thought to "later Gnostic"[9] theories. This authentic Pauline epistle antedates Gnosticism.

"Powers of the air . . ." This is the same as "power of darkness" (Luke 22:53; Col. 1:13) and the "spiritual hosts of wickedness in the heavenly places" (6:12). This possible meaning was pointed out by Bruce, who based it upon the fact that the word Paul used for "air" is not *aither*, meaning the clear upper air, but *aer*, which means the obscure, misty, lower air.[10] The logic of construing Paul's meaning here as "darkness" is further supported by the truth noted by Barry:

---

[5]Francis W. Beare, *op. cit.,* p. 639.

[6]Theodore E. Wedel, *Interpreter's Bible* (New York: Abingdon Press, 1953), Vol. X, p. 640.

[7]*Ibid.*

[8]John William Russell, *op. cit.,* p. 476.

[9]Francis W. Beare, *op. cit.,* p. 640.

[10]F. F. Bruce, *The Epistles to the Ephesians* (Old Tappan, N.J.: Fleming H. Revell Co., 1961), p. 48.

Air here describes a sphere, and therefore a power, below the heaven and yet above the earth. The word and its derivatives carry with them the ideas of cloudiness, mist and even darkness. Hence it is naturally used to suggest the evil power as allowed invisibly to encompass and move about this world, yet overruled by the power of the true heaven, which it vainly strives to overcloud and hide from the earth.[11]

Thus inherently, the designation of Satan as prince of the powers of the air (in the sense suggested above) is precisely accurate and instructive. Satan's awesome power is above that of men, but below that of Christ. Furthermore, Paul's reference later in this epistle (6:12) to "spiritual hosts of wickedness in the heavenly places" is more accurately understood, in the light of this, as not being on a parity with the dominion of Christ (also in the heavenly places), but confined to that lower, obscure heavenly place in view here.

"The spirit that now worketh . . ." A spirit is a living being; and from this it is plain that Paul considered Satan to be at work in the men of his generation; and we are certain that he is no less at work now.

Barclay pointed out that these first three verses have a description of the life without Christ, the same being: (1) a life lived on the world's standards and with the world's values, (2) a life under the dictates of the prince of powers of the air, (3) a life of disobedience, (4) a life at the mercy of *desire*. "To succumb to that desire is inevitably to come to disaster."[12] (5) a life that follows the desires of the flesh, and (6) a life which deserves only the wrath of God. To this list there should also be added: "It is a life which follows the desires of the mind" (v. 3). The unregenerated mind itself is at enmity with God; and the imaginations of it are a source of rebellion against God.

"Lusts of the flesh . . . desires of the flesh . . ." These certainly include the gratification of bodily appetites; but, as Lipscomb said, "The flesh, the world and the devil are not different classes of sin, but aspects of sin; and any one is made at times to represent all."[13]

---

[11]Alfred Barry, *op. cit.,* p. 23.

[12]William Barclay, *The Letters to the Galatians and Ephesians* (Philadelphia: Westminster Press, 1954), p. 116.

[13]David Lipscomb, *New Testament Commentaries* (Nashville: The Gospel Advocate Company, 1939), *Ephesians,* p. 40.

With regard to the powerful spiritual hosts over whom Satan is said to be their prince, Macknight identified these with the fallen angels of Jude 6 and 1 Peter 5:8, supposing that "they have arranged themselves under the direction of one chief"[14] the better to carry on their evil work. He also supposed that Satan might have been the leader of the angels who rebelled against God, hence "the devil and his angels" (Matt. 25:41).

"By nature, children of wrath . . ." Apart from God, there is nothing in nature that leads men into paths of righteousness; and rejection of the knowledge of God by the pre-Christian world promptly issued in their unbelievable debauchery.

"We also all once lived . . ." How could Paul have included himself here with the godless pre-Christian Gentiles? Of course, in the sense of all men being guilty before God, the Jew and Gentile alike were without merit; but that is not the meaning of this place. Paul had always sought to have a pure conscience before God, and he was a practicing Pharisee of the noblest and purest motives; and one may not escape the certainty that in this place Paul was including himself with the pre-Christian Gentiles in an accommodative sense. The writings of Paul abound in examples of this same fundamental courtesy and consideration on his part; and one may only marvel at the blindness that refuses to see it in a passage like Hebrews 2:3.

Verses 4-5, *But God, being rich in mercy, for his great love wherewith he loved us, even when we were dead through our trespasses, made us alive together with Christ (by grace have ye been saved).*

"Dead through our trespasses . . ." "This describes the existing state from which we were made alive with Christ."[15] The same thought is in Romans 5:10 where our being enemies was the existing state from which we were reconciled to God.

"By grace have ye been saved. . ." In this Paul referred to salvation from *past sins* and induction into the kingdom of Christ. The apostle Peter mentioned this as salvation from one's "old sins" (2 Peter 1:9). As Lipscomb said:

---

[14]James Macknight, *Apostolical Epistles with Commentary* (Grand Rapids: Baker Book House, 1969), Vol. III, p. 278.

[15]F. F. Bruce, *Answers to Questions* (Grand Rapids: Zondervan Publishing House, 1972), p. 104.

We are already saved from our past sins, but we must continue faithful to the end; for the Saviour says, "Be thou faithful unto death, and I will give thee the crown of life" (Rev. 2:10).[16]

Paul's reference to salvation in the past perfect tense as something done and accomplished already has no reference to final destiny but to the primary obedience that makes a true child of God. See under verse 8.

Verse 6, *And raised us up with him, and made us to sit with him in the heavenly places, in Christ Jesus.*

"Raised us up with him . . ." Paul was speaking of obeying the gospel in the preceding verse, of being saved from "old sins," of becoming a part of Christ, being made alive "with Christ," etc. In that light, this clause is a plain categorical reference to Christian baptism, the same being the means by which God makes the penitent believer to be "in Christ." How astounding are the comments which would make "raised up with" Christ in this place to mean: "the resurrection of believers at the last day,"[17] "a spiritual transformation,"[18] "believers are viewed (here) as already seated there (in heaven) with Christ,"[19] "in spirit already, and ere long our bodies too will be raised"[20] — but the true meaning is given by Paul himself thus:

We were buried with him through baptism into death: that like as Christ was raised from the dead through the glory of the Father, so we also might walk in newness of life (Rom. 6:4).

Having been buried with him in baptism, wherein ye were also raised with him, through faith in the working of God who raised him from the dead . . . you, I say, did he make alive together with him (Col. 2:12, 13).

The full meaning of this verse is that Christians who have been baptized into Christ, therein being "made alive together with Christ" and being "raised up with him," are partakers of the full rights and privileges of the heavenly kingdom. Men

---

[16]David Lipscomb, *op. cit.,* p. 42.

[17]James Macknight, *op. cit.,* p. 282.

[18]Francis W. Beare, *op. cit.,* p. 643.

[19]F. F. Bruce, *op. cit.,* p. 50.

[20]John Wesley, *One Volume New Testament Commentary* (Grand Rapids: Baker Book House, 1972), *in loco.*

have removed baptism from their own theology, but they have not removed it from that of Paul.

Verse 7, *That in the ages to come he might show the exceeding riches of his grace in kindness toward us in Christ Jesus.*

"Exceeding riches . . . in kindness . . ." The marvelous tenderness and consideration of God for his erring human children must ever inspire with admiration, wonder and awe the soul that becomes conscious of the fullness and glory of such wonderful love.

"In Christ . . ." Like a constant drumbeat, this Pauline concept is hammered into every line of his writings. The love, the goodness, the hope, the forgiveness, the joy, the salvation — everything is in Christ.

"In the ages to come . . ." The apostle Paul did not anticipate the end of the world in a few days, or a few weeks, or in his lifetime, but on the other hand considered that God's grace would be available in the salvation of sinful men for "ages to come." This is only one of a very great many such texts and intimations in the NT which demonstrate the perverse error, both of those who charge all of the sacred writers with expecting the Second Coming any minute and those who refer this to "the ages that will follow Christ's Parousia."[21]

Verses 8-9, *For by grace have ye been saved through faith; and that not of yourselves, it is the gift of God; not of works that no man should glory.*

The jubilation with which some hail this text would be much more restrained by a little careful study of it. There is no release in this text from obligations God has bound upon sinners who desire to be saved. It cannot mean, nor does it say, that "faith only" saves sinners, and that even that faith is supplied by the Lord, not by sinners, being "not of yourselves"! Because of arrogant and persistent error which men strive to fasten upon this beautiful passage a careful study of it is included here.

The error of men in their interpretations of this passage is evident in such comments as "our salvation . . . is appropriated

---

[21]William Hendriksen, *New Testament Commentary, Ephesians* (Grand Rapids: Baker Book House, 1967), p. 120.

by us through faith alone."[22] "Here is the basis for the watchword of Reformation theology: *solo gratia, sola fide, soli Deo gloria* ('by grace alone, through faith alone, to God alone be glory')."[23] The OT injunction was "Thou shalt not yoke the ox with the ass"; but, in the so-called "watchword" of Reformation theology the ox is yoked with two asses, namely *solo gratia* and *sola fide*. If salvation is by grace alone, it cannot, at the same time be of faith; and if it is of faith alone, it cannot, at the same time, be of grace also. Could a man be married to Ruth *alone* and to Ann *alone* at the same time? Thus the "watchword" is a contradiction on its face; and, besides that, the so-called "scriptures" *grace only* and *faith only,* are bastard scriptures, being nowhere mentioned in the word of God, with the lone exception of James 2:24, where that sacred writer says "we are not justified by faith alone."

But what does the text say?

"By grace have ye been saved through faith . . ." Some of the critical scholars declare the past perfect tense here to be un-Pauline; [24] but, while it is true that Paul often spoke of salvation as a continuing process (as in 1 Corinthians 1:18 and Romans 5:9), he was here speaking of being "saved" in the sense of having obeyed the gospel. Jesus said, "He that believeth and is baptized shall be saved" (Mark 16:16); and Paul was here addressing people who had believed and had been "raised with Christ" by baptism into newness of life (v. 6); and, therefore, in the sense of Paul's thought here, it was mandatory to use the past perfect. The primary salvation accomplished when a sinner believes and obeys the gospel is complete, final and perfect, *as regards his old sins.* The use of the past perfect makes it certain that *that* primary salvation was referred to here.

"By grace . . ." The connotations of this word as used in the NT include the principles: (1) of human beings (all of them) being unworthy of the salvation God provides, (2) of the impossibility of any man's meriting or earning salvation, even if he had a million lives to live, and (3) that salvation bestowed upon men originated in the heart of God and that it flows out from God to men, being from God and of God alone. It is clear then that God's grace

---

[22]F. F. Bruce, *op. cit.,* p. 51.

[23]*Ibid.*

[24]Francis W. Beare, *op. cit.,* p. 645.

is to all men, for all men alike, and that it is available for every person who was ever born on earth (Titus 2:11). If then, salvation is by grace only, all men are already saved; for God's grace has appeared to all. Christ himself, however, taught that *all* men will not be saved; and the only intelligent reconciliation of those twin facts lies in accepting the premise of human salvation's being *conditional*, that is, made to turn upon human acceptance of it through human compliance with the conditions upon which God through Christ and the apostles promised it. The Reformation heresy was simply that of removing or negating *all conditions* of salvation except the sinner's subjective trust/faith, thus proclaiming what was called "salvation through faith alone." Such preconditions of salvation as repentance, confession, baptism and the acceptance by the convert of his Christian obligations — all these are declared to be "works" and therefore unnecessary to be performed as conditions of salvation, and this despite the truth that none of them is a "work" at all, except in the sense that the sinner's faith is also a "work."

"Through faith . . ." The most likely meaning of this phrase, as attested by the *Emphatic Diaglott* rendition of it, is "through the faith,"[25] that is, "through the Christian faith," or the Christian religion. One thing is absolutely certain: this cannot mean the subjective trust/faith of sinners. Three reasons deny such an interpretation: (1) the Diaglott rendition is supported by the Vatican manuscript which has the article (the); and furthermore the inclusion of it is often understood anyway so that the absence of the article in some manuscripts does not deny it; and, in all probability, the translators would have supplied it (as permitted) if they had properly understood the meaning of it. (2) The qualifying clause next given, "and that not of yourselves," absolutely denies that the faith of sinners is in view here. See under the clause below. (3) Recent extensive studies by George Howard of the University of Georgia disclose that the usual meaning of "faith" in the NT is not sinner's trust/faith at all, but fidelity.[26] "Faith" as used in the vocabulary of current theological jargon to mean sinner's trust/faith experienced inwardly and subjec-

---

[25]*Emphatic Diaglott* (Brooklyn: Watchtower Bible and Tract Society, n.d.), p. 649.

[26]George Howard, article: "The Faith of Christ" in *Expository Times,* Vol. 7, pp. 212-214, April, 1974.

tively is not a NT concept at all. Also, it is impossible to reconcile such a perverted understanding of the word "faith" in this clause, because of the qualifier thundered in the next clause.

"And that not of yourselves . . ." The placement of this modifying clause applies it to faith, no matter whether the word for "that" is rendered as here, or "this" *as it should be rendered.* Both the Nestle Greek Interlinear Greek-English Testament and the Emphatic Diaglott translate the word "this" making it absolutely mandatory to understand "the faith" as being that which is "not of yourselves." Those who have already interpreted "faith" here as sinner's faith, however, are under the necessity of removing the meaning of this qualifier which so effectively denies their interpretation; and they have labored prodigiously in a losing cause:

(1) Macknight injected a word foreign to the Greek text, mistranslating the verse thus, "By grace are ye saved through faith, and *this affair* is not of yourselves, etc." He added, "I have supplied *this affair* (making it mean) *your salvation through faith* is not of yourselves!"[27] Well, that's one way to deal with a troublesome text! Others have sought to base their objections to the obvious meaning upon grammatical considerations.

(2) Robertson made faith in this passage sinner's faith, saying, "Grace is God's part, faith is ours," basing his conclusion on the fact of the adverb, *this* (mistranslated *that* in the RV) being of neuter gender, and thus not corresponding to the word faith which is feminine gender, flatly affirming that there is no reference at all in this place to faith as used in that same clause, but referring to salvation as used in the clause before![28] Lenski called this "careless," and then used the same argument himself! The simple truth is that no rule of grammar requires an adverbial phrase to agree *in gender* with its antecedent. This writer has long insisted that it is grammar, not Greek, that foils the work of many interpreters. F. F. Bruce exposed the poverty of this argument from grammar thus:

> The fact that the Greek word for faith (*pistis*) is feminine, while the prounoun *that* is neuter here, is no barrier to regarding *faith* as the gift of God. The phrase "and that" is really adverbial! A similar usage by Paul is in Philippians 1:28 thus:

---

[27]James Macknight, *op. cit.*, p. 282.
[28]As quoted by William Hendriksen, *op. cit.*, p. 121.

> A token . . . of your salvation, and that from God; and
> in that reference *that* is similarly neuter, while both token
> (*endeixis*) and salvation (*soteria*) are feminine.[29]

(3) Hendriksen and others, being aware of the total failure of the argument from grammar to sustain their thesis, support still another theory, credited to A. Kuyper, Sr., which makes "faith" in this verse to mean "faith exercised by the sinner" (which is the essential error in all of these theories) "is not of yourselves but is God's gift."[30] This, of course, is the prize winner, being, without doubt, the most unbelievable of all these false explanations. If allowed, it would make the NT say that men are saved by faith, but there is no need really for them to believe, since God himself gives the faith he requires! The human theories would then have to be revised to teach that men are saved by faith only; but men do not even have to believe, for God gives them faith! This to be sure would remove all conditions without exception, making salvation of all men to depend utterly upon the action of God. The conception that "faith" in this place means some kind of subjective (inward) faith exercised by a person must really be dear to its adherents who will subscribe to any theory as ridiculous, unscriptural and unbelievable as this.

There is only one possible way of understanding "faith" as the subjective response of a person (in this passage), and that is by referring it to the faith of *Jesus Christ*. If this is done, of course, then the availability of Christ's faith as the basis of human redemption is indeed the gift of God. Such an interpretation would have the grace of not contradicting the scriptures; but, in all likelihood, the simple meaning here is "the Christian faith," which came about as a gift of God to mankind, and not as a result of any human contribution whatever. See more on "faith of Christ" under Galatians 2:16, 2:20.

"Not of works, that no man should glory . . ." This refers to works of the Law of Moses, to nothing else; and the expression itself had become a kind of proverb in Paul's writings during those long years of his struggles against Judaizing teachers. It is simply outrageous that a scholar will ignore this and apply

---

[29]F. F. Bruce, *op. cit.*, p. 104.
[30]William Henriksen, *op. cit.*, p. 122.

this verse (9) to mean that "God rejects every work of man."[31] Paul never taught anything like that. He said "work out your own salvation" (Phil. 2:12), and he also praised the Thessalonians for their "work of faith" (1 Thess. 1:3). If God rejects "every work of man," Paul never heard of it! Alfred Barry caught the true meaning here perfectly, thus:

> In this verse we have the echo of the past Judaizing controversy; it sums up briefly the whole argument of Romans 3:27 to 4:25. There is another reminiscence, but more distinct and detached in Philippians 3:2-9.[32]

"That no man should glory . . ." This intention of the Father absolutely removes the primary steps of Christian obedience from any possibility of inclusion in the words "not of works," because there is nothing in any of the steps of primary obedience which by even the wildest stretch of human imagination can be construed as "glorying," or providing any basis for human glorying.

"Faith . . ." not in one's self, but in the crucified Saviour — any ground of glorying here?

"Repentance . . ." entails godly sorrow for sins committed, issuing in a reversal of the human will — any ground of glorying?

"Confession . . ." is not a confession of how saved one is, or what wonders the Lord has done for one, but of faith in Jesus Christ as the Son of God — any ground of glorying here?

"Baptism into Christ . . ." In this act, which is the sinner's only in the sense that he is commanded to "have himself baptized," he is passive, silent, meek, helpless; with hands folded over a penitent heart, he permits his entire person to be buried in baptism, this action showing that he does not trust himself for salvation any more than he would trust a dead body, fit only to be buried — any ground of glorying here? NO! NO! NO! Those who are glorying in this generation are not those who are obeying the gospel in order to be saved, as the scriptures teach; but, on the other hand, they are those who are screaming to high heaven that they are being saved in a better way, by doing nothing except "believing" or "trusting." They are glorying in being saved without "obeying the gospel"; and they are glorying against those whom they denounce and decry as "legalists"

---

[31]*Ibid.*, p. 123.
[32]Alfred Barry, *op. cit.*, p. 26.

because they do render obedience to these primary commandments and strive to teach all men to do likewise.

This writer has never known a Christian throughout many
years of preaching and teaching God's word who ever gloried in
rendering primary obedience to the gospel, or who for one
moment believed such obedient actions on his part "earned" salvation, or "placed God under obligations to him," or put him in
a position of "deserving" or "meriting" eternal redemption. The
implied (or stated) slander of Christians who believe that Christ
meant what he said when he declared that "He that believeth
and is baptized shall be saved" is not merely arrogant and dis-
honest, but it is also without love. Since the groups who believe
and practice obedience to the primary conditions of redemption
most certainly include "faith in Christ Jesus" as being the very
first of those preconditions, are such believers then disqualified
as Christians because they also obeyed the Lord's word in those
areas? Such is the love that men have for their theory that they
will denominate anyone who denies it as a Pharisee, a legalist
and a truster in works. This evident hatred of those who accept
for themselves and teach others the "obedience of faith" betrays
the true allegiance and sonship of them that manifest it. *They*
are the true Pharisees of our day. "Beware of the leaven of the
Pharisees."

Verse 10, *For we are his workmanship, created in Christ Jesus
for good works, which God afore prepared that we should walk
in them.*

"Good works . . ." One who is a Christian works under the
same imperative compulsion as that which rested upon the Christ
who said, "We must work the works of him that sent me" (John
9:4). Any theory which divorces the works a Christian must do
from having any connection with his salvation is a false theory.
It is true, to be sure, that even the good works of Christians are
in no sense adequate grounds of God's justification lavished upon
them in Christ; but they are conditions antecedent to eternal life,
which may indeed, for cause, be waived by the Father in love, but
which may not, under any circumstances, be rejected with
impunity by arrogant men who simply decide they will do it "by

---

[33]Francis Foulkes, *Tyndale NT Commentaries, Ephesians* (Grand Rapids:
Wm. B. Eerdmans Publishing Company, 1963), p. 77.

faith alone." Most of the commentators who advocate the "faith only" heresy are very broadminded (!) in dealing with this verse. They say: "The essential quality of the new life is good works." "If we are not living a life of good works, we have no reason to believe that we have been saved by grace."[34] "Paul reminds us that works have a place in God's salvation."[35] Etc., etc. Well, what is that place? Paul spelled it out, thus:

> God will render to every man according to his works: to them that by patience in well-doing seek for glory and honor and incorruption, eternal life: but unto them that are factious and obey not the truth, but obey unrighteousness, shall be wrath and indignation, tribulation and anguish, upon every soul of man that worketh evil, of the Jew first and also of the Greek (Rom. 2:6-9). Also see 2 Corinthians 5:10.

The truth is clear enough for all who wish to know it.

Verses 11-12, *Wherefore remember, that once ye, the Gentiles in the flesh, who are called Uncircumcision by that which is called Circumcision, in the flesh, made by hands; that ye were at that time separate from Christ, alienated from the commonwealth of Israel, and strangers from the covenants of the promise, having no hope and without God in this world.*

There is a progression in these two verses describing the pre-Christian state of Gentile Christians. "*Physically* they lacked the ancient sign of the covenant; *politically* they had no part in Israel's national or religious life, and *spiritually* they had no knowledge of the true God."[36] Also in verse 12 (beginning after the words "made by hands") "there is a fivefold negative description with a cumulative effect, the situation becoming graver and more terrible; and the last clause is the climax."[37]

"Wherefore remember . . ." It might be good for any Christian to pause now and then and look up to God and remember the way it was with himself before he began to follow Christ. Few indeed are they who remember nothing for which they feel strong emotions to praise God and thank him for all his benefits.

---

[34]W. G. Blaikie, *op. cit.,* p. 64.

[35]Williard H. Taylor, *Beacon Bible Commentaries,* Vol. IX (Kansas City: Beacon Hill Press, 1965), p. 174.

[36]George E. Harpur, *A New Testament Commentary, Ephesians* (Grand Rapids: Zondervan Publishing House, 1969), p. 463.

[37]W. G. Blaikie, *op. cit.,* p. 63.

"Uncircumcision . . . Circumcision . . ." Circumcision was the sign of God's covenant with the children of Israel; but instead of accepting their responsibility of teaching all nations of the true God, they usurped for themselves alone the privileges of the true knowledge of God and became exclusive, arrogant, proud and conceited, looking down upon Gentiles with the utmost contempt and detestation. No modern person can fully appreciate the exclusiveness of ancient Israel; but the following paragraph from Barclay provides some suggestion of what it was like:

The Jew said that God created Gentiles as fuel for the fires of hell, that of all the nations God made, he loved Israel alone, that the best of serpents crush and the best of Gentiles kill, that it was not even lawful to aid a Gentile women in labor because it would only bring into the world another Gentile. The barrier was absolute. If a Jewish boy married a Gentile girl, a funeral for that boy was carried out. Even setting foot in a Gentile's house defiled a Jew![38]

Most of the "glorying" Paul had in mind in his letters regarded such inordinate conceit as that depicted by Barclay above. Paul, having himself been a participant in such thinking, understood it completely and totally rejected, repudiated and forsook it; and, when something of the same arrogant pride, conceit and vainglory which once pertained to Israel began to rear its serpentine head among Gentile Christians, Paul struck a blow against it, much of the book of Romans having that as the objective.

"Separate from Christ . . ." Gentiles, prior to Christianity, had no longing for a Messiah, as did the Jews.

"Alienated from the commonwealth of Israel . . ." The use of this expression shows that Paul was already thinking of the commonwealth of the new Israel, the spiritual Israel, which is the church, which is not exclusively the possession of any race or class of men, but for "whomsoever will." All nations, races and divisions of men are invited to membership in the new commonwealth. By bringing into view in these verses the Jews and Gentiles (Circumcision and Uncircumcision), Paul indicated that all other similar distinctions are likewise abrogated in Christ. The Jewish exclusiveness was actually hardly worse than that of the educated Greeks who divided the whole world

---

[38]William Barclay, *op. cit.,* p. 125.

as "Greeks and barbarians," or that of the Romans who classified all men as either "citizens or non-citizens." Summarized,
any of these classifications actually meant, "We vs. all other
people on earth"!

"Strangers from the covenant of the promise . . ." All of the
great and precious promises of the OT, looking to the blessing
of "all kindreds of the earth," were literally unknown by the
Gentiles. The Jews knew, or should have known, that God also
had plans for their salvation, but no evangelical message ever
went out from Jerusalem under the old covenant.

"Having no hope . . ." The pessimism of the entire pre-
Christian Gentile world is one of the saddest and most wretched
chapters of human history. In the vanity of his own intellectual
conceit, ancient man rejected the knowledge of God, which at one
time he most certainly did have; and the story of what then
followed is recounted in the first two chapters of Romans. Every
man should read it as a prophecy of what will surely happen to
"modern man" when he has finished with removing God from
his thoughts.

"Without God . . ." translates a single word in the Greek
(*atheists*), the same being the only NT occurence of it. This word
was commonly used by Christians to describe the pagans.

When Polycarp, the aged bishop of Smyrna, was led into the
arena before a howling multitude clamoring for his death, the
Roman Procurator took pity on his gray hairs and invited him
to save his life by renouncing Christ and saying, "Away with
the atheists." (The pagans called the Christians atheists.) But
Polycarp waved his hands toward the bloodthirsty throng in the
arena, and cried, "Away with the atheists!" thus turning the
word back upon those who used it.[39]

For full discussion of the godlessness of the pre-Christian
Gentiles, see the first two chapters of Romans, with comments
in this series.

Verse 13, *But now in Christ Jesus ye that once were far off are
made nigh in the blood of Jesus.*

The OT scriptures seem to have been constantly in Paul's
mind; and in this verse the background was apparently this
passage:

---

[39]Francis W. Beare, *op. cit.,* p. 653.

Peace to him that is far off, and to him that is near saith the Lord; and I will heal him. But the wicked are like the troubled sea when it cannot rest . . . There is no peace, saith my God, to the wicked (Isa. 57:19-21).

Thus Paul showed the salvation of Gentiles to have been in God's plan always, Gentiles being clearly included in Isaiah's prophecy of those whom God would heal. Peter also, in the Pentecostal sermon, extended the terms of admission to God's kingdom to "all that are afar off" (Acts 2:39).

"Far off . . ." From the above, it is clear that in both OT and NT these words are a reference to Gentiles, but the implications and connotations of the expression are far greater than that of a mere term of identification. In the ancient cultures of both the pagans and the Jews, that which was "far off" was held to be detestable. Both Horace and Virgil described the opening lines of pagan worship ceremonies thus:

> Hence! O hence! Ye profane!
> I abominate the profane vulgar,
> And drive them from the temples.[40]

The English word "profane" derives from the Latin *procul a fano,* which is literally *far from the temple.*[41] The utter depravity of the whole pre-Christian Gentile civilization is expressed by the words "far off."

"Made nigh in the blood of Christ . . ." It is the blood of Christ which cleanses from sin, making it possible for the profane to enter the temple of God; it was the ransom paid for the redemption of the souls under bondage to sin; it was the purchase price paid for his church. The blood references in the NT are precious, and only the spiritually reprobate are capable of rejecting them as in any manner offensive.

Verse 14, *For he is our peace, who made both one, and brake down the middle wall of partition.*

"Our peace . . ." The mind of the great apostle still lingered upon the glorious prophecies of Isaiah (see under verse 13, above); and in such a frame of mind Paul would most certainly have included in his thoughts the prophecy of the Son of God who

---

[40]Adam Clarke, *Commentary on the Whole Bible,* Vol. XI (New York and London: Carlton and Porter, 1830), p. 780.
[41]*Ibid.*

had assured his apostles that the Jewish temple itself would be utterly devastated and destroyed within the time-span of a single generation after Jesus spoke (Mark 13:30), and that the destruction would be so complete that not one stone would be left on top of another (Mark 13:2). Furthermore, as Paul wrote, he could not have failed to recall that he himself had barely escaped with his life when the Jews wrongly accused him of taking a Gentile beyond the "middle wall of partition" in the temple (Acts 21:28f). And yet . . . here he was dictating a letter to a congregation containing many Gentiles, all of whom, together with himself and many other Jews, were now, all of them, members of that greater temple *in Christ*! As one of the most prominent and successful Pharisees of his generation, Paul would also have had first-hand information about the rending of the temple veil that hung between the Holy of Holies and the Holy Place, a sensational event that took place at the moment of Christ's death (Matt. 27:51), the significance of this being in the fact that the sacred veil was the largest, highest, most important and most symbolical of all the "middle walls of partition" (of which there were several) in the ancient Jewish temple. Thus, when God rent it in twain, *all of the middle walls* of separation were broken down and destroyed. A little fuller comment on this situation is purposefully included here with the intention of showing the absurdity of a critical remark such as:

> It is improbable, however, that the figure (of the broken down middle wall of partition) would have occurred to any Christian writer while the wall itself was still standing: the expression therefore points to a post-Apostolic dating of this epistle![42]

Only if Paul had been a spiritual ignoramus could he have failed to know at this time of his first imprisonment when this letter was written that God had broken down the middle wall of partition between the Jews and Gentiles. Paul's whole apostolical mission had been carried forward in the stern and certain conviction that God had broken it down; and for anyone to imagine that Paul would have needed the actual destruction of the temple itself (which occurred after Paul's death) to suggest the figure which he employed in this passage it would first have

---

[42]Francis W. Beare, *op. cit.*, p. 655.

to be supposed that Paul was a spiritual dunce. The whole Christian world knew that the temple was doomed to destruction by Christ's prophecy; and not even all of the cunning and power of the Jews and Gentiles alike who tried to save it could prevent the prophecy's fulfillment. Not only by Paul, but by *every Christian*, the Jewish temple was looked upon as *already destroyed!* Inherent in such a criticism as that just quoted is not only the bias which prompted it but an amazing lack of spiritual discernment. All such criticisms of the word of God have a quality of solving "problems" by creating greater and more numerous problems. For example, if it is assumed, for the moment only, and for the purpose of argument, that some post-Apostolic writer wrote Ephesians, attributed it to Paul the apostle, sent it forth, and achieved universal acceptance of it as a genuine Pauline letter by the churches of all nations for nineteen centuries, — if such a monstrous and improbable supposition should be allowed, then it would be true that the book of Ephesians was produced by a true genius who gave humanity some of the noblest teaching in all of the sacred scriptures, but that this *genius* (!) did not even know that Paul died before the Jewish temple was destroyed, and that he betrayed the fraudulent nature of his deception by the reference in verse 14!

Verse 15. *Having abolished in his flesh the enmity, even the law of commandments contained in ordinances; that he might create in himself of the two one new man, so making peace.*

"Abolished in his flesh . . ." The thought here is similar to that in Hebrews 10:20, where the new and living way is said to have been opened up through the veil, that is to say, his flesh, thus lending probability to the view of Russell that Paul was referring to the veil of the temple ("middle wall" in verse 14) which was rent when Christ died. He said:

> Re: "middle wall of partition . . ." This probably is a symbolical reference to the partition in the temple which set apart the court of the Gentiles. Its destruction was typified in the rending of the veil of the temple at the time of the crucifixion (Matt. 27:51).[43]

---

[43]John William Russell, *op. cit.*, p. 477.

"Abolished the enmity . . ." "No iron curtain, color bar, class distinction or national frontier of today is more absolute than the cleavage between Jew and Gentile in antiquity."[44] Christ abrogated, annulled and replaced the entire Jewish system with another institution, that of the New Covenant, in which all former distinctions were canceled.

"Abolished . . . the law of commandments . . ." This refers to the totality of the entire Jewish system of religion, and is not restricted in meaning to "the ceremonial law," or any lesser part of Judaism. All of that system was nailed to the cross of Christ. See CH, 8:8ff.

"That he might create . . ." The spiritual creation "in Christ" is of equal rank in the holy scriptures with the creation of the universe itself, as recorded in Genesis.

"In himself of the twain . . ." "The twain" are the Jews and the Gentiles, both of whom are now united as one new man "in Christ."

"So making peace . . ." Thus the key words of Isaiah 57:19-21 continue to sparkle in Paul's writings here: "them that are far off . . . them that are near . . . peace . . ."

Verse 16, *And might reconcile them both in one body unto God through the cross, having slain the enmity thereby.*

"Reconcile . . ." All of the enmity and hatred of previous class distinctions are dissolved and disappear through the creation of a new man, the Christian, who is then no longer a Jew nor a Gentile but a participant of the newness of life in Christ Jesus.

"In one body . . ." This is equivalent to the church, the commonwealth of the new Israel, the spiritual body of Christ, the community of new creatures forming God's creation through Christ upon the earth.

"Through the cross . . ." The centrality of the cross of Christ is an essential Christian concept. No person can be a "new man" till he is willing to forsake the old man, an act referred to by Christ as "to deny" one's self. The cross was literally the death of Christ; but for all Christians, the cross means the renunciation of self, the denial of self, followed by union with Christ, in

---

[44]F. F. Bruce, *op. cit.,* p. 54.

Christ and as Christ, in which state the new man has a new life, a new name, a whole set of new value-judgments, actually a new mind, the mind of Christ.

"Having slain the enmity thereby . . ." The instrument of Christ's triumph over sin was the cross, in which all evil, of every kind, was brought to naught, potentially at the present time, and in the absolute sense eventually.

Verse 17, *And he came and preached peace to you that were afar off, and peace to them that were nigh.*

The key words of Isaiah 57:19-21 are still a kind of refrain, repeated over and over by Paul in this passage.

"He came and preached peace . . ." Christ's entry into the world to bring the word of the Father to sinful humanity had a far greater purpose than merely making peace between Jews and Gentiles, worthy and epochal as such an achievement would be. As Blaikie expressed it:

> The repetition of the word "peace" (in this passage) is expressive; if the subject had merely been peace between two classes of men, we should not have had the repetition. The repetition denotes peace between each of the two classes, and a third party, viz. God.[45]

Verse 18, *For through him we both have our access in one Spirit unto the Father.*

This verse is exceptional in that Christ, the Holy Spirit and the Father are all named in it.

Verse 19, *So then ye are no more strangers and sojourners, but ye are fellow-citizens with the saints, and of the household of God.*

As Taylor observed, there are no less than three metaphors of unity in verses 19-21, expressed as (1) common citizenship, (2) membership in a single household, and (3) mutual parts of one holy temple.[46]

Paul was a Roman citizen and had received signal blessings from such a relationship. Thus it was natural that he should have compared the privileges of being in Christ to citizenship

---

[45]W. G. Blaikie, *op. cit.,* p. 66.
[46]Williard H. Taylor, *op. cit.,* p. 181.

in a kingdom much higher and holier than any other ever known on earth. It was one of Paul's favorite metaphors (see Phil. 3:20).

"Of the household of God . . ." This is a reference to God's family, extended and expanded to include all who would be saved. A similar word was used in antiquity to describe the "family" of slaves belonging to some mighty ruler, or wealthy landowner. Several such "households" are mentioned in Romans chapter 16. "The household of Chloe" (1 Cor. 1:11) is also mentioned.

Verse 20, *Being built upon the foundation of the apostles and prophets, Christ Jesus himself being the chief corner stone.*

"The foundation of the apostles and prophets . . ." There are five foundations of the Christian faith mentioned in the NT: (1) The foundational teaching is composed of the teachings of Christ delivered through the apostles and prophets of the new dispensation (Matt. 7:24-26). (2) The foundational fact is that Jesus Christ is the Son of the living God (Matt. 16:13-20). (3) The foundation person is Jesus Christ our Lord (1 Cor. 3:11). (4) The foundational personnel was made up of the apostles and prophets of the NT, as revealed here. (5) The foundational doctrines of Christianity (six of these) are enumerated in Hebrews 6:1, 2.

Significantly, many different metaphors are needed to set forth the many facets of Christ's relationship to his people on earth. He is called the bridegroom, the lord of the vineyard, the foundation, the cornerstone, the good shepherd, the true vine, the door of the sheep, the pioneer, the forerunner, the head of the body, etc., etc.

"Corner stone . . ." In this verse, perhaps the ancient cornerstone was the basis of the metaphor. It was more than what is usually called a cornerstone now. Several lines of the building were bound together, completed and held together by the cornerstone. For more extended comment on this subject, see CR, chapter 9 "Christ the Living Stone."

Verse 21, *In whom each several building, fitly framed together, groweth into a holy temple in the Lord.*

---

[47]F. F. Bruce, *op. cit.,* p. 105.

"Each several building . . ." There is no compelling reason to follow the RV in this rendition. The RSV has "the whole structure"; the NEB has "the whole building"; and the AV has "all the building." F. F. Bruce discussed this variation thus:

> The evidence for and against the omission of the article is rather evenly balanced, although on the whole the case appears to be stronger for its omission. But there is some NT authority for the meaning "all," even when the article is absent, so that the rendering "all the building" would be possible whichever reading be preferred.[47]

On the basis of the context, it seems to this writer that the preferable view is presented in AV, RSV and NEB. After all, it is the unity of all things in Christ which Paul stressed; and the holy temple of the Lord would therefore seem more logically represented under the figure of a whole building, rather than as a conglomeration of many buildings, as in "each several building." If the RV has accurately translated for us Paul's true meaning, on the other hand, then the words of David Lipscomb would appear to be the best understanding of them:

> The NT clearly recognizes each separate congregation as the body of Christ. God through his Spirit dwells in each distinct and separate church (in the sense of congregation). The church is the body of Christ in the community where it exists. It is not a foot in Corinth, an arm in Ephesus, an eye in Philippi, or an ear in Antioch. . . . A child of God in a strange land has only to worship God himself and multiply the word of God in the hearts of others; and the result is a church of the living God, complete without reference to any other organization in the world.[48]

Verse 22, *In whom ye also are builded together for a habitation of God in the Spirit.*

Regarding the basic concept of the church of our Lord being the true temple of God, see full comment on this in CA, 7:44ff, also under the heading "The Church the Temple of God" under 1 Corinthians 3:16 in this series of commentaries.

"In whom . . ." is the equivalent of "in Christ"; and thus we have here another verse in which the Father, the Son and the Holy Spirit are designated.

---

[48]David Lipscomb, *op. cit.*, p. 54.

CHAPTER 3

This whole chapter is a prayer, but between the first and second words of it, Paul made a characteristic digression in which he gave further teaching on the mystery of redemption (1-13), concluding this part of the letter with what has been called "the boldest prayer ever prayed" (14-21).

Verse 1, *For this cause, I Paul, the prisoner of Christ Jesus in behalf of you Gentiles —*

Actually, Paul's prayer began back in 1:15; and following several digressions, he was about to resume it here; but he hardly got started before going into another digresssion on the mystery of Christ.

"For this cause . . ." The thought will be resumed in these same words in verse 14.

"I Paul . . ." Some radical and irresponsible critics of the NT affirm that these words were forged to this epistle by some later author who passed it off as having been written by Paul; but no believer in Christ could possibly have been guilty of such fraud and deception. The utter poverty of such an allegation is so obvious that some of the scholars who accept such a monstrous opinion feel called upon to explain how such a thing could have happened. This is typical of such "explanations":

> It was published under Paul's name as a tribute of love and admiration by a disciple of great gifts, deeply imbued with the mind and spirit of the great apostle . . . (he wrote) to give expression to ideas of Christ and of the church which had been developing in the apostle's mind (!) . . . he would feel that he was no more than the vehicle of his master's (!) thoughts and therefore might legitimately address the church in his name![1]

Such a canard as that makes out no acceptable justification for the fraud, deception, dishonesty and wickedness of imposing a document upon Christian people as having been written by Paul, when it wasn't. It is hard to make a judgment regarding the greater immorality, whether it pertains to the alleged deceiver the critics would make the author of Ephesians, or to

---

[1]Francis W. Beare, *Interpreter's Bible*, Vol. X (Nashville: Abingdon Press, 1950), p. 600.

the critics themselves who are morally capable of alleging such nonsense as the *justification* of such a sin. Comments like that cited above tell us far more about critics than they do of the authorship of Ephesians, thus: (1) Such comment shows that the critics approve of such deceptions, enabling them to speak in glowing terms of the true fidelity and devotion of such alleged deceivers. (2) It shows that their conception of morality is compatible with such fraud. It could be done (indeed *was done,* they say) "legitimately"! (3) It raises the question of how much "legitimate fraud" the critics themselves have perpetrated in their devious efforts to cast reflection and discredit upon the NT. If men do not believe God's word, let them say so; but may they also have the courage to spare us who believe it the kind of insult to human intelligence inherent in a proposition like that quoted above.

"Paul, the prisoner of Christ . . ." As Barclay said, "A single word or idea can send Paul's thoughts off at a tangent"[2]; and the bare mention of his being a prisoner triggered a whole galaxy of related thoughts, giving us another marvelous Pauline digression. The writing of this epistle is beyond forgery, imitation, or counterfeiting. Paul alone *could have* written this epistle.

When Paul wrote this, he was awaiting trial under Nero, and in all probability fully aware of the ultimate martyrdom that awaited him; but there is no word of complaint here. In fact, he is not Nero's prisoner at all, but the prisoner of Christ! When Paul suffered, from whatever cause, it was all for Christ. How noble was that soul which lived in such a climate of personal loyalty and devotion to the Lord! As Barclay put it, "The Christian has always a double life and a double address."[3] To all outward appearance Paul was a prisoner of the Roman government, but that is not the way Paul looked at it, at all. He thought of himself as suffering and being imprisoned for the sake of Christ. This thought of the origin of his imprisonment ended with Paul's being freed for a while.

"In behalf of you Gentiles . . ." Beare denied that this could be "a real mode of address" by Paul;[4] but such an opinion betrays ignorance of what Paul was saying. The use of "you" with

---

[2]William Barclay, *The Letters to the Galatians and the Ephesians* (Philadelphia: The Westminster Press, 1954), p. 140.

[3]*Ibid.,* p. 141.

[4]Francis W. Beare, *op. cit.,* p. 664.

Gentiles was not for the purpose of addressing the whole Gentile creation, but for the purpose of limiting the meaning of "in behalf of," restricting it primarily to his Gentile converts. It was Paul's standing up for the truth that Gentiles should be brought into the Lord's church without regard to the Jews and the Law of Moses that precipitated the savage hatred of him on the part of unconverted Israel. It was friendship for Trophimus, a Gentile, which resulted in the false charges against him in the temple, that first brought him into the power of the Roman government. In a very real sense, every Gentile on earth is indebted to Paul for the salvation which we have received in Christ. As Barclay truly said, "Had there been no Paul, it is quite conceivable that there would have been no world-wide Christianity, and that we would not be Christians today."[5] Paul's great mission, assigned by Christ who called him to the apostleship, was to "the Gentiles." *That* is what is in view here. It was precisely that Gentile thing which formed so important an element of the Great Mystery that dominated the rest of this parenthesis.

In addition to Paul's defense of the right of "the Gentiles" to be received "into Christ," that defense having precipitated his first arrest and imprisonment, it was predominantly Paul's religious views on this very question which were the grounds of all of the persecutions that confronted him, both Jewish and Roman. If the Jewish hierarchy had been willing to allow Christianity as compatible in any manner with Judaism, there would have been no Roman opposition. As Martin pointed out:

> If the Gentile Christians were stated to be non-Jewish, then they came under Roman laws about illegal religions; but so long as they were regarded as a Jewish sect, they were immune from such laws with their death penalty.[6]

Thus it was actually true that all of Paul's persecutions, first to last, were part and parcel of his mission to the Gentiles.

Verse 2, *If so be that ye have heard of the dispensation of that grace of God which was given me to you-ward.*

"If so be that ye have heard . . ." From this, it is falsely alleged that this letter could not have been addressed to the

---

[5]William Barclay, *op. cit.,* p. 144.

[6]George E. Harpur, *A NT Commentary, Ephesians* (Grand Rapids: Zondervan Publishing House, 1969), p. 464.

Ephesians, since they had most certainly heard of the mystery Paul was about to emphasize. Such a view, however, is due to overlooking the true meaning of the word "if" as used here and in many other NT passages. Macknight translated this place "Seeing ye have heard . . ."[7] Even Beare admitted that it means "Assuming that you have heard . . ."[8] Many reputable scholars translate the "if" here as "since," or "inasmuch." William Hendriksen devoted a number of pages to a thorough study of this.[9]

Verses 3-4, *How that by revelation was made known unto me the mystery, as I wrote before in few words, whereby, when ye read, ye can perceive my understanding in the mystery of Christ.*

"By revelation . . ." Paul always emphasized that the wonderful truth he brought to men was from God, not of himself, that it was given to him by Christ, disclaiming any credit whatever as belonging to himself. Yet, it was absolutely *necessary* that Paul emphasize the world-shaking importance of that truth. When he implied (in the words "when ye read") that men should study his writings, it was not vainglory or egotism on his part, but the mere statement of a basic obligation every Christian has to study divine revelation in the scriptures.

"The mystery . . . the mystery of Christ . . ." One cannot fail to be amused at the "problem" some scholars (?) find with this! As Foulkes said:

> Mystery here is defined differently from its definition in Colossians, leading to the assertion that the difference is so great as to make common authorship impossible.[10]

Foulkes rejected such a simplistic understanding of the mystery, asking, "Can they not be different aspects of the central revelation?"[11] Of course, that is exactly what they are. Not merely two but a dozen complex and interlocking elements of the Great Mystery were revealed by the apostle Paul; and as for the quibbles about one element being stressed here, another there, such problems are as laughable as that of the six blind men

---

[7]James Macknight, *Apostolical Epistles with Commentary, Ephesians* (Grand Rapids: Baker Book House, 1969), p. 286.

[8]Francis W. Beare, *op. cit.,* p. 665.

[9]William Hendriksen, *NT Commentary, Ephessians* (Grand Rapids: Baker Book House, 1967), p. 151ff.

[10]Francis Foulkes, *The Epistles of Paul to the Ephesians* (Tyndale) (Grand Rapids: Wm. B. Eerdmans Publishing Company, 1963), p. 93.

[11]*Ibid.*

describing the elephant. "The Mystery of Christ includes far more than the fact that Gentiles were fellow partakers with Jews of the promise in Christ Jesus."[12] This writer has published *The Mystery of Redemption*[13] containing a full discussion of this subject.

"I wrote before in few words . . ." Like many of Paul's statements, this is capable of a number of meanings, and no one can be certain exactly what he intended. The usual understanding is that this refers to a mention of the mystery earlier in this same letter (1:9f); but of course, there is nothing to keep it from referring to another letter not preserved through history. This uncertainty poses a problem, then, concerning what was intended when Paul wrote, "When ye read."

"When ye read . . ." It is not fair to leave this without calling attention to a possible meaning of this proposed by F. J. A. Hort who believed that it means, "in a semi-technical sense, the reading of the Holy Scriptures."[14] The more radical critics have screamed themselves hoarse about such an interpretation; but it is logical, in keeping with other significant passages of the NT, and probably correct! Christ himself, quoting from the prophecy of Daniel, said, "Let him that readeth understand," both Matthew and Mark giving the quotation exactly as Jesus made it. The most obvious and ridiculous error supposed to support the so-called Markan theory is that of making Jesus' quotation from Daniel a parenthesis injected by Matthew or Mark, with the accompanying conclusion that one or another of the sacred evangelists copied the other! May God deliver his children from that kind of "reasoning"! Both Matthew and Mark gave that quotation, because, in all likelihood, the admonition to Christians was constantly reiterated from the very first, requiring them to read, study and search the scriptures daily, etc. Jesus, it will be remembered, asked the lawyer, "How readest thou?" It was, therefore, a proverb from the first with Christians that they should constantly read the scriptures (at first, the OT, and

---

[12]David Lipscomb, *NT Commentaries, Ephesians* (Nashville: The Gospel Advocate Company, 1939), p. 57.

[13]James Burton Coffman, *The Mystery of Redemption* (Austin: Firm Foundation Publishing House, 1976).

[14]Francis W. Beare, *op. cit.,* p. 666.

in time all of the writings of the apostles and NT prophets as well). In the light of these facts which cannot be denied, how naturally, Paul should have included the clause, "when ye read."

Verse 5, *Which in other generations was not made known unto the sons of men, as it hath now been revealed unto his holy apostles and prophets in the Spirit.*

The scriptural definition of "mystery" is apparent here, the mystery being God's plan of redeeming men, once concealed, now revealed.

"As it hath now been revealed . . ." All of the commentaries examined by this writer fail to see the essential limitations imposed by this clause. What Paul said here is not that the present revelation of the mystery is final and complete, but that the previous generations did not possess a revelation of it "as it hath now been revealed." Revelation 10:7 states that the mystery of God will be finished, or "is finished" in the days of the voice of the seventh angel, when he is about to sound; and it will hardly be denied by any that this means it is not finished now! Marvelous as the Christian revelation surely is, there is no ground for men assuming conceitedly that they "know all about it."

"Holy apostles and prophets in the Spirit . . ." Far from claiming to be the unique source of God's revelation of the great mystery, Paul here declared that the "holy apostles and prophets" of the first Christian generation (all of them) were likewise participants in having received from God this glorious revelation. Paul was both an apostle and a prophet; but Paul did not here preempt the title "holy" unto himself; but there was no honorable way in which he could have denied it to that sacred group to which he himself surely belonged. Bruce has a perceptive comment thus:

> The reference to the "holy apostles and prophets" has been felt to have an impersonal ring about it, making it difficult to imagine Paul himself writing it; but the difficulty lies rather in our twentieth century English ears than in first century NT Greek. There is nothing formal or liturgical about Paul's use of the adjective "holy," and nothing unnatural about the way in which he associates the other apostles and prophets with himself.[15]

---

[15]F. F. Bruce, *The Epistles to the Ephesians* (Old Tappan, N.J.: Fleming H. Revell Co., 1961), p. 61.

Verse 6, *To wit, that the Gentiles are fellow-heirs, and fellow-members of the body, and fellow-partakers of the promise in Christ Jesus through the gospel.*

"To wit . . ." This has the meaning of "that is to say," or "namely." It is often used in legal documents for the purpose of introducing a detailed statement, or formal list.

"Fellow heirs . . . fellow members . . . fellow-partakers . . ." It would have been difficult indeed to have piled together three expressions more eloquent of the absolute equality of privilege and blessing to be shared and shared alike by Jews and Gentiles in Christ. Of course, the OT prophets had plainly foretold the salvation of Gentiles; and, in Romans, Paul cited references from all three of the major OT divisions in which there were definite and undeniable foreshadowings of his own mission to the Gentiles; "but the thing not visible in the OT was that the Gentile sharing of these blessings involved the creation of 'one new man' (2:15),"[16] and that there would be no separate organization for either Jews or Gentiles, both being incorporated into the one body, the church.

As Alfred Martin put it: "The mystery was not that the Gentiles should be saved — there is much in the OT concerning that, particularly in Isaiah — but that they should be joined with Jews in one body!"[17]

Verse 7, *Whereof I was made a minister, according to the gift of the grace of God which was given me according to the working of his power.*

In verses 2, 7 and 8, Paul stressed the grace, that is the divine favor, bestowed upon him by the Father through Christ. "The apostle of the Gentiles enlarged upon the greatness of his special mission. Thrice here he calls it a grace given to him."[18] Also compare Galatians 2:7-9 and Colossians 1:24.

Verse 8, *Unto me who am less than the least of all saints, was the grace given, to preach unto the Gentiles the unsearchable riches of Christ.*

---

[16]*Ibid.*

[17]Alfred Martin, *Wycliffe Bible Commentary, NT* (Chicago: Moody Press, 1971), p. 736.

[18]J. R. Dummelow, *Commentary on the Holy Bible* (New York: The Macmillan Company, 1937), p. 963.

"Less than the least of all saints . . ." It is a mistake to render this "the very least of all saints,"[19] for it was clearly Paul's intention here to invent a word for pressing his utter rejection of any personal glory regarding the wonderful grace given. He compared a superlative, which is illegal grammatically (!); but Paul was above many of the rules so respected by men generally. "Less than the least" is similar to "more than the most" or "higher than the highest," etc. But, in this connection, what about that forger who wrote Ephesians, the one mentioned by Beare, who so loved and honored Paul, etc., etc.? What did he do to his beloved teacher with a remark like this? The falsehood inherent in the theory of pseudonymous authorship of Ephesians shines in a passage like this, like the nakedness of the king in the fable (of the invisible clothes). As Bruce said, "No disciple of Paul's would have dreamed of giving the apostle so low a place";[20] furthermore, it is obvious to any thoughtful person that "no Christian who ever lived" would have given Paul so low a place! That is, none except the holy apostle himself who wrote the epistle.

"Unsearchable riches of Christ . . ." The blessings of salvation in Christ are extravagantly above all human ability to evaluate them. "Usually precious things are rare, their rarity increasing their value; but here that which is most precious is boundless."[21] The literal meaning of "unsearchable" is: "*trackless, inexplorable*, not in the sense that any part is inaccessible, but that the whole is too vast to be mapped out and measured."[22] Paul's thought in this connection was that such unsearchable riches were to be provided for all mankind through his preaching. There was a sense in which he could give such incredible wealth to everyone on earth! This was why Paul so appreciated and honored the office which God gave him, that of the apostleship.

Verse 9, *And to make all men see what is the dispensation of the mystery which for ages hath been hid in God who created all things.*

---

[19]George E. Harpur, *op. cit.,* p. 464.

[20]F. F. Bruce, *op. cit.,* p. 63.

[21]W. G. Blaikie, *Pulpit Commentary,* Vol. 20 (Grand Rapids: Wm. B. Eerdmans Publishing Company, 1950), p. 105.

[22]Francis W. Beare, *op. cit.,* p. 669.

"To make all men see . . ." The message of salvation is to be preached to human beings, not angels, spirits or other non-terrestrial beings. It is important to keep this in mind in the study of the next verse.

"The dispensation of the mystery . . ." Paul's many references in the NT to the mystery of God, the mystery of the faith, the mystery of Christ, the great mystery, the mystery of godliness, etc., etc., are among the most interesting passages in the NT. Essentially, Christ himself is the mystery, a thumbnail biography of Christ actually being called the mystery in 1 Timothy 3:16, the six several items of that biography being various elements of the mystery.

"Which for ages hath been hid in God . . ." God's plan of human redemption existed always in the purpose of God, the fact of its being hidden indicating that there were beings who might indeed have understood it if God had chosen to reveal it. "God does not owe it to anyone to explain why for a long time the mystery was concealed."[23] It was concealed not only from the Gentiles, but also concealed from the Jews; and according to 1 Peter 1:12, it was also concealed from the angels in heaven. It was even concealed from the holy prophets of the OT who were given revelations in words which they did not fully understand concerning this very mystery (1 Peter 1:10-12).

"Hid in God who created all things . . ." The reason for injecting this word about the creation would appear to be "to indicate the relation of the matter in hand to the mightiest works of God. This is no trifling matter; it connects with God's grandest operations."[24] In fact, all through Paul's writings there prevails the impression that the saved in Christ are a part of infinite plans, all creation, even previous intelligent creations (as angels) being destined to share a common purpose with the redeemed when God shall sum up all things "in Christ." No pretense of being able to explain such things is affected by this writer.

Verse 10, *To the intent that now unto the principalities and the powers in the heavenly places might be made known through the church the manifold wisdom of God.*

---

[23]William Hendriksen, *op. cit.,* p. 158.
[24]W. G. Blaikie, *op. cit.,* p. 106.

The fact of the gospel's promulgation upon earth being, in some manner, for the purpose of "making known" to "principalities and powers in the heavenly places" God's manifold wisdom has not been satisfactorily explained; at least, this student of the scriptures has not seen any satisfactory explanation of it. We shall take a look at some of the teachings men have allegedly found in this verse:

John Locke: The governments and powers in the heavenly places are the Jewish religious leaders.

Macknight: They are the different orders of the angels in heaven.[25]

Calvin, Hodge, Grosheide and Lenski thought this refers to the good angels in heaven.[26]

A. T. Robertson understood the reference as to "evil powers or fallen angels, exclusively."[27]

Such variety of opinions suggests that the true interpretation might lie in a different direction altogether. In verse 9, as already noted, Paul gave the purpose of gospel preaching to be that of making "all *men* see." Verse 10 could be nothing more than a dramatic, rhetorical burst of eloquent hyperbole, having much the same meaning as if he had written:

We shall shout the gospel message to the highest heavens and extol the glory of the church as the demonstration of God's manifold wisdom to the highest beings in the universe!

This view has one thing in common with those already cited — *it may be wrong;* but at least it makes as much sense as anything else at hand on the subject. Certainly the whole subject of the impact of the gospel of Christ upon creations above and beyond our own human creation, of which so little is known, and concerning which God has not given us very much information, lies totally beyond the exploration projected for this series of commentaries.

"The manifold wisdom of God . . ." Hendriksen pointed out that the word here rendered "manifold" actually means "mulit-colored, or much variegated," translating the phrase, "the iridescent wisdom of God."[28] This calls attention to the infinite

---

[25]James Macknight, *op. cit.*, p. 303.
[26]William Hendriksen, *op. cit.*, p. 158.
[27]*Ibid.*
[28]*Ibid.*, p. 159.

diversity and sparkling beauty of the wisdom of God. Bruce favored "the many-colored wisdom of God."[29] Since wisdom has no *literal* color, it is clear that Paul was speaking figuratively in this passage.

Verse 11, *According to the eternal purpose which he purposed in Christ Jesus our Lord.*

The preeminence of the Lord Jesus Christ and his having been, from all eternity, the focal center of God's redemptive purpose are affirmed in this verse. There are also overtones of the pre-existence and godhead of the Lord Jesus Christ in this declaration.

Verse 12, *In whom we have boldness and access in confidence through our faith in him.*

This verse mistranslates the last phrase which should follow the RV margin and read "through the faith of him," that is, through the faith of Christ, meaning the faith Christ himself possessed and demonstrated. Justification as accomplished, not by sinner's faith, but by the perfect faith and obedience of the Son of God is a subject that has been treated somewhat in depth in the commentaries on Romans and also in Galatians, to which reference is made for those wishing to pursue the subject further. See under Galatians 2:16, in this volume. There is no justification whatever for rendering this verse "through our faith in him." The Greek NT says no such thing. See in CR 3:22ff. Taylor, Wesley, Macknight and many others, along with the AV, testify to the correct translation as "faith of him," despite the fact that some who admit the true rendition still manage to deny the meaning of it!

"In whom we have boldness . . ." Like many other passages in the Pauline writings, this corresponds very closely to the book of Hebrews (4:16). Christian boldness is revealed as being at least partially the responsibility of the Christian himself to maintain it, encourage it in others, and to manifest it openly in all places and circumstances. It is the spiritual equivalent of the confidence displayed by a good athlete who "talks up a good game" with his teammates, manifesting at all times a winning attitude.

---

[29]F. F. Bruce, *op. cit.*, p. 64.

"Access . . ." This is Paul's word for the privilege of approaching God in prayer, of coming boldly to the throne of grace, of possessing the right to petition the Father in one's own person through identity with the Lord Jesus Christ and needing no go-between, mediator, priest or any other person whomsoever as any kind of dispenser of spiritual privilege, or even as an aid in such things. Christians are *priests* unto God in Christ Jesus who is the "one mediator"; and no other mediators are needed. Not the name of any saint, nor the use of any religious device, nor the requirement of any human creed can circumvent or countermand this fundamental right of the redeemed in Christ, who without any qualification whatever have "access with boldness" unto God "in Christ Jesus." Is this through their own faith in Christ? NO, but by reason of the perfect faith and obedience of Christ, and in the meaningful sense, *actually* Christ, as being a part of his spiritual body.

Verse 13. *Wherefore I ask that ye may not faint at my tribulations for you, which are your glory.*

What a beautiful and selfless thought is this! The rigors of a Roman prison, though somewhat tempered in Paul's case, were nevertheless extremely galling, the very fact of being chained twenty-four hours a day to a Roman sentry was itself a terrible punishment. Paul at this time seems to have been kept, either within the vicinity of the Pretorian barracks, or within the compound that housed the royal bodyguard of the Caesars. In the final imprisonment which came some years later, Paul is thought to have been kept in a dungeon. However, the grand apostle's thoughts were not of his own trials and sufferings, but of the intimidation that such sufferings might cause among his converts. He was not concerned about Paul, but about them! Surely, there is a love here that approaches that of the dear Saviour himself.

Verse 14-15, *For this cause I bow my knees unto the Father, from whom every family in heaven and on earth is named.*

"I bow my knees . . ." Paul had begun to finish this prayer back in verse 1, but he interrupted it for the magnificent digression regarding the great mystery in Christ; now he repeated the words, "For this cause," and completed the marvelous prayer.

The Jews often stood to pray (Matt. 6:5; Luke 18:11-13); but kneeling for prayer is often indicated in the NT, although it was not unknown at all in the OT. Solomon knelt in the prayer of dedication for the temple (1 Kings 8:54). Stephen at his martyrdom (Acts 7:60), Peter when he raised Dorcas (Acts 9:40), Paul on farewell occasions (Acts 20:36; 21:5), and our Lord himself in Gethsemane (Luke 22:41) knelt in prayer. However, other acceptable attitudes or postures are also indicated, such as "lifting up the hands" (1 Tim. 2:8), "falling on the face" (Luke 5:12), etc.

"Unto the Father . . ." Paul here prayed to God, not as the Father of mankind, generally, but in the spiritual sense of being the spiritual Father of his children in Christ. "In the spiritual, or redemptive sense, God is definitely not the Father of all men."[30] This is an important distinction. It is not the brotherhood of all men (in the sense of having the same Creator) that blesses human relationships. It is the brotherhood of men "in Christ" that brings peace and amity. "The brotherhood of man," apart from the qualifier of their being brothers "in Christ Jesus," is a sadistic joke. The Jewish-Arab conflict is a prime example of the brotherhood of man apart from Jesus Christ.

"Of whom every family in heaven and on earth . . ." The RV has changed this from the AV renditions, "the whole family in heaven and on earth," upon textual grounds which many scholars recognize as valid. However, Blaikie, in *Pulpit Commentary,* dogmatically declared that there are no constraining reasons for the change. "The context requires the sense of 'whole family'."[31] He also cited examples of instances in Matthew 2:3, Luke 4:13, Acts 2:36, 7:22, and Ephesians 2:21 where the absence of the article (as here) denoted the totality of a thing. As Hendriksen said, the trouble with the "every family" rendition is that there is hardly any way to know what may be meant by it. "How many families? . . . are the Jews a family? . . . the Gentiles? . . . do the angels form a family? . . . . several families? etc., etc."[32] John Wesley's unique thought on this is quite interesting. Using the

---

[30]William Hendriksen, *op. cit.,* p. 167.
[31]W. G. Blaikie, *op. cit.,* p. 107.
[32]William Hendriksen, *op. cit.,* p. 167.

AV rendition, he nevertheless came up with a number of different families, all one, in the sense of being God's children. He
wrote:

> The whole family of angels in heaven, saints in Paradise,
> and believers on earth is named (of the Father), being "the
> children of God," a more honorable title than children of
> Abraham, and depending on him as the Father of the family.[33]

Wesley's interpretation has the advantage of explaining the
passage no matter which way it is translated, and this would
seem to commend it as the most probable meaning of it.

Verse 16, *That he would grant you, according to the riches of
his glory, that ye may be strengthened with power through his
Spirit in the inward man.*

"The inward man . . ." Clarke's definition of the "inward
man" is as good as any. He wrote:

> Every man is a compound being, having a body and a soul.
> The outward man is that alone which is seen and considered
> by men. The inward man is that which stands particularly with
> reference to God and eternity.[34]

All of the Ephesians whom Paul had converted had been
made partakers of the Gift Ordinary of the Holy Spirit, granted
to them as an earnest of their redemption at the time they were
baptized into Christ (see Acts 2:38, 39; Eph. 1:13). The prayer
in this verse is to the effect that the Spirit of God within them
would be a source of power, more firmly establishing them in the
faith.

Wedel spoke of the confusion and uncertainty many feel
with regard to such a thing as the "indwelling" Spirit of God
thus:

> The concept of the Holy Spirit is at best vague in popular
> understanding; and even theologians can be puzzled by such
> phrases as are in this verse . . . And the expression, "Christ may
> dwell in your hearts" (next verse) can be equally puzzling.[35]

---

[33]John Wesley, *One Volume NT Commentary* (Grand Rapids: Baker Book
House, 1972), *in loco.*

[34]Adam Clarke, *Commentary on the Whole Bible* (London: Carlton and
Porter, 1829), Vol. VI, p. 447.

[35]Theodore O. Wedel, *Interpreter's Bible,* Vol. X. (Nashville: Abingdon
Press, 1953), p. 676.

See extended remarks on this problem under Galatians 5:23, above. There are no less than eight designations for the same scriptural phenomenon, two of them being in these verses 16 and 17.

Verse 17, *That Christ may dwell in your hearts through faith; to the end that ye, being rooted and grounded in love.*

Christ dwelling in Christian hearts is one and the same thing as the Spirit's dwelling in them. The first fruit of the Spirit is love (Gal. 5:23); and here the great result of the "indwelling Christ" is that of the Christian's being "rooted and grounded in love." Again reference is made to the comment on this under Galatians 5:23.

Significantly, in verses 14-17, above, there are references to the Father, the Son, and the Holy Spirit; and although the names seem to be used almost interchangeably, yet there is a preeminence pertaining to the Father, as well as distinct differences between the Son and the Holy Spirit.

Verse 18, *May be strong to apprehend with all the saints what is the breadth and length and height and depth.*

"Breadth, length, etc., of what . . . .?" Beare thought it was "truth."[36] Lipscomb believed it was the love of Christ;[37] Adam Clarke considered it to be the "church of God";[38] Macknight saw in this a comparison of the church with the dimensions of the temple of Diana;[39] the early "church fathers referred these words to the cross."[40] From all this, it is perfectly evident that "Since Paul purposely omitted all definition, leaving the phrase in absolute generality, no answer can be perfectly satisfactory."[41] Perhaps if we were to cite all of these possible meanings and were privileged to ask the apostle which one is correct, he might very well answer, "Why all of them, of course!" Of all the things mentioned as the possible object of these words, men are unable to know the infinite dimensions of them; but Christ in our hearts

---

[36] Francis W. Beare, *op. cit.,* p. 679.
[37] David Lipscomb, *op. cit.,* p. 66.
[38] Adam Clarke, *op. cit.,* p. 447.
[39] James Macknight, *op. cit.,* p. 307.
[40] Alfred Barry, *Ellicott's Commentary on the Whole Bible,* Vol. VII (New York: The Macmillan Company, 1958), p. 35.
[41] *Ibid.*

can help us to understand how infinitely above men are the things of God.

Verse 19, *And to know the love of Christ which passeth knowledge, that ye may be filled with all the fulness of God.*

"The love of Christ" being made here the object of the verb "know" indicates quite clearly that "the love of Christ" is not primarily the thing under consideration in the previous verse, despite the fact of the vast majority of scholars taking exactly that position. As Blaikie said:

> When "the love of Christ" is made the subject of a separate part of the prayer, and is not in the genitive, but in the objective case, governed by a verb of its own, this explanation is not to be entertained.[42]

"That ye may be filled with all the fullness of God ..." This is the grand climax of a prayer which reaches the most exalted heights. Paul here prayed for the Christians to whom he wrote that they might be filled with "all the fullness of God." No wonder this has been called the boldest prayer ever prayed. Dummelow was doubtless correct in interpreting this to mean: "That ye may be filled up to all the fullness of God, i.e., to the perfection of the divine attributes (Matt. 5:48)."[43] See discussion of "Perfection of Christians" under 1:4, above.

THE DOXOLOGY

Verses 20-21, *Now unto him that is able to do exceeding abundantly above all that we ask or think, according to the power that worketh in us, unto him be the glory in the church and in Christ Jesus unto all generations for ever and ever. Amen.*

"Exceeding abundantly ..." As Bruce said, "This is another one of Paul's "super-superlatives," coined to express God's capacity to transcend all that we ask or think."[44] As Paul concluded the prayer, it never occurred to him that in asking God to make the Christians as perfect as God himself he had exceeded, in his request, the ability of God to grant it; on the other hand, he was convinced that God could do far more than any mortal might ask.

---

[42]W. G. Blaikie, *op. cit.,* p. 108.
[43]J. R. Dummelow, *op. cit.,* p. 963.
[44]F. F. Bruce, *op. cit.,* p. 70.

"The power that worketh in us . . ." Paul did not undervalue the divine nature of the power of God in human life, the same being the most remarkably powerful influence that men can know. In this marvelous doxology, Paul did not leave the church out. Great as the power of God in human life assuredly is, it works in those who are "in Christ," being particularly *their* endowment. Being "in Christ," is the same as being "in the church" — this is another truth that is emphasized in this doxology. It is precisely in this great truth that Protestantism has failed. All of the systems which set aside the church, or propose salvation apart from it, are disconnected, and shall always be disconnected from the mainstream of Christianity.

Over the main portal of the Central Church of Christ in Houston are engraved these words:

UNTO HIM BE THE GLORY IN THE CHURCH AND IN CHRIST JESUS
UNTO ALL GENERATIONS FOREVER AND EVER. AMEN.

This is perpetually God's will. There is no generation, however far in the future, which can be exempt from the imperative here. It is God's will that glory to himself shall be in the church and in Christ Jesus; and men who do not consent to this are not in harmony with God's will.

There are not two places in which to glorify God. "In the church" and "in Christ Jesus" designate the same theater of operations. Those "in Christ" are also in the church; and those not "in the church" are not "in Christ."

"Amen . . ." For comment on this, please see CH, 13:25.

CHAPTER 4

Paul's writings defy any strict organization, due to the nature of their composition as dictated epistles. Nevertheless, there is certainly a broad outline in evidence here, the first three chapters dealing with Christian doctrine, and the last three with Christian morality and behavior. Of course, there is some mingling of the two.

It should be noted that Paul placed doctrine first. All human morality derives from the authority of God; and, apart from mortal responsibility to the Creator, there is, strictly speaking, no such thing as right or wrong conduct, immorality or morality! This underlies the total helplessness of men, apart from God, to direct their own affairs. The ultimate authority for evaluating the deeds of men as either praiseworthy or blameworthy cannot lie within men, but must be grounded externally in the will of the Father in heaven. It was therefore by design that Paul first wrote of Christian doctrine, then of Christian morals. "This is the true order."[1]

Verse 1, *I therefore, the prisoner in the Lord, beseech you to walk worthily of the calling wherewith ye were called.*

"To walk worthily . . ." "Walking" is frequently used in the NT as a designation of the Christian's total behavior pattern. To walk "worthily" is therefore to exhibit the kind of life that would do honor to the holy religion of Christ which they had accepted.

All of the high hopes, aspirations and ideals for God's holy church upon this earth, however, must finally succeed or fail in a degree determined, at least in part, by the kind of people who make up the church. Paul "next turned to the character of the Christian which is necessary if the church is to fulfill her great task."[2]

Verse 2, *With all lowliness and meekness, with longsuffering, forbearing one another in love.*

---

[1]John Wesley, *One Volume Commentary on the NT* (Grand Rapids: Baker Book House, 1972), *in loco.*

[2]William Barclay, *The Letters to the Galatians and Ephesians* (Philadelphia: The Westminster Press, 1954), p. 157.

181

These qualities of Christian character are the opposite of those sought and glorified by the non-Christian; and in the pagan culture that provided the setting for the Ephesian congregation, such qualities were actually despised.

"Lowliness . . ." Barclay tells us that "In Greek there is no word for humility which has not some suggestion of meanness attached to it."[3] Humility is a becoming virtue in Christians because it reflects their evaluation of themselves in respect of the infinitely righteous and holy God. It is the fountain from which are derived all of the Christian virtues. Conceit on the part of a child of God is a denial of the faith. There is also a very proper and necessary self-esteem which enters into Christian character (Rom. 12:3).

"Meekness . . ." Martin chose "gentleness" as a synonym for this word;[4] "It is closely connected with the spirit of submissiveness."[5] Moses was described as "meek" (Num. 12:3); and perhaps in the character of the mighty lawgiver can be seen the true qualities which are indicated by this word. Certainly, "weakness" is not one of them. It does not mean docile, easy to handle or merely "cooperative." It refers to moral authority and power issuing in restraint as far as human temptations are concerned.

"Longsuffering . . ." "This word is used of God's patience with men" (Rom. 2:4; 9:22; 1 Tim. 1:16; 1 Peter 3:20; 2 Peter 3:15).[6] "If God had been a man, he would long since have wiped out the world for all its disobedience!"[7] Paul's use of the word here in the sense of a Christian virtue suggests that Christians should be tolerant, forgiving, and understanding of one another's mistakes and sins. A Christian who is always "up tight" about the mistakes of others can create a disaster in any congregation. He, in fact, *is* a disaster!

"Forbearing one another in love. . ." In a word, this means that a Christian should accept his place with other Christians, having an attitude that grants to them the same "right to belong" which he claims for himself.

---

[3]*Ibid.*, p. 159.

[4]Alfred Martin, *Wycliffe Commentary, Ephesians* (Chicago: Moody Press, 1971), p. 739.

[5]Francis Foulkes, *Tyndale NT Commentaries, Ephesians* (Grand Rapids: Wm. B. Eerdmans Publishing Company, 1963), p. 109.

[6]*Ibid.*

[7]William Barclay, *op. cit.*, p. 164.

Verse 3, *Giving diligence to keep the unity of the Spirit in the bond of peace.*

Our holy Saviour prayed for unity among the believers in Christ; and here it appears that unity was a major concern of the most gifted of the apostles; and it may be inquired, in the light of this, why is there so much disunity in the world? In a word, we do not know. It is obvious to all who ever contemplated it that there are no magic devices available for bringing unity out of chaos. Furthermore, it appears in this verse that unity is not produced by Christians, but by the Spirit of God, and Christians are merely admonished to keep it. "Whether there will ever be in this world any outward organic unity of the visible church, we do not know. The selfishness and pride of men are against it."[8]

"Giving diligence . . ." carries the idea of "trying" or "endeavoring," leaving out any requirement that "unity" must be achieved. As a matter of truth, some types of proposed unity are not even desirable. There was a fierce unity in the medieval church.

Verses 4-5, *There is one body, and one Spirit, even as also ye were called in one hope of your calling; one Lord, one faith, one baptism.*

"One body . . ." This is the spiritual body of Christ, the church, made up of Jews, Gentiles, all men and even includes the saved who no longer live on earth.

"And one Spirit . . ." The reference to the third person of the godhead seems to anticipate "Lord" (v. 5) and "God" (v. 6). In any case, the Spirit here is that being called "the Holy Spirit" in the NT, who like Christ and like the Father, dwells in Christian hearts.

"One hope of your calling . . ." This is the hope of eternal life in Christ. There is simply no other lesser thing that may correctly be defined as the "one hope" of Christians.

"One faith . . ." is thought to refer to the Christian religion and not the the subjective trust/faith of individual Christians. Wesley said it refers to "the universal church";[9] and there is no

---

[8]Henry H. Halley, *Halley's Bible Handbook* (Grand Rapids: Zondervan Publishing House, 1927), p. 564.

[9]John Wesley, *op. cit., in loco.*

doubt that the meaning of subjective trust/faith usually read into this word is frequently not in it at all. However, Hendriksen has a convincing analysis indicating that it *is* trust/faith Paul had in mind. He wrote:

> The fact that "faith" is mentioned immediately after "Lord," and is immediately followed by "baptism," all in a very short sentence, would seem to indicate that all three are a very closely knit unit.[10]

This therefore carries the full impact of Mark 16:16, where Christ said, "He that believeth and is baptized shall be saved." The Lord and faith and baptism are all in a very short sentence there, faith and baptism appearing as coordinates in both passages. Furthermore, this understanding of the passage has the advantage of explaining why there is no reference to the Lord's Supper, an omission which is very puzzling to many commentators:

> Why does he not also include the Lord's Supper?[11]

> "Baptism" means "spirit baptism," based on the fact that Paul does not refer to the Lord's Supper here in this list of unities.[12]

> It is often asked why no reference was made here to the other great sacrament of the gospel (the Lord's Supper).[13]

Foulkes pointed out the explanation by Westcott, which is doubtless correct. He said, "The apostle is speaking of the initial conditions of the Christian life, whereas the Holy Communion belongs to the support and development of the Christian life."[14] For the same reason, Christ had no need to mention the Lord's Supper in Mark 16:16, "He that believeth and is baptized shall be saved." The fact that hinders many from seeing this is that they have failed properly to discern that baptism is one of the divinely imposed *preconditions of salvation*.

"One baptism . . ." The reason why many commentators make this mean Holy Spirit baptism, the earnest of the Spirit, the Pentecostal outpouring, etc., is cited above. The obvious

---

[10]William Hendriksen, *NT Commentary, Ephesians* (Grand Rapids: Baker Book House, 1967), p. 187.

[11]*Ibid.*

[12]Willard H. Taylor, *Beacon Bible Commentary*, Vol. 9 (Kansas City: Beacon Hill Press, 1965), p. 205.

[13]Francis Foulkes, *op. cit.,* p. 113.

[14]*Ibid.*

meaning of the passage is Christian baptism; that is, the baptism which is the initiatory rite of admittance into the Christian religion. As Bruce said, "If 'one baptism' here had meant Spirit-baptism to the exclusion of water baptism, it would have been associated with 'one Spirit,' and not with 'one Lord'."[15]

THE ONE BAPTISM

No less than seven baptisms are mentioned in the NT (for enumeration of these, see CH, 1:1-2). The statement here that there is "one" means that only one pertains to the Christian life in the present dispensation. There cannot be any escape from the conclusion that this is the baptism of the Great Commission, as given by both Mark and Matthew. That Christ would have mentioned a baptism in that context which is not the "one" baptism is unthinkable. Furthermore, it has just been pointed out that "Lord . . . faith . . . baptism" in this passage answers perfectly to Mark 16:16. The one baptism is therefore the one that the church itself is commanded to administer and that destroys any notion to the effect that baptism in the Spirit or by the Spirit is meant; because there has never been a church since the times of the apostles that could baptize anyone in the Holy Spirit, the same being something God promised that he would do (Matt. 3:11). The "one baptism" is the one Christ commanded his followers to administer to "all nations" (Matt. 28:18-20). A comparison of the post-Reformation writings with that of the wisest scholars of antiquity starkly reveals the bias toward Luther's invention of salvation by "faith only," which mars the exegesis of many writers in this later period.

Verse 6, *One God and Father of all, who is over all, and through all, and in all.*

The seventh of these great unities is God himself. The Pauline teaching that all men "live and move and have their being in God" is implicit in a verse like this. The very fact of the existence of life proves that God is.

"One God . . ." The unity of God, as reiterated in the first commandment of the Decalogue, was thus emphasized at a time when the world was steeped in polytheism. This great truth

[15]F. F. Bruce, *The Epistle to the Ephesians* (Old Tappan, N.J.: Fleming H. Revell Co., 1961), p. 80.

burst upon the pagan darkness of pre-Christian times like sheet
lightning at midnight (Deut. 6:4). "The Lord our God is one
Lord!" The OT, however, does not deny the NT conception of the
godhead as a plurality. The word for God's oneness in the OT
is *echad*, the same being a compound unity (as in "The people
is one" — Gen. 11:6). Therefore, Deuteronomy 6:4, and similar
passages, may not be alleged as a denial of that plurality
associated with deity in the NT.

Verse 7, *But unto each one of us was the grace given according to the measure of the gift of Christ.*

It is incorrect to construe this as a reference to supernatural
gifts. Paul was not dealing with that kind of gift in this letter,
because the thrust of its message was toward all future generations, and the age of miraculous gifts was rapidly passing. Some
of these no doubt still existed, but they are not in focus here.
What Paul said of all gifts coming from Christ, of course, applied
to all kinds of gifts; but as Blaikie said, "Grace does not refer
merely to supernatural gifts, but also to the ordinary spiritual
gifts of men . . . what each gets, he gets for the good of all."[16] The
fact that the supernatural gifts are not any longer needed does
not detract from the glory of those gifts which are called ordinary, but which have blessed the church in all ages.

Verse 8, *Wherefore he saith,*
    When he ascended on high, he led captivity captive,
    And gave gifts unto men.

"This quotation is from Psalm 68:18; but Paul altered it, from
Thou didst take gifts to *He gave gifts!*"[17] Wesley's explanation
is the usual one; but it is perhaps better to understand this as
a scripture that Paul was here writing, not one that he was
merely quoting. This would be to understand "wherefore he
saith" as meaning "Thus saith the Lord," after the manner of
OT prophets. There is an obvious allusion here to one of Paul's
favorite comparisons, that of the conquering Christ leading the
type of triumphal parade affected by Roman emperors.

Again and again, we have noted in Paul's letters passages
which the scholars have attempted to identify as "garbled"

---

[16]W. G. Blaikie, *Pulpit Commentary* (Grand Rapids: Wm. B. Eerdmans
Publishing Company, 1950), Vol. 20, p. 148./
[17]John Wesley, *op. cit., in loco.*

or "altered" quotations from the OT. It is very probable, however, that here the inspired Paul was *writing new scripture*, not merely *quoting* old passages. Naturally, the new scripture would use terminology used by other sacred writers, the thought being distinctly *new* as it is in the passage before us. The importance of this regarding the authorship of this epistle will not be lost on the discerning student. No pseudonymous writer could have done such a thing *innocently*; such an act, if it had been done, would necessarily have been grounded in a deliberate purpose of fraud and deception. As Bruce pointed out, the first three words of this verse may be translated in either of two ways, thus: "Wherefore he (i.e., God) saith, or Wherefore it (i.e., Scripture) saith."[18] Since it is clear that the scriptures do not say what Paul wrote here, the conclusion is reasonable that the first of these renditions is the correct one.

"Led captivity captive . . ." See discussion of "The Triumph Metaphor" under 2 Corinthians 2:14 in CC. Interpreting this as Paul's own scripture, not a quotation, we shall look to this metaphor, which was one of Paul's favorites, for the probable meaning here. Christ is represented as the mighty conqueror, leading in his train of captives "captivity" itself, a personification of all of the bondage which oppresses human life, such as "captivity to death," the imprisonment of our mortality, "the captivity to sin" (2 Tim. 2:26), etc.

And gave gifts unto men . . ." This is the part of the so-called quotation that is in no sense whatever "a quotation." Referring this passage to the OT (Ps. 68:18) "reveals the picture of a victorious king ascending the mountain of the Lord in triumphal procession, attended by a long train of captives, receiving tribute from his new subjects."[19] The conquering Christ, however, is represented as distributing gifts to men. The NT is the record of the rich and glorious nature of the gifts of Christ to those who love him. His "unsearchable riches" are freely lavished upon his own. See below on "ascended."

Verse 9, *(Now this, he ascended, what is it but that he also descended into the lower parts of the earth?*

---

[18]F. F. Bruce, *op. cit.,* p. 82.
[19]*Ibid.*

"Now this, he ascended . . ." Taylor paraphrased this clause as meaning "As to this matter of ascension."[20] Paul in this verse made an argument to the effect that the ascension of Christ proved that Christ had also descended to the earth. His argument was *not* that any ascension proves a descent. If he meant such a thing as that, it would not have been true. The ascension of Christians to be with the Lord in eternity does not prove that they *also descended*, etc.

Misunderstanding of Paul's argument lies behind a remark like this: "That an ascent implies a descent . . . strange and unconvincing as the argument appears to the modern reader, it is pure midrash!"[21] Such a view is only blindness to the glory of one of the great NT texts. Paul did not argue that "an ascension implies a descent"; any child would know better than that, and Paul was no intellectual child. What then was his argument?

Paul, along with the whole NT church, believed in the pre-existence of Christ with God, before the world was, worshiping him as Lord, Saviour, King, Creator of the universe, Sustainer of the universe, or as Paul himself titled him, King of kings and Lord of lords (1 Tim. 6:15). Now, when it is declared of Jesus Christ the Lord that *he ascended,* the unescapable and necessary deduction is imperative: *that he also descended!* How otherwise could a member of the Godhead ascend? How could the Holy One, with God in the beginning, "the same was God"; how could *he* have ascended without first descending? This verse, therefore, far from being "pure midrash," is one of the most eloquent passages in the NT touching upon the glorious Christian doctrine of the Ascension of Jesus Christ and of his pre-existence from all eternity with the Father.

Verse 10, *He that descended is the same also that ascended far above all the heavens, that he might fill all things.)*

See under verse 9 for the thrust of Paul's argument. These words counteract any thought that by his ascension to heaven Christ thereby, in any sense, deserted the earth. On the contrary, he fills the entire universe. As Barclay expressed it, "The

---

[20]Williard H. Taylor, *op. cit.,* p. 207.
[21]Francis W. Beare, *Interpreter's Bible*, Vol. X (New York: Abingdon Press, 1953), p. 688.

ascension of Christ meant not a Christ-deserted, but a Christ-filled world."[22] The manner of Christ's "filling" all things, of course, is not in a physical sense. It is his all-pervading power and sovereign authority; it is his omniscience and universal presence in all places simultaneously — these are the qualities of our Lord in view here (see Matt. 18:20).

Verse 11, *And he gave some to be apostles; and some, prophets; and some, evangelists; and some pastors and teachers.*

This is a characteristic Pauline insertion, prompted by his mention a moment earlier of Christ "filling all things," which of necessity meant that he filled the church. How did Christ do such a thing? He did it in the manner in view here, through the faithful preaching of men in all generations who would declare the saving message.

As Bruce observed, there are two pairs of offices in view here: (1) apostles and prophets, and (2) evangelists and pastor-teachers.[23] The first pair were effective in the founding of the church, and the second pair are required in all generations. The omission of "some" before "teachers" indicates that the meaning is teaching-pastors, or pastor-teachers. The failure of some to see that the word "pastor" is a NT synonym for "elder" or "bishop" has led to some rather fanciful comments, such as:

> The fact that neither bishops nor elders are mentioned is an indication that we are still some distance removed from the developed organization that we find around the turn of the first century.[24]

All kinds of scholarly misconceptions are evident in a remark like the above. The "organization" of the Lord's church did not "develop" but was given from the very first. Paul ordained elders among the churches established on his first missionary tour (Acts 14:23). In fact, the verse before us says: "He gave," that is, the Lord gave the offices mentioned, including that of elder or bishop, called here pastor-teachers.

Verses 12-13, *For the perfecting of the saints, unto the work of ministering, unto the building up of the body of Christ; till we all attain unto the unity of the faith, and of the knowledge of the*

---

[22]William Barclay, *op. cit.,* p. 171.

[23]F. F. Bruce, *op. cit.,* p. 85.

[24]Francis W. Beare, *op. cit.,* p. 691.

*Son of God, unto a fullgrown man, unto the measure of the stature
of the fulness of Christ.*

In these verses is set forth the purpose of the Lord in the
sending forth of apostles, prophets, evangelists and elders,
mentioned in the preceding verse, that purpose being the building up of the body of Christ, which is the church. But the passage
goes dramatically beyond that. It is not apostles, etc., *alone* who
are to do the ministering in the Lord's church. "Perfecting of the
saints unto the work of ministering" means that:

> Not only those called apostles, prophets, evangelists and
> pastor-teachers, but the entire church should be engaged in
> spiritual labor. The universal priesthood of believers is stressed
> here.[25]

Another very important thing in this passage regards the
rendition of verse 13b. The AV has "unto a perfect man" where
the RV has "unto a full-grown man." There can be little doubt
that the AV is correct, because the measure of "the fullness of
the stature of Christ," mentioned next, can be nothing if not
absolute perfection. As Barclay said, "The aim of the church for
its members is nothing less than perfection."[26] It is true that the
Greek word here may be rendered *fullgrown*, as in RV; but it is
also rendered *perfect*, in the sense of being applicable to God himself (Matt. 5:48).[27] The meaning here has to be *perfect*; nor is this
an idle distinction. See article on "The Perfection of Christians"
under 1:4, above.

Verses 14-15, *That we may be no longer children, tossed to and
fro and carried about with every wind of doctrine, by the slight
of men, in craftiness, after the wiles of error; but speaking truth
in love, may grow up in all things into him, who is the head, even
Christ.*

There are two things which contribute to the seduction of
Christians away from the holy faith. These are: (1) the natural
instability of many persons who are captivated by novelty, easily misled, swayed by popular fashion, etc. As Barclay said of
such people, "They are always under the influence of the last

---

[25]William Hendriksen, *op. cit.,* p. 198.

[26]William Barclay, *op. cit.,* p. 177.

[27]W. E. Vine, *An Expository Dictionary of NT Words* (Old Tappan, N.J.:
Fleming H. Revell Co., 1940), Vol. III, p. 173.

person with whom they talked."[28] (2) Then there are the deceivers themselves, ruthless, cunning, unprincipled sons of the devil who, while often appearing in sheep's clothing, are nevertheless "ravening wolves." The language Paul used here makes any apology for the deceivers a gratuitous endorsement of evil. Note:

> Our translation is inadequate. The meaning is: "They make use of every shifting device to mislead" (Weymouth). There are not only those around you who lead you astray but mean to do it (Moule). They lay deliberate traps on purpose to guide you away from Christ whom they do not love.[29]

The greatest mistake that any Christian can make is to assume that teachers of error are sincere. While true enough that some of them are, it is equally true that many are not.

"Speaking the truth in love . . ." The wholesome life of absolute integrity, truthfulness before all men, love toward all men — what priceless gems of character are these; and where in all the wide, wide world may one look for a life like that except in the humble and faithful service of the Son of God?

Verse 16, *From whom all the body fitly framed and knit together through that which every joint supplieth, according to the working in due measure of each several part, making the increase of the body unto the building up of itself in love.*

In this wonderful expression of the glory and beauty of the body of Christ, "Language cannot express the full truth."[30] A moment before Paul spoke of Christ as "the head." He is also the whole body. He is all in all.

It should also be noted here that "every joint" and "each several part" make it very clear that Paul expected every member of the body of Christ to make its own contribution to the building up of the whole.

Verse 17, *This I say therefore, and testify in the Lord, that ye no longer walk as the Gentiles also walk, in the vanity of their mind.*

Some old versions had inserted the word "other" before *Gentiles*; but as Bruce has accurately observed, "Christians

---

[28]William Barclay, *op. cit.,* p. 178.

[29]Willard H. Taylor, *op. cit.,* p. 211.

[30]J. R. Dummelow, *Commentary on the Holy Bible* (New York: The Macmillan Company, 1937), p. 964.

constitute a third race on the earth, no longer Jews, no longer
Gentiles. Even the *also* of the RV is misleading."[31] The meaning here is simple enough. "No longer live the old pagan life."

Verses 18-19, *Being darkened in their understanding,
alienated from the life of God, because of the ignorance that is in
them, because of the hardening of their heart; who being past feeling gave themselves up to lasciviousness, to work all uncleanness
with greediness.*

Here is a reference to the pre-Christian Gentiles who at first
knew God, rebelled against him, turned away from him, eventually being hardened, first through their own wickedness, and
later receiving a judicial hardening of God himself who thus
punished their disobedience. See extended discussion of that
deplorable condition of the pre-Christian Gentiles in CR, 1:21ff.
These two verses are a thumbnail reference to a matter Paul
discussed at length in Romans, chapter 1.

"Hardening of their heart . . . gave themselves up . . ." See
special related articles on these topics: "When God Gives Men
Up" (CR, 1:28), and "The Hardening of Israel" CR, chapter 11.

Verses 20-24, *But ye did not so learn Christ; if so be that ye
heard him, and were taught in him, even as truth is in Jesus: that
ye put away, as concerning your former manner of life, the old
man that waxeth corrupt after the lusts of deceit; and that ye be
renewed in the spirit of your mind, and put on the new man, that
after God hath been created in righteousness and holiness and
truth.*

"Ye did not so learn Christ . . ." The "ye" here is emphatic.
"Certainly, you, among whom I myself labored, did not learn
Christ in such a manner as to allow living like Gentiles!" As
Blaikie said, "To learn Christ" means "to learn all about Christ
through complete acceptance and obedience of his teachings."[32]

"If so be that ye heard him . . ." This is not a conditional but
an idiomatic saying with the impact of "As surely as you have
heard him."[33]

"The old man to be put off . . ." This was the old man that
lived like the Gentiles, as Paul had just described.

---

[31]F. F. Bruce, *op. cit.,* p. 91.

[32]W. G. Blaikie, *op. cit.,* p. 151.

[33]William Hendriksen, *op. cit.,* p. 212.

"The new man to be put on . . ." Note that the "new man" is not man's doing at all, but God's. "That after God hath been created!" This simply means to "put on Christ." How is this done? Note:

Christians put on Christ in baptism (Gal. 3:26, 27).

They put on the name of Christ (Matt. 28:18-20).

They put on (or receive inwardly) the mind of Christ (Phil. 2:5).

They put on "the body of Christ" in the sense of belonging to his spiritual body, the church.

They put on the manner of daily living that Christ exhibited.

They put on Christ in the sense of being "in Christ."

Verse 25, *Wherefore, putting away falsehood, speak ye truth each one with his neighbor: for we are members one of another.*

Harpur pointed out that Paul made the application in practical living concerning what he meant by putting off the old man and putting on the new man. From this verse through 5:20, the contrast between the two is dramatically presented:

falsehood vs. truth (4:25).
resentment vs. self-control (4:26, 27).
stealing vs. generosity (4:28).
evil speech vs. edification (4:29, 30).
malice vs. love (4:31-5:2).
impurity vs. chastity (5:3-14).
imprudence vs wisdom (5:15-17).
debauchery vs. joy (5:18-20).[34]

Always speaking truth relieves one of the task of remembering what he has already said! The violator of this holy law will discover that the principle of truth within him perishes, leaving him helpless to discriminate between reality and fantasy. Satan is a liar and the father of lies.

"With his neighbor . . ." This does not restrict truthtelling to conversation with neighbors only, leaving one free to lie to those whom he does not recognize as neighbors. The injunction means always speak the truth.

Verse 26, *Be ye angry, and sin not: let not the sun go down upon your wrath.*

---

[34]George E. Harpur, *A NT Commentary, Ephesians* (Grand Rapids: Zondervan Publishing House, 1969), p. 466.

This verse can be misread, as if it said, "Be sure to be angry now and then, but do not sin!" It appears that the meaning is, "When you are angry, be sure that you commit no sin." Anger is a time when sin strongly presents itself as a temptation to violence or other retaliatory action directed against the object of one's anger.

Anger is even attributed to God himself; therefore the teaching cannot mean that it is a sin to be angry. There are things which certainly should arouse the emotion of anger in Christian hearts. About the most ineffective person on earth would be one incapable of being angry.

"Let not the sun go down . . ." Even when anger comes, it must be terminated quickly. Sundown is the time for removing anger from the heart. When anger remains, it can corrupt and destroy every virtue of the soul.

Verse 27, *Neither give place to the devil.*

Paul recognized the devil as a personal enemy of Christians; and in this he followed the Saviour who taught men to pray, "Deliver us from the evil one" (Matt. 6:13). Satan in this verse appears as a being operating against Christians; and the admonition is that they should not allow any room for the devil's operations, as would be done if anger should be retained in the heart.

Verse 28, *Let him that stole steal no more: but rather let him labor, working with his hands the thing that is good, that he may have whereof to give to him that hath need.*

The ignorant person called upon to read this chapter publicly almost broke up the meeting when he read:

"Let him that stole, steal; no more let him labor with his hands!"

This is repeated here to show how much depends, at times, upon the proper punctuation; and it should always be remembered that the original writers of the NT did not punctuate it, punctuation marks having been added much later.

It is very obvious from this entire section that the persons who were addressed in this epistle were quite possibly doing some of the very things Paul condemned here. We are bound to be struck by these implications. Beare said, "The church was welcoming into her fellowship members of the criminal classes."[35] Words like these have the impact of "cease and desist from all sin." While those who "had been" criminals were welcome, their sins were not welcome.

The word of God reveals some acceptable methods of acquiring property, these being: (1) by inheritance, (2) by work, (3) by reception of it as a gift, (4) through merchandising, (5) through investment, etc.; two of the acceptable methods and one of the unacceptable methods appear in this verse, the latter being, of course, stealing.

Verse 29, *Let no corrupt speech proceed out of your mouth, but such as is good for edifying as the need may be, that it may give grace to them that hear.*

The Christian is an ambassador at all times of the faith which he has professed. All conversation provides an opportunity of imparting grace to people who might stand desperately in need of it; and for the child of God to waste the vast majority of all such occasions through idle, frivolous, empty, meaningless conversation is a standing tragedy on earth. And what is even worse is the indulgence of conversation which is vulgar, profane or obscene.

"That it may give grace . . ." The Christian should never lose sight of the sad fact of a world lost in sin, without the Lord, needing some word, some ray of light, some word of grace that will point to the Lamb of God that takes away sin.

Verse 30, *And grieve not the Holy Spirit of God, in whom ye were sealed unto the day of redemption.*

"Ye were sealed . . ." See under 1:13, above, for more extended remarks on this, also in CR, 3:23f.

"Grieve not the Holy Spirit . . ." Any of the sins Paul was forbidding in these verses would, of course, grieve the Holy Spirit in the heart of any Christian committing them; but the thought here seems especially directed against filthy conversation.

In addition to "grieving" the Holy Spirit, mentioned here, the NT reveals a number of other ways in which men may sin against the Holy Spirit:

They may lust against him (Gal. 5:16).
They may resist him (Acts 7:51).

---

[35]Francis W. Beare, *op. cit.,* p. 700.

They may lie to him (Acts 5:3).
They may try him (Acts 5:9).
They may insult him (do despite unto) (Heb. 10:24).
They may blaspheme against him (Mark 3:29).
They may "quench" him (1 Thess. 5:19).

"The day of redemption . . ." "This means the day of judgment in which our redemption will be completed."[36]

Verse 31, *Let all bitterness, and wrath, and anger, and clamor, and railing, be put away from you with all malice.*

Such conditions of the inward life as that indicated by the prohibitions listed here are the bane of earthly existence. What incredible waste and loss of all that is precious flow out of the undisciplined lives of unregenerated men; and, tragic as that is, it must be held even more deplorable that many Christians have never learned to live above the behavior Paul proscribed in this powerful verse. We are indebted to Henriksen for excellent definitions of the sins here enumerated.

"Bitterness . . ." is the settled disposition of one who is resentful.

"Anger . . ." is strong, sudden antagonism, explosive, potential murder.

"Wrath . . ." is like a roaring furnace, settled indignation.

"Clamor . . ." is yelling at others.

"Railing . . ." is "blasphemy" in the Greek, meaning "speaking against God or man."

"Malice . . ." takes delight in inflicting hurt or injury.[37]

Verse 32, *And be ye kind one to another, tenderhearted, forgiving each other, even as God also in Christ forgave you.*

These are the opposites of the things forbidden in verse 31.

"Kind one to another . . ." Nothing blesses mankind any more than ordinary kindness, which is not in any sense ordinary, but the most extraordinary endowment that any Christian possesses.

"Tenderhearted . . ." How much at variance with the pagan cultures of antiquity was this Christian virtue is pointed out by Macknight thus:

---

[36]John Wesley, *op. cit., in loco.*
[37]William Hendriksen, *op. cit.*, p. 223.

This precept is very different from that of Epicitus who speaks to this purpose, "If one is in affliction, thou may say to him that thou hast pity on him; but take care not to feel any pity."[38]

Forgiving . . . as Christ forgave you . . ." The longest parable Matthew recorded, that of "The Unmerciful Servant" (Matt. 18:21-35), concludes with these words: "So shall also my heavenly Father do unto you, if ye forgive not every one his brother from your heart." The watchword for Christians, and for all men, is "Forgive or forfeit forgiveness!"

"As Christ forgave . . ." The great motivation for all virtue is in Christ, especially that for forgiveness. All thought of malice toward others should perish in the flood of joy that sweeps over the soul which has been cleansed and forgiven of all sins.

---

[38]James Macknight, *Apostolical Epistles and Commentary, Ephesians* (Grand Rapids: Baker Book House, 1969), p. 329.

CHAPTER 5

"Walk" as a metaphor of general behavior is used in this chapter to admonish Christians to (1) walk in love (1-2), (2) walk in the light (3-14) and (3) walk in wisdom (15-21). In verse 22, Paul began instructions relative to three classes of reciprocal obligations: (1) those between husbands and wives (22-33), (2) those between children and parents (6:1-4), and (3) those between servants and masters (5-9). Only the first of these is in this chapter.

Verses 1-2, *Be ye therefore imitators of God, as beloved children; and walk in love, even as Christ also loved you, and gave himself up for us, an offering and a sacrifice to God for an odor of a sweet smell.*

"Imitators of God . . ." The NT teaches that the only practical revelation of God is that of Christ himself; and, in view of this, "imitating God" is a commandment to be fulfilled by "walking in love," just as Christ loved us and gave himself for us. Certainly, the teaching here is not to the effect that weak and fallible mortals should in any sense "play God" by usurping to themselves judgments that pertain to God alone.

As Mackay said, "To copy God is to be like a Person, to reflect his image."[1] Christians should strive to be like God in forbearance, goodness and love.

The reference to Jewish sacrifices in verse 2 has puzzled commentators who have variously understood the nature of Christ's sacrifice (as mentioned here) to be "a sacrifice of consecration (Ex. 29), a peace-offering (Lev. 3) or a sin-offering (Lev. 4)."[2] Alfred Barry has presented a very interesting and convincing argument based on a similar expression in Hebrews 10:5, and the OT reference there, and upon the peculiar Hebrew usage of these terms, concluding that, "Therefore, we have here a complete summary — all the more striking and characteristic

---

[1]John Mackay, *God's Order* (New York: The Macmillan Company, 1953), p. 170.

[2]John William Russell, *Compact Commentary on the NT* (Grand Rapids: Baker Book House, 1964), p. 481.

because incidental — of the doctrine of the Atonement."[3] Christ was not merely one kind of sacrifice, or offering, but every kind.

Verses 3-4, *But fornication, and all uncleanness, or covetousness, let it not even be named among you, as becometh saints; nor filthiness, nor foolish talking or jesting, which are not befitting; but rather giving of thanks.*

This is another of Paul's catalogues of vice, none of them, not even all of them together being any complete list of sins, but merely typical. Other lists are in Romans 1:29ff, 1 Corinthians 5:11ff, 6:9ff, Galatians 5:19ff and Colossians 3:5ff. Fornication is prominently mentioned in practically all of these, due to its prominence in the pagan culture from which Gentile converts to Christianity had been recruited. As Bruce said:

> We may think it strange to see covetousness so closely associated with these vices, but Paul is simply moving from outward manifestations of sin to their inner springs in the cravings of the heart.[4]

It will be recalled that Christ also did this, tracing murder to the angry thought behind it, and adultery to the lustful heart (Matt. 5:21-27ff).

"Not even named among you . . ." This indicates that such vices as are enumerated here are forbidden to Christians and that it is not fitting that their minds should dwell upon such things or that their tongues should talk about them.

"Filthiness . . . foolish talking . . . jesting . . ." Filthiness of moral character leads inevitably to filthiness of conversation; and Paul also condemned that. The smutty story, the foolish jesting, the empty nonsense that passes in some quarters for conversation — all of these are proscribed and forbidden. Dummelow interpreted the reference to jesting, etc., as jesting about such sins as were just mentioned. "Do not get near these topics for the sake of being amusing."[5] Macknight rendered jesting as "double meanings," citing that as the meaning of "artfully

---

[3]Alfred Barry, *Ellicott's Commentary on the Whole Bible*, Vol. XIII (Grand Rapids: Zondervan Publishing House, 1959), p. 46.

[4]F. F. Bruce, *The Epistle to the Ephesians* (Old Tappan, N.J.: Fleming H. Revell Co., 1961), p. 102.

[5]J. R. Dummelow, *Commentary on the Holy Bible* (New York: The Macmillan Company, 1937), p. 964.

turned discourse" (Greek), specifically identifying these as "chaste expressions which convey lewd meanings."[6]

Whereas the Puritans went too far in their over-strict interpretation of Paul's words here, it may not be denied that our own generation has erred in the other direction. This passage condemns much of the conversation of many Christians, which at best, in many cases, is "borderline." Bruce believed that, "Above all, all light and irreverent talk about sacred things is to be utterly reprobated."[7]

Verse 5, *For this ye know of a surety, that no fornicator, nor unclean person, nor covetous man, who is an idolator hath any inheritance in the kingdom of Christ and God.*

"The phrase *kingdom of Christ and God* occurs only here in the NT."[8] It does not indicate two kingdoms, but rather that the kingdom of Christ and the kingdom of God are one and the same. The deity of Christ is implied in such a construction. Beare claimed that this verse is opposed to Paul's statement in 1 Corinthians 15:23, 24 that Christ would "finally deliver the kingdom to God," affirming that such a view is here "abandoned."[9] Such a notion is unscientific, illogical and contrary to scripture. The kingdom of Christ and God, from its inception, was never understood any other way except as the kingdom of both Christ and God.

Verse 6, *Let no man deceive you with empty words: for because of these things cometh the wrath of God upon the sons of disobedience.*

"Empty words . . ." refers to the arguments of those opposing the truth by defending the immorality of the pagan culture surrounding the church of those days.

"Because of these things . . ." means because of the gross sins just enumerated by the apostles.

"The wrath of God upon the sons of disobedience . . ." implies more than the ultimate overthrow of evil at the final judgment.

---

[6]James Macknight, *Apostolical Epistles with Commentary and Notes* (Grand Rapids: Baker Book House, 1969), p. 333.

[7]F. F. Bruce, *op. cit.,* p. 103.

[8]Willard H. Taylor, *Beacon Bible Commentary,* Vol. 9 (Kansas City: Beacon Hill Press, 1965), p. 230.

[9]Francis W. Beare, *Interpreter's Bible* (New York: Abingdon Press, 1950), Vol. X, p. 707.

Repeatedly, throughout history, when the measure of a people's wickedness had overflowed, God wiped them out in some grand historical upheaval. Paul would mention this a few moments later.

Verses 7-9, *Be not ye therefore partakers with them; for ye were once darkness, but are now light in the Lord: walk as children of the light (for the fruit of the light is all goodness and righteous and truth).*

These verses prove the coherence of the whole paragraph beginning with verse 3. Up to this point, Paul was describing the "unfruitful works of darkness" (v. 11); and the argument of this passage is, "Do not take up the old ways again; you once practiced all that; you know how useless and unfruitful such works are; and you now belong to a new order of things; "Ye are the light in the Lord." The glorious results (fruit) of the new way of living in Christ are all "goodness, righteousness and truth"!

Verse 10, *Proving what is well-pleasing unto the Lord.*

As "children of light," by continuing to walk in the Christian way, the very achievements of such living would "prove" what was pleasing to God, first to themselves, and secondarily, to all who became aware of what they were doing.

Verse 11, *And have no fellowship with the unfruitful works of darkness, but rather even reprove them.*

"Reprove . . ." This word means "expose," and probably should be so translated. There can be no neutrality between the sons of light and the sons of darkness. As Hendriksen said:

> Sin must be exposed. One is not being nice to a wicked man by endeavoring to make him feel what a fine fellow he is. The cancerous tumor of sin must be removed. It is not really an act of love to smooth things over, as if the terrible evil of the sons of disobedience is really not so bad.[10]

Verse 12, *For the things which are done by them in secret it is a shame even to speak of.*

Although this verse is surely true of all wicked men, Macknight, and others, have detected a close connection here with the

---

[10]William Hendriksen, *Exposition of Ephesians* (Grand Rapids: Baker Book House, 1967), p. 233.

various mystery cults of paganism. His paraphrase of verse 11-12 brings this out thus:

And have no fellowship with those who celebrate the heathen mysteries, which being transacted in the darkness of night are really the unfruitful works of darkness, as they bring no fruit to the initiated, except eternal death: But rather reprove them. For the impure and wicked actions which are secretly done in the mysteries by the initiated, are so abominable, that it is base even to mention them.[11]

Verse 13, *But all things when they are reproved are made manifest by the light: for everything that is made manifest is light.*

"Everything that is made manifest (by the light) is light . . ." This means "Everything that the light reveals becomes itself light!" Of course, this is literally true. Nothing can be seen, except through its *reflection* of light; and that which reflects light (as the moon) is in itself light. As Dummelow noted, this very thing had happened to the Christians who received this letter. "Light turns darkness into light; this is what had happened to Paul's readers.[12]

Verse 14, *Wherefore he saith, Awake thou that sleepest, and arise from the dead, and Christ shall shine upon thee.*

"Wherefore he saith . . ." Here again, we have the phenomenon of Paul an apostle of Christ producing scripture, in exactly the same way as the prophets of the OT, and introducing his words with exactly the same formula, "Thus saith the Lord," "God saith," etc. As Hendriksen said, "There is no sound reason here to interpret this in any other way than in 4:8."[13] See under 4:8, above, for another example of the same phenomenon.

Despite the obvious, however, the translators and commentators have done a number of strange things with this verse. (1) They have accused Paul of misquoting scripture; (2) they have suggested that the words here are an early Christian song; and to accommodate that view, they have translated the words of the above clause as "Wherefore *it* saith!"; (3) they have said, "Through error or forgetfulness, the writer has mistaken this fragment of a Christian hymn to be a quotation from the OT!"[14]

---

[11]James Macknight, *op. cit.,* p. 337.
[12]J. R. Dummelow , *op. cit.,* p. 965.
[13]William Hendriksen, *op. cit.,* p. 234.
[14]Francis O. Beare, *op. cit.,* p. 711.

We categorically reject such interpretations, there being utterly no reason whatever why such views should be trusted.

Verses 15-16, *Look therefore carefully how ye walk, not as unwise, but as wise; redeeming the time, because the days are evil.*

Christ himself divided the whole human family along this fundamental line of cleavage, "the wise and the foolish," the wise being those who "hear the sayings of Jesus and do them," the foolish being those who hear and do not (Matt. 7:24ff). Paul here referred to that same basic division of mankind, showing that Christians themselves are in no manner exempt from doing God's will.

"Redeeming the time . . ." "This does not carry the idea of paying a particular price, but of 'making the most of' the time."[15] How true this was of the time when Paul penned these words. Within a very few years, Rome would be burned, and Nero would drown the Christians in blood to divert suspicion from himself that he personally had set it on fire. Jerusalem would fall to the armies of Vespasian and Titus; and the accumulated wrath of God for centuries of rebellion would finally overflow against Israel. Many who read these words for the first time would soon suffer persecution and death. The days were indeed evil; and only a little while remained before the storm would overwhelm the world, only a little while to walk in the light and joy of the loving service of Christ the Lord.

Verses 17-18, *Wherefore be ye not foolish, but understand what the will of the Lord is, And be not drunken with wine, wherein is riot, but be filled with the Spirit.*

"Be not foolish . . ." Cited here as persons falling into the classification of "foolish" are the drunken. Who are they? Our current society recognizes no drunkards, only "alcoholics"; but persistent indulgers in alcohol receive no comfort from what Paul declared here. It is not even "the drunkard" who is condemned in this place, but the person who "gets drunk," or becomes intoxicated. While true enough that the NT does not forbid the use of wine (see below), the person who becomes intoxicated (even once) has violated the admonition here.

---

[15]Willard H. Taylor, *op. cit.,* p. 234.

The overseer (elder) therefore must be above reproach . . . not one (who lingers) beside (his) wine (1 Tim. 3:2; Titus 1:7). Deacons similarly (must be) dignified, not . . . addicted to much wine (1 Tim. 3:8); and urge aged women similarly (to be) reverent in demeanor . . . not enslaved to much wine (Titus 2:3).

"Wherein is riot . . ." Alcohol is the greatest single killer in the United States today. It produces more sorrow than may be attributed to any other single source on earth. It corrupts government, aggravates poverty, destroys spirituality and eventually destroys any society stupid enough to indulge the unrestrained use of it.

"But be filled with the Spirit . . ." Not spirits, but the Holy Spirit is the true watchword. "Satan is ever substituting the bad for the Good. Getting drunk is associated with unrestrained living . . . it marks the person who, if he so continues, *cannot be saved.*"[16]

It has been asked, "If the Holy Spirit indwells us, why does Paul command us to be filled with the Spirit?" Bruce answers this question thus:

> Being filled with the Spirit implies more than being indwelt by him. In some believers' lives he has little more than a foothold, being almost crowded out by a number of concerns. Paul is eager that his converts should be under the undisputed control of the Spirit.[17]

Verse 19, *Speaking one to another in psalms and hymns and spiritual songs, singing and making melody with your heart to the Lord.*

"Speaking one to another . . ." This reference is probably to the custom of Christians "singing by turns a hymn to Christ, as to a god."[18] "By turns" is also rendered "antiphonally"; but from 1 Corinthians 14:26, the custom was actually that of singing by turns.

"Psalms, hymns, and spiritual songs . . ." Although these can be differentiated, there is no need to do so. The teaching declares

---

[16]William Hendriksen, *op. cit.*, p. 239.

[17]F. F. Bruce, *Answers to Questions* (Grand Rapids: Zondervan Publishing House, 1972), p. 107.

[18]Pliny's Letter to the Emperor Trajan, 112 A.D. Henry Bettenson, *Documents of the Christian Church* (New York and London: Oxford University Press, 1947), p. 6.

that not all songs are acceptable in the worship of God, but only those with spiritual value.

Regarding the question whether or not the public assemblies or worship services of the Christians are referred to here, it seems best to construe the passage as having exactly that application. To make it applicable to all types of gatherings would be to prohibit a Christian from singing any kind of music except sacred music, a prohibition that does not appear in the passage at all. With Lipscomb and many others it is viewed here as instruction regarding the public worship of the Christians.[19]

"Singing . . ." The meaning of this term is to produce music vocally; and regardless of ancient meanings attributed to the word *psallo*, rendered "making melody" used here in conjunction with it, no translator has ever rendered this verb any other way. God's command for Christians is that they should sing, and if playing instruments of music is an acceptable part of divine worship, it is difficult to understand why it would not have been so stated in this place. Arguments from the ancient meaning of *psallo* are, as F. F. Bruce declared, "irrelevant to the question of instrumental music, one way or the other."[20]

WHY INSTRUMENTAL MUSIC IN THE WORSHIP OF GOD IS REJECTED

1. There is nothing strange or unusual about some Christians rejecting mechanical music as in any manner appropriate or permissible in Christian worship. The entire Protestant world maintains exactly the same religious position with reference to use of the Rosary of the Virgin Mary, the sign of the cross, the burning of sacred incense, the sprinkling of holy water, the sacrifice of the mass, prayers for souls in purgatory, the lighting of holy candles . . . and a hundred other innovative additions to Christianity, as being not taught in the NT. The identically same arguments which support the non-use of such devices as those here cited are valid when applied to the use of mechanical instruments of music in God's worship. The burden of proof therefore rests upon those who reject some of the historical church's innovations, but do not reject them all. To many devout souls, it appears

---

[19]David Lipscomb, *NT Commentaries, Ephesians* (Nashville: The Gospel Advocate Company, 1937), p. 106.
[20]F. F. Bruce, *op. cit.,* p. 107.

mandatory to reject *all* innovations (Matt. 15:9). No one has ever denied that the use of mechanical instruments in worship was unknown to the NT age and that the first historical appearance of them in Christian worship came during the eighth century.

2. It is accepted by many that the use of musical instruments in the OT was an innovative change from David and that the change was not approved by the Lord. This, of course, is vigorously denied by some; but their denials are refuted by the truth that the Orthodox Hebrew Communion through the centuries has clung to the non-use of mechanical instruments, maintaining that God did not approve of them; and *they know the teaching of the OT on that point better than any modern scholars.*

3. Mechanical music as worship of God is antithetical, by nature, to spiritual religion. From times immemorial, many centuries before Christ came, instruments of music were conspicuously associated with pagan worship (Dan. 3:7); and for the first six and one-half centuries of the Christian faith on earth, they were just as conspicuously omitted from Christian worship. Although Paul did not have such things in mind when he declared that "God is not worshiped with men's hands," the text truly applies to this question (Acts 17:25, AV). The introduction of mechanical instruments into the worship of Christ involves the service and skills of technical and profession craftsmen who tend to emphasize "art" more and more, and "worship" less and less, resulting usually in the professionalizing of the "singers" as well as the players; and anyone who has ever known the internal workings of a big city church choir can testify to the blight that inevitably follows. There was never anything on earth more "unspiritual."

There are many other persuasive and convincing things to be said on this question, but the above are cited here because they were determinative in the thinking of this writer, at a time when he was a member of a "choir" and struggling with this question himself.

Verses 20-21, *Giving thanks always for all things in the name of our Lord Jesus Christ and to God, even the Father; subjecting yourselves one to another in the fear of Christ.*

"Giving thanks always for all things . . ." This cannot mean that a Christian should give thanks because illness, suffering, loss and adversity of many kinds may have fallen upon him, but that he should give thanks for "all things" *in every situation* that may afford a proper ground of gratitude to God. Thus: When one is young, let him thank God for youth; when he is old, let him thank God that he has been permitted so long to live; in health, for strength and joy; in sickness, for the ministry of physician, nurse, loved ones and friends; in poverty, for the privilege of living "like Jesus"; in wealth, for God's endowments; in death itself, for the hope of eternal life, etc., etc.

Such an admonition as this might seem impossible of obeying, "did we not know full well that Paul had learned to do this, even in the most unpropitious circumstances."[21]

"Subjecting yourselves one to another in the fear of Christ . . ."

"Paul ceaselessly preached 'submission,' or 'subjection,' to Roman authority (Rom. 13:1-7; 1 Cor. 14:32-34; 16:16; Titus 3:1).[22] This clause is the topical heading for the next three paragraphs of the epistle, as pointed out in the chapter introduction. The first of the three reciprocal relationships discussed is that of husbands and wives, beginning in the next verse.

Verses 22-23, *Wives, be in subjection unto your own husbands, as unto the Lord. For the husband is the head of the wife, as Christ also is the head of the church, being himself the saviour of the body.*

"Wives be in subjection . . ." This is to be understood in the light of the obligation, given a moment later, for the husband to love his wife even as Christ loved the church. There never was any kind of effective organization that functioned without a head. From ants and bees in the insect world to central governments, an effective social unit of any kind requires a head; and it could not have been otherwise with regard to the human family, the oldest of God's organizations among men, being prior to that of any state, or of the church. By the appointment of God himself, the husband was named head of the family. Societies which have reversed this are known as matriarchal; but by definition they are inferior.

---

[21]*Ibid.*, p. 112.
[22]J. R. Dummelow, *op. cit.*, p. 964.

"As unto the Lord . . ." "This does not mean that they should yield to their husbands the same deference as they would yield to Christ himself, but that deference is a duty which they owe to the Lord."[23]

"As Christ is the head of the church . . ." Marriage from the very beginning was prophetical of the spiritual relationship between Christ and his church (the great "mystery" of v. 32). Paul begins here to build that analogy.

"The saviour of the body . . ." Here, "The implication seems to be that the husband is the protector and defender of his wife."[24]

Verse 24, *But as the church is subject to Christ, so let the wives also be to their husbands in everything.*

In the continuing analogy, the true life of the church is her head, who is Christ; and the true achievement and fulfillment of the wife is in her husband. This is the Christian view of the family. The current social unrest could indicate that this ancient concept will be overturned; but if it is ever supplanted by another, women will not, in any sense, gain by the change. Apart from the teachings of Jesus Christ and the apostles, the status of woman in society has tended to be lower and lower; and there can be no doubt whatever that if woman should reject her place in the Christian home, as taught in the NT, the same forces which in the past destroyed and degraded her in practically every society on earth would again overwhelm and crush her. Like the poor prodigal who resented the restrictions of his incumbency in the father's house, but found those of the "far country" to be far more cruel and oppressive, woman may choose to forsake the gains of the centuries in the Father's house for the fancied delights of "the far country"; but, if so, she will find, as did the prodigal, that Satan is still in the swine business!

Verses 25-26, *Husbands, love your wives, even as Christ also loved the church, and gave himself up for it; that he might sanctify it, having cleansed it by the washing of the water with the word.*

---

[23]F. F. Bruce, *op. cit.*, p. 114.
[24]*Ibid.*

The measure of love that husbands are commanded to give their wives is that of Christ's love of the church. A love that would die for the beloved! Any submission or subjection that a devoted wife might give to her husband would be more than rewarded and justified by such a love as that. Hendriksen was right when he declared, "More excellent love than this is inconceivable."[25]

"That he might sanctify it . . ." The sanctification in view here is the original consecration of the alien sinner to God's service at the time of his conversion. Any notion of the sanctification here meaning any special state of holiness beyond that first and decisive setting apart unto God is incorrect.

"Having cleansed it by the washing of the water with the word . . ." This is a reference to Christian baptism. "This can scarcely be anything other than baptism; that is what the language would most naturally have conveyed to the original readers."[26]

"With the word . . ." is understood in two different ways, some holding that it means baptism in response to "the preaching of the gospel,"[27] and others supposing that it refers to the confession "with the mouth" by converts prior to and at the time of their being baptized. This prompted Goodspeed's translation thus:

> Just as Christ loved the church and gave himself for her, to consecrate her, after cleansing her with the bath in water through her confession of him.[28]

It is hard to say which meaning Paul might have intended here for both are true, in the sense of being appropriate.

It is difficult to understand why commentators became exercised about this verse, pausing after allowing that the meaning cannot possibly be anything other than Christian baptism, to include a paragraph or so affirming their repudiation of "baptismal regeneration." "Baptismal regeneration" is not a relevant scriptural question today. As far as this writer

---

[25]William Hendriksen, *op. cit.,* p. 250.

[26]F. F. Bruce, *op. cit.,* p. 114.

[27]Francis Foulkes, *Tyndale NT Commentaries, Ephesians* (Grand Rapids: Wm. B. Eerdmans Publishing Company, 1963), p. 158.

[28]Edgar J. Goodspeed, *The NT, An American Translation* (Chicago: University of Illinois Press, 1923), *in loco.*

knows, nobody in this century has believed anything even remotely resembling the theory of "baptismal regeneration." The teaching of true believers to the effect that a person must believe and be baptized in order to be saved has no connection with baptismal regeneration. Baptismal regeneration theorists believed that "the external application of water, accompanied by the appropriate words, is sufficient to bring about regeneration."[29] Since the Dark Ages, whoever believed a thing like that? On the other hand, regeneration, a work of God, takes place in the sinner at the time of, and *when he is baptized.* Water baptism is most certainly a precondition of receiving regeneration and forgiveness from God; and ten thousand angels swearing it is not true could not change that; but it is not water which regenerates, it is God who does so *when* the sinner is baptized. It is very encourageing to see a great Baptist scholar, such as Beasley-Murray, who is willing to admit that such a distinction is valid. He said:

Baptism is the occasion when the Spirit brings to new life him that believes in the Son of man.[30]

If through man's failure to obey the Lord by being baptized that *occasion* never comes, then neither will newness of life arrive!

Hendriksen also, after the usual disclaimers regarding "baptismal regeneration," rendered the meaning of this verse thus:

Christ loved the church and gave himself up for her in order that he might by means of the rite of baptism with water sanctify and cleanse her.[31]

Amen! There cannot be any doubt that such is the true meaning here. But the giving of its proper NT place to Christian baptism requires no disclaimers. As Lipscomb said, nothing more is attributed to baptism in this passage[32] than in many other NT passages, such as:

He that believeth and is baptized shall be saved (Mark 16:15, 16).

---

[29]F. F. Bruce, *op. cit.,* p. 116.
[30]G. R. Beasley-Murray, *Baptism in the NT* (Grand Rapids: Wm. B. Eerdmans Publishing Company, 1973), p. 278.
[31]William Hendriksen, *op. cit.,* p. 251.
[32]David Lipscomb, *op. cit.,* p. 113.

Repent and be baptized every one of you in the name of Jesus Christ unto the remission of sins, and ye shall receive the gift of the Holy Spirit, etc. (Acts 2:38).

Arise and be baptized and wash away thy sins, calling on the name of the Lord (Acts 22:16).

Etc.

In connection with this verse see Titus 3:5, and discussion there.

Verse 27, *That he might present the church to himself a glorious church, not having spot or wrinkle or any such thing; but that it should be holy and without blemish.*

The absolute perfection of the church is prophesied here; but the manner of achieving this is left out of sight. It is revealed by Paul in Colossians 1:28. See comment under that verse. Also see article on "Perfection of Christians," under Ephesians 1:4.

Verses 28-29, *Even so ought husbands also to love their own wives as their own bodies. He that loves his own wife loveth himself: for no man ever hated his own flesh; but nourisheth and cherisheth it, even as Christ also the church.*

The analogy which had been in Paul's mind as far back as verse 23, above, is about to be stated emphatically here and in the following four verses. First, there is the practical consideration that: just as Christ provides for every need of the church, nourishing and blessing her in all times and places by all means, so also the husband is obligated to make the care of his wife the principal concern and most urgent business of his whole life. In loving her, he is, after all, only loving himself.

Verses 30-31, *Because we are members of his body. For this cause shall a man leave his father and mother, and shall cleave to his wife; and the two shall be one flesh.*

Here (verse 31) Paul quoted verbatim the passage from Genesis 2:24, making it the scriptural basis of the grand analogy between Adam I and Adam II, between Eve and the bride of Christ.

"Because we are members of his body . . ." Paul here says of the bride of Christ, what Adam said of his bride, "bone of my bones . . . flesh of my flesh" (Gen. 2:23). Without the inspiration of one like Paul, men would probably never have known the magnificent analogy concealed in the creation story itself as a prophecy and prefiguration of the church. Paul had long understood the "mystery" mentioned here, having brought it to light by various earlier references to it. In 2 Corinthians (11:3), he pointed out that Satan's seduction of the bride of the first Adam suggested the seduction by Satan of the bride of the second Adam (the church).

ADAM AND EVE . . . CHRIST AND THE BRIDE

Adam naturally provides the great type of Christ. Just as Adam was progenitor of all living, so Christ is the author of life in himself. As in Adam all die, so in Christ shall all be made alive. When Eve was formed, a deep sleep fell upon Adam, and Eve was taken from his side. In the redemptive act on the cross, the deep sleep of death came upon Christ; his side was pierced; blood and water came forth, these emblems of the two great Christian ordinances of baptism and the Lord's supper, making it possible to see (in a figurative sense) that the church came forth from the side of Christ. Satan beguiled Eve, and likewise the church, luring her into the great apostasy. There are extensive analogies in this, one of them appearing particularly in these verses, that being the oneness of Adam with his bride forming a prophecy of the oneness of Christ and the church.

Verses 32-33, *This mystery is great: but I speak in regard of Christ and the church. Nevertheless do ye also severally love each one his own wife even as himself; and let the wife see that she fear her husband.*

Hendriksen pointed out that the Vulgate mistranslation of the passage, "This mystery is Great" reads thus *sacramentum hoc magnum.*[33] "It is upon this sole basis that the Roman church set up the claim that marriage is a sacrament."[34] As Hendriksen said, "If the simple fact had been observed that *Mystery* is the word Paul used here, (such) a mistake would never have occurred."[35]

---

[33]William Hendriksen, *op. cit.,* p. 256.
[34]James Macknight, *op. cit.,* p. 346.
[35]William Hendriksen, *op. cit.,* p. 256.

The RSV rendition of "This mystery is great" reads, "I take it to mean"! However, as Foy E. Wallace said, "Paul did not take it to mean anything; he said exactly what the great mystery is."[36] The exalted view, both of marriage and of the church of Jesus Christ, shines forth in this text. The sacredness of marriage is seen in God's design of it, from the very beginning, to be a figure of the union of Christ and his church; and the glorious importance of the church appears in the fact of its having been in the design of God from the very beginning. Despite all of these wonderful thoughts, however, Paul, will still conclude with a practical thought:

"Nevertheless do ye also severally love each one his own wife . . ." Let the husband think of himself as the protection, defender and provider for his wife, even as Christ is of the church.

"And let each wife see that she fears her husband . . ." This has none of the connotations usually associated with "fear" in common speech today. "It means *reverence* and *respect*. It is the kind of fear that the Bible so frequently calls on individuals to show before God."[36]

---

[36]Foy. E. Wallace, Jr. *A Review of the New Versions* (Fort Worth: Foy E. Wallace, Jr. Publications, 1973), p. 445.

[37]Francis Foulkes, *op. cit.,* p. 163.

CHAPTER 6

Of this whole chapter it may be said, as Dummelow said of the last verse, "It is a worthy conclusion to this immortal Epistle!"[1] Paul here continued his discussion of reciprocal relationships: (2) between children and parents (1-4), and (3) between slaves and masters (5-9). His final great admonition to strength in the Lord through putting on the whole armor of God (10-20) was followed by practical words regarding the bearer of the letter (21-22), and the benediction (23-24).

Verse 1, *Children obey your parents in the Lord for this is right.*

As in all three of the reciprocal duties discussed here, Paul began with the duties of that group who were supposed to submit or obey. "*Obedience* is a stronger word than *submission* which was given as the duty of the wife."[2] James M. Gillis outlined a program for the healing of modern society as follows:

The salvation of society is in the family and the reconstruction of family virtues, parental authority, and filial obedience. The family is the nucleus of all society. You can have no prosperous state unless the family is healthy. You can have no effective church unless the family is sound . . . The family is the organic cell from which all human societies are constructed.[3]

"For this is right . . ." There will never be a time when it is right for children to disregard, dishonor, and disobey their parents. "Parents give their children three things: they bring them into being, provide them nourishment, and afford them instruction."[4] There are three concentric rings describing the situations in which all men should learn discipline and obedience, these being the home, the school and society. If one does not learn obedience at home, he becomes a troublemaker

---

[1]J. R. Dummelow, *Commentary on the Holy Bible* (New York: The Macmillan Company, 1937), p. 966.

[2]Alfred Martin, *Wycliffe Bible Commentary, NT* (Chicago: Moody Press, 1971), p. 749.

[3]James M. Gillis, *The Ten Commandments* (New York: The Paulist Press, 1931), p. 49.

[4]Thomas Aquinas, *The Ten Commandments of God* (London: Burnes, Oates, and Washbourne, Ltd. 1937), p. 50.

in school; and from there he soon graduates to the police court. A great deal of the world's sorrows could be prevented if all children were taught to obey their parents.

"In the Lord . . ." Paul did not have in view here anything except Christian homes. He did not teach that children should obey instructions which contradict basic Christian principles.

Verse 2, *Honor thy father and mother (which is the first commandment with promise).*

Some have been puzzled by this reference to "the first commandment with promise."

> It is asked, Does not the second commandment contain a promise, too? Or, if the reference there to the mercy of God being shown to thousands of generations is to be regarded as a statement rather than as a promise, then is not the fifth the *only* one of the ten with a promise?[5]

Perhaps the best understanding of this is to take "with promise" not to be a modifier of "first commandment," thus being parenthetical. This would leave the flat declaration that "this is the first commandment," meaning, "This is the first commandment *for children.*" This would make Paul's meaning to be, "Children obey your parents in the Lord, for that is the first commandment for children; also, there is a promise connected with it." Certainly, Paul was not saying here that the Fifth Commandment in the Decalogue is the first, except in the sense indicated. For more complete discussion of the Fifth Commandment, please see CD, pp. 58-70.

Verse 3, *That it may be well with thee, and thou mayest live long on the earth.*

This promise is as true now as it was when included in the Decalogue. Multiplied thousands of untimely and tragic deaths of young people would be avoided, or could have been avoided, by their simple obedience to the sacred instructions here. Disobedient, arrogant and heedless children, refusing to be restrained by parental wishes of any kind, are almost certain to violate basic rules of survival on the earth.

---

[5]Francis Foulkes, *The Tyndale NT Commentaries, Ephesians* (Grand Rapids: Wm. B. Eerdmans Publishing Company, 1963), p. 164.

Verse 4, *And ye fathers, provoke not your children to wrath: but nurture them in the chastening and admonition of the Lord.*

In this matter of making basic human obligations to be *reciprocal* rather than limited to the ones required to obey, the Christian religion swept away the whole philosophy of pre-Christian ages. In 5:25, Paul laid it upon husbands that they must love their wives, even as Christ loved the church enough to die for it! Here he confronted parents, fathers particularly, with their obligations to their children. They must instruct and discipline them "in the Lord," having the most urgent respect to the rights and feelings of the children. A moment later, he would thunder the obligations of masters toward their slaves (6:9). The epic nature of these admonitions is seen in the fact that in the society of Paul's day, wives, children and slaves had no rights.

STATUS OF WIVES, CHILDREN AND SLAVES

All women, wives in particular, were in practical fact the chattels of their husbands, without economic or civil rights of any kind whatever, subject to divorce or abuse upon any pretext and without recourse or protection of any kind. What Christianity has done for women has been extolled in the songs and literature of all nations; but the same glorious transformation of the status of children and slaves was also achieved by those sacred scriptures before our eyes in this very chapter. See CJ, 4:27.

The rights of children were also non-existent in ancient society.

A Roman father had absolute power over his family. He could sell them as slaves, work them in the fields, even in chains. He could take the law into his own hands (he was the law), punish as he liked, and even inflict the death penalty on a child![6]

The notion that a father had any obligation toward a child simply did not exist in non-Jewish elements of ancient pagan society. As a result of the prevailing attitude, many unwanted or despised children were exposed at birth to the elements, wild beasts, or other forms of horrible death.

---

[6]William Barclay, *The Letters to the Galatians and Ephesians* (Philadelphia: The Westminster Press, 1954), p. 208.

It was exactly the same way with slaves.

> A slave is no better than a beast; the old and sick must be thrown out to starve; when a slave is sick, it is a waste to give him rations; masters had power of life and death over slaves; Augustus killed a slave for killing a pet quail; Pollio flung a slave *alive* to the savage lampreys in his fish pond because he dropped and broke a crystal goblet. One Roman nobleman's wife killed a slave because she lost her temper. Slaves used as maids often had their cheeks torn, their hair torn out, or were branded with hot irons at the caprice of their heartless and cruel masters.[7]

Now, it was to a world which from the remotest antiquity had operated upon such principles as these, regarding wives, children and slaves, that the great apostle of Christianity thundered the mighty oracle of these magnificent chapters. In the name of Christ, he asserted the obligations of husbands, fathers and masters, thereby announcing the character of the basic rights of wives, children and slaves. In all literature apart from the word of God, where is anything that compares to what is taught here? No wonder this letter has lived two thousand years; and, as for the nonsense that it was not written by Paul, one may only ask, "Who, in the name of God, *could have written it* except Paul?"

Verse 5, *Servants, be obedient unto them that according to the flesh are your masters, with fear and trembling, in singleness of your heart, as unto Christ.*

This injunction addressed to slaves and masters "does not imply either approval or disapproval of the institution of slavery itself."[8] Those who understand Christianity as any kind of an attack upon the established institutions in society, should take account of the fact that the most shameful and disreputable institutions of ancient culture were in no case frontally assaulted by Christianity. Some who should know better are embarrassed by this; but there were reasons grounded in the greatest wisdom, why such an open attack was not made. See discussion of this in CC, under 1 Corinthians 7:21.

---

[7]*Ibid.,* p. 214.

[8]Francis W. Beare, *Interpreter's Bible,* Vol. X (New York: Abingdon Press, 1963), p. 732.

"With fear and trembling . . ." "This is not advice for the slave to cringe before his master, but is to be taken in close relationship with the words, *as unto Christ.*"[9]

"In singleness of your heart . . ." This means, "Not merely through fear of punishment, but from a principle of uprightness."[10]

"As unto Christ . . ." All work must be done, by all men, slaves included, as being performed under the eye of God. Every piece of work a Christian does must be good enough for God to see. The economic and labor problems of the world, especially acute today, are not primarily economic at all. The problem which the world faces is a religious problem. Barclay observed that:

> We will never make men good workmen by increasing pay, bettering conditions or heightened rewards. It is a Christian duty to see to these things, of course; but in themselves they will never produce good work. The only secret of good workmanship is that it is done for God.[11]

Verse 6, *Not in the way of eyeservice, as men-pleasers; but as servants of Christ, doing the will of God from the heart.*

"Eyeservice . . ." refers to the slave (or other workman) who is diligent to appear busy only when the boss is looking. It is the opposite of work done out of good will with love and integrity.

"Men-pleasers . . ." A motive far higher than winning approval of inspectors or superiors marks the work of Christians, that of considering every task as "the will of God," and striving to please him in the execution of it.

Verse 7, *With good will doing service, as unto the Lord, and not unto men.*

This is further emphasis and elaboration of what Paul had just written. All work done by the Christian is to be done "as unto the Lord," that is, "as service of the Lord." This is one of the noblest principles of Christianity, making all employment to be the service of God. Not merely those who perform public service for the church, or those who stand in some formal

---

[9]*Ibid.,* p. 733.

[10]Adam Clarke, *Commentary on the Whole Bible* (London: Carlton and Porter), *in loco.*

[11]William Barclay, *op. cit.,* p. 215.

relationship to religious activity, not merely these, but all men who engage in honest work, doing it well and cheerfully, are servants of God, no less than they.

Verse 8, *Knowing that whatsoever good thing each one doeth, the same shall he receive again from the Lord, whether he be bond or free.*

Although there is a sense in which good, honest and cheerful work of a slave might bring some limited reward during earthly life, "It is ultimately the judgment seat of Christ that the apostle has in view here."[12] Whatever men may do, Christ will reward all of his workmen at last. It is the consciousness which would enable the workman, even though he was a slave, "to work zestfully and cheerfully even for a master who was unreasonable in his demands and impossible to please."[13]

Verse 9, *And ye masters, do the same things unto them, and forbear threatening: knowing that he who is both their Master and yours is in heaven, and there is no respect of persons with him.*

This is the oracle of God that turned the world upside down. All obligations involving human beings are a two-way street. Slaves have duties, but so also, do their masters! What an earth-shaking concept that was, and IS! Toward their slaves, masters were commanded: "Give them the same good will, love and loyalty that you hope to receive from them."[14] Behind a commandment like this lay the infinite dimensions of those tremendous new value-judgments which were brought to mankind from above by Jesus Christ the Lord. *The infinite value of human life!* Who ever heard of such a thing? It had never been heard of until the apostles of Christ preached it in the heathen darkness, having themselves received it of the Lord. The mighty corpus of the ancient empire trembled under the impact of a shot like this verse which Paul launched from the end of a prisoner's chain; and when a shaft of light such as this penetrated the darkness, men knew instinctively that a new age had dawned.

However, it should be noted that it was not the truth alone which could change the world; it was *the truth in Christ the Lord!*

---

[12]F. F. Bruce, *The Epistle to the Ephesians* (Old Tappan, N.J.: Fleming H. Revell Co., 1961), p. 124.

[13]*Ibid.*

[14]Francis W. Beare, *op. cit.*, p. 735.

The duty of masters to their slaves, fathers to their children and husbands to their wives, etc., was not just splendid theory. The living Christ at the right hand of God would require of every man an accounting of his deeds at the judgment of the Great Day. No man would escape it!

Shallow and unperceptive persons of our own times tend to be critical of NT teaching because no hard, definitive commands are uttered demanding the abolition of slavery; but it was clear to Christ and the apostles that *laws* never made men better; only an inward change could accomplish such a purpose as that. Paul's instructions here did not free slaves; but, as Dummelow said, "It freed slavery of its evils,"[15] and set in motion forces that would ultimately destroy, not only slavery, but other evil institutions as well.

In this connection, the resurgence of humanism in these times should be noted. Turning away from God, men are obsessed with the notion that, in themselves, they can make everything all right, with their laws, social gains and planned programs of all kinds; but it is no more possible to accomplish worthwhile human societies away from God than it is to produce a crop of apples from uprooted trees. "The NT presents the demands of the kingdom of God as prior to those of a utopian society on this earth . . . Love of God is still the first and great commandment, love of neighbor *second.* Worshiping and serving the creature more than the Creator, however, drowned the pre-Christian world in debaucheries; and, if indulged, *it will do it again!*

Verse 10, *Finally, be strong in the Lord, and in the strength of his might.*

The admonition Paul was about to give here had been in mind throughout the epistle. He mentioned the strength of God (1:19; 3:16) and the putting on of "the new man" (4:24) earlier; but now he would give final instructions for arming the Christian for the warfare against the forces which opposed him. "The cosmic purpose of God involves the believer with the spiritual hierarchy of the unseen world organized under the power of Satan."[17]

---

[15]J. R. Dummelow, *op. cit.,* p. 966.

[16]Theodore O. Wedel, *Interpreter's Bible*, Vol. X (New York: Abingdon Press, 1953), p. 733.

[17]George E. Harpur, *A NT Commentary, Ephesians,* (Grand Rapids: Zondervan Publishing House, 1969), p. 468.

Verse 11, *Put on the whole armor of God, that ye may be able to stand against the wiles of the devil.*

"The armor of God . . ." The Christian does not oppose evil in his own strength, but in the strength of the Lord. Only the armor of God is sufficient to the warfare involved.

"The wiles of the devil . . ." One may experience only irritation and disgust at a remark like this: "Neither of these nouns is used by Paul; each occurs twice in this epistle (4:14, 27). In place of 'the devil' Paul always used the personal name 'Satan'."[18] The incredible thesis that lies behind a comment like that is that Paul could not have written Ephesians, because *there are two nouns in it that he did not use in his other writings!* It is assumed by such theorizers that although Paul knew the devil's personal name and used it frequently, he did not know that Satan was "the devil," and that he could not thus have identified him here. Such a notion is outrageously fantastic. Note the following deduction that such a theory (if accepted) would require:

The pseudonymous writer who allegedly forged Ephesians in Paul's name is represented as one "deeply imbued with the mind and spirit of the great apostle, closely acquainted with his letters, etc."[19] Of course, this unknown fraud also had to be a *great genius* ever to come up with the kind of world-shaking truth revealed in this epistle; and yet, this great genius who knew all about Paul was stupid enough to say "devil" instead of Satan, which it is alleged Paul *never* did! Thus the thoretical genius was a stupid ass, after all. The evil critics of God's word will have to come up with something a lot more reasonable than this to deserve any credibility whatever. Besides all that, the writer of Hebrews (2:14) used the word "devil"; and the conviction of this writer that Paul wrote that epistle is continually strengthened by further studies of the word of God. Paul's use of the word "devil" in this passage has its bearing in that same direction. The whole critical word game of counting and cataloging words is, in its entirety, artificial, contrived and absolutely undependable. *Any writer may use words in any letter that he never used before!* Of course, they talk about "probability"; but what is the

---

[18]Francis W. Beare, *op. cit.,* p. 737.
[19]*Ibid.,* p. 600.

"probability" that any fraudulent forger could have produced a book like Ephesians?

"The wiles of the devil . . ." This refers to the strategems employed by the evil one with the design of destroying the faith of Christians. Paul was familiar with many of the devices by which Satan had sought to hinder and thwart his apostolical labors. He mentioned a glaring instance of this (1 Thess. 2:18), knew that the most intimate human relationships could be exploited to the detriment of Christianity (1 Cor. 7:5), and pointed out that the devil could even take the form of an angel of light so as to lead believers away from the truth (2 Cor. 11:3, 14).

So-called "moderns" who are so far above the word of God that they reject all possibility of an unseen kingdom of evil presided over by a malignant personal foe (Satan), are not "wise" in any sense, but are blinded and deceived by "the god of this world."

Verse 12, *For our wrestling is not against flesh and blood but against principalities, against the powers, against the world-rulers of this darkness, against the spiritual host of wickedness in the heavenly places.*

In this verse, Paul described the spiritual enemy. He had already mentioned the "devil"; but Satan has many allies, "the spiritual hosts of wickedness." It is an unpardonable error to suppose that Paul here had any reference to the mythological gods of the Greeks and Romans, or to any of the complicated theories of vain speculators regarding the unseen creation. Of *them*, Paul affirmed *nothing*. It is a fact beyond denial that the ancient pagan world was organized along patterns of evil, and the whole pagan complex of antiquity was fitted together, dovetailed and interwoven in such a manner as to forbid the notion that such a sprawling, powerful, effective and arrogant pagan society was merely accidental. Satan had organized it. Furthermore, evil is still organized; and organization presupposes an organizer.

"Principalities . . ." There are various dominions of evil, that is, certain classifications of it. Paul's use of some of these words here appears to be figurative; nevertheless, there were and are genuine realities behind them.

"World-rulers of this darkness . . ." Barry interpreted this as a "poetic expression of the idea conveyed by the expression 'prince of this world,' applied by Jesus himself to Satan (John 12:31; 14:30; 16:11)."[20] The power of Satan is limited to them who yield themselves to do evil; and in no sense does Satan share ultimate authority with God. This whole passage, including the discussion of the armor, is figurative, setting forth the Christian's struggle against evil as a warfare; and this passage is a description of the foe.

In heavenly places . . ." This expression, as Paul used it, sometimes means "in the very presence of God," but in others it is limited to what might be called, loosely, the Christian religion; and it is so limited here. Satan is not conducting any war in heaven against God! However, religion, in the broad sense, provides a very extensive and convenient field of satanic operations, the great apostasy itself having been produced in the church herself.

Verse 13, *Wherefore, take up the whole armor of God that ye may be able to withstand in the evil day, and, having done all, to stand.*

The nature of the Christian warfare is further evident in this. It is not so much an attack against evil, as it is a warding off and foiling of evil's attack against the Christian which is indicated by the emphasis upon "stand." The forces of evil on earth have been mightily offended and wounded by the gospel of Christ; bitterness and hatred against the truth are to be expected everywhere.

"In the evil day . . ." The notion that Paul here referred to "the time which the horoscope has designated as dangerous, when the unlucky star is in the ascendant,"[21] is ludicrous. Nothing could have been any further from the mind of the apostle! What is meant, of course, is the day of crisis or decision; and, as Hendriksen pointed out: "In order to stand one's ground in the day of evil or crisis, let him stand his ground *today!*"[22]

---

[20]Alfred Barry, *Ellicott's Commentary on the Whole Bible,* Vol. VIII (Grand Rapids: Zondervon Publishing House, 1959), p. 57.

[21]Francis W. Beare, *op. cit.,* p. 739.

[22]William Hendriksen, *NT Commentary, Ephesians* (Grand Rapids: Baker Book House, 1967), p. 286.

Over and beyond this, there also looms the certainty of the final judgment on the last day.

Verses 14-17, *Stand therefore, having girded your loins with truth, and having put on the breastplate of righteousness, and having shod your feet with the preparation of the gospel of peace; withal taking up the shield of faith, wherewith ye shall be able to quench all the fiery darts of the evil one. And take the helmet of salvation, and the sword of the Spirit, which is the word of God.*

"Which is the word of God . . ." These last six words are descriptive, not merely of the sword of the Spirit, but of the whole armor of God, and of each several part of it also. Note the following:

TRUTH . . . What is this, if it is not the sacred word?

RIGHTEOUSNESS . . . The Biblical definition of righteousness is "all the commandments of God" (Ps. 119:172).

THE GOSPEL OF PEACE . . . This is the word of God.

FAITH . . . "Faith comes by hearing God's word" (Rom. 10:17).

SALVATION . . . Paul wrote to Timothy that "From a babe thou hast learned the sacred writings which are able to make thee wise unto salvation" (2 Tim. 3:15). Thus salvation comes only of the sacred writings which are the word of God.

THE WORD OF GOD . . . This is also the sword of the Spirit.

No passage in all the Bible any more dramatically teaches the absolute necessity of the Christian's thorough knowledge of the word of God. Not having it, he is naked, barefooted, bareheaded and helpless before the enemy.

From *Pilgrim's Progress*, it will be recalled that the armor with which the Christian was outfitted in the House Beautiful had no protection for his back. Christians are not protected if they flee from the foe; they are expected to stand against every attack.

"The sword of the Spirit . . ." It should be noted, especially, that the word of God is the means by which God's Spirit enables Christians to stand against the enemy and overcome. There is nothing here to support the view that God's Spirit, apart from the word of God, will ever enable the child of God to overcome. Our generation needs to return to the word of God.

Verse 18, *With all prayer and supplication praying at all seasons in the Spirit, and watching thereunto in all perseverance and supplication for all the saints.*

As Hendriksen noted, the word "all" is used four times in this verse.[23]

ALL kinds of prayers and supplications are to be used: public prayers, private prayers, intercessory prayers, prayers of thanksgiving, every kind!

ALL seasons are the season of prayer: all times of the day, all conditions and circumstances, all occasions, all states of mind, etc.

ALL perseverance: through times of discouragment or defeat when it seems that all is lost, when victory has smiled or when it has failed . . . let nothing hinder the prayer life.

ALL the saints are to be remembered in prayer. What an intercessor was Paul. His letters abound with the word that he is praying for those whom he remembers and for those who will receive his letters.

Even though the Christian has put on the whole armor of God, he cannot win the victory except through a constant reliance upon prayer. A prayerless Christian is a contradiction of terms.

Verse 19, *And on my behalf, that utterance may be given unto me in opening my mouth to make known with boldness the mystery of the gospel.*

As Paul constantly prayed for others, he earnestly desired that others should constantly pray for him. The reason why he felt especially in need of prayer was stated in the next verse. He was an ambassador of the Highest, yet he was chained to a Roman soldier; but Paul was not intimidated by the disparity between his true status and that which might have seemed to be his status. Chained though he was, Paul, in those letters he was dispatching from his Roman cell, was destroying the great pagan empire; and there can be little doubt that Paul fully understood this.

"The mystery of the gospel . . ." This is another reference to the mystery of Christ, the mystery of God, etc., as Paul variously identified it. See under 1:9, above.

Verse 20, *For which I am an ambassador in chains; that in it I may speak boldly, as I ought to speak.*

---

[23]*Ibid.,* p. 280.

See under preceding verse. This was during Paul's first imprisonment in Rome, "during which Colossians, Philemon, Ephesians and Philippians were written; and, although not as severe as his second imprisonment, he was nevertheless a prisoner."[24] From Acts 28:20, it is inferred that Paul was continually chained to a guard.

Paul did not pray for the easement of his burden, but for the grace to proclaim the word of God boldly in spite of it.

Verses 21-22, *But that ye also may know my affairs, how I do, Tychicus, the beloved brother and faithful minister in the Lord, shall make known unto you all things: whom I have sent unto you for this very purpose, that ye may know our state, and that he may comfort your hearts.*

This message is nearly identical with Colossians 4:7f, indicating that Tychicus was also the bearer of other letters besides this one. Tychicus was a native of Asia (Acts 20:4), is named among the delegates to the Gentile churches who went with Paul to Jerusalem, and was mentioned as a messenger of Paul in 2 Timothy 4:12 and Titus 3:12. Bruce observed that, "On the present occasion, he was probably Paul's special envoy to churches in the province of Asia which were planted in the course of Paul's Ephesian ministry."[25]

"Whom I have sent . . ." This may sound strange, since Tychicus was still with Paul when this was written. "This is the epistolary aorist tense . . . at the time they read this letter, he will have been sent."[26]

Verses 23-24, *Peace be to the brethren, and love with faith, from the Father and the Lord Jesus Christ. Grace be with all them that love our Lord Jesus Christ with a love incorruptible.*

Hendriksen's noble comment on these verses is:

The peace that passes all understanding, the love that is the greatest of the three greatest, and the faith that overcomes the world, these three precious treasures *are given away* to any one who sincerely requests them of God the Father and the Lord Jesus Christ.[27]

---

[24]*Ibid.*, p.282.
[25]F. F. Bruce, *op. cit.*, p. 135.
[26] Alfred Martin, *op. cit.*, p. 753.
[27]William Hendriksen, *op. cit.*, p. 286.

The significant thing here, of course is the reverse order in which Paul's favorite words are enumerated. In Romans 1:7, 1 Corinthians 1:3, 2 Corinthians 1:2, Galatians 1:3, and Colossians 1:2 — in all these, the order of the words is invariably "grace," then "peace." Here it is the other way; and, as Dummelow said, "An imitator would have copied the other epistles in this."[28] No one but Paul himself would have dared reverse the order of these words; therefore, this conspicuous departure from his usual mode of expression has, in this instance, the impact of an apostolical signature.

"Love incorruptible . . ." What an amazing word is this!

It is those who love with an imperishable love that are meant: there must be neither decrease nor decay; and "those who were chosen in him before the foundation of the world" (1:4) retain their love for him undiminished after the world itself has passed away![29]

---

[28]J. R. Dummelow, *op. cit.,* p. 966.
[29]William Hendriksen, *op. cit.,* p. 286.

BIBLIOGRAPHY . . . EPHESIANS

The following authors and sources were quoted in the text of the commentary on Ephesians:

Barclay, William, *The Letters to the Galatians and Ephesians* (Philadelphia: The Westminster Press, 1954).

Barry, Alfred, *Ellicott's Commentary on the Whole Bible,* Vol. VIII (Grand Rapids: Zondervan Publishing House, 1959).

Barth, Marcus, *The Broken Wall* (London: Collins, 1960).

Beare, Francis W., *Interpreter's Bible,* Vol. X. (New York: Abingdon Press, 1953).

Blaikie, W. G., *Pulpit Commentary,* Vol. 20, *Ephesians* (Grand Rapids: Wm. B. Eerdmans Publishing Company, 1950).

Bruce, F. F., *The Epistle to the Ephesians* (Old Tappan, N.J.: Fleming H. Revell Co., 1961).

Clarke, Adam, *Commentary on the Whole Bible* (London: Carlton and Porter, 1829), Vol. VI.

Foulkes, Frances, *Tyndale NT Commentaries, Ephesians* (Grand Rapids: Wm. B. Eerdmans Publishing Company, 1963).

Harpur, George E., *NT Commentary, Ephesians* (Grand Rapids: Zondervan Publishing House, 1969).

Hayes, D. A., *Paul and His Epistles* (Grand Rapids: Baker Book House, 1969).

Hendriksen, William, *NT Commentary, Ephesians* (Grand Rapids: Baker Book House, 1967).

Howard, George, article: "The Faith of Christ" in *Expository Times,* Vol. 7, April, 1974.

Lipscomb, David, *NT Commentary, Ephesians* (Nashville: Gospel Advocate Company, 1939).

Mackay, John, *God's Order* (New York: The Macmillan Company, 1953).

Macknight, James, *Apostolical Epistles with Commentary and Notes, Ephesians* (Grand Rapids: Baker Book House, 1969).

Martin, Alfred, *Wycliffe Bible Commentary, NT* (Chicago: Moody Press, 1971).

Robinson, J. Armitage, *St. Paul's Epistle to the Ephesians* (London: The Macmillan Company, 1903).

Russell, John William, *Compact Commentary on the NT* (Grand Rapids: Baker Book House, 1964).

Taylor, Willard H., *Beacon Bible Commentary,* Vol. IX (Kansas City: Beacon Hill Press, 1965).

Vine, W. E., *An Expository Dictionary of NT Words* (Old Tappan, N.J.: Fleming H. Revell Co., 1940).

Wedell, Theodore O., *Interpreter's Bible,* Vol. X (Nashville: Abingdon Press, 1953).

Wesley, John, *One Volume NT Commentary* (Grand Rapids: Baker Book House, 1972).

Philippians

INTRODUCTION

The city of Philippi: (a) the pre-Christian history of this place dates back to Philip II of Macedon (382-336 B.C.),[1] father of Alexander the Great. The location of the place figured prominently in its early history. Philip II, the first undisputed master of ancient Macedonia, decided to expand his kingdom and needed the financial muscle to do it. The gold mines of Mt. Pangaeus would provide it. Therefore, he took over a very ancient village on the mountain slopes, *Krenides* (meaning *springs*), named it Philippi, made a city out of it and established himself as undisputed owner of the vast wealth of the gold mines of Pangaeus which yielded over one thousand talents of gold a year, really an incredibly large sum of money. Using his great wealth for purposes of bribery and for the perfection of the military phalanx which he had invented, Philip soon had the power to take the world of his day, a project he was not permitted to finish, due to his murder in 336 B.C.; but he left the twin instruments of the military and the gold by which his son Alexander the Great would effect his conquest of the entire world.

Roman domination of Philippi followed their winning the battle of Pydna (168 B.C.); but the failure of the gold mines drastically reduced the size and importance of it. In 42 B.C., the decisive battle between imperialists Octavius and Anthony and the supporters of the republic, Cassius and Brutus, took place near Philippi, resulting in the establishment of the empire and elevation of Octavius as Caesar Augustus by the Roman senate some 15 years later.[2] It was this battle which focused the attention of Augustus upon Philippi, leading to his making it a Roman colony, settling some of his retired soldiers upon the surrounding lands, and lavishing Roman money upon the rebuilding and enlargement of it.

A Roman colony in those times was a fortunate city, subsidized by the imperial treasury, honored with all kinds of privileges, exemption from taxes, freedom from the regulations of the provincial governors, and political autonomy with regard

---

[1]*Encyclopaedia Britannica,* Vol. 17, p. 724.
[2]*ISBE,* p. 2369.

to an extensive list of their personal affairs. The meanest citizen
of a place like Philippi would have been conscious of the dignity
and favorable status of his city. The local rulers took titles like
the great lords in Rome; the people wore Roman costumes;
theaters and stadiums, built after Roman models, featured the
same kind of entertainment seen in the capital. Following the
battle of Actium (September 2, 31 B.C.),[3] Augustus, firmly
enthroned with absolute power, constituted Philippi a colony,
"settling it with partisans of Antony, his final rival, who were
evicted from Italy."[4] This very interesting and significant fact
illuminates Paul's analogy of "our citizenship is in heaven"
(3:20). Christians are like the citizens, those partisans of Antony,
who had been banished from Rome and were living, with certain
privileges of course, in a hostile environment, but whose hearts
were still in Rome.

(b) In the times when Paul, Luke, Timothy and Silas entered
Philippi with the gospel (50 A.D.), a hundred years of imperial
patronage had endowed Philippi with an importance consistent
with its strategic location as a mighty bastion of Roman power
in Macedonia. Philippi dominated the trade routes, and was a
sectional headquarters of the famed Roman road, the Egnatian
Way,[5] the great 500-mile-long highway from the Adriatic sea
through Thrace to the Bosphorus, located some ten miles inland
from the town of Neapolis (new town). Luke referred to the place
as "the first of the district" (Acts 16:12), leading to the supposition that Luke was a citizen of Philippi.

(c) The glorious history of the Philippian church was not to
continue indefinitely. Today, the place is not inhabited and is
marked by the ruins of an amphitheater and a great temple with
inscriptions.[6]

The character of the Philippians: Due to their history there
were traces of the humble virtues which marked Rome's early
history. The men were manly, the women womanly; and like the
centurions so often mentioned in the NT, many of them with
military background exhibited the stern qualities of rugged

---

[3]*Encyclopaedia Britannica*, Vol. 1, p. 134.
[4]E. M. Blaiklock, *Cities of the NT* (Old Tappan, N.J.: Fleming H. Revell Co.,
1965), p. 40.
[5]*Ibid.*
[6]*Encyclopaedia Britannica*, Vol. 17, p. 724.

dependability, honesty, liberality and faithfulness. The retired Roman soldiery of that period was a repository of the noblest virtues and qualities of life which had been handed down from the past, being a far different breed of men from the soft, reprobate society fostered by the Caesars. ISBE lists the following among the characteristic qualities of the Philippians of the times of Paul:

(a) It is the least Jewish of any of the places featured in the Pauline literature. It will be recalled that when Paul first preached there, no synagogue was available, indicating that there were fewer than ten Jews in Philippi. In place of it there was a place of prayer by the river.

(b) Women were very prominent in the congregation from the first, Lydia's home being the base of operations for Paul's evangelism of the city. This is consistent with what we know of the status of women in Macedonian society."[7] Some believe that the slave-girl, out of whom Paul cast the Python spirit, was also a member, although the NT does not support this view. Significantly, Luke gave much more attention to women in his gospel than others gave, and this could have been due to his background as a citizen of Philippi. Kennedy observed that, "From the evidence of the epistle, devoted women of heathen extraction (as their names show; see 4:2) stood in the forefront of Christian work; and this was not peculiar to Philippi."[8]

(c) The hardness and dependability of Macedonian men who were part of the Philippian church were commented upon by Hausrath, who said, "They represented the noblest and soundest part of the ancient world. 'Ye have always obeyed' (2:12) . . . They were men of sterner mold than could be found in Asia Minor."[9]

(d) Diversity marked the Philippian population. "The converts doubtless manifested the same diversity of nationality and the same differences in social position."[10] There were elements of the old pagan populations, residual elements of the Roman military, tradesmen (such as Lydia) and members of the Imperial Civil Service.

---

[7]*ISBE*, p. 2372.
[8]H. A. A. Kennedy, *The Expositor's Greek New Testament* (Grand Rapids: Wm. B. Eerdmans Publishing Company, 1967), Vol. iii, p. 401.
[9]*ISBE*, p. 2372.
[10]*Ibid.*, p. 2373.

(e) The population, as well as the converts, were derived from deeply religious stock, the religious zeal of the Philippians being attested even by the excavations in that area. As Kennedy observed:

> The rocks near the ancient site of Philippi are a "veritable museum of mythology." There are traces of a temple dedicated to Silvanus, one of the most popular deities of the Imperial epoch . . . an Oriental god Mên had his votaries there, and the most revered of the sanctuaries of Dionysus, favorite Thracian divinity, was also there.[11]

(f) An extraordinary liberality characterized them. "Even Paul was astonished at their giving, declaring that they gave out of much affliction, that they abounded in giving, and that they were rich only in their liberality (2 Cor. 8:2)."[12] This very letter of Philippians is a monument to their devoted Christian giving. Surely, adding all these qualities together, one finds it easy to see why Paul had a special place in his heart for these Philippians.

Founding of the church at Philippi: A full account of this is found in Acts 16th chapter; and extended comments were made on all of the interesting events of that founding in CA, chapter 16. Although, as Blaiklock reminded us, "It cannot be stated with certainty that Philippi saw the first preaching of Christianity in Europe,"[13] there being the definite possibility that Christ was preached in Rome before Paul's arrival at Phillipi; nevertheless, the success of the gospel at Philippi is definitely the first in Europe of which we have so full and vivid an account. An additional sidelight on Paul's release from imprisonment in Philippi by the magistrates was given thus, by Hendriksen:

> Can it be that the Codex Bezae is correct when it suggests that the authorities had seen a connection between the earthquake and the missionaries, and that in their fear they had arrived at the conclusion that Paul and Silas were what they claimed to be?[14]

This is a very plausible possibility and should be noted in connection with Acts 16th chapter.

---

[11]H. A. A. Kennedy, *op. cit.,* p. 400.

[12]*ISBE,* p. 2373.

[13]E. M. Blaiklock, *op. cit.,* p. 42.

[14]William Hendriksen, *NT Commentary, Philippians* (Grand Rapids: Baker Book House, 1962), p. 14.

Authorship and canonicity of Philippians. Very little needs to be said about this, "The Pauline authorship of Philippians has not been seriously questioned by reputable scholars."[15] "Of the genuineness of this epistle there can be no shadow of doubt."[16] "In no case is Pauline authorship doubted."[17] There is no need to multiply testimony to the generally accepted truth of Paul having indeed been the author of Philippians. On some minor points, however, the unity of the epistle has been questioned as, for example, in the allegation of the great Christology of chapter 2 being quoted from a popular Christian hymn of the earliest era. We disagree with Foulkes who thought that "We should regard 2:6-11 as a hymn with the humiliation and exaltation of Christ as its theme."[18] See comment under those verses for reasons why the hymn theory is rejected, the principal one of course being that there is simply no evidence whatever to support it.

Answers to criticisms: (a) The mention of "elders and deacons" in 1:1 is alleged as proof of a late first-century date of the epistle; but such allegations are founded in scholarly ignorance of the truth that Paul ordained elders in every church he planted on the very first missionary journey (Acts 14:23), and that long before that the elders were governing the congregation in Jerusalem (Acts 11:30). The critical notion that the development of the church organization was a later first-century development is rejected.

(b) The epistle shows traces of Gnosticism (2:5-8); but as Hendriksen said, "Such a weird interpretation contradicts the context."[19]

(c) The epistle is a post-Pauline attempt to reconcile Jewish-Christian and Gentile-Christian parties, typified respectively by Euodia and Syntyche (4:2); but the context plainly reveals that both of these names apply to women who belonged to the congregation in Philippi and that neither one of them had ever headed a party opposed to Paul, being on the contrary "laborers together" with him!

---

[15]John A. Knight, *Beacon Bible Commentary,* Vol. IX, *Philippians* (Kansas City: Beacon Hill Press, 1965), p. 281.

[16]B. C. Caffin, *Pulpit Commentary,* Vol. 20, *Phillipians* (Grand Rapids: Wm. B. Eerdmans Publishing Company, 1950), p. xii.

[17]Frances Foulkes, *New Bible Commentary, Revised* (Grand Rapids: Wm. B. Eerdmans Publishing Company, 1970), p. 1127.

[18]*Ibid.*

[19]William Hendriksen, *op. cit.,* p. 31.

Date and occasion of writing: Caffin made the date to be "thirty years after the ascension and ten years after the founding of the Philippian congregation," that is, in the year 60 A.D.[20] Dummelow thought it was written in 61 or 62;[21] Barry placed the writing of it as 62, or 63;[22] the view accepted in this series was ably expressed by Kennedy as follows:

> C. H. Turner writing in Hastings Bible Dictionary on *Chronology of the NT* adopted 58 as the year of the recall of Felix and the arrival of Festus in the province of Judaea; Paul would thus have reached Rome in 59; hence, in all likelihood, Philippians was written towards the close of the year 61.[23]

This view also agrees with that of Hewlett who placed the writing of this epistle within the years of Paul's imprisonment mentioned in Acts 28:39, carrying with it also the affirmation that Philippians was written from Rome.[24] The recent speculations as to its having been written from Caesarea or Ephesus have failed to impress this writer as having any validity whatever. As Kennedy said, "It is all but universally agreed that this epistle was written in Rome."[25]

From the above it is clear that Philippians is one of the four prison epistles: Philippians, Colossians, Philemon, and Ephesians, three of these "in all probability being dispatched at the same time to their respective destinations by the hand of Tychichus,"[26] leaving the question of whether Philippians was before or after the three. Despite the learned arguments of Lightfoot to the effect that Philippians was earlier than the three, the position that seems most probable was thus enunciated by Kennedy, "Paul expected a speedy termination of his case";[27] and that brings us near to the end of the period of imprisonment, thus making Philippians later, not earlier, than the other three.

---

[20]B. C. Caffin, *op. cit.,* p. i.

[21]J. R. Dummelow, *Commentary on the Holy Bible* (New York: The Macmillan Company, 1937), p. 967.

[22]Alfred Barry, *Ellicott's Commentary on the Whole Bible,* Vol. III, *Philippians* (Grand Rapids: Zondervan Publishing House, 1959), p. 61.

[23]H. A. A. Kennedy, *op. cit.,* p. 406.

[24]H. C. Hewlett, *A NT Commentary, Philippians* (Grand Rapids: Zondervan Publishing House, 1969), p. 471.

[25]H. A. A. Kennedy, *op. cit.,* p. 403.

[26]William Hendriksen, *op. cit.,* p. 29.

[27]H. A. A. Kennedy, *op. cit.,* p. 405.

For those interested in extensive arguments to the contrary, reference is made to the monumental work of Bishop J. B. Lightfoot.

Theological value of Philippians: Despite the truth of this epistle being in the form of a somewhat rambling and informal personal letter, it has some of the profoundest teachings of Holy Writ. The great Christological passage of 2:6-11 "comes from a mind full of the grand conception of the glory of Christ . . . this and Philippians 3:9 go to show that the characteristic doctrines of St. Paul's Epistles were as far as possible from being abstract theorems or passing phases of thought."[28] They were practical, everyday doctrines appealed to here as the basis of Paul's exhortations, the fact of such eternal doctrines being already widely accepted in the church being implicit in this use of them.

Outline of Philippians: Full agreement with Dummelow is here expressed. He said, "The epistle does not admit of formal analysis."[29]

Special features of Philippians: The emphasis upon joy, the frequent use of "in Christ" or its equivalent, and the oft-repeated compound name of Lord Jesus Christ must be mentioned as special features. All of these will be duly noted in the notes on the text.

Why study Philippians? There are many reasons for studying all of God's word; but Hendriksen has an admonition on this question which richly deserves to be remembered and repeated:

1. It reveals the secret of true happiness; and how this secret may be obtained is clearly disclosed in this letter.

2. It reveals the man who had learned this secret. Philippians is one of the most personal of all Paul's letters.

3. It reveals the Christ who taught Paul this secret. Thus, there was in this letter revealed the true secret of one who could truly say: I'VE FOUND IT![30]

Abbreviations: See at the front of this volume.

---

[28]J. R. Dummelow, *op. cit.,* p. 968.
[29]*Ibid.*
[30]William Hendriksen, *op. cit.,* p. 3.

CHAPTER 1

This marvelous epistle begins, as Paul usually begins, with a salutation followed by thanksgiving and supplication upon behalf of the readers. The first chapter also records Paul's remarkable soliloquy. As pointed out in the Introduction, it is useless to divide this letter in the pattern of a classical outline. Philippians is not an essay or treatise of any kind but a personal letter to beloved friends; and it runs along in the same somewhat rambling fashion of any personal letter. Nevertheless, some of Paul's profoundest teaching is presented in this priceless little letter.

Verse 1, *Paul and Timothy, servants of Christ Jesus, to all the saints in Christ Jesus that are in Philippi, with the bishops and deacons.*

"Paul . . ." is the sole author of the epistle, the name of Timothy who was with him at the time being added as a courtesy. Also, Mounce noted, "Timothy might have acted as Paul's secretary."[1]

"Timothy . . ." This name is associated with that of Paul in several other Pauline letters (Colossians 1:1, Philemon 1:1, 2 Corinthians 1:1, and in both the Thessalonians 1:1). Timothy was deeply interested in the Philippians, having been with Paul when their congregation was established (Acts 16:11-40), and in all probability having visited them again and again.

"Servants of Jesus Christ . . ." The word rendered "servants" here is actually "slaves"; but the sinister connotations of that word make the other rendering preferable. Paul's true authority as an apostle was fully known and recognized at Philippi, and therefore there was no need for his stressing the authority as he had done in Corinthians and Galatians. For some reason, Paul did not here distinguish between himself as an apostle and Timothy as a brother, but humbly wrote: "Paul and Timothy, servants of Christ Jesus." The word "slaves" which Paul used here is not as good a translation as "servants" because (in English) *slaves* carries the "associate ideas of involuntary service, forced

---

[1]Robert H. Mounce, *Wycliffe Bible Commentary* (Chicago: Moody Press, 1971), p. 756.

subjection and even harsh treatment,"[2] none of which are applicable to the servants of Christ.

"To all the saints . . . at Philippi . . ." As Barclay said, "*Saint* is a misleading quotation."[3] It carries the idea of stained glass windows and a higher mortal sanctity; but in the NT usage of the word, "It does not designate any high level of ethical achievement, but persons who in Christ have been set apart unto the new life."[4] Thus it indicates the goals, rather than the attainments of Christians. It is clear enough that Paul used "saints" as a designation for all Christians, and that it denoted living members of the body of Christ.

"All . . ." Lipscomb commented on the importance of this word as found here, and in 1:2, 7, 8, and 25, 2:17, and 4:21 as attesting the "beautiful spirit of unity"[5] at Philippi.

"With the bishops and deacons . . ." Some scholars have attempted to late-date Philippians, supposing that there was no clear-cut organization in the primitive churches until post-apostolical times; but such efforts are ill-founded, being based on false premises. Elders of the church were ordained on the very first missionary tour Paul made (Acts 14:23); and, even before that, the government of a church by its elders is clearly evident in Acts 11:30. As for the fact that Paul did not usually mention the deacons and elders, as he did here, there was without any doubt a reason for it. Macknight pointed out that most of Paul's letters were addressed to the Christians, not their officers, in order to prevent "the bishops and deacons from imagining that the apostolical writings were their property, and that it belonged to them to communicate what part of them to the people that they saw fit."[6] Not even any prior right of interpretation pertained to bishops and deacons.

"Bishops . . ." In the NT, this term is synonymous with *elders* and *shepherds*. "It is a fact now recognized by theologians of all

---

[2]William Hendriksen, *NT Commentary, Philippians* (Grand Rapids: Baker Book House, 1962), p. 44.

[3]William Barclay, *The Letters to the Philippians, Colossians and Thessalonians* (Philadelphia: The Westminster Press, 1975), p. 10.

[4]Robert H. Mounce, *op. cit.,* p. 756.

[5]David Lipscomb, *A Commentary on the NT Epistles*, Volume IV (Nashville: The Gospel Advocate Company, 1964), p. 156.

[6]James Macknight, *Apostolical Epistles with Commentary,* Volume III (Grand Rapids: Baker Book House, 1969), p. 402.

shades of opinion that in the NT the same officer in the church is indifferently called bishop (overseer) or presbyter (elder) . . . the one a term of dignity, the other of age."[7] There are six (perhaps seven) NT synonyms for the title that belonged to the NT office. They are:

> Bishop (translated overseer).
> Presbyter (translated elder).
> Pastor (translated shepherd).
> Steward (Titus 1:7).

Significantly, there were a plurality of bishops in Philippi, demonstrating the fact that no such thing as the "metropolitan bishop" of later ages was evident there when Paul wrote these lines.

As for the reason why Paul elected to mention these congregational officers in this letter, it was probably connected with the gift of money which he had received from that church, a gift which, in all probability, was suggested, administered and dispatched by the elders and deacons, thus making it very appropriate that they would have been greeted in this salutation.

"Deacons . . ." These officers are not mentioned elsewhere in the NT, except in 1 Timothy 3:8, 12ff; but many scholars insist on tracing their work back to Acts 6:2.[8] The word from which this is rendered is also translated "servant" or "minister" in the NT.

Verse 2, *Grace to you and peace from God our Father and the Lord Jesus Christ.*

Frequent comments on this characteristic Pauline greeting have been made in this series of commentaries. For example, see CR 1:1 and CC, 1 Corinthians 1:2. Scholars are inclined to make a big thing out of the order of "grace" and "peace" as they appear in most of Paul's greetings. As Boice said, "The final point is this: grace comes before peace . . . . In God's order of things God's hand is always there before any spiritual blessings."[9] True as such an observation be, however, it may be doubted that Paul

---

[7] J. B. Lightfoot, *St. Paul's Epistle to the Philippians* (Grand Rapids: Zondervan Publishing House, 1963), pp. 95, 98.

[8] Frances Foulkes, *New Bible Commentary, Revised* (Grand Rapids: Wm. B. Eerdmans Publishing Company, 1970), p. 1129.

[9] James Montgomery Boice, *Philippians* (Grand Rapids: Zondervan Publishing House, 1971), p. 32.

consciously intended this understanding of these words as used in his salutations. Significantly, Paul reversed them in Ephesians 6:23, 24. See comment under those verses.

Verses 3-5, *I thank my God upon all my remembrance of you, always in every supplication of mine on behalf of you all making my supplication with joy, for your fellowship in furtherance of the gospel from the first day until now.*

Significant in this apostolical prayer is the absence from it of any list of things Paul needed to receive from God, and the predominance of those things for which Paul felt the need of giving thanks to God! Paul's prayers were more like a list of things he has already received and for which thanksgiving was offered. One is struck with the startling difference of many prayers heard today.

"With joy . . ." Joy is the key word of Philippians; and Barclay has given a beautiful outline of the joy Paul communicated in this loving letter:

CHRISTIAN JOY INCLUDES:

The joy of prayer (1:4)
The joy that Jesus Christ is preached (1:18).
The joy of faith (1:25).
The joy of seeing Christians in fellowship together (2:2).
The joy of suffering for Christ (2:17).
The joy of news of a loved one (2:28).
The joy of Christian hospitality (2:29).
The joy of the man who has been baptized into Christ (3:1, 4:1).
The joy of the man who has won one soul for the Lord (4:1).
The joy inherent in every gift (4:10), this being not in regard
    merely to its value but to the fact of another's caring.[10]

Christian joy is an emotion unspeakably higher than that which may be occasioned by mirth, pleasure, fun, hilarity, gladness, laughter, delight, and the whole family of related emotions unworthy to be compared to Christian joy, that glorious emotion which is not only eternal but sacred, pure and holy as well.

In verses 3-5, Paul's words seem to be more than usually earnest and impassioned. He dwells long and fondly on the subject; "He repeats words and accumulates clauses in the intensity of his feeling."[11]

---

[10]William Barclay, *op. cit.,* p. 13.
[11]J. B. Lightfoot, *op. cit.,* p. 82.

"For your fellowship . . ." Many have written on the techni-cal meaning of this word as inclusive of liberality and many other virtues, such as sharing; but Boice has a priceless note on it thus:

> Fellowship means more than a sharing of something, like the fellowship of bank robbers dividing the loot. It means a sharing *in* something, participating in something greater than the people involved and more lasting than the activity of any given moment . . . it means being caught up into a communion created by God![12]

"You all . . ." (v. 3) is the plural of *you*, there being no other definite plural of this word in the English language, "you both," "you three," etc., being definite and limited. It is used nine times in Philippians.

"From the first day until now . . ." "This refers to the first day of Paul's preaching in Philippi (Acts 16:13)."[13] Amazingly, this church had contributed financially to Paul's support throughout their acquaintance with the apostle. All men should take this lesson to heart. The true extent of one's love of the Lord is measured by "the amount of sacrifice he is prepared to make to help in the progress of the gospel."[14]

Henriksen's analysis of the characteristics of that "fellow-ship" enjoyed by those "in Christ" reveals it as:

> A fellowship of grace, of faith, in prayer and thanksgiving, of believers with each other, in love one for another, in help-ing each other, of contributing to each other's needs, of help-ing promote the gospel, of separation from the world, and of that eternal warfare of believers struggling side by side against a common foe.[15]

Verse 6, *Being confident of this very thing, that he who began a good work in you will perfect it until the day of Jesus Christ.*

Paul does not here refer to himself as the founder of the church at Philippi, though in a sense he *was* the founder. Paul, however, preferred to give the glory to God, recognizing the

---

[12]James Montgomery Boice, *op. cit.,* p. 36.

[13]James William Russell, *Compact Commentary on the NT* (Grand Rapids: Baker Book House, 1964), p. 487.

[14]R. P. Martin, *The Tyndale NT Commentaries, Philippians* (Grand Rapids: Wm. B. Eerdmans Publishing Company, 1959), p. 61.

[15]William Hendriksen, *op. cit.,* p. 52.

Father as the one who actually converted them and brought them to a saving knowledge of the Saviour.

Boice flatly declared that this verse is one "of the three greatest in the Bible,"[16] teaching the doctrine of the final perseverance of the saints. This student, however, fails to find any suggestion of such a doctrine in this passage. It should be noted here that Paul's confidence was not in the Philippians but in God. It was the conduct of those Philippians up to that point which inspired Paul with confidence concerning their ultimate destiny. As Hendriksen put it:

> Your perseverance in sympathetic participation in the work of the gospel (v. 5) has convinced me that you are the objects of divine preservation (v. 6). These two must not be separated.[17]

It is true that God did foreordain and predestinate *such souls* to eternal life; but there was absolutely nothing in God's so doing to *compel* the Philippians to be *such souls!* That is not what Paul declared here; but rather his declaration is that the evidence proved the Philippians to be *such souls,* as attested by their conduct throughout his acquaintance with them, and that God would surely reward them eternally, such a confidence, of course, being contingent upon the fact of the Philippians continuing to be *such souls.*

"Until the day of Jesus Christ . . ." This can hardly be anything except the final day of the Second Advent of Christ, called in the NT "the judgment." That is "the day" toward which all the world moves. It is a gross mistake, however, to read this, as Paul's expecting the Second Coming in the lifetime of his Philippian converts. As Lightfoot said, "It must not be hastily inferred from this that St. Paul confidently expected the Lord's advent during the lifetime of his Philippian converts."[18]

Verse 7, *Even as it is right for me to be thus minded on behalf of you all, because I have you in my heart, inasmuch as, both in my bonds and in the defence and confirmation of the gospel, ye are all partakers with me of grace.*

"You all . . ." See under verse 5, above.

---

[16]James Montgomery Boice, *op. cit.,* p. 40.
[17]William Hendriksen, *op. cit.,* p. 51.
[18]J. B. Lightfoot, *op. cit.,* p. 84.

"I have you in my heart . . ." Paul's deep affection for the Philippians is easy to understand. Nothing caused them to waver in their constant help of his preaching mission. Not even Paul's imprisonment had caused them to cut off their support.

"Partakers with me of grace . . ." As Mounce said, "They were partakers with Paul in grace, not partakers of Paul's grace."[19]

Verse 8, *For God is my witness, how I long after you all in the tender mercies of Christ Jesus.*

The rendition here is a vast improvement over the AV, the verse being a remarkable witness of the Christian's unity with the Lord, and, in fact, his identity with the Lord. Many scholars have been struck with the impact of this passage. Caffin stated the implications of the verse thus: "Not I, but Christ liveth in me. Paul is so united with Christ that he feels with the heart of Christ and loves with the love of Christ."[20] Lightfoot paraphrased it as follows:

> Did I speak of having you in my heart? I should rather have said that in the heart of Christ Jesus I long for you. This is a powerful metaphor describing perfect union. The believer has no yearnings apart from his Lord; his pulse beats with the pulse of Christ; his heart throbs with the heart of Christ.[21]

Paul's profession of love for the Philippians was genuine; and, as Calvin said, "It tends in no small degree to secure faith in the doctrine when the people are persuaded that they are loved by the teacher."[22]

Verse 9, *And this I pray, that your love may abound yet more and more in knowledge and in all discernment.*

Pink's amazing deductions from this verse are to the effect that in contrast to the amazing love of the Philippians, they had an inadequate understanding of the mind of Christ, and that Paul longed for a better balance in their characters. "Therefore he prayed (not as most of *us* need to pray — that our love may be in proportion to our light) but that their intelligence may be

---

[19]Robert H. Mounce, *op. cit.,* p. 758.
[20]B. C. Caffin, *Pulpit Commentary,* Vol. 20, *Philippians* (Grand Rapids: Wm. B. Eerdmans Publishing Company, 1950), p. 3.
[21]J. B. Lightfoot, *op. cit.,* p. 85.
[22]William Hendriksen, *op. cit.,* p. 57.

commensurate with their affections."[23] He compared the Philippians to certain simple but sincere Christians of all ages whose affections exceeded their knowledge. Their state, if such is the proper understanding of it, was just the opposite of that of the Corinthians whose vaunted "knowledge" contrasted with their inadequate love one of another.

"That your love may abound . . ." The Greek word rendered "love" here is *agape*, not *eros* or *philo*.[24] Despite any deficiencies in their "knowledge," Paul heartily approved of the abounding love of the Philippians.

Verse 10, *So that ye may approve the things that are excellent; that ye may be sincere and void of offence unto the day of Christ.*

"Approve the things which are excellent . . ." This is very similar to "distinguish things that differ" as Paul wrote in Romans 2:18; and both here and there, "It is impossible to decide exactly what Paul means."[25] One thing is evident, Paul wanted the Philippians to grow in knowledge in order to avoid offense in living the Christian life. Russell thought that Paul's words in 4:8 show what is meant by "the things which are excellent," as used here.[26]

"Sincere . . ." It has often been pointed out that this word is derived from two Latin words, *sin* (without) and *cere* (wax). Italian marble vendors and certain merchants of porcelain fell into the habit of hiding flaws in their merchandise by filling cracks and blemishes with a certain kind of wax; but the more reputable dealers advertised their wares as *sin cere* (without wax); and from this derived the meaning of the English word "sincere." The true meaning of it is "without deception" or "without hypocrisy."

"Unto the day of Christ . . ." This is another reference to the judgment and final advent of Jesus our Lord.

Verse 11, *Being filled with the fruits of righteousness, which are through Jesus Christ, unto the glory and praise of God.*

---

[23]Arthur W. Pink, *Gleanings From Paul* (Chicago: Moody Press, 1967), p. 200.

[24]John A. Knight, *Beacon Bible Commentary,* Vol. IX, *Philippians* (Kansas City: Beacon Hill Press, 1965), p. 295.

[25]John Murray, *The Epistle to the Romans* (Grand Rapids: Wm. B. Eerdmans Publishing Company, 1968), p. 82.

[26]James William Russell, *op. cit.,* p. 487.

As Pink said, "This verse, along with verse 10, sets before us a powerful incentive to live hourly with the judgment seat of Christ before us, . . . that we may not be ashamed at his coming."[27]

"Fruits of righteousness . . ." As Knight observed, "This righteousness is that by Jesus Christ in contrast to that which is by the law (3:9)."[28] In order, therefore, to have fruit of *that* righteousness, the believer must be "in Christ," identified with him. See under 3:9.

This expression also carries with it the idea of the end of the world being a harvest (Matt. 13:39) and a reaping (Gal. 6:4-9). Here Paul prayed upon behalf of the Philippians that "At that day they might appear filled with all the fruits of righteousness which are by Jesus Christ. What an incentive to holiness to keep *that* before us."[29]

Verse 12, *Now I would have you know, brethren, that the things which happened unto me have fallen out rather unto the progress of the gospel.*

"The things which happened unto me . . ." And what were those things? The last half of the book of Acts gives a great many of the near incredible things that happened unto Paul, revealing his life as an odyssey surpassing that of any other, save Christ alone, who ever lived on earth. In addition, 2 Corinthians 11:23-30 briefly mentions many other things not even hinted at in Acts. Only a man of the profoundest humility could have made this casual reference to such a list of sufferings and hardships as that which marked Paul's life. Rather than dwelling upon them here, Paul rejoices that the net result of all he has endured has been the spread of the gospel of Christ.

Verse 13, *So that my bonds became manifest in Christ throughout the whole praetorian guard, and to all the rest.*

"The praetorian guard . . ." The AV's rendition of this as "the palace," has been rejected on what appears to be sufficient grounds; but the mention of "saints in Caesar's household" (4:22) surely indicates that the word of the gospel was assuredly known "in the palace," whether or not this verse states the fact.

---

[27]Arthur W. Pink, *op. cit.,* p. 221.
[28]John A. Knight, *op. cit.,* p. 297.
[29]Arthur W. Pink, *op. cit.,* p. 221.

Lightfoot, especially, did extensive work to prove that "praetorian" as used here is reference to a body of men, and not to a place; and most commentators follow Lightfoot's lead on this. Despite this, the opinion persists that such a view could be challenged.

Paul, although blessed with some liberty, was nevertheless chained to a Roman soldier at all times, his captor being changed several times a day, and thus providing Paul with a captive audience which included, in time, practically the whole praetorian guard, a body of troops assigned to the person of the emperor. It is not hard to understand how Paul would have taken advantage of such an opportunity.

"And to all the rest . . ." This usually is understood as meaning the rest of the praetorian troops; but it might have a wider application to many others who were in Rome at that time. Hayes, understanding this as "the whole praetorian guard," stated that it must have taken some time for this to become possible.[30] This, of course, seems to place the writing of Philippians near the end of a period of imprisonment.

"My bonds became manifest in Christ . . ." This refers to the fact that the reasons for Paul's imprisonment became generally known as unconnected with any kind of crime or misdemeanor and derived solely from his faithfulness in preaching the gospel of Christ. Such a truth would have endeared him to many in the praetorian.

Verse 14, *And that most of the brethren in the Lord, being confident through my bonds, are more abundantly bold to speak the word of God without fear.*

Wesley explained the renewed vigor and courage of "most of the brethren in the Lord" as being due to the fact that "They saw in Paul, as they had never seen before, the presence, power and sufficient grace of Christ."[31]

The fact that such a notable character as Paul was permitted for at least a couple of years to continue day by day preaching the gospel while in the custody and control of the emperor's

---

[30]D. A. Hayes, *Paul and His Epistles* (Grand Rapids: Baker Book House, 1969), p. 431.

[31]John Wesley, *One Volume NT Commentary* (Grand Rapids: Baker Book House, 1972), *in loco.*

bodyguard very effectively spread the news abroad that it was safe to preach the word. However, those circumstances of relative tolerance of the gospel would before long give way to the great persecution under Nero. Paul would suffer martyrdom, and countless Christians would seal their faith with their blood. That Paul surely had premonitions of such a drastic change appears in this very letter (v. 20); but, for the moment, the grand apostle would glorify God, rejoicing in the opportunities to preach the word of salvation to all who would hear it.

Verse 15, *Some indeed preach Christ of envy and strife; and some also of good will.*

The NT does not reveal any of the details concerning those who preached Christ of "envy and strife"; and speculation leads us nowhere. Boice cited writings of Suetonius and Clement in support of the view that "Paul perished as a result of the jealousy and strife that existed among Roman Christians."[32] Whether such jealousy arose from Judaizing elements of the church opposing Paul's teaching, or from certain "leaders" of the church in Rome who found themselves eclipsed by Paul's success and influence through winning many converts in the praetorian guard and even the palace is impossible to determine.

Envy and strife caused trouble in those days, and so do they still cause trouble now. As Boice observed:

> Never in the history of the world have the opportunities been greater for the proclamation of the gospel; yet never has the believing church been more irrelevant and divided . . . the bitter fruits of the strife and envy that divide today's believers.[33]

Verses 16-17, *The one do it of love, knowing that I am set for the defence of the gospel; but the other proclaim Christ of faction, not sincerely, thinking to raise up affliction for me in my bonds.*

The factious party in view here had the purpose of making Paul's imprisonment more distasteful and burdensome, no doubt hoping to influence his judges against him, their conduct in this being as contemptible as any that could be imagined.

"Set for the defence of the gospel . . ." Foy E. Wallace deplored the rendition of this in RSV which drops out of sight altogether

---

[32]James Montgomery Boice, *op. cit.*, p. 69.
[33]*Ibid.*

the stern and determined purpose of the word "set," making it read, "I am put here!"[34]

Lightfoot indentified the factious preachers of this passage as belonging to the Judaizing party, giving reasons for the difference in Paul's rejoicing in their preaching (as stated in the next verse) and his scathing denunciation of the Judaizers in Galatians; but the reasons for such a change of Paul's viewpoint are not sufficient. Therefore, it seems far more preferable to look for the source of the envy and strife against Paul in some other quarter. Caffin and many others have followed Lightfoot's lead in this, supposing that:

> Their motives were not pure; they wished to make Paul feel the helplessness of imprisonment, and to increase his affliction by opposing his doctrines, and by forming a party insisting on the observance of the ceremonial law.[35]

Verse 18, *What then? Only that in every way, whether in pretence or in truth, Christ is proclaimed; and therein I rejoice, yea, and will rejoice.*

One must agree with Hayes who said, "This is one of the noblest utterances of one of the greatest men."[36] There is a toleration in Paul's words here which would bless the whole world if more widely imitated.

Verse 19, *For I know that this shall turn out to my salvation, through your supplication and the supply of the Spirit of Jesus Christ.*

Knight preferred the translation, "turn out to my deliverance";[37] thus not taking away the truth that Paul was most certainly a saved person already at the time these words were written. Regardless, however, of the confidence some modern Christians seem to have about the certainty of their salvation, Paul evidently preferred the viewpoint that his salvation was something which still pertained to the future. See under 3:12ff. Of course, it is true that Christians are already "saved in Christ"; but it is also true that they "shall be saved" at the last day.

---

[34]Foy E. Wallace, Jr., *A Review of the New Versions* (Fort Worth: Foy E. Wallace, Jr. Publications, 1973), p. 445.

[35]B. C. Caffin, *op. cit.,* p. 5.

[36]D. A. Hayes, *op. cit.,* p. 434.

[37]John A. Knight, *op. cit.,* p. 303.

Verse 20, *According to my earnest expectation and hope that in nothing shall I be put to shame, but with all boldness, as always, so now also Christ shall be magnified in my body, whether by life, or by death.*

The great truth evident in this verse was concisely stated by Boice: "Christ must be magnified in the bodies of those who believe in him, or he will not be magnified at all."[38] God is not magnified in political movements, earthly cathedrals, temples or church houses, but in the *bodies* of Christians. "Ye are the temple of the Holy Spirit!" God did not dwell even in the temple of Solomon (Acts 7:47, 48). "Solomon in the prayer of dedication acknowledged that heaven and earth could not contain God, much less a building he had constructed."[39] As Boice stressed:

Throughout history this truth has been perverted over and over. Men have often made the mistake of identifying the hand of God with the development of Reformation churches, the cause of democracy, the movement for prohibition, pacifism, or even civil rights. But God is not magnified in these . . . God's hand is seen only in the lives of men who honor God.[40]

Paul's determination that whether he lived or died he would honor Christ provoked the Great Soliloquy in the next few verses.

PAUL'S GREAT SOLILOQUY

Verses 21-24, *For me to live is Christ, and to die is gain. But if to live in the flesh, — if this shall bring fruit from my work, then what I shall choose I know not. But I am in a strait betwixt the two, having the desire to depart and be with Christ; for it is very far better: yet to abide in the flesh is more needful for your sake.*

In Shakespeare's *Hamlet*, the Prince of Denmark delivered a soliloquy in which he viewed both the present life and the after-death state as equally undesirable and terrifying. When considering the evils of life, he could incline toward death, except for the soul-shattering thought that evil dreams would torture him. Thus Hamlet stands as the typical unregenerated man, oppressed by life, but afraid to die. Here, the matchless Paul rises

---

[38]James Montgomery Boice, *op. cit.*, p. 80.
[39]*Ibid.*, p. 81.
[40]*Ibid.*, p. 80.

above such a dilemma, viewing both life and death as the means of magnifying the Lord Jesus.

"To live is Christ . . ." Salvation through Christ is, briefly stated, a sinner's denial of himself, renunciation of himself, and complete submission to the will of Christ, being "baptized into" Christ, thus being saved, not as *himself*, but as *Christ*. That fact surfaces in Paul's brief clause here.

"To die is gain . . ." "Anyone who can truthfully say, 'For me to live is Christ' can also say, 'To die is gain'."[41] Therefore, this Pauline statement is more than a mere complaint of his being imprisoned. "To depart and be with Christ is very far better!" (v. 23). No Christian should dread death. Whatever Paul could have meant by such words as these, the confidence is justified that the after-death state of Christians will be "very far better" than any earthly life, however blessed.

"Very far better . . ." "This is the highest superlative which it is possible to form in any language . . . from which we may infer that Paul knew of no middle state of insensibility between death and the resurrection."[42] It can hardly be imagined that Paul would have considered such a middle state of total insensibility to be preferable to remaining in the world to proclaim the gospel of Christ. Despite this, however, there seems to be indicated some kind of intermediate state in such passages as 1 Thessalonians 4:14, 16 and 1 Corinthians 15:51, 52. We must confess, as did Dummelow, that "Our best notions of the other world are dim and confused."[43]

"To depart and be with Christ . . ." Of course, this is a mere euphemism for death; but, as Martin noted, "It is a military term for striking camp, and a nautical expression for releasing a vessel from its mooring."[44] Barry stated that this expression is found in only one other NT passage, Luke 12:36, "When he shall return (break up) from the wedding. The body is looked upon as a mere

---

[41]F. F. Bruce, *Answers to Questions* (Grand Rapids: Zondervan Publishing House, 1972), p. 109.

[42]James Macknight, *op. cit.*, p. 413.

[43]J. R. Dummelow, *Commentary on the Holy Bible* (New York: The Macmillan Company, 1937), p. 972.

[44]R. P. Martin, *op. cit.*, p. 78.

tabernacle. Each day is a march nearer home, and death is the last striking of the tent on arrival."[45]

Verse 25, *And having this confidence, I know that I shall abide, yea, and abide with you all, for your progress and joy in the faith.*

"And abide with you all . . ." seems to be a poetic way of saying he would remain alive; because, as Macknight said, "He did not mean to tell the Philippians that he would leave off traveling among the churches he had planted and make his residence with them alone."[46]

"In the faith . . ." Both NEB and Phillips make this read "your faith" instead of "the faith," for the obvious purpose of applying the passage to the subjective trust/faith of believers, rather than allowing the true meaning to stand. This most certainly is not a reference to subjective faith in the heart of Christians but has the meaning of "the Christian religion."

Verse 26, *That your glorying may abound in Christ Jesus in me through my presence with you again.*

"Glorying . . ." here is a better translation than "rejoicing" of the AV, "which is too mild an expression to describe what the Philippians would feel if Paul were restored again to the church."[47]

Although it is evident that Paul here expressed confidence of seeing the Philippians again, it should be remembered that his inspiration did not reveal exactly what would take place upon every future occasion contemplated by the apostle. He made his plans like Christians today make their plans. Therefore, it is best to view this as a confident expectation on Paul's part of seeing the Philippians again, and not as a dogmatic prophecy that he would indeed do so. If indeed it was a prophetic promise of his seeing them, we may be certain that he did so; although, of course, we are far from having a complete record of all that Paul did, or all that he wrote. The sacred NT provides only limited glimpses of his glorious life.

Verse 27, *Only let your manner of life be worthy of the gospel of Christ: that, whether I come and see you or be absent, I may*

---

[45]Alfred Barry, *Ellicott's Commentary on the Whole Bible*, Vol. III, *Philippians* (Grand Rapids: Zondervan Publishing House, 1959), p. 71.

[46]James Macknight, *op. cit.*, p. 414.

[47]R. P. Martin, *op. cit.*, p. 81.

hear of your state, that ye stand fast in one spirit, with one soul striving for the faith in the gospel.

Manner of life . . . worthy of the gospel . . ." One thing is supremely important. "No matter what happens, either to Paul or the Philippians, they must live worthily of their faith and profession."[48]

"Stand fast . . ." One thing Paul expected of every Christian was that he should stand fast in the faith. It was a foregone certainty that Satan would use every device to induce Christians to waver or defect. The world at that time, as it always has been, was a hostile environment for Christianity. The Christian life could be lived successfully only by those who were determined to fight with all of their strength in order to maintain their integrity. It is clear here that Paul expected the Philippians to do just that.

"Striving for the faith of the gospel . . ." Dummelow declared that this does "not mean Christian doctrine. . . but faith as a power in the soul";[49] however such an interpretation is surely wrong, being only another instance of modern commentators trying to make every reference to faith in the NT a subjective trust/faith inwardly experienced by Christians.

According to Lightfoot and others, "the faith" is here objective, that which is believed, the content of the gospel message, as in Jude 3, "to contend for the faith:" if so, it may be the earliest NT instance of this use of the word.[50]

Verse 28, *And in nothing affrighted by the adversaries: which is for them an evident token of perdition, but of your salvation, and that from God.*

"An evident token of perdition . . ." The thought here is that the fearlessness of the Christians would be an omen of perdition to the persecutors, and at the same time an evidence of their own salvation.

"And that from God . . ." Only God could give them the fearlessness which Paul here enjoined; and some apply these words to their fearlessness; however, the proximity of "salvation" to the phrase indicates that it is their salvation which is here affirmed as coming "from God."

---

[48]William Barclay, *op. cit.,* p. 29.

[49]J. R. Dummelow, *op. cit.,* p. 972.

[50]H. C. Hewlett, *A NT Commentary, Philippians* (Grand Rapids: Zondervan Publishing House, 1969), p. 473.

Verses 29-30, *Because to you it hath been granted in the behalf of Christ, not only to believe on him, but also to suffer in his behalf: having the same conflict which ye saw in me, and now hear to be in me.*

Here one glimpses the impact of terrible persecutions upon the soul of the beloved apostle. "This allusion, of course, is to the lawless scourging and imprisonment of Acts 16:22-24."[51] That outrage deeply impressed itself upon Paul's heart, as indicated, at the very first, by his demand that the magistrates apologize and by subsequent references to it in 1 Thessalonians 2:2 and 2 Timothy 3:10.

The same implacable and evil hatred of the darkness against the light was the motivation of persecutions against both Paul and the Philippians. His own sufferings were the same as theirs with regard to cause and motivation of both.

"On behalf of Christ . . ." Paul's evident purpose here was to bring home to the Philippians the high dignity and privilege of suffering for the cause of the Lord. By these words, he shared with them the fellowship of suffering in the name of Christ.

---

[51]Alfred Barry, *op. cit.,* p. 72.

CHAPTER 2

This exceedingly important chapter containing some of the profoundest Christological teaching in the word of God begins with an earnest plea for unity, in which Paul stated a fourfold basis of his appeal with an intensity indicating that "There was serious personal strife for place among the Philippian Christians."[1] (1-4). The example of humility exhibited by the Saviour was cited as motivation for their unity (5-11), this offhand, matter-of-fact appeal standing as one of the most astounding testimonials to the pre-existence and deity of Jesus Christ that could be imagined. Paul continued his appeal for the Philippians to exercise diligence in Christian service and for them to become shining lights in an evil world (12-18). Plans concerning Timothy and Epaphroditus were discussed in the final verses of the chapter (19-30).

Verse 1, *If there is therefore any exhortation in Christ, if any consolation of love, if any fellowship of the Spirit, if any tender mercies and compassions.*

Collectively, the fourfold premise of this verse adds up to this: "Look, if there is anything at all to your Christianity . . .!"

"If . . ." "This is rhetorical and in no way expresses doubt."[2] Paul was here appealing to those very things which he considered most certain in the area of Christian experience. This was a common Hebrew method of making a statement in the affirmative, as when Jesus said, "If I go, I shall come again" (John 14:3), making the certainty of his going the pledge also of his Second Coming.

Lightfoot paraphrased this quadruple list of "ifs" thus:

If your experiences in Christ appeal to you with any force, if love exerts any persuasive power upon you, if your fellowship in the Spirit is a living reality, if you have any affectionate yearnings of heart, any tender feelings of compassion, listen and obey![3]

---

[1]John A. Knight, *Beacon Bible Commentary,* Vol. IX, *Philippians* (Kansas City: Beacon Hill Press, 1965), p. 315.

[2]James William Russell, *Compact Commentary on the NT* (Grand Rapids: Baker Book House, 1964).

[3]J. B. Lightfoot, *St. Paul's Epistle to the Philippians* (Grand Rapids: Zondervan Publishing House, 1963), p. 107.

Thus it is clear that Paul here based this appeal for unity upon all of the sacred elements of true Christianity and upon their highest and best impulses as men.

"Fellowship of the Spirit . . ." Martin is no doubt correct in his comment on this that "The meaning must be 'fellowship with participation in the Spirit' rather than 'fellowship wrought by the Spirit'."[4] Thus the admonition is that the Philippians should be "in the Spirit," not that the Spirit should be "in them"! See under verse 5, below.

Henriksen pointed out that Paul's stirring appeal here has a "fourfold incentive and a three-fold directive, the latter being (i) oneness (v. 2), (ii) lowliness of mind or disposition (v. 3), and (iii) helpfulness (v. 4)."[5]

Verse 2, *Make full my joy, that ye may be of the same mind, having the same love, being of one accord, of one mind.*

By commanding them to be in the Spirit, Paul touched upon the basic theological foundation of Christian unity. There is only "one Spirit" (Eph. 4:4). Other passages bearing upon this basic unity are Romans 12:5 and 1 Corinthians 12:13.

Verse 3, *Doing nothing through faction or vainglory, but in lowliness of mind each counting other better than himself.*

"Faction and vainglory . . ." These twin vices have been spoilers of the church of God in all ages. Petty strivings for place and preferment, jockeyings for advantage, pushing and shoving for prestige or attention — how many congregations of believers in Christ have been blighted or destroyed by the sins Paul mentioned here?

Hendriksen asked a pertinent question on his verse: "But how can a man who knows that he is industrious regard the rather lazy fellow-member as being better than himself?"[6] Of course, Paul's rule here does not mean that every Christian must think that every member besides himself is better *in every particular* than he is! However, a proper evaluation of our brothers in Christ will reveal that every person *in one particular or*

---

[4]R. P. Martin, *The Tyndale NT Commentaries, Philippians* (Grand Rapids: Wm. B. Eerdmans Publishing Company, 1959), p. 91.

[5]William Hendriksen, *NT Commentary, Philippians* (Grand Rapids: Baker Book House, 1962), p. 99.

[6]William Hendriksen, *op. cit.,* p. 100.

another is better than ourselves. In opportunity, in privilege, in the endowment of youth, strength, intelligence, or other of life's benefits, every Christian in *some specific sense* is better than any other; and thus this rule enhances one's true regard, not merely of his brother, but of himself as well.

Verse 4, *Not looking each of you to his own things, but each of you also to the things of others.*

As Wesley said, "The *also* sanctions some reasonable amount of attention to one's own interests!"[7] True as this is, however, it is concern for and interest in other people and *their* interests which pay the greatest dividends to the Christian. Would a person who habitually practiced the injunction of Paul in this verse be popular with his peers? Hendriksen gave the answer thus: "True Christianity is still the best answer to the question, 'How can I win friends and influence people?' "[8]

If all Christians would concentrate upon thinking of those particulars in which others are better than themselves and of speaking of such things, a climate of heavenly love and appreciation would soon replace the faction and vainglory which Paul sought to eradicate by this injunction.

Verse 5, *Have this mind in you, which was also in Christ Jesus.*

As Wesley said, "From this verse to verse 11, Paul presents the great renunciation of Christ as the supreme example of the unselfishness to which he has exhorted the Philippians in verse 4."[9]

"Have this mind in you . . ." This is one of eight scriptural expressions describing the redeemed in Christ. For a full list and discussion of these, see under Galatians 5:23, this volume.

"Which was also in Christ Jesus . . ." The proper verb in this clause must be "is" rather than "was"; because, while true enough either way, the eternity and pre-existence of Christ clearly enunciated in the whole passage suggest "is" rather than "was." Hendriksen translated it "is."[10] The Greek in this clause

---

[7]John Wesley, *One Volume NT Commentary* (Grand Rapids: Baker Book House, 1972), *in loco.*

[8]William Hendriksen, *op. cit.,* p. 101.

[9]John Wesley, *op. cit., in loco.*

[10]William Hendriksen, *op. cit.,* p. 102.

has no verb at all,[11] the reason being that no *single tense* of the verb "to be" is adequate in this clause. Of himself, Jesus said, "I am . . . I was . . . and behold I am alive forever more" (Rev. 1:17, 18). Thus Jesus Christ is, was and ever will be. See also Hebrews 13:8.

Having the mind of Christ in one is equivalent to the indwelling of the Holy Spirit, as well as to the indwelling of the Father and the Son in Christian hearts. The Christian's being "in Christ," "in God," "in the Holy Spirit," or having "the word of Christ dwell in" him are also equivalent in every way. See under Galatians 5:23, above.

THE SO-CALLED HYMN

Verse 6, *Who existing in the form of God, counted not the being on an equality with God a thing to be grasped.*

Many scholars insist that "Paul here quotes a previously composed hymn";[12] but outside the attractiveness of plausible imagination, there is no hard evidence of any kind to commend such a view. It is true, of course, that the passage is composed of balanced phrases having a kind of rhythm and that they could have been sung; but what does that prove? Matthew's entire narrative of the crucifixion has been sung and continues to be one of the most popular oratorios. Again, it is true that this passage shows evidence of having been carefully thought out; but the reader is referred to CR 1:6, for review of another Pauline passage showing the most careful and deliberate construction even exceeding the passage here in that quality. The rejection of the "hymn theory" has the utility of refuting those who wish to deny the Pauline authorship of this passage; and, since there is no proof whatever of its ever having been an ancient hymn, this writer rejects the hymn theory as having no merit whatever.

"Being in the form of God . . ." As Knight said:

The Greeks had two words for "form," one of them referring to mere external appearance, as when a mirage takes the appearance of water . . . the other suggests that the appearance

---

[11]Alfred Marshall, *The Nestle Greek Text with a Literal English Translation* (Grand Rapids: Zondervan Publishing House, 1958), *in loco.*

[12]Frances Foulkes, *New Bible Commentary, Revised* (Grand Rapids: Wm. B. Eerdmans Publishing Company, 1970), p. 1132.

is the true revelation of the object itself, the form participating in the reality. It is the second word (*morphe*) which Paul here employs.[13]

This is of course a dogmatic statement of the deity of Jesus Christ. As Hewlett said, "It includes the whole nature and essence of deity, and is inseparable from them."[14] There are at least nine other NT passages affirming the deity of Christ; for a list of these, see CH 1:8.

"Counted not being on an equality with God . . ." These words refer to "being in the form of God," and are a statement (in different words) of the status of our Lord in his pre-existent state before the incarnation. It is a gross misinterpretation to construe these words as reference to anything else.

"A thing to be grasped . . ." Modern exegesis has, to a large extent, attempted to pervert this clause, making it mean that Jesus (in his pre-existent state) "could have grasped at equality with God by self-assertion, but declined to do so."[15] Such a misinterpretation, however, makes "equality with God" something that Christ did not have in his pre-incarnate state (flatly contradicting "existing in the form of God"), but something which presented itself to him as a temptation. The true meaning of this place is that, although Christ had existed from the beginning as God (John 1:1), he did not count the prerogatives of deity "something to be grasped" or "tenaciously retained,"[16] because one would not need to grasp what is already his. As Martin expressed this viewpoint (while denying it), "He had no need to grasp at equality with God because he already possessed it."[17]

This student has carefully read the arguments from the meaning of *harpagmos*, and while convinced that Paul might have used a Greek word here with a double meaning (hence the two diverse interpretations), it is only another of countless instances in scripture where the Holy Spirit left room for men to make a moral judgment. After all, as Kennedy said:

---

[13]John A. Knight, *op. cit.*, p. 381.
[14]H. C. Hewlett, *A NT Commentary, Philippians* (Grand Rapids: Zondervan Publishing House, 1969), p. 474.
[15]R. P. Martin, *op. cit.*, p. 97.
[16]*Ibid.*
[17]*Ibid.*

Much trouble would be saved if interpreters instead of
merely investigating the refinements of Greek metaphysics
. . . were to ask themselves, "What other terms could the apostle
have used to express his conceptions?"[18]

The truth of this passage shines like the sun at perihelion,
and it is nearly incredible that anyone could miss it. Note the
following:

(1) The mistaken position of some scholars is concisely stated
by both Bruce and Martin:

The basic idea of the word (*harpagmos* in v. 6) is that of seizing what one does not possess . . .[19] Equality with God is not
a position which the pre-existent Christ had and gave up.[20]

A bastard translation of this place in the manner of such
interpretations voids and contradicts Paul's entire arugment in
this passage. As Macknight said:

The apostle is not cautioning the Philippians against covet-
ing what they were not in possession of, but exhorting them,
after the example of Christ, to give up for the benefit of others
what they were in possession of, or had a right to.[21]

Furthermore, if Christ did not have equality with God, such
an equality being only something that he might have "snatched
at" (NEB), then our Lord's not grasping at equality with God
could not have been an instance of humility, "but merely the
absence of a mad impiety."[22]

(2) After all of the tiresome arguments of scholars pontificat-
ing about the meaning of an obscure Greek word, the truth still
stands, as expressed by Barclay who affirmed that: "It can mean
that Jesus did not need to snatch at equality with God, because
he had it as a right."[23] This of course is exactly what it does
mean.

---

[18]H. A. A. Kennedy, *The Expositor's Greek New Testament* (Grand Rapids:
Wm. B. Eerdmans Publishing Company, 1967), Vol. 435.

[19]F. F. Bruce, *Answers to Questions* (Grand Rapids: Zondervan Publishing
House, 1972), p. 109.

[20]R. P. Martin, *op. cit.,* p. 97.

[21]James Macknight, *Apostolical Epistles with Commentary,* Volume III (Grand
Rapids: Baker Book House, 1969), p. 23.

[22]B. C. Caffin, *Pulpit Commentary,* Vol. 20, *Philippians* (Grand Rapids: Wm.
B. Eerdmans Publishing Company, 1950), p. 60.

[23]William Barclay, *The Letters to the Philippians, Colossians and Thessalonians* (Philadelphia: The Westminster Press, 1975), p. 36.

(3) Furthermore, there are parallels to the thought of this passage in other Pauline passages, as follows:

(a) "For ye know the grace of our Lord Jesus Christ, that though he was rich, yet for your sakes he became poor, that ye through his poverty might become rich" (2 Cor. 8:9). Here, as well as in the passage before us, the great parabola appears.

These verses have been called the great parabola of scripture, for they picture the descent of our Lord Jesus Christ from the highest position in the universe down . . . down . . . down to his death on the cross, and then carry the mind of the reader up again to see Christ seated once more upon the throne of his glory![24]

(b) "When he ascended on high, he led captivity captive, and gave gifts to men. (Now that he ascended, what is it but that he also descended into the lower parts of the earth?" Eph. 4:8, 9). See notes on this passage, above. Paul's argument here is that Christ could not have ascended without first descending, the same being exactly the same affirmation of the pre-incarnation glory and godhead of Jesus which appears in the related passages here cited, especially in Philippians 2:6-11.

Verse 7, *But he emptied himself, taking the form of a servant, being made in the likeness of men.*

This verse strongly suggests Isaiah 42:1: "Behold my servant whom I uphold; mine elect, in whom my soul delighteth; I have put my spirit upon him: he shall bring forth judgment to the Gentiles." It should be distinguished, however, that Christ did not actually become in any sense a servant to any man; rather his life was humble, clothed in meekness and poverty, encompassed with hatred and hostility, and marked by an earthly status fully comparable with that of slaves. He even suffered the death of a condemned slave, though he was King of kings and Lord of lords.

"Emptied himself . . ." Of what did Christ empty himself?

The diversity of opinions among interpreters in regard to the meaning of this passage is enough to fill the student with despair, and to afflict him with intellectual paralysis.[25]

One thing is clear enough. The use of *morphe* in connection with servant shows that the manhood of Jesus was no less real

---

[24]James Montgomery Boice, *Philippians* (Grand Rapids: Zondervan Publishing House, 1971), p. 125.

[25]F. F. Bruce, (as quoted by John A. Knight), *op. cit.,* p. 319.

and actual than his godhead.[26] Agreement is also felt with Mounce that Christ did not empty himself of divine attributes, because, as he said, "He that hath seen me hath seen the Father" (John 14:9). Christ emptied himself of his glory (John 17:5), exactly the same renunciation Paul was enjoining upon the Philippians.

"In the likeness of men . . ." "This word, of course, does not imply that our Lord was not truly man, but, as Chrysostom said, that he is more than a man."[27]

Verse 8, *And being found in fashion as a man, he humbled himself, becoming obedient even unto death, yea, the death of the cross.*

Here in this verse also, the essential truth of the whole passage bearing upon the eternal power and godhead of Christ shines in the use of the word "obedient." "Only a divine being can accept death as *obedience*; for ordinary men it is a *necessity!*"[28] The death of Christ was not something inflicted upon the Son of God, but the voluntary laying down of his life for the salvation of men (John 10:17f); therefore, it was, on the part of Christ, obedience to the Father's will.

However, Paul will not stop with this emphasis upon the humiliation and death of Christ; the great parabola reaches to the right hand of the Majesty of the Heavens, and the apostle will not pause until he brings that into focus again.

Verse 9, *Wherefore also God highly exalted him, and gave unto him the name which is above every name.*

"Exalted him . . ." The exaltation here is contrasted not with the pre-existent eternal godhead of Christ, but with the humiliation of his incarnation, the one new element in it being in this, that "He is exalted in the very nature in which he died."[29] Thus human nature has been elevated and made to sit on the right hand of God in the person of Christ.

---

[26]Robert H. Mounce, *Wycliffe Bible Commentary* (Chicago: Moody Press, 1971), p. 765.

[27]B. C. Caffin, *op. cit.,* p. 60.

[28]R. P. Martin (quoting Lohmeyer), *op. cit.,* p. 102.

[29]James Macknight, *op. cit.,* p. 427.

"The name which is above every name . . ." Dummelow said, "This name is the completed title, The Lord Jesus Christ."[30] The name in view here "is Lord, *kurios,* the OT name for God."[31] "In light of verse 11, the supreme name is that of 'Lord.' The root meaning of this term (*kurios*) was used in LXX to translate the divine name Yahweh."[32] The word "Lord" denotes rulership based upon competent and authoritative power. The identity of the expression *Lord Jesus Christ* with the sacred unpronounceable name of GOD as known to the Jews was commented upon thus by Taylor:

God changed the ineffable name into a name utterable by man, and desirable by the world; the majesty is all arrayed in robes of mercy. The tetragrammaton, adorable mystery of the patriarchs, is made firm for pronunciation and expression when it becomes the name of the Lord's Christ![33]

This writer, because of John 17th chapter, strongly inclines to Dummelow's identification of this name as "The Lord Jesus Christ." For extensive notes on "thy name," see CJ 17:3f. Christ himself first revealed the sacred compound title Jesus Christ in John 17:3, the very night in which he declared himself to be the Christ.

Verse 10, *That in the name of Jesus every knee should bow, of things in heaven and things on earth and things under the earth.*

"In the name of Jesus . . ." It is wrong to read this "at the name of Jesus," giving rise to the superstitious practice of genuflecting at every mention of the name "Jesus." "In the name of" means "by the authority of," and one thing in view here is that prayers shall be universally offered in the sacred name of the Lord Jesus Christ.

Barclay has a precious passage on the term "Lord," thus:

This great title by which Jesus came to be known in the early church was *kurios.* (1) It began by meaning *master* or *owner.* (2) It became the official title of the Roman emperors; (3) it became the title of the heathen gods; and (4) it was the title used to translate the sacred four-letter unpronounceable

---

[30]J. R. Dummelow, *Commentary on the Holy Bible* (New York: The Macmillan Company, 1937), p. 973.

[31]Robert H. Mounce, *op. cit.,* p. 765.

[32]R. P. Martin, *op. cit.,* p. 104.

[33]H. A. A. Kennedy, (quoting Taylor), *op. cit.,* p. 439.

name of God in the OT. So then when Jesus was called *Kurios* (Lord), it meant he was the Master and Owner of Life, the King of kings, the true Lord in a way which heathen gods could never be; he was nothing less than Divine.[34]

As to the meaning of things in heaven . . . earth . . . under the earth, etc., such actions as knees bending and tongues confessing are universally associated with human beings. "Therefore, unless it can be proved that these words are highly poetical, the view which refers these designations to *persons* (and not things) deserves the preference."[35] It is also possible that Macknight's understanding this as a reference to "angels, men and devils" could be correct.[36] However construed, the words speak of the absolute and total supremacy of our Lord Jesus Christ.

Verse 11, *And that every tongue should confess that Jesus Christ is Lord, to the glory of God the Father.*

The use of "should" in this place does not imply any uncertainty. As regards the present life only, the teaching of this place details what men ought to do, "should" do, and not what they will do; for it is a fact that many live and die without confessing the Saviour. However, there are overtones of eternity in the passage, and with reference to the ultimate future, all men, high and low, good or bad, saved or unsaved "shall" surely confess Christ to the glory of God the Father. See Revelation 6:15-17.

Here is the great truth that comforted and sustained the weary prisoner chained to a Roman guard; this was the reason why martyrs died with the blessed name of Jesus on their lips; and here is the basic conviction of the redeemed of all ages, namely, that Jesus Christ our Lord is supreme, our only Lord, seated at the right hand of God.

However, we cannot agree with some scholars who take "Jesus is Lord" to be the total creed, and the first-creed, of the early church. Of course, such a view is tailor-made to fit the foolish notion that the religion of Christ grew, developed or evolved." It did no such thing. True Christianity was revealed in its entirety by Christ; and, while true enough that the apostles required some time fully to understand and practice

---

[34]William Barclay, *op. cit.,* p. 39.
[35]William Hendriksen, *op. cit.,* p. 115.
[36]James Macknight, *op. cit.,* p. 429.

his teachings, none of the apostles ever went beyond the basic revelation by Jesus Christ himself.

In this context, everything mentioned in this Philippian letter was commonly accepted Christian doctrine. Even the profound teaching of the pre-incarnation glory and godhead of Christ as related to his humiliation, death and ultimate glorification — all of this was a part of the basic fundamental creed of the first Christians. How else could Paul have referred to such things, not as new doctrine but as a well-known, long-received argument favoring their humility? Remember it was only 30 years since Christ was crucified when Paul wrote this letter. The writings of Paul are the effective refutation of any notion that the Christians did not generally refer to Jesus as Lord until long after the resurrection. Christ himself thus referred to himself in Matthew 7:21 and many other places in the NT.

Boice has a matchless paragraph on this as follows:

> What do these verses contain? The answer is that they contain most of the distinctive articles of the Christian creed. They teach the divinity of Christ, his pre-existence, his equality with God the Father, his incarnation and true humanity, his voluntary death on the cross, the certainty of his ultimate triumph over evil and the permanence of his ultimate reign. Then how foolish in the light of these statements are the views of scholars who attempt to dismiss the distinct doctrines of Christianity as late developments in the history of an historically conditioned and slowly evolving church. There was no evolution of these doctrines . . . the doctrines themselves were always known (from Christ himself). Christianity is Christ — this Christ; and these things were believed about him from the beginning.[37]

Verse 12, *So then, my beloved, even as ye have always obeyed, not as in my presence only, but now much more in my absence, work out your own salvation with fear and trembling.*

To be sure this verse gives the lie to the heresy of being saved by faith alone; and the somewhat humorous efforts of those holders of the heresy to diminish the impact of this place is discernible in the following comments:

> *Salvation* (in this verse) has emphasis on that aspect of salvation which is called *sanctification.*[38]

---

[37]James Montgomery Boice, *op. cit.,* p. 126.
[38]William Hendriksen, *op. cit.,* p. 121.

Salvation, not in personal terms . . . this can hardly be taken in a personal sense!³⁹

Here is no denial of justification by faith, for it is Christians, not unbelievers, who are being addressed. *Salvation* is something they already possess.⁴⁰

The very word *salvation* signifies that we cannot save ourselves. This does not mean that we can and must effect our salvation.⁴¹

Far more acceptable are such comments as:

Work out your own salvation. Though salvation is through Christ it must be worked out by obedience (Heb. 5:8). *With fear and trembling.* That is, earnest anxiety.⁴²

Work out your own salvation. Christ's work of atonement is finished . . . *Your own*; it is each man's own work; no human friend, no pastor, not even an apostle, can work it for him. *With fear and trembling.* Have an eager, trembling anxiety to obey God in all things.⁴³

If there is any outstanding commandment of God through Christ and the apostles which sinners neglect, refuse or reject through disobeying it, may they be persuaded by Paul's word in another place to the effect that those "who obey not the gospel" will be utterly destroyed (2 Thess. 1:8). And just what is the gospel? In a general sense it is all that Christ through the apostles commanded; but specifically the reference is to believing, repenting, confessing Christ and being baptized into him. How unspeakably foolish are those who fancy that since they "believe" there is no need for them to obey a command like baptism!

Verse 13, *For it is God who worketh in you both to will and to work, for his good pleasure.*

God indeed works in and through the obedient, but this is far from being a denial that men must obey God. Through the ages the problem has been this: if one must (in addition to believing in Christ) be baptized in order to be saved, that, in the view of some, would make man his own Savior; but such a view is not

---

³⁰R. P. Martin, *op. cit.,* p. 111.

⁴⁰John A. Knight, *op. cit.,* p. 323.

⁴¹Frances Foulkes, *op. cit.,* p. 1133.

⁴²James William Russell, *op. cit.,* p. 489.

⁴³B. C. Caffin, *op. cit.,* p. 61.

justified. For example, when the man born blind washed in the pool of Siloam (John 9:1-12), that did not make him his own healer; although none can deny that he could not have been healed without doing what Christ commanded. The same principle applies to the scripture: "He that believeth and is baptized shall be saved" (Mark 16:16). See comment in this series of commentaries on both of these passages.

This verse was called a paradox by Barry, thus:

> In this famous paradox, Paul calls men to work by their own will, just because only God can grant them power both to will and to do. The origination of all in God, and the free action (which is in some sense origination) of man, are both truths recognized by our deepest consciousness, but to our logic irreconcilable.[44]

Scholars are entirely too sensitive about "work" and sinners, or Christians either, "saving themselves." No apostle, or other NT evangelist, had any of the foolish notions on this subject which clutter the minds of so many today. In the first sermon ever preached, the apostle Peter said, "Save yourselves from this crooked generation" (Acts 2:40). Paul's mention here (almost immediately) of "crooked and perverse generation" shows that his thinking here was exactly parallel to that of Peter on Pentecost. In fact, these two verses supplement and explain each other.

Verses 14-15, *Do all things without murmurings and questionings: that ye may become blameless and harmless children of God without blemish in the midst of a crooked and perverse generation, among whom ye are seen as lights in the world.*

"Murmurings . . ." Here, as practically always in the scripture, guilt is attached to the vice of murmuring. For a discussion of this sin, see CA 6:1. "Questionings . . ." would seem to be just one form of murmuring.

"That ye may become . . . children of God . . ." As Hendriksen said, "Some commentators fail to see how *children of God* can in any sense *become* children of God."[45] But, as the same writer noted: "A child of God should strive to become a child of God without blemish!"[46]

---

[44]Alfred Barry, *Ellicott's Commentary on the Whole Bible*, Vol. III, *Philippians* (Grand Rapids: Zondervan Publishing House, 1959), p. 75.

[45]William Hendriksen, *op. cit.,* p. 124.

[46]*Ibid.*

Verse 16, *Holding forth the word of life that I may have whereof to glory in the day of Christ, that I did not run in vain neither labor in vain.*

"Holding forth the word of life . . ." This is explanatory of the clause in the preceding verse to the effect that the Philippians "are seen as lights in the world." The light which they are able to shed abroad is not of themselves but of the word of God which they have received. A problem well known to many scholars involves an alternative translation of "holding forth," which would make it "holding fast"; but the resolution of it is unimportant, the meaning being about the same either way it is rendered. As Mounce explained it:

> If Paul is continuing the metaphor (of the Christians being lights in the world), then the place should be translated "holding forth" like a torch held out before the bearer . . . But if the final clause is parenthetical (Lightfoot) and the apostle is contrasting the Christians with the perverse generation, it will be translated "holding fast."[47]

"Run in vain . . . labor in vain . . ." Paul did not mean by this that his ultimate redemption depended in any manner upon the fidelity of the Philippians, but that if they should not live properly his "running" and "labors" would prove to be in vain as far as the Philippians were concerned. Therefore, this verse does not bear upon the so called doctrine of the final perseverance of the saints.

Verses 17-18, *Yea, and if I am offered upon the sacrifice and service of your faith, I joy and rejoice with you all; and in the same manner do ye also joy and rejoice with me.*

There is in view here a sacrifice, whether like that in Exodus 29:40, or like one of the animal sacrifices offered to pagan gods, is not specified; because a "drink offering" was a prominent feature of both. Russell thought that Paul had the Jewish sacrifice in mind, saying: "Paul's meaning is figurative, referring in humility to his service as the drink-offering which was added to the burnt offering."[48] However, whether the reference is "to the Jewish libation poured out *beside* the altar, or the pagan libation poured out *over* the sacrifice, makes no

---

[47]Robert H. Mounce, *op. cit.,* p. 766.
[48]James William Russell, *op. cit.,* p. 290.

difference."[49] The meaning is the same both ways. In either case, Paul was comparing all of his own great toils and sacrifices to the drink offering (which was the tiniest part) and their labors to the main sacrifice!

Paul was an unqualified marvel. He drew great spiritual lessons from the Olympic games, from the triumphal processions of emperors, and in this amazing passage from the temple sacrifices! However, it is very important to see that *"I be offered* is a verb in the passive voice and figurative in meaning. Paul is not offering anything, whether his own life or the Philippians' faith!"[50]

The great lesson for all in the passage was presented by Barclay as follows:

> Paul was perfectly willing to make his life a sacrifice to God; and, if that happened, to him it would be all joy, and he calls on them (v. 18) not to mourn at the prospect but rather to rejoice. To him every call for sacrifice or toil was a call to his love for Christ; and therefore he met it, not with regret or complaint but with joy.[51]

Verse 19, *But I hope in the Lord Jesus to send Timothy shortly unto you, that I also may be of good comfort when I know your state.*

In the two preceding verses, Paul contemplated his own martyrdom as a realistic possibility; but here the mood changed to one of hope and confidence, for his being able to send Timothy would mean that his state had improved enough to make this possible. It is therefore impossible to make Paul's statements about his prospects the basis of dating the epistle. Like any person in similar circumstances, Paul, from time to time, would have wavered between the extremes of despair and confidence. Note here that Paul anticipated still being alive at a time when Timothy would return with good news.

Timothy had been with Paul extensively during his travels and was at the time indicated here performing some valuable service for the apostle. It would have been a genuine sacrifice for Paul to part with him for a journey to Philippi. Nevertheless, such was his concern for them that he was willing to do so.

---

[49]William Hendriksen, *op. cit.,* p. 127.
[50]R. P. Martin, *op. cit.,* p. 120.
[51]William Barclay, *op. cit.,* p. 46.

Verses 20-21, *For I have no man like-minded, who will care truly for your state. For they all seek their own, not the things of Jesus Christ.*

Paul referred to those around him as "brethren" (4:21), but they were far short of the zeal and dedication of a man like Timothy. Paul has been accused of petulance on account of this evaluation of his associates; but it is a mistake to make anything out of this except what it is, a matter-of-fact statement concerning the attitude of some of the apostle's contemporary brethren. Furthermore, the same evaluation would apply to a great many so-called "brethren" in our own times.

As Caffin said, "Paul's spiritual isolation increases our wonder and admiration for the strain of holy joy that runs through Philippians."[52] It is also a mistake to apply Paul's words here to everyone associated with him in the NT. "We must suppose that faithful helpers like Luke were not in Rome at this time having been sent away for a little while on some business."[53] As Mounce put it, "Paul's no *one* here is not a sweeping condemnation of fellow laborers, but it means that of those *available* there was no one like Timothy."[54] Despite this, as Dummelow said, "Doubtless some of Paul's brethren had declined the mission from reasons that Paul considered selfish."[55]

Verses 22-24, *But ye know the proof of him, that, as a child serveth a father, so he served me in furtherance of the gospel. Him therefore I hope to send forthwith, so soon as I shall see how it will go with me: but I trust in the Lord that I myself shall come shortly.*

"Ye know the proof of him . . ." The whole world of NT churches in those days knew the proof of Timothy. The word translated "proof" was used of gold and silver that had been tested and could be accepted as current coin."[56] Timothy had been with Paul in Philippi when that church was founded (Acts 16:1ff); he was in Thessalonica and Beroea (Acts 17:1-14), and

---

[52]B. C. Caffin, *op. cit.,* p. 63.
[53]James Macknight, *op. cit.,* p. 434.
[54]Robert H. Mounce, *op. cit.,* p. 767.
[55]J. R. Dummelow, *op. cit.,* p. 974.
[56]John A. Knight, *op. cit.,* p. 329.

in Corinth and Ephesus (Acts 18:25; 19:21, 22); and even at the time Paul wrote this letter he was standing by Paul in Rome (Phil. 1:1).

"Him therefore I hope to send . . ." Implicit in these words is the fact that Paul could not, at the moment, send Timothy. Macknight believed that "This was because Aristarchus, Titus and Luke were all absent from Rome at this time,"[57] leaving only Timothy to look after Paul. Of course, Epaphroditus was available, and him Paul sent.

"I trust . . . that I myself shall come shortly . . ." "This hope, in all probability, was fulfilled (Titus 3:12)."[58] Lipscomb has a great paragraph on Paul's probable thoughts at this juncture:

> We do not know what he meant by *shortly*. The uncertainty as to what whim might strike Nero was nothing to count upon. He no longer counts on going to Spain as he once had planned (Rom. 15:28); his heart now turns to this old field of labor (Phile. 22) . . . those grievous wolves of whom he warned the Ephesian elders (Acts 20:29,30) had taken advantage of his absence and were causing much trouble and confusion among the churches of Asia.[59]

Verse 25, *But I counted it necessary to send you Epaphroditus, my brother and fellow-worker and fellow-soldier, and your messenger and minister to my need.*

Paul must have regarded Epaphroditus very highly. Note the five titles given to him.

"I counted it necessary to send . . ." This is what the scholars call an epistolary aorist and refers to something Paul was in the process of doing, not to something already done. Another instance of it is in verse 28. In all likelihood, Epaphroditus was the one who bore this letter to the Philippian church; but since, at the time of the Philippians' reading it, the sending of Epaphroditus would indeed (at that time) be spoken of in the past tense.

"Epaphroditus . . ." This name occurs only here in the NT, although there are two other instances of the shortened form of it in Colossians and Philemon. Since it was a rather common

---

[57]James Macknight, *op. cit.,* p. 436.
[58]B. C. Caffin, *op. cit.,* p. 63.
[59]David Lipscomb, *A Commentary on the NT Epistles,* Vol. IV (Nashville: The Gospel Advocate Company, 1964), p. 194.

name, scholars are very reluctant to allow that there may be a connection with the man mentioned here.

"Messenger . . ." The Greek word from which this comes is actually "Apostle"; but, as Epaphroditus was certainly not an apostle in the ordinary sense, it is supposed that Paul used the title here as complimentary. They are definitely wrong who interpret this word as meaning "that Epaphroditus was diocesan bishop of Philippi."[60] There is no evidence of any diocesan bishop having been appointed or honored during NT times. The nearest thing to such a thing is the honor given to James the Lord's brother; but in his case, it appears that the respect paid to him was derived from the fact of his having been a physical half-brother of the Lord Jesus Christ, and not from any office like that of a metropolitan bishop.

EPAPHRODITUS

Certainly Epaphroditus was a spiritual leader at Philippi, probably one of the elders. He had been commissioned by the church there to bring a gift of money to Paul and to remain with him for an unspecified time to look after Paul's needs and to assist in any way possible. While engaged in that service, he became dangerously ill, possibly from attending Paul during an illness, or from over-exertion. The friends of Epaproditus in Philippi heard of his illness, and became concerned and anxious regarding his condition. God graciously restored him to health. As was quite natural, he wanted to return to Philippi as soon as he became able to travel. Paul, in complete accord, sent him back, probably as the bearer of this letter, and heaping praise and commendation upon him as in the passage before us.

Verse 26, *Since he longed after you all, and was sore troubled, because ye had heard that he was sick.*

"Was sore troubled . . ." "Erasmus said the Greek word so translated means to be almost killed with grief."[61] It should be remembered that homesickness was certainly a factor in the grief of Epaphroditus, a homesickness that would have been grievously aggravated by his illness.

---

[60]B. C. Caffin, *op. cit.,* p. 64.
[61]James Macknight, *op. cit.,* p. 437.

Verse 27, *For indeed he was nigh unto death: but God had mercy on him; and not on him only, but on me also, that I might not have sorrow upon sorrow.*

Paul's ascription of Epaphroditus' recovery to the special providence and mercy of God is characteristic. All healing is of God; but there are some recoveries which give every evidence of having been granted by the Father in answer to prayer; and so, it seems, was the case of Epaphroditus.

Again, on this passage, Hendriksen raises an important question: "Why did not Paul perform a miracle on behalf of Epaphroditus, instead of permitting the illness to continue?"[22] The answer lies in the purpose of miracles, which were never given for the personal needs of God's apostles and preachers, but only for the purpose of "confirming the word" (Mark 16:20). Timothy suffered from a stomach illness and Trophimus was left at Miletum sick, just as Epaphroditus was allowed here to suffer the normal course of his illness.

Verse 28, *I have sent him therefore the more diligently, that, when ye see him again, ye may rejoice, and that I may be the less sorrowful.*

The altruism of the great apostle shines in this, as Hendriksen noted: "Easing the mind of the Philippians and imparting gladness of heart to them meant more to Paul than any personal service he might have been able to derive by the continued attendance upon him of Epaphroditus."[63]

Verse 29, *Receive him therefore in the Lord with all joy; and hold such in honor.*

Dummelow thought that:

The apostle heaps commendations upon Epaphroditus, apprehending seemingly that he might have a cool reception (vv. 29-30), since he is going home prematurely and without having rendered all the service expected.[64]

It is very difficult, however, for this writer to agree with that, because the severe "nigh-unto-death" illness of Epaphroditus would certainly have made it very difficult for any right-minded

---

[62]William Hendriksen, *op. cit.*, p. 141.

[63]*Ibid.*, p. 143.

[64]J. R. Dummelow, *op. cit.*, p. 974.

person to have faulted his desire to return home before the mission was totally completed.

Verse 30, *Because for the work of Christ, he came nigh unto death, hazarding his life to supply that which was lacking in your service toward me.*

"Hazarding his life . . ." The word here actually means "gambling his life" for Paul's sake. The use of the particular Greek word (parabolos) has led some scholars to identify Epaphroditus' work as like that "of an association of men in Alexandria known as the Parabolani. Among the hazardous duties of this 'suicide squad' was the nursing of the sick during epidemics."[65]

When certain types of epidemics frightened the pagan populations, terrible things happened. Barclay tells this:

> In A.D. 252 plague broke out in Carthage; the heathen threw out the bodies of their dead and fled in terror. Cyprian, the Christian bishop, gathered his congregation together and set them to burying the dead and nursing the sick.[66]

Whether anything like this was involved in the illness contracted by Epaphroditus is unknown; but we may be sure of one thing, "He was a brave man; for anyone who proposed to offer himself as an attendant of a man waiting trial on a capital charge was laying himself open to considerable risk of facing the same charge."[67]

---

[65]Robert H. Mounce, *op. cit.,* p. 769.
[66]William Barclay, *op. cit.,* p. 50.
[67]*Ibid.,* p. 48.

CHAPTER 3

In this chapter, Paul sounded again "the prevalent note of the epistle, 'rejoice in the Lord,' added a few supplementary counsels and acknowledged the contribution sent through Epaphroditus."[1] However, beginning in verse 4, there is a typical Pauline diversion.

Verse 1, *Finally, my brethren, rejoice in the Lord. To write the same things to you, to me indeed is not irksome, but for you it is safe.*

"Finally, my brethren ..." On this, Mounce refers to a quotation to the effect that "Paul is the father of all preachers who use 'finally, my brethren,' as an indication that they have found their second wind!"[2] It is ridiculous, of course, to make such a common habit the basis of denying the rest of the epistle. Many preachers have said, "Now, finally ..." and then continued half an hour; and there is no reason to suppose that Paul might not have done the same thing here, especially in a personal letter.

"Rejoice in the Lord ..." The significant words here, especially are "in the Lord." The type of rejoicing Paul is speaking of is possible only for those who have been baptized into Christ. As Boice expressed it:

> Joy is founded to a very great degree on sound doctrine . . . Joy is a supernatural delight in God and God's goodness; and it is a very different things from happiness . . . supernatural joy is to steep ourselves in the teachings of the Bible.[3]

It is amazing how often in the scriptures joy is associated with knowledge and study of God's word, a familiar example being, "The statutes of the Lord are right, rejoicing the heart" (Ps. 19:8). Both here and in 2:18 "rejoice" has the status of an apostolical order or commandment. A Christian who will not "rejoice in the Lord" is a contradiction! Paul himself, suffering

---

[1]J. R. Dummelow, *Commentary on the Holy Bible* (New York: The Macmillan Company, 1937), p. 975.

[2]Robert H. Mounce, *Wycliffe Bible Commentary* (Chicago: Moody Press, 1971), p. 769.

[3]James Montgomery Boice, *Philippians* (Grand Rapids: Zondervan Publishing House, 1971), p. 190.

privations, imprisonment and hardships, led the way in this most distinctive of all Christian virtues.

"To write the same things . . ." has given exegetes a lot of trouble as to what Paul meant. Agreement is here expressed with Caffin who said, "The words refer to the constant admonition of this epistle, 'Rejoice in the Lord'."[4] Moffatt's translation is in line with this meaning; and, despite the fact of Lightfoot's supposing that Paul here alluded to warnings against dissensions in the church,[5] there is really no convincing reason why the clause should not be applied to "rejoice in the Lord."

As Barclay said, "Like any good teacher, Paul was never afraid of repetition."[6] Jesus repeated over and over again, often changing his words to convey new facets of truth; and one of the remarkable blindnesses of so-called higher criticism of the NT is inability to see various gospel statements as due to Jesus' well-known habit of repetition and not due to one or another gospel writer's blundering efforts to "copy" what another writer recorded. Thus Luke's record of one of Jesus' sermons "on the plain" is not a variant account of Matthew's account of the sermon on the mount, but is a variant of the blessed Saviour's teachings, both gospel accounts being absolutely accurate records of exactly what Jesus said on two different occasions. This simple, obvious truth devastates utterly whole volumes of intricate criticisms made without benefit of light from this fact, a fact Paul bluntly stated in this verse.

"For you it is safe . . ." Lightfoot, of course, made this an objection to viewing the repetition mentioned here as applicable to the command to "rejoice," saying that "Such an injunction has no direct bearing on the *safety* of the Philippians, and its repetition could hardly be suspected of being irksome to the apostle."[7] The danger, however, that Paul guarded against through his oft-repeated admonitions was that of drifting away from the truth; and Lightfoot's objection fails to take this into account.

---

[4]B. C. Caffin, *Pulpit Commentary,* Vol. 20, *Philippians* (Grand Rapids: Wm. B. Eerdmans Publishing Company, 1950), p. 111.

[5]R. P. Martin, *The Tyndale NT Commentaries, Philippians* (Grand Rapids: Wm. B. Eerdmans Publishing Company, 1959), p. 135.

[6]William Barclay, *The Letters to the Philippians, Colossians and Thessalonians* (Philadelphia: The Westminster Press, 1975), p. 52.

[7]J. B. Lightfoot, *St. Paul's Epistle to the Philippians* (Grand Rapids: Zondervan Publishing House, 1963), p. 125.

Verse 2, *Beware of the dogs, beware of the evil workers, beware of the concision.*

Here is more repetition, the threefold 'beware" being one of the most dramatic warnings in scripture. What a tragedy is the butchering of this text by so-called translators. The RSV, for example, changed this to "Look out for the dogs!" As Foy E. Wallace, Jr., said, "This is an example of ruining the language and literary quality of the scriptures."[8] "Beware" is a far better word in this place than "look out for."

"Dogs . . . evil workers . . . concision . . ." Many believe that these are not three classes of enemies but three designations of one class, that class being rather effectively identified by the word "concision," which is a derogatory reference to circumcision and points squarely at the Judaizers who were the gospel enemies beyond all others of that era. The secular, nationalistic Jews were also enemies but when Paul referred to them, his references to circumcision were more respectful. As Martin said: "But what did infuriate him was the insistence that the rite be enforced on Gentile Christians in order to make them 'full Christians'."[9]

"Concision . . ." This means "Those who mutilate the flesh" (RSV); "The verb is used in LXX of cuttings forbidden by Mosaic law."[10]

"Dogs . . ." "This applies to those of unholy tastes and desires, of whom Jesus warned the multitude in the Sermon on the Mount: 'Give not that which is holy unto the dogs' (Matt. 7:6)."[11] Furthermore, the status of dogs in that ancient culture was a far different thing from what it is in our own. The dog in America today is a loved and appreciated creature; but the dog was held to be most contemptible in ancient times. The Jews referred to Gentiles as "dogs"; the prophet Isaiah compared the false shepherds of Israel to dumb dogs, lazy dogs and greedy dogs (56:9-11); and the Psalmist designated the enemies of the Messiah, stating that "the dogs have encompassed" him (22:16).

---

[8]Foy E. Wallace, Jr., *A Review of the New Versions* (Fort Worth: The Foy E. Wallace, Jr., Publications, 1973), p. 446.

[9]R. P. Martin, *op. cit.,* p. 136.

[10]Robert H. Mounce, *op. cit.,* p. 769.

[11]James William Russell, *Compact Commentary on the NT* (Grand Rapids: Baker Book House, 1964), p. 494.

"Ill-workers . . ." The opinion of Dummelow cannot be ruled out that there are three classes of gospel enemies in this passage, the expression here meaning the establishment of national Israel (1 Thess. 2:14-16). "Unbelieving Jews are here intended, radically opposed to the gospel of Christ. . . . Jewish hostility was violent beyond measure in Macedonia (Acts 17)."[12] If this view should be accepted, then the three classes of enemies would be:

dogs . . . those of unholy desires and appetites.
ill-workers . . . the unbelieving Jews who tried to exterminate the gospel.
the concision . . . the believing Jews who sought to pervert it.

Despite the widespread opinion to the contrary, Dummelow's views appear convincing to this writer.

Verse 3, *For we are of the circumcision, who worship by the Spirit of God, and glory in Christ Jesus, and have no confidence in the flesh.*

Both the Judaizers and the unbelieving Jews supported their opposition to Christianity by appealing to their circumcision as proof of their standing within the covenant of Abraham. They called themselves "the circumcision" "as proof of their right descent from Abraham and the only objects of God's favor."[13] Here Paul challenged them.

"We are the circumcision . . ." Christians, not those fleshly descendants of Abraham, are the true Israel of God. This is a theme which Paul developed extensively in Romans; and for a further discussion of this subject see CR 2:25ff and 9:7ff.

Macknight's paraphrase of this is:

The Judaizers, being destitute of the qualities signified by circumcision, have no title to the name and should be shunned. But we are the true circumcision, who worship God in Spirit and in truth, and boast in Christ Jesus as our Saviour, and have no reliance upon our descent from Abraham.[14]

Verse 4, *Though I myself might have confidence in the flesh: if any other man thinketh to have confidence in the flesh, I yet more.*

---

[12]J. R. Dummelow, *op. cit.,* p. 975.
[13]James Macknight, *Apostolical Epistles with Commentary,* Volume III (Grand Rapids: Baker Book House, 1969), p. 440.
[14]*Ibid.,* p. 445.

In this and the following verses, Paul defended himself against any who might have said, "Paul is decrying privileges to which he himself cannot lay claim. He minimizes them because he never had them and cannot get them. The grapes are sour!"[15] As Barclay put it, "Paul set out his credentials, not in order to boast, but to show that he had had every privilege that a Jew could enjoy, and had risen to every attainment to which a Jew could rise."[16]

Verses 5-6, *Circumcised the eighth day, of the stock of Israel, of the tribe of Benjamin, a Hebrew of the Hebrews; as touching the law, a Pharisee; as touching zeal, persecuting the church; as touching the righteousness which is in the law, found blameless.*

The incredible importance of the conversion of Saul of Tarsus in the early rise and spread of Christianity is seen in this very paragraph. It was who and what Paul was which disarmed and frustrated the Jewish opposition. Paul was the equal or superior of every Jew on earth, and his wholehearted acceptance of Christ as the true Messiah of Israel annihilated in one fantastic act of acceptance every argument of the Jewish hierarchy who denied it.

"Circumcised the eighth day . . ." The ancient Jew placed an inordinate amount of emphasis on this, even affirming that no circumcised person could be lost!

"Of the stock of Israel . . ." As Barry noted, "These words are emphatic . . . a true scion of the covenanted stock, the royal race of the Prince of God."[17]

"Of the tribe of Benjamin . . ." This tribe gave Israel their first king (Saul), their wisest man, Mordecai, and they remained faithful despite the departure of the ten tribes; but their greatest contribution to both Israel and the whole world was the apostle Paul.

"A Pharisee . . ." Paul was one of the noble Pharisees, the same being one who sincerely and honestly tried to measure up to all of the strict and scrupulous teachings of this demanding group. For discussion of other types of Pharisees, see CM 3:7. The

---

[15]William Hendriksen, *NT Commentary, Philippians* (Grand Rapids: Baker Book House, 1962), p. 155.

[16]William Barclay, *op. cit.,* p. 57.

[17]Alfred Barry, *Ellicott's Commentary on the Whole Bible,* Vol. III, *Philippians* (Grand Rapids: Zondervan Publishing House, 1959), p. 80.

Sadducees were materialists, politically minded unbelievers, who denied many teachings of the scriptures. The Pharisees were far better than they, but the Sadducees held most of the high offices.

"As touching zeal, persecuting the church . . ." Whereas many of the Pharisees held religious convictions like Paul, they did nothing about it. Paul fanatically pursued his faith by persecuting the church.

"As touching righteousness which is the law . . ." Paul was here speaking of the Law of Moses, not of "law-works" or of "law-righteousness" as these words are frequently read in an effort to make Paul's reference here inclusive of the law of Christ; but Paul was speaking in this passage of the Mosaic regulations. See under verse 9, below.

"Blameless . . ." By this, Paul did not lay claim to perfection, but on the other hand affirmed by this that his record was without charge of violation.

Verses 7-8, *Howbeit what things were gain to me, these have I counted loss for Christ. Yea verily, and I count all things to be loss for the excellency of the knowledge of Christ Jesus my Lord: for whom I suffered the loss of all things, and do count them but refuse, that I may gain Christ.*

No earthly honor, or preferment, no mortal achievement, no wealth, social standing or earthly glory would the great apostle exchange for the knowledge of Christ.

"The loss of all things . . ." It cannot be known what all this might have included. Was his wife, or family, included in the things he lost? No one can say, but the haunting possibility exists. Whatever he lost for the sake of gaining Christ, Paul considered his status as a child of God far above and beyond any privilege he might have lost.

Verses 8b-9, *That I may gain Christ and be found in him, not having a righteousness of mine own, even that which is of the law, but that which is through the faith of Christ, the righteousness which is from God by faith.*

We agree with Monroe who flatly declared that "here is Paul's most concise statement of justification by faith";[18] and

---

[18]Robert H. Mounce, *op. cit.,* p. 771.

there is, therefore, all the more reason why men should take heed to the meaning of it. The undeniable fact is that RV, RSV and most of the so-called modern translations pervert the meaning of this passage by rendering "faith in Christ" instead of "faith of Christ"; and for a justification of the rendition followed here, see under Galatians 2:16, and in the extended note 3 at the end of Galatians chapter 3.

"And be found in him . . ." The great Pauline expression "in Christ," or as here "in him," which is found more than one hundred fifty times in his letters, identifies the place of redemption as being "in the Lord." The NT reveals no way of being "in the Lord" except through being baptized "into him"; and, therefore, the conclusion is absolutely mandatory that Paul is addressing these words to people who have been baptized into Christ with the admonition that they strive to be "found in him," either when death overtakes them or the Lord shall come. The teaching of all of the holy NT writers agrees perfectly with this admonition. As the apostle John expressed it:

> And I heard a voice from heaven saying, Write, Blessed are the dead who die in the Lord from henceforth: yea, saith the Spirit, that they may rest from their labors; for their works follow with them (Rev. 14:13).

"Righteousness . . . of the law . . ." That is, of the Law of Moses. The contrast here is not between obeying the ordinances of the gospel of Christ and being saved by "faith alone"; but the contrast is between trusting in the ceremonies of the Law of Moses for salvation as contrasted with believing and obeying the gospel of Christ.

"That (righteousness) which is through the faith of Christ . . ."

As Boice said, "The are two kinds of righteousness,"[19] that which comes of men, and that which is achieved by God. The righteousness which saves was not achieved by men, but by Christ; therefore, it is called here the "righteousness of Christ," or the "righteousness of God through the faith of Christ." One who wishes to be saved must become a participant in the righteousness achieved through the faith and perfect obedience of Christ. For five hundred years, the monstrous heresy has prevailed that men achieve that perfect righteousness merely

---

[19]James Montgomery Boice, *op. cit.*, p. 200.

through believing subjectively in Christ, Paul revealed how *truly* men become sharers in Christ's righteousness. They renounce self, deny themselves, believe in Christ and obey the gospel by being baptized into Christ, thus becoming Christ, in the sense of being "in him" and identified with Christ. The righteousness that saves is not theirs but Christ's; and even in the case of Christ's righteousness, it was not achieved by faith only but by faith and our Saviour's perfect obedience. Thus every man who will be saved shall not be saved as Joe Doakes, but as Jesus Christ. See extensive discussion of this in Galatians and Ephesians but also in CR 3:22ff.

"The righteousness which is from God by faith . . ." This clause, with its reference to sinner's faith, is the irrefutable denial that it is sinner's faith mentioned in the preceding clause. The comment of Hendriksen to the effect that it is here merely "repeated for the sake of emphasis"[20] cannot be allowed, because in several other similar passages there is a distinct differentiation between the saving faith and righteousness "of Christ," as distinguished from that of sinners. See under Galatians chapter 3. There can be no doubt that the same distinction is evident here.

"By faith . . ." Even here, the meaning is not the mere subjective faith of sinners; for, as Boice said: "The most common distortion of faith in our day is the attempt to make it *subjective.*"[21] The usual theological jargon of the current era makes faith to be absolutely subjective; but nothing could be farther from the truth. George Howard, as cited earlier in this volume, has effectively proved that in the NT Greek, the word for faith almost never has the sense of subjective believing. The true meaning is nearer to our word "fidelity" or "faithfulness," meanings which Paul plainly included in the expression, "the obedience of faith," with which he both began and concluded the Book of Romans.

"Faith of Christ . . ." Although this is translated "faith in Christ" by many versions and translations, it would be just as correct to translate "knowledge of Christ" (v. 8) and "cross of Christ" (v. 18) as the knowledge or cross "in Christ" as it is to make "of Christ" read "in Christ." In all these cases, the Greek word for Christ stands without the article; and, as a glance at the

---

[20]William Hendriksen, *op. cit.,* p. 166.
[21]James Montgomery Boice, *op. cit.,* p. 208.

Greek New Testament shows, the preferable rendition is "of Christ."[22] The AV renders this verse "faith of Christ"; and this student is simply unwilling to allow that any of the modern translators is in any manner superior in knowledge of the Greek to the translators of the Authorized Version, nor have their discoveries uncovered anything whatever that justifies perverting these texts by rendering them "faith in Christ." May the discerning student beware.

Verses 10-11, *That I may know him, and the power of his resurrection, and the fellowship of his sufferings, becoming conformed unto his death; if by any means I may attain unto the resurrection from the dead.*

As Barry pointed out, "The order of these verses is notable and instructive."[23] The three mountain peaks of interest are (1) the resurrection of Christ, (2) the fellowship of Christians with him in sufferings and (3) the glorious resurrection unto eternal life at the last day. The three-fold emphasis discernible in these verses provides a thumbnail abbreviation of the apostolical gospel, an abbreviation which by extension can be made to include nearly everything in the entire NT. Note:

I. The Resurrection of Christ.

This, of course, includes all of the gospel record which preceded and led up to the resurrection, all of which, especially the sufferings and death of our Lord, were in a sense validated, confirmed and endowed with eternal significance by the resurrection. This focal emphasis on Christ's resurrection was not exclusively Pauline, but characterized all the NT writers. Peter tied the entire Pentecostal sermon to the resurrection of Christ (Acts 2:24), making forgiveness of sins and the reception of the earnest of the Holy Spirit derivative from the fact of our Lord's resurrection, ascension and sending the Comforter; and, while true enough that Peter promised forgiveness and the gift of the Spirit as blessings to be received subsequently to and in consequence of the recipient's believing, repenting, and being baptized into Christ, the sacred word makes it clear enough that the sinner's part in such marvelous blessings is limited to his

---

[22]Alfred Marshall, *The Nestle Greek Text with a Literal English Translation* (Grand Rapids: Zondervan Publishing House, 1958), p. 785.

[23]Alfred Barry, *op. cit.,* p. 82.

fulfillment of the preconditions prior to receiving them, and that Christ, not the sinner, is the fountain source from which all blessings flow.

It would be impossible to trace in a single chapter the amazing manner of Paul's making all to depend on Christ's resurrection. Everything depends on it; without it, we are still in our sins (1 Cor. 15:17); it is the pledge of our justification and forgiveness (Acts 13:30, 38, 39), etc.

2. Suffering with Christ.

This is the "partaking of Christ's sufferings," "the conformity to his death," the "taking up the cross," and being "crucified with Christ," as stressed throughout the NT (1 Peter 4:13; Rom. 8:17; 2 Cor. 1:5; Col. 1:24; 2 Tim. 2:11). It was expected that every Christian should suffer as a result of his faith; indeed it was a proverb or "faithful saying" that "*If we suffer*, we shall also reign with him" (2 Tim. 2:12).

3. Attainment to the Resurrection from the Dead.

This means the final and glorious resurrection of the redeemed at the last day, an event so nobly referred to by Paul a few moments later in verses 20, 21. Another Pauline reference to this is: "If we have become united with him in the likeness of his death, we shall be also in the likeness of his resurrection" (Rom. 6:5). Also in 1 Corinthians 15:12-23, Paul made the resurrection of Christ, appealed to as a fact which not even the enemies of the faith could deny, to be a pledge of the Christian's own resurrection at the last day. See notes in this series on those references.

Verse 12, *Not that I have already obtained, or am already made perfect: but I press on, if so be that I may lay hold on that for which also I was laid hold on by Christ Jesus.*

"Not that I have already obtained . . ." Paul never viewed the Christian prize of eternal salvation as being something that one might "get" in any final and irrevocable act. The Pauline view, in evidence here, was that the Christian life was a race to be won, a life to be lived, a course to be completed, and that no one ever had it made till the probation of life was completed. There was no lack of confidence in Paul, as evidenced by these words; but this was merely his way of saying that he was still running the Christian race.

"Or am already made perfect . . ." There are two different uses of "perfect," here and in verse 15, the word being the same in both cases. In the 12th verse, Paul is speaking of that personal and individual perfection which God will give to every Christian on the last day; but in verse 15 he is claiming, not merely for himself but also for all of the Philippians (or at least the majority of them) the full attainment of that same perfection; but in this instance the reference is to the perfection of Christ which rightfully belongs to every Christian.

In Matthew 5:48, Jesus laid down the law that underlies eternal salvation, the law of absolute perfection, "even as God is perfect." No one ever attained such perfection in his own right, except the Lord; but every Christian enjoys that status as a result of his being baptized "into Christ," identified with Christ, and in a sense, being Christ! It was to that status which Paul referred in verse 15; but in this verse (12) Paul referred to every Christian's final perfection in heaven (see under Colossians 1:28, this volume). Also see article on "perfection" under Ephesians 1:4, this volume.

Verse 13, *Brethren, I count not myself yet to have laid hold: but one thing I do, forgetting the things which are behind, and stretching forward to the things which are before . . ."*

"I count not myself yet to have laid hold . . ." See comment on this same thought expressed at the beginning of verse 12.

"Laid hold . . ." This was a favorite expression with Paul. He viewed the priceless gift of eternal life as a prize to be seized eagerly and without delay, something to be taken with determination never to let go of it. It was that same determined seizing and laying hold of which had characterized the Saviour's "laying hold on" him for the preaching of the truth, hence the words in the preceding verse, "I was laid hold on by Jesus Christ."

"Forgetting the things which are behind . . ." Paul was not one to live in the past. The past he properly appreciated; but his thoughts continued to dwell upon the future. The great prize still lay forward at the finish line.

Just how did Paul forget the past? "Well, he certainly did not forget his knowledge of the Bible, nor God's grace or God's great mercies . . . his writings prove this."[24] Boice thought Paul's

---

[24]James Montgomery Boice, *op. cit.,* p. 227.

forgetting was "ceasing to let the things which in the past over-shadow the present. He let the past, both good and bad, be past, constantly looking forward to the work God had for him to do."[26] All Christians need the grace to do the same thing.

Verse 14, *I press on toward the goal unto the prize of the high calling of God in Christ Jesus.*

As Hendriksen expressed it, "Paul's intense yearning and striving for spiritual perfection is expressed now under the symbolism of the familiar footrace."[26] Commentators often illustrate this passage by bringing forward vivid acounts of the ancient Olympic contests in various cities of the ancient empire; but the modern Olympics which have been brought into millions of homes through the wonder of television are just as excellent illustrations, in which the agony of defeat and the ecstasy of victory are seen as starkly today as when viewed by the apostle nearly two millenniums ago. Of course, in this verse, it is the eagerness and determination of the contestant to win which dominate the thought. See CH, chapter 12, "The Christian Race," for a more extended look at the analogy of the Christian life compared to a footrace.

Verse 15, *Let us therefore, as many as are perfect, be thus minded: and if in anything ye are otherwise minded, this also shall God reveal unto you.*

We agree with Mounce that "There is no reproachful irony here (Lightfoot)." The perfection in Christ was a very real and genuine thing to Paul; and thus it should be to every Christian. Again, reference is made to the article on this subject under Ephesians 1:4 in this volume.

"This also shall God reveal . . ." Lipscomb applied this to all "having a sincere desire to know and to do God's will, and without any wish or preference except to do the will of God."[27] He cited John 7:17 and Hosea 6:3 as confirming his conclusion. Mounce arrived at a similar conclusion, thus: "The condition for future enlightenment is to walk according to present light."[28]

---

[25]*Ibid.*

[26]William Hendriksen, *op. cit.,* p. 170.

[27]David Lipscomb, *A Commentary on the NT Epistles,* Volume IV (Nashville: The Gospel Advocate Company, 1964), p. 210.

[28]Robert H. Mounce, *op. cit.,* p. 772.

Indeed, if one does not walk in the light he already has, it may be considered certain that God will not provide more light than he is willing to use.

Verse 16, *Only, whereunto we have attained by that same rule let us walk.*

While, admittedly, "the precise meaning of this compressed verse is doubtful,"[29] it appears to this writer that Paul here instructed the Philippians to keep on walking in the light they already had received and by which they had come thus far. Darrell Royal, famed University of Texas football coach, was once asked about a key post-season game, wanting to know if he had any new plays, etc. Royal answered, "Well, we plan to dance with who brung us!" It seems that this was what Paul meant here. Sometimes when churches grow and attain some measure of what the world would call prosperity, they wish to brighten up their image in the community, sometimes even softening the old doctrines preached by those who built the church; but the homely wisdom of staying with that which is already proved was here enunciated by an apostle.

Verse 17, *Brethren, be ye imitators of me, and mark them that so walk even as ye have us for an ensample.*

"Imitators of me . . ." See other comment on this in this series in CC, 1 Corinthians 4:16, 10:11; also under Ephesians 5:1, this volume.

"Mark them that so walk . . ." Significantly, there is some positive marking as well as negative that should engage the attention of Christians. Marking them that cause divisions (Rom. 16:17) has ever been the delight of some of the church's professional "markers" in all generations; but here an opposite kind of marking is stressed. If churches and those who love the church were more diligent to honor and promote those who "walk even as" Paul walked, it may be that so much of the other type of marking would not be necessary.

Verse 18, *For many walk, of whom I told you often, and now tell you even weeping, that they are enemies of the cross of Christ.*

---

[29]*Ibid.*

"For many walk . . ." These are the evil walkers, and Christians are admonished also to mark these (Rom. 16:17), that is, to identify them in order to thwart their evil devices against the church.

Macknight's paraphrase is valuable, thus:

> For many teachers walk very differently, who I have often said to you, and now even weeping I repeat it, are enemies of the cross of Christ, both by teaching that men are pardoned only through the Levitical sacrifices, and by refusing to suffer with Christ for the truth.[30]

"Those described here were not Judaizers; this would have elicited a different reaction than weeping."[31] This, of course, is a different view from that expressed in Macknight's paraphrase; but there is no reason why both classes of evil-workers were not in Paul's view. (Nevertheless, Lightfoot also took the persons denounced in this passage to be "the antinomian reactionists, the same as those in Romans 16:18).''[32] Those were the persons, professing to be wise, and yet by no means innocent in their wisdom. In any case, a more complete description of those "enemies" is in the next verse.

Verse 19, *Whose end is perdition, whose god is the belly, and whose glory is in their shame, who mind earthly things.*

This description includes all of every name and doctrine whose interest and concern are focused upon the earth and earthly considerations alone. The apostolical description fits a great many people who would be chagrined and embarrassed to admit it; but it is evident to all except themselves that their one and only interest is centered in the present life on earth.

Verse 20, *For our citizenship is in heaven; whence also we wait for a Saviour, the Lord Jesus Christ.*

"Citizenship . . . in heaven . . ." Russell pointed out that this illustration "was drawn from the fact that the Philippians' citizenship was in Rome. Paul developed the same idea in Hebrews 13:14."[33]

---

[30]James Macknight, *op. cit.,* p. 457.

[31]Robert H. Mounce, *op. cit.,* p. 773.

[32]J. B. Lightfoot, *op. cit.,* p. 155.

[33]James William Russell, *op. cit.,* p. 492.

"Whence also we wait for a Saviour . . ." The Second Coming is the background of this. Paul represents himself and the Philippians as living in a state of expectancy, awaiting the coming of the Son of God from heaven, who would raise the dead, appoint the hypocrites their portion in hell, and redeem the righteous unto eternal glory. While true enough that no apostle ever taught that Christ was sure to come within the age wherein they lived, nevertheless they certainly taught that it was possible to be "at any time," that men should live expectantly in regard to it, and that they should be ready at all times for the coming of the Lord. This was sound doctrine then; and it still is.

Boice was correct in diagnosing the cause of much of the malaise which has fallen upon modern Christianity, thus:

> In our day, belief in the Second Coming of Jesus Christ has faded into a remote and sometimes irrelevant doctrine in many large segments of the Christian church; and it is entirely possible that our present lack of courage and lack of joy flow from this attitude.[34]

Verse 21, *Who shall fashion anew the body of our humiliation, that it may be conformed to the body of his glory, according to the working whereby he is able even to subject all things unto himself.*

"The body of our humiliation . . ." Dummelow's interesting remarks on this appear to be true:

> The apostle keenly felt the humiliation of man's mortal state. The idea of the body of glory was given him by the form of the heavenly splendor in which he had seen the Lord Jesus on the Damascus road.[35]

The AV is surely in error on this. "It is not our *vile body* that is to be changed . . . the body is not vile, and the Bible nowhere says it is."[36] Nevertheless, the mortal body is sooner or later in every life a source of humiliation and ultimately death. See CC, 2 Corinthians 5:4ff.

"Changed . . ." This change must occur in either one of two ways: (1) as a result of death itself, following which the body

---

[34] James Montgomery Boice, *op. cit.*, p. 247.
[35] J. R. Dummelow, *op. cit.*, p. 977.
[36] D. A. Hayes, *Paul and His Epistles* (Grand Rapids: Baker Book House, 1969), p. 439.

crumbles into dust, or (2) as a result of the change mentioned in 1 Corinthians 15:52. This writer will spare the reader any detailed explanation of just how that will occur! But, whether following death, or the change of the living at the Second Coming, all men shall be endowed with the new life at the resurrection and a body "as it pleases God."

CHAPTER 4

This chapter is a fitting conclusion for the whole epistle. I. There are three final exhortations (a) to unity (vv. 1-3), (b) to joy (vv. 4-7), and (c) to conformity with all that is good after the apostle's model (vv. 8-9). II. Finally comes thanks for the Philippian offerings: (a) the admission that he could not claim their gift as a necessity (vv. 10-13), (b) a rehearsal of their former liberality (vv. 14-17), and (c) a blessing upon their present sacrifice offered through him to God (vv. 18-20). The salient features of this chapter outline are taken from Barry.[1]

Verse 1, *Wherefore, my brethren beloved and longed for, my joy and my crown, so stand fast in the Lord, my beloved.*

Paul heaped loving title upon loving title to express his affections for the Philippians, there being no less than five expressions of endearment. Significantly, they are Paul's joy at the time present, but in prospect of the Second Advent they will be (at that time) his *crown.* The Greeks had two words for crown, one signifying the diadem of the emperor, and the other referring to the garland that decorated the winner in an athletic contest, the latter being "*stephanos,* the wreath of victory in the games."[2] Barclay pointed out a second meaning of *stephanos,* just as applicable here as the other:

> It was the crown with which guests were crowned when they sat at a banquet, at some time of great joy. It is as if Paul said that the Philippians were the crown of all his toil . . . that at the final banquet of God they were his festal crown.[3]

"So stand fast . . ." We cannot help being a little surprised at this; for, as Boice said, "If we were writing the passage and were using Paul's image, we should likely speak of invasion, marching or conquest. Paul does not do that, but speaks correctly

---

[1]Alfred Barry, *Ellicott's Commentary on the Whole Bible,* Vol. III, *Philippians* (Grand Rapids: Zondervan Publishing House, 1959), p. 85.
[2]H. C. Hewlett, *A NT Commentary, Philippians* (Grand Rapids: Zondervan Publishing House, 1969), p. 479.
[3]William Barclay, *The Letters to the Philippians, Colossians and Thessalonians* (Philadelphia: The Westminster Press, 1975), p. 70.

of standing!"[4] It has been pointed out that Christ conquers new
territory; his followers stand firm in holding what Christ gains.
This is not the only possible analogy of Christian evangelism,
but it is surely one. Perhaps, in the personal sector, this is the
most important analogy; because the great challenge for the
Christian is not that of overcoming someone else with a knowledge of the truth but with himself standing faithfully for the
Lord till life's end.

Verses 2-3, *I exhort Euodia, and I exhort Syntyche, to be of the
same mind in the Lord. Yea, I beseech thee also, true yokefellow,
help these women, for they labored with me in the gospel, with
Clement also, and the rest of my fellow-workers, whose names are
in the book of life.*

Despite the unpleasantness regarding the difficulty mentioned, this passage is one of the most precious in the NT,
because of its mention of the book of life.

"I exhort Euodia . . . Syntyche . . ." The repetition of "I
exhort" was probably for the purpose of avoiding any semblance
of partiality, or any hint of taking sides. No one can say just who
these ladies were; but their trouble is easy enough to understand.
They had a falling out or disagreement over some point of
doctrine or practice, and the animosity between them had
become a problem in the whole church. Boice believed that the
shadow of this personal friction falls upon several passages prior
to this passage where Paul dealt with it. In 1:8, 27, 2:2 and 3:16,
there have already been exhortations to unity and walking by
the same rule; but in this passage Paul boldly confronted the
difficulty and demanded a reconciliation.

Caffin considered the repeated "I exhort" as a probable
indication that both ladies were at fault.[5]

"True yokefellow . . ." Just who was this? Hewlett allowed
that it could have been Luke;[6] Wesley made a conjecture that
it was Silas;[7] Clement of Alexandria taught that this referred

⁴James Montgomery Boice, *Philippians* (Grand Rapids: Zondervan Publishing House, 1971), p. 260.

⁵B. C. Caffin, *Pulpit Commentary,* Vol. 20, *Philippians* (Grand Rapids: Wm.
B. Eerdmans Publishing Company, 1950), p. 156.

⁶H. C. Hewlett, *op. cit.,* p. 479.

⁷John Wesley, *Explanatory Notes Upon the NT (Napierville, Ill: Alec. R.
Allenson, Inc., 1950), in loco.*

to Paul's wife![8] Dummelow said it was probably a proper name on which Paul made a pun, as in the case of Onesimus (profitable).[9] It is hardly necessary to add that we do not know who it was. If this writer were asked to guess at it, the answer would be Epaphroditus, following Lipscomb and Lightfoot.

"In the Lord . . ." This expression absolutely dominates Paul's writings. In verse 1, Paul commanded the Philippians to "stand fast" in the Lord; and here those two women at odds with each other were told to be of the same mind "in the Lord." All spiritual achievements result from being in the Lord. As Knight said, "It is implied here that outside Christ there can be no unity; one cannot love man without loving God."[10] Most disputes are insoluble, except from the discipline that comes of being "in the Lord."

"These women . . . labored with me in the gospel . . ." Not merely these two women, but Lydia also had been an extensive helper of Paul's gospel labors at Philippi. It is not necessary in the case of these, any more than that of Lydia, to suppose that they aided Paul in the public preaching. Paul could not forget their helpfulness, their love of the truth and their sacrifices on his behalf; but now all that was wrecked by an unfortunate disagreement. No wonder Paul attempted to heal it.

"With Clement also . . ." Despite the fact of Lightfoot's opinion that Paul was here enlisting Clement to aid in the reconciliation, the language, as it stands, is a reference to Clement having been, along with Paul, helped by the two sisters in disagreement. One encounters extensive comment with reference to Clement's identity, the conclusion usually being that he is not the same as the famed Clement of Rome.

CLEMENT

Ever since the times of Origen (185-251), who was a disciple of Clement of Alexandria,[11] there has been a positive identification of the Clement mentioned in the above passage with

---

[8]B. C. Caffin, *op. cit.,* p. 155.

[9]J. R. Dummelow, *Commentary on the Holy Bible* (New York: The Macmillan Company, 1937), p. 977.

[10]John A. Knight, *Beacon Bible Commentary,* Vol. IX, *Philippians* (Kansas City: Beacon Hill Press, 1965), p. 346.

[11]Vergilius Ferm, *An Encyclopaedia of Religion* (New York: Philosophical Library, 1943), p. 177.

Clement of Rome who lived until the year 101 and who himself wrote a letter to the Corinthians.

Despite the unwillingness of most modern scholars to allow it, Barry insisted that "the fact of Clement's being in Alexandria (apparently) at the time of Paul's writing is no serious objection."[12] Philippi was a Roman colony, and he might well have been there part of the time on business. "Furthermore the chronology is not decisive against the identification, although it would make Clement very old when he wrote his epistle."[13] Barry summed it all up by saying:

> The identification may stand as not improbable, while the commonness of the name Clement makes it far from certain.[14]

"And the rest of my fellow-workers . . ." Paul's mention, a moment before, of the two sisters in disagreement having helped his own labors, and with Clement also, immediately brought into view a large number of others who had been Paul's fellow-laborers, no less than Clement! Any preacher can see the immediate problem of avoiding calling all those personal names with the almost certain result of leaving out someone who should also have been mentioned. Paul cut the Gordian knot by declaring that God has the whole record in the Book of Life. Beautiful!

"Whose names are in the book of life . . ." For extended comment on the book of life, see CH, chapter 12, under "Book of Life." Significantly there is a register of the redeemed kept by God himself without error. As Martin said, "Christian service may pass unnoticed on earth; but the important thing is that God takes note, and will praise at the last (1 Cor. 4:5)."[15] One's having his name inscribed in the book of life does not, of itself alone, assure eternal life. As Caffin said, "This does not necessarily involve the doctrine of an unconditional, irreversible predestination, or the phrase *to blot out of my book* (Rev. 3:5) could not be used."[16]

Verse 4, *Rejoice in the Lord always: again I will say, Rejoice.*

---

[12]Alfred Barry, *op. cit.,* p. 86.

[13]*Ibid.*

[14]*Ibid.*

[15]R. P. Martin, *The Tyndale NT Commentaries, Philippians* (Grand Rapids: Wm. B. Eerdmans Publishing Company, 1959), p. 167.

[16]B. C. Caffin, *op. cit.,* p. 156.

"In the Lord . . ." The type of rejoicing commanded here is possible only for the redeemed in Christ. After almost 2,000 years, the incredibly beautiful power of this letter still shines. How could such a document have been written from a prison? Surely its writer was "in the Lord Jesus Christ."

Verse 5, *Let your forbearance be known unto all men. The Lord is at hand.*

"Moderation" is a better word than "forbearance" here, because it covers a lot more ground. The Christian is to be moderate in all things, acting with restraint, and without bigotry, avoiding all excesses and extremes of every kind. The Christian community should be known "unto all men," not for demanding their rights, but for their moderation.

"The Lord is at hand . . ." As Foulkes said, "This may refer to the nearness of the Lord to the believer, or to the nearness of his coming."[17] Since the inspired apostle deliberately chose words that may thus have a double meaning, it is only a crooked exegesis which can latch onto one or another of these, insisting that invariably it has this or that meaning. The scholars who are diligent to prove the holy apostles "mistaken" about the soon-coming of the Lord invariably make such an expression as this, or the *Maranatha* of 1 Corinthians 16:23, a flat declaration that Christ was soon to appear in the Second Advent. The careful student of God's word should avoid either extreme, always making allowances for the fact that inspiration gave us an expression capable of two meanings. Could this have been otherwise than by deliberate design?

Verse 6, *In nothing be anxious; but in everything by prayer and supplication with thanksgiving let your requests be made known unto God.*

"In nothing be anxious . . ." In Matthew 6:25-34, our Lord gave extensive admonition on the subject of anxiety; and reference is here made to the comment on those passages in CM 6:25ff. In order to avoid anxiety here, Paul followed exactly the instruction given by the Lord during his ministry.

---

[17]Frances Foulkes, *New Bible Commentary, Revised* (Grand Rapids: Wm. B. Eerdmans Publishing Company, 1970), p. 1138.

We must agree with Hendriksen that Paul's instruction here
does not forbid "kindly concern . . . genuine interest in the
welfare of others."[18]

THANKSGIVING IN EVERYTHING

"In everything . . ." It appears that Paul saw prayer as the
fitting human response to every conceivable situation that might
arise in life; and the position of this phrase at the beginning of
a long clause would make it applicable throughout the clause,
with the meaning that "thanksgiving" should characterize every
prayer, no matter what unusual or extreme life-situation might
have triggered the prayer. But how can anyone be thankful "in
everything"? This writer is indebted to George Henry Stephen-
son for a sermon delivered at Highland congregation in
Memphis, Tennessee, which stressed the following:

In youth one may thank God for the brightness and prospect
of life beckoning to the future.

In age one may thank God that life has extended so long.

In health one may thank God for the greatest of physical
blessings.

In illness one may thank God for wise physicians, kind
nurses and the tender concern of loved ones.

In wealth one may thank God for having been made the
steward of such large accounts.

In poverty one may thank God for him, who though he was
rich became poor that he might make many rich, and for his
special promise, "Blessed are ye poor."

In the event of great loss one may thank God for blessings
he is yet permitted to retain.

In death itself the Christian can thank God for the hope of
eternal life.

At all times and places, in all circumstances and situations,
the Christian will thank God for Jesus Christ our Lord, for the
Father who gave him, for the life he lived, the death he died,
his resurrection from the dead, and for his everlasting gospel
which we have received.

"Let your requests be made known unto God . . ." But, does
not God already know everything? In a sense, of course, he does;
but the command of God, as uttered here through an apostle,
explains the manner chosen by the Father, through which he

---

[18]William Hendriksen, *NT Commentary, Philippians* (Grand Rapids: Baker
Book House, 1962), p. 194.

will know "the requests" of his children. Note too, that this apostolical order says nothing of making known one's *needs* or *desires*. God already knows about them; but our "requests" . . . they do not even become requests until they are made known to God in the prayers of his people.

WHAT SHOULD BE REQUESTED OF GOD?

The forgiveness of sins. Christians are commanded to pray for the forgiveness of their sins (Acts 8:22); but the unbaptized, even though they are belivers, are not so commanded. The believing Saul of Tarsus had been on his knees three days and nights; but God's messenger neither invited him to continue his petition, nor did Saul receive any answer. On the contrary, the inspired preacher commanded him to "arise and be baptized and wash away his (thy) sins" (Acts 22:16).

The forgiveness of the sins of others. Both our Lord (Luke 23:34) and the martyr Stephen (Acts 7:60) prayed for the forgiveness of the sins of others.

The wisdom of God. "If any man lack wisdom, let him ask of God, that giveth to all men liberally and upbraideth not, and it shall be given." (James 1:5,6).

Relief from bitter experiences. Jesus himself prayed that "the cup" might pass from him (Matt. 26:39).

Our daily bread. This line from the Lord's Prayer probably has the larger meaning of "food for today." In any event, prayer for all of life's basic necessities, such as food, clothing and shelter, is authorized by this model prayer.

Laborers in the vineyard. "Pray ye therefore the Lord of the harvest, that he will send forth laborers into his vineyard" (Matt. 9:38).

Laborers already working. Paul admonished the Ephesians to "Pray for ME, that utterance may be given unto me that I may open my mouth boldly, to make known the mystery of the gospel" (Eph. 6:19).

For mercy. "Come boldly to the throne of grace that we may obtain mercy and find grace to help in time of need" (Heb. 4:16).

For the sick. "The prayer of faith shall save the sick" (James 5:14, 15).

Deliverance from temptation. "Lead us not into temptation, but deliver us from the evil one" (Matt. 6:13).

For them that despitefully use us. This includes prayer for enemies. See Matthew 5:44.

In everything. The text before us stresses the need of prayer in all of life's conditions and circumstances. Any list, therefore, of things we should pray for must be partial and incomplete. "Everything" certainly covers a lot of territory. Only one other specific will be noted.

For rulers and authorities. Paul singled out as an object of prayer, in all probability, because it is easily overlooked, especially in a corrupt age like that of the NT era. He said:

> I exhort therefore, that first of all prayers, intercession and giving of thanks be made for all men, for kings, and for all that are in authority, that we might lead a quiet and peaceable life in all godliness and honesty. For this is good and acceptable in the sight of God our Saviour (1 Tim. 2:1-3).

Two examples of prayers for "all that are in authority" are included here:

> Eternal Father, Thou art He before whom the generations of men rise and fade away. From everlasting to everlasting, Thou art God. From Thee comes every good and perfect gift. To Thee, we lift our hearts in thanksgiving. Of Thee, we pray forgiveness of our sins.

> O God, bless the President of the United States, the Members of Congress, and the judiciary. Bless these servants of the people that they may have wisdom to know what is right, courage to do what is right, and sufficient support of their constituents to sustain them in what is right. Endow these Thy servants with grace and knowledge to the end that the wounds of our bleeding world may be healed and peace on earth prevail. May Thy name be glorified and Thy kingdom be increased throughout all nations. God bless the United States of America and this House of Representatives. Through Jesus Christ our Lord. Amen. (Prayer by Burton Coffman in the House of Representatives, May 26, 1953.)

> Almighty God, and our eternal Father: We praise and bless Thy holy name for all the benefits Thou hast granted unto the sons of men. We pray especially for that measure

of Thy divine Providence which will enable all these Thy servants and ministers of Thy gracious will to know what is right, to have the courage to attempt what is right, and to be endowed with the strength to accomplish it. Bless this great City to the end that it might continue in peace and prosperity according to Thy holy will. In the name of Jesus Christ our Lord. Amen. (Invocation by Burton Coffman at meeting of New York City Council, January 8, 1965.)

WAYS IN WHICH GOD ANSWERS PRAYER

How does God answer prayer? First of all, God answers prayer literally, as when Joshua prayed for the sun to stand still, Elijah prayed for drouth, or rain, and when Jonah prayed to God from the belly of the great fish. NT confirmation of God's literal answer of prayer is in the following:

The supplication of a righteous man availeth much in its working. Elijah was a man of like passions with us, and he prayed fervently that it might not rain; and it rained not on the earth for three years and six months. And he prayed again; and the heaven gave rain, and the earth brought forth her fruit (James 5:16-18).

God answers prayer by a refusal to grant the petition. In 2 Corinthians 12:7-10 Paul detailed the fact of his earnest prayers that God would take away his thorn in the flesh, a thing God declined to do.

God also answers prayer by sending something different from what was requested. For example, in Gethsemane Jesus prayed for the "cup" to pass from him; instead of allowing this, God sent an angel to strengthen the Lord. Similarly, men may pray for lighter loads, but God may send them greater strength.

God answers prayer gradually. Hawthorne's allegory of *The Great Stone Face* illustrates this principle. Little Ernest longed to see a man who exemplified the character visible in the Great Stone Face. Gradually, after long years, Ernest himself became that character.

God answers prayer after delay. It seems strange that God would delay to answer Christian prayers, but it may not be denied. The angel sent to stay the hand of Abraham about to offer Isaac delayed until the latest possible moment. The wine had run completely out at Cana before the Lord answered his mother's implied request. When Jacob wrestled with an angel, day was breaking before the issue was decided. In the NT, Jairus came to the Lord; and during Jesus' delay, his daughter died. Here also may be the explanation of *why* the Lord often delays the answer to prayer; it is that he may give something far more wonderful, or far better, than what was requested. In the case of Jairus' daughter, a resurrection was far better and far more wonderful than a healing would have been.

God also answers prayer through natural laws and processes. When fields yield richly; when people enjoy good health; when nature pours out abundant blessings; all of these things are God's answer to his children's prayers for daily bread, nor should the Giver be overlooked merely because the normal processes of nature through which his blessings were conveyed are recognized and partially understood.

By way of summarizing the ways in which God answers prayer, *some of the ways* are:

He may answer it literally.
He may refuse to grant the petition.
He may send something different from what was requested.
He may answer it gradually.
He may answer it after a long delay.
He may answer through natural laws and processes.

Verse 7, *And the peace of God which passeth all understanding, shall guard your hearts and your thoughts in Christ Jesus.*

"The peace of God . . ." This was described by Hendriksen as "The smile of God reflected in the soul of the believer, the heart's calm after Calvary's storm, the conviction that God who spared not his own Son will surely also, along with him, freely give us all things (Rom. 8:32)."[19]

"Passeth all understanding . . ." Those who see it manifested in the lives of Christians cannot understand such peace exhibited despite the slings and arrows of outrageous fortune encountered by them; even those who possess it cannot fully understand it; but those who have experienced it would not exchange it for anything that the world has to offer.

"Shall guard your hearts . . ." The scholars tell us that this is translated from a military term signifying a sentinel guarding a city. As Philippi was a Roman colony, populated with many

---

[19]*Ibid.*, p. 196.

retirees from the military establishment of Rome, this must rank as another marvelous analogy drawn by Paul from things which he observed in his travels. Such metaphors as those of the athletic contests in Olympian games or the triumphal processions of generals and rulers are also included.

"In Christ Jesus . . ." Paul's favorite expression again appears here. To understand all that is meant by these words is to grasp in its fullness the whole theology of the apostle Paul, and indeed all the NT writers. One may only be amazed that so many commentators pay no attention at all to these most important words. Out of Christ there is nothing; in him is the life eternal; and men (let all men hear it) are "baptized into Christ," as Paul himself declared (Rom. 6:3). What about faith? No unbeliever *can* be baptized, and no believer is in Christ till he is baptized into him.

Verse 8, *Finally, brethren, whatsoever things are true, whatsoever things are honorable, whatsoever things are just, whatsoever things are pure, whatsoever things are lovely, whatsoever things are of good report; if there be any virtue, and if there be any praise, think on these things.*

"Finally . . ." Paul had written this in 3:1; but as Caffin put it, "Again and again he prepares to close his epistle, but he cannot at once bid farewell to his beloved Philippians."[20]

Thought control is clearly the practice Paul enjoined here. If men would live correctly in God's sight, let them *think* of those qualities which possess positive value. Thinking of such things will lead to speaking of them, as exemplified in the lives of associates, thus contributing to the joy and unity of Christian fellowship.

Foulkes pointed out that the strong word (*logizomai*) Paul used here, translated "take such things into account" is Paul's way of saying, "Let such things shape your attitudes."[21]

Of special interest in Paul's list given here is the word *aretē*, translated "virtue." This is found nowhere else in Paul's letters and in only two other NT references (1 Peter 2:9; 2 Peter 1:3), despite the fact of its being "a frequent word in classical and

---

[20]B. C. Caffin, *op. cit.,* p. 157.
[21]Frances Foulkes, *op. cit.,* p. 1138.

Hellenistic Greek."[22] Lightfoot believed that Paul "seems studiously to avoid this common heathen term for moral excellence."[23] From this Lightfoot interpreted Paul's meaning to be, "Whatever value may reside in your old heathen conception of virtue, whatever consideration is due to the praise of men, etc."[24] Barry concurred in this discernment, saying that Paul's introduction of *virtue* and *praise* after the hypothetical "if there be any" indicated that these last two words "occupy less firm and important ground"[25] than the others (due, of course, to pagan conceptions of what the terms meant).

Despite the above, however, this writer holds this list of desirables in the highest respect, the words in their commonly accepted denotations and connotations standing for the very greatest human excellence known to men. God help all men to let their thoughts dwell upon such things as Paul enumerated here.

Verse 9, *The things which ye both learned and received and heard and saw in me, these things do: and the God of peace shall be with you.*

This is the equivalent of Paul's frequent admonitions to follow (or imitate) him as he followed (or imitated) Christ. See under 3:17, above.

"The God of peace . . ." In verse 7, Paul had written "the peace of God"; and, as Barry said, "The inversion is striking."[26] The peace of God passes all understanding, but the God of peace is more, peace being that which is given, and God being the giver.

Verse 10, *But I rejoice in the Lord greatly, that now at length ye have revived your thought of me; wherein ye did indeed take thought, but ye lacked opportunity.*

Paul reserved his expression of thanks to the Philippian congregation for their financial aid, quite properly, to the very last of his letter. The doctrinal part of the letter being finished, Paul

[22]R. P. Martin, *op. cit,*, p. 172.
[23]J. B. Lightfoot, *St. Paul's Epistle to the Philippians* (Grand Rapids: Zondervan Publishing House, 1963), p. 162.
[24]*Ibid.*
[25]Alfred Barry, *op. cit.,* p. 87.
[26]*Ibid.*

in this verse turned to those intensely personal things between himself and the Philippians.

"Ye have revived . . ." Some scholars detect a vein of criticism or disappointment in this, as if Paul has said, "Well, I am glad you have come alive." If there is any thought like this here, then Paul promptly took the sting out of it by pointing out that, actually, there had been "no opportunity" to help him any sooner. Furthermore, as Knight wrote: "Paul wrote 'ye were also careful (*ephroneite*)' . . . using the imperfect tense, which suggests his willingness to believe that the Philippians all along had desired to help but were hindered."[27]

Verse 11, *Not that I speak in respect of want: for I have learned, in whatsoever state I am, therein to be content.*

"Not that I speak in respect of want . . ." This statement has elicited two opinions of scholars: (1) "Paul uses the word *content* (a moment later) in the sense of his being independent of circumstances; but his all-sufficient resources are by the grace of Christ who lives in him."[28] (2) Sir William M. Ramsay believed that Paul had inherited, or otherwise come into possession of, a large sum of money, founding his opinion on the fact of Luke's attendance upon Paul and other conditions of Paul's imprisonment. Despite the plausibility of Ramsay's deductions it would appear that the preferable view is that after (1), above.

Verse 12, *I know how to be abased, and I know also how to abound: in everything and in all things have I learned the secret both to be filled and to be hungry, both to abound and to be in want.*

Strange as it may appear to us, Paul was, in this verse, disclaiming any need of the Philippians' gifts, rejoicing in the reception of it for the benefit to *them*, not to himself! This is simply astounding. As Mounce put it, "While not dependent on the gift, or even seeking it, Paul rejoiced in that such sacrifices were well-pleasing to God and beneficial to the giver."[29]

Verse 13, *I can do all things in him that strengtheneth me.*

---

[27]John A. Knight, *op. cit.,* p. 349.

[28]Frances Foulkes, *op. cit.,* p. 1138.

[29]Robert H. Mounce, *Wycliffe Bible Commentary* (Chicago: Moody Press, 1971), p. 775.

This is a summary of what Paul had just been writing with regard to his having an inward sufficiency "in the Lord" to cope with any of life's circumstances, no matter how severe, and no matter how favorable. Paul truly felt that it was impossible for life to confront him with *anything* that he and the Lord could not handle! Those who think they find traces of Stoicism in Paul's attitude here know nothing, either of Stoicism or of the heart of the great apostle. As King correctly noted, "Christ is the source of Paul's power; it is Christ who is continually infusing power into him."[30] The key words of this verse, as so often in Paul's writings, are "IN HIM."

Verse 14, *Howbeit ye did well that ye had fellowship with my affliction.*

"My affliction . . ." Note Paul does not say "want," leaving room for what he had already implied, namely, that he did not actually *need* their gift. Hendriksen saw this verse as Paul's statement that their gift had "relieved his need";[31] but it seems more accurate to see it as encouraging in his affliction (imprisonment). Whether or not Paul could have survived without the gift (after all, Rome was feeding him), he nevertheless deeply appreciated this evidence of loving concern on the part of his dear Philippians.

Verses 15-16, *And ye yourselves also know, ye Philippians, that in the beginning of the gospel, when I departed from Macedonia, no church had fellowship with me in the matter of giving and receiving but ye only; for even in Thessalonica ye sent once and again to my need.*

From the very beginning of Paul's experience at Philippi, the people there were noted for their liberality and hospitality. It was from the house of Lydia that Paul preached the gospel there. Even before Paul was out of Macedonia, they began sending him money. As Hendriksen said, "Truly the stamp of Luke's and Lydia's commendable generosity was upon this congregation."[32]

Verse 17, *Not that I seek for the gift; but I seek for the fruit that increases to your acccount.*

---

[30]John A. Knight, *op. cit.,* p. 350.
[31]William Hendriksen, *op. cit.,* p. 207.
[32]*Ibid.*

Again Paul stressed the truth that he did not covet their money, and yet he was glad for what they had done. Their eternal reward was enhanced and extended as a result of their generous treatment of the apostle.

Verse 18, *But I have all things, and abound: I am filled, having received from Epaphroditus the things that came from you, an odor of a sweet smell, a sacrifice acceptable, well-pleasing to God.*

The apostle "credits the givers with the proper spirit, that is, the attitude of faith, love and gratitude."[33] Notice how giving is described in the terms of the worship of God, being a "sacrifice," "an odor of a sweet smell," a figurative reference to the incense burned in the tabernacle, symbolical of the prayers of God's people.

Verse 19, *And my God shall supply every need of yours according to his riches in glory in Christ Jesus.*

Hendriksen made a distinction between God's general providence over all of his creation, including even plants and animals, and "the very special providence of which believers are the objects,"[34] applying the latter to the Philippians as promised in this verse. Paul's teaching in 2 Corinthians 9:6-10, coupled with this emphatic blessing upon the Philippians, surely supports such a view. However, as Hendriksen further commented on this:

> This does not mean that the Philippians would now be justified in becoming lazy. "God's word does not advocate fanaticism, nor does it say that one should throw his pocketbook into the nearest river and then announce that he is going to live by faith" (Tenney). To be sure, God was taking care of Paul, but one of the ways in which he was doing so was exemplified by the gift from Philippi.[35]

Verse 20, *Now unto our God and Father be the glory for ever and ever. Amen.*

This short, beautiful doxology, so characteristic of Paul's letters, is concluded with the solemn "Amen." For comment on "Amen," see CH 13:25.

---

[33]*Ibid.,* p. 209.
[34]*Ibid.,* p. 210.
[35]*Ibid.*

Verses 21-23, *Salute every saint in Christ Jesus. The brethren that are with me salute you. All the saints salute you, especially they that are of Caesar's household. The grace of the Lord Jesus Christ be with your spirit.*

Hendriksen, like many others, has supposed that Paul might have written these final verses with his own hand, as he sometimes did, thus making such an inscription a kind of signature.

Knight wrote that "One would expect in a personal letter such as this to find in the closing salutations a number of names."[36] Despite the fact of many scholars accepting such a proposition, such an expectation as that mentioned by Knight is as fantastically unreasonable as any that could be contrived by the imagination. In no other scholarly assumption is there such a vacuum of intelligent reasoning as in this. Think a moment. If Paul saluted a few friends by name at the end of this epistle, it would have been an insult to a hundred others whom he personally knew in Philippi. We have already seen under 4:3 how the great apostle had avoided getting involved with writing any more personal names (see comment); and for him gratuitously to have included a list of names here was unthinkable. Any minister who ever served a large church with hundreds of his personal friends members of it will instantly recognize what an unconscionable blunder it would have been for Paul to tack on a list of personal greetings here, unless he had been planning to name "all of those" whom he knew and loved at Philippi. Thus the objection voiced by Knight uncovers no fault of the apostle's but it does show the fuzzy thinking of many scholars on this point.

"Salute every saint . . ." "Only here in the NT does *hagios* (saint) occur in the singular (fifty-seven times in the plural), and even here it is prefaced by *every*, a strong reminder that Christianity is a corporate affair."[37]

"Saints in Caesar's household . . ." As Barclay said, "This is what we would call the Imperial Civil Service."[38] Caesar's houshold was all over the empire, wherever his servants or officers were carrying out the emperor's orders. Despite this, it

---

[36]John A. Knight, *op. cit.,* p. 352.
[37]Robert H. Mounce, *op. cit.,* p. 777.
[38]William Barclay, *op. cit.,* p. 87.

should be remembered that Paul was in Rome when this was written, justifying the conclusion that "Christianity had infiltrated into the highest positions in the empire."[39]

Lightfoot took a step in the direction of indentifying some of these with some of the individuals saluted in Romans 16th chapter. See CR under that reference. If slaves of a nobleman in the provinces were willed to the emperor, then upon the death of the nobleman, the slaves would be transferred to Rome, but still retain their family identity, as the "household of Aristobulus" for example; and Lightfoot thought some of the "household" mentioned here might formerly have lived at Philippi. He wrote:

> This supposition best explains the incidental character of the allusion. Paul obviously assumes that his distant correspondents know all about the persons thus referred to. If so, we are led to look for them in the long list of names saluted by St. Paul some three years before in the epistle to the Romans.[40]

"The Lord Jesus Christ . . ." The prevalence of this expression in Philippians is significant. Almost every other line in the epistle has it in one form or another, making it rank along with "in Christ" as a distinctive mark of the Pauline theology. All men should praise God for the remarkable beauty and effectiveness of this priceless personal letter preserved through so many dangers and centuries to bless the saints of all ages.

---

[39]*Ibid.*
[40]J. B. Lightfoot, *op. cit.,* p. 173.

BIBLIOGRAPHY . . . PHILIPPIANS

The following authors and sources were quoted in the text of the commentary on Philippians:

Barclay, William, *The Letters to the Philippians, Colossians, and Thessalonians* (Philadelphia: The Westminster Press, 1976).

Barry, Alfred, *Ellicott's Commentary on the Whole Bible*, Vol. VIII, *Philippians* (Grand Rapids: Zondervan Publishing House, 1959).

Blaiklock, E. M., *Cities of the New Testament* (Old Tappan, N.J.: Fleming H. Revell Co., 1965).

Boice, James Montgomery, *Philippians* (Grand Rapids: Zondervan Publishing House, 1971)

Bruce, F. F., *Answers to Questions* (Grand Rapids: Zondervan Publishing House, 1972).

Caffin, B. C., *The Pulpit Commentary*, Vol. 20, *Philippians* (Grand Rapids: Wm. B. Eerdmans Publishing Company, 1950).

Dummelow, J. R., *Commentary on the Holy Bible* (New York: The Macmillan Company, 1937).

Encyclopaedia Britannica (Chicago: William Benton, 1961).

Ferm, Vergilius, *An Encyclopedia of Religion* (New York: Philosophical Library, 1943).

Foulkes, Francis, *New Bible Commentary, Revised* (Grand Rapids: Wm. B. Eerdmans Publishing Company, 1970).

Hayes, D. A., *Paul and His Epistles* (Grand Rapids: Baker Book House, 1969).

Hendriksen, William, *NT Commentary, Philippians* (Grand Rapids: Baker Book House, 1962).

Hewlett, H. C., *A NT Commentary, Philippians* (Grand Rapids: Zondervan Publishing House, 1969).

International Standard Bible Encyclopaedia (Chicago: The Howard Severance Company, 1915).

Kennedy, H. A. A., *The Expositor's Greek Testament*, Vol. III (Grand Rapids: Wm. B. Eerdmans Publishing Company, 1967).

Knight, John A., *Beacon Bible Commentary,* Vol. IX, *Philippians* (Kansas City: Beacon Hill Press, 1965).

Lightfoot, J. B., *St. Paul's Epistle to the Philippians* (Grand Rapids: Zondervan Publishing House, 1963).

Lipscomb, David, *A Commentary on NT Epistles*, Vol. IV (Nashville: The Gospel Advocate Company, 1964).

Macknight, James, *Apostolical Epistles with Commentary* Vol. III (Grand Rapids: Baker Book House, 1969).

Marshall, Alfred, *The Nestle Greek Text with an English Translation* (Grand Rapids: Wm. B. Eerdmans Publishing Company, 1970).

Martin, R. P., *The Tyndale NT Commentaries, Philippians* (Grand Rapids: Wm. B. Eerdmans Publishing Company, 1959).

Mounce, Robert H., *Wycliffe Bible Commentary, NT* (Chicago: Moody Press, 1971).

Murray, John, *The Epistle to the Romans* (Grand Rapids: Wm. B. Eerdmans Publishing Company, 1968).

Pink, Arthur, *Gleanings from Paul* (Chicago: Moody Press, 1967).

Russell, James William, *Compact Commentary on the NT* (Grand Rapids: Baker Book House, 1964).

Wallace, Foy E., Jr., *A Review of the New Versions* (Fort Worth: Foy E. Wallace, Jr., Publications, 1973).

Wesley, John, *Explanatory Notes Upon the NT* (Napierville, Ill.: Alec R. Allenson, Inc.).

Wesley, John, *One Volume NT Commentary* (Grand Rapids: Baker Book House, 1972).

Colossians

INTRODUCTION

Authenticity. Absolutely nothing of any significance has ever been said against the authenticity of this epistle. Criticisms? Of course, there have been many vain efforts to reduce or destroy the confidence in which the Christians of nearly two thousand years have received this work as a genuine epistle of Paul; and a few of these will be noted under *criticisms,* below; but the investigation of such criticisms should be dissociated from the question of *authenticity,* a subject to which they are totally unrelated.

Authorship. This letter purports to be from the apostle Paul; and only in an imagination running wild is it possible to associate the letter with any other person than that of the blessed apostle himself. The historical situation is Pauline, the people named in the letter were companions and associates of Paul; the bearer of the letter was Paul's Tychicus, a faithful postman who carried other Pauline letters also. The Christology of the epistle, the emphasis upon being "in Christ," the conception of Christ as the "head" of the church which is his "body," and likewise every line of the whole letter are indelibly stamped with the mind of Paul.

Supportive, corroborative opinion in harmony with the above views may be cited in abundance, as for example:

There need be no misgivings in accepting the Pauline authorship of the epistle. The doubts formerly entertained by the critics have largely disappeared, and the number increases of those who fully admit its genuineness. The time is probably not far distant when this will be regarded as settled by common consent.[1]

The authenticity (of Colossians) was not questioned until the second quarter of the 19th century . . . sober criticism has come today to realize that it is impossible to deny the Pauline authorship of this epistle.[2]

Some objections have been raised . . . but the criteria for judging style are not accurate enough to place the authenticity in jeopardy . . . We may therefore with confidence accept the ascription of the epistle to Paul as genuine.[3]

---

[1]J. R. Dummelow, *Commentary on the Holy Bible* (New York: The Macmillan Company, 1937), p. 980.

[2]*ISBE,* p. 677.

[3]Donald G. Guthrie, *New Bible Commentary, Revised* (Grand Rapids: Wm. B. Eerdmans Publishing Company, 1970), p. 1139.

The consensus of Christian scholarship is that Paul is the author of this epistle; the method and content are Pauline ... The early church attests its authenticity; and it is included in the most important *P 46 papyrus*, The Chester Beatty Papyrus.[4]

Criticisms. A few of the common allegations of critical scholars will be noted for the sake of young students who might have encountered them; but, as noted above, critics of the NT have long ago overreached themselves; and today the whole pseudo-science of source criticism stands naked and discredited before every Christian scholar on earth. It is not so much the intelligence of source critics which is questioned, for doubtless some of them are brilliant intellectuals; however, it is the *basic rules* of the critical games in which they are engaged which have *come unglued*. A substantial part of the major assumptions underlying current source criticism is naive, simplistic, unrealistic and absolutely untrustworthy.

(1) For example, some of the word games of the critics are preposterous. Twelve verses at the end of Mark are rejected, partially on the grounds that three words in the passage were not in Mark's vocabulary! This is on a parity with rejecting the preamble to the Declaration of Independence because it has four words which were not in the vocabulary of Thomas Jefferson! Rejection of Pauline authorship of this epistle on the basis that 34 words in it are not found elswhere in Paul's writings is just as ridiculous. (2) Questionings based upon variations in style and form are likewise undependable. As Ashby said: "Stylistic criteria are not very firm grounds of critical proof in any circumstances."[5] (3) The critical device of trying to make Colossians to be Paul's refutation of a late second-century gnosticism, thus anachronistic and un-Pauline, is also wicked, unreasonable, unprovable. To begin with, the critics do not know that much about gnosticism which existed before Christianity as well as after it, and which, in various forms, has been present in all generations. Besides that, in a few instances, critics have even

---

[4]John B. Nielson, *Colossians in Beacon Bible Commentary*, Vol. IX (Kansas City: Beacon Hill Press, 1965), p. 359.

[5]Ernest G. Ashby, *A NT Commentary* (Grand Rapids: Zondervan Publishing House, 1969), p. 481.

resorted to mistranslations of the sacred text in order to bolster their theories. This will be noted in the text of the commentary below.

SPECIFIC CRITICISMS

1. There are 34 words in Colossians not found elsewhere in Paul's writings, and not even elsewhere in NT. Well, what of it? Paul was "fighting a unique heresy at Colossae."[6] Words needed nowhere else were needed here, both to define and to refute the error. As Hendriksen put it:

> Percy is entirely correct when he states, "It can be safely affirmed, that from the aspect of lexicography no serious argument against the genuine character of this epistle can be advanced."[7]

2. In 1963, a critic came up with the idea that an author would use the conjunction "and" at a constant ratio to the numbers of words written, and denied the Pauline authorship of Colossians on the fact that the "ratio" varied from that in other Pauline letters! But, writing in *Time* magazine, March 29, 1963, William Toedtman rejected such a conclusion with the words, "So *kais* (ands) are the most unreliable figures to pour into a computer."[8] In computerese it is *GIGO*, that is *garbage in, garbage out*!

3. The heresy combated in Colossians was second-century gnosticism; thus first-century Paul could not have been the author. The major premise of this criticism is false. Colossians was not directed against the gnosticism of the second-century; because, as Hendriksen pointed out, "They made extensive use of Colossians."[9] Dr. Frank Pack also stressed that, "Historically, such an idea as gnosticism may have come from Christianity as a deviate idea."[10] As Alfred Barry's excursus on this subject proves, all of the phases of gnosticism which Paul touched upon in Colossians "refer only to the errors of Judaeo-Gnosticism . . .

---

[6]William Hendriksen, *Colossians and Philemon* (Grand Rapids: Baker Book House, 1962), p. 29.

[7]*Ibid.*

[8]*Ibid.*, p. 31.

[9]William Hendriksen, *op. cit.*, p. 31.

[10]Frank Pack, "The Gospel of John in the Twentieth Century" in *The Restoration Quarterly*, Vol. 7, No. 4 (Abilene: The Restoration Quarterly Corporation, 1963), p. 179.

Gnosticism in its early stages while still allied to Judaism,"[11] and therefore contemporary with Paul.

The City of Colossae. A group of three cities, Laodicea, Hierapolis and Colossae, located about a hundred miles east of Ephesus, had relatively strong congregations of Christians in apostolic times. In ancient times, Colossae was the largest and most important; but by the times of the apostle Paul, its importance had declined; however, Pliny "classed it among the most famous towns in the district,"[12] having reference, no doubt, to its history rather than its size. The most important thing that ever happened there was the reception of this letter from the apostle Paul.

Founding of the Church at Colossae. There seems little doubt that Paul himself was acquainted with the Colossians. Far from denying this, 2:1, 2 actually affirms it as Macknight proved. See in text below. In all probability, Paul had occasion to visit the Colossians while residing two full years at Ephesus (Acts 19:10); and if not, then certainly some of the Colossians had opportunity to hear Paul.

Date. Most conservative scholars agree that Colossians was written from Rome during Paul's first imprisonment which makes the date of it somewhere near the years 60 or 61 A.D. Barry and Hendriksen each gave 61-63 as the approximate date. ISBE gives 58 A.D. as a possibility. Since this letter was in a sense the twin of Ephesians, both being dispatched by the same hand and the same carrier at the same time, the date of both must be the same. This writer favors the date 58.

Relationship to Ephesians. By the very fact of Ephesians and Colossians having been written by the same author at the same time, approximately, and addressed to churches within a hundred miles of each other, having the same problems and existing under similar conditions, it is inevitable that the letters would bear a close similarity to each other. Of course, the similarity has been the basis of all kinds of wild speculation about one of these letters being copied from the other. As Barry said:

---

[11]Alfred Barry, *Ellicott's Commentary on the Whole Bible,* Vol. III (Grand Rapids: Zondervan Publishing House, 1959), p. 123.

[12]J. R. Dummelow, *op. cit.,* p. 980.

The letters present, on the one hand, the most striking similarities, and, on the other hand, differences almost equally striking and characteristic — thus contradicting all theories of derivation of one from the other, and supporting very strongly the idea of independent contemporaneousness and coincidence of thought.[13]

Plan and Themes. About the only outline Paul used in his letters was that of laying down the doctrine of what to believe in the first part, and then laying down the rules of proper behavior in the latter part of his letters. The Christology is very high in Colossians, making Christ the full possessor of "godhead." "The body of Christ" with himself as "head" is also prominent. Many other fundamental Christian teachings are also included. They are wrong, however, who would make the conception of "Christ's spiritual body" to be Pauline exclusively. As Ellis said, "This motif is deeply embedded in the structure of NT theology . . . its roots lie in the teaching of the Lord himself."[14]

Pertinence. All of the sacred scriptures are relevant to all ages and conditions of men; and the great reason for studying the word of God was announced by Paul himself in 2 Timothy 2:15; however, our own age will find a special relevance in Colossians. Like those ancient Christians, the citizens of our own times are tempted to trust the philosophy and vain deceit of men, to rely upon the so-called "knowledge" which holds itself above and opposed to the word of God, and to adulterate Christianity with all kinds of human additives. As Nielson expressed it:

> The Colossian errors are also today's errors. In the face of so many cults, the issue becomes again the perennial one: "What think ye of Christ? whose son is he?" (Matt. 22:42) . . . Colossians is superbly suited to make that identification possible.[15]

Thus, it is with profound thanksgiving to the Providence which has preserved for nearly two thousand years the priceless truth contained in this letter to the Colossians, that we again look closely at the words which have inspired and blessed Christians through the ages.

---

[13]Alfred Barry, *op. cit.,* p. 91.
[14]E. Earle Ellis, *Wycliffe NT Commentary* (Chicago: Moody Press, 1971, p. 781.
[15]John B. Nielson, *op. cit.,* p. 361.

CHAPTER 1

This is one of the most important chapters in the Holy Writ, because of the Christology which reaches a climax of surpassing importance in v. 28.

It begins with the usual Pauline greetings (1-2) and occasions of thanksgiving for the Colossians (3-8); next comes a profound paragraph on the preeminence of the Son of God (9-23), and then the superb mention of the mystery and the secret of human perfection to be achieved "in Christ" (24-29).

Verse 1, *Paul, an apostle of Christ Jesus through the will of God, and Timothy our brother.*

"Paul, an apostle . . ." It is not necessary to refer to Paul as "Saint Paul," for such a title actually downgrades him. All Christians are "saints," but not all are apostles. "Apostle" was the high title given by Christ himself to his chosen representatives, and it carries with it the idea of plenary authority. A second reason for using the title "Apostle Paul" is that it is the title used by himself, and therefore the one preferred by himself. Still a third reason is that it emphasizes the truth that Paul was Christ's representative, not the representative of the church. He was not an apostle appointed by ecclesiastical authority, but a plenary representative of Christ, chosen and appointed by divine authority. Thus the medieval conceit that the Holy Scriptures belonged to the church and were in some sense the property of it and therefore subject to their exclusive interpretation is defeated and destroyed by the apostolical title itself. Of course, it was medievalism that downgraded Paul from "apostle" to "saint," thus putting him on a parity with any deceased Christian. It is high time to restore the biblical emphasis and speak of "Paul the apostle of Christ."

"Timothy our brother . . ." The Greek has "Timothy the brother," and by this word Paul dissociated Timothy from any responsibility or authority for the letter to the Colossians, Paul being the exclusive author of it in the sense of its teachings pertaining to him alone.

As Barry noted, "In a special epistle like this, Timothy would be joined with Paul, as usual; but in a general epistle to the churches of Asia, the apostle alone would rightly speak."[1] Despite this view, it is incorrect to think of Timothy's name, in any sense, being joined with that of Paul, except as a courtesy in places where Timothy was known.

Another error is that of denying "apostle" as any kind of title. Guthrie said, "Apostle is no formal title, but a claim to divine authority."[2] On the contrary, "Apostle" is indeed a title, bestowed by the Saviour himself (Luke 6:13). Although of Greek origin, the word "apostle" was most certainly known by our Lord, and its use in Luke's gospel is not anachronistic. See CL 6:13, for more on this.

Verse 2, *To the saints and faithful brethren in Christ that are at Colossae. Grace to you and peace from God our Father.*

"The saints and faithful brethren . . ." Hendriksen pointed out that "The definite article *the* is omitted before *brethren*,"[3] indicating that not two classes, but only one class is addressed. As Wesley put it, "*Saints* refers to their union with God . . . *brethren* refers to their union with fellow-Christians."[4]

"In Christ . . . at Colossae . . ." Hayes commented thus:

> They were in Christ as surely as they were in Colossae. They had their residence in Colossae and walked about in Colossae; but they had received Jesus in their hearts as Lord, and they also walked in him as they went about their business day by day.[5]

As Barclay said, "Wherever a Christian is, he is in Christ."[6] That is why outward circumstances cannot destroy a Christian. No matter what happens in his environment, to his property, or even to his body, he, through it all, remains safe in Christ Jesus.

---

[1]Alfred Barry, *Ellicott's Commentary on the Whole Bible,* Vol. III, *Philippians* (Grand Rapids: Zondervan Publishing House, 1959), p. 96.

[2]Donald Guthrie, *New Bible Commentary, Revised* (Grand Rapids: Wm. B. Eerdmans Publishing Company, 1970), p. 1141.

[3]William Hendriksen, *Colossians and Philemon* (Grand Rapids: Baker Book House, 1964), p. 44.

[4]John Wesley, *Explanatory Notes Upon the NT* (Napierville, Illinois: Alec. R. Allenson, Inc., 1950), *in loco.*

[5]D. A. Hayes, *Paul and His Epistles* (Grand Rapids: Baker Book House, 1959, Reprint from Copyright Edition, 1915), p. 369.

[6]William Barclay, *The Letters to the Philippians, Colossians and Thessalonians* (Philadelphia: The Westminster Press, 1975), p. 104.

Although specifically addressed to the Christians in Colossae, this letter was also intended for the nearby congregations at Laodicea (4:16), and in fact for the Christians of all times and places.

Verses 3-4, *We give thanks to God the Father of our Lord Jesus Christ, praying always for you, having heard of your faith in Christ Jesus, and of the love which ye have toward all the saints.*

Some commentators have supposed that Paul copied his habit of beginning his letters with prayers of thanksgiving from the stylized letters of that period, each containing an expression of thanks to some pagan deity; but strong agreement is felt with Ashby who declared that Paul's prayers were "no merely conventional opening." The omission of such prayers in Galatians and 2 Corinthians indicates that they were included "only when the progress of the converts was a real cause for thanksgiving."[7]

"Faith . . . hope . . . love . . ." make up Paul's famed triad, found in these two verses and the verse following, and reminding one of 1 Thessalonians 1:3, 1 Corinthians 13:3, etc.

Hendriksen observed that Paul's letter to Titus also omitted the prayer of thanksgiving; thus it is correct to say that "In all of Paul's epistles, with the exception of Galatians and Titus, the opening salutation is followed, either immediately or very shortly, by a thanksgiving and/or doxology."[8]

"Having heard of your faith . . ." This is interpreted to mean that Paul did not have first-hand knowledge of the Colossians, but such an interpretation is probably incorrect. As Macknight said, "It was Paul's custom when absent from the churches which he had planted to make inquiry as to their state."[9] Thus it is very possible that Paul here referred to their continuing in the faith and not to their being converted. Colossae was a Phrygian city; and the NT emphatically declares that Paul "went throughout Phrygia" (Acts 16:6).

"Your faith in Christ Jesus . . ." It is refreshing to find a scholar such as Ashby firmly declaring what is undoubtedly true in this passage, as well as in a great many other NT scriptures, namely, that:

---

[7]Ernest G. Ashby, *A NT Commentary* (Grand Rapids: Zondervan Publishing House, 1969), p. 483.

[8]William Hendriksen, *op. cit.,* p. 46.

[9]James Macknight, *Apostolical Epistles with Commentary,* Vol. III (Grand Rapids: Baker Book House, 1969), p. 479.

Christ is the sphere in which this faith works rather than its object; in other words "faith" derives its significance from their position "in Christ."[10]

"Faith" that saves the Christian is not a subjective trust/faith in his heart, but a faith properly exercised by one who is "in Christ." "Faith in Christ," properly understood, usually means the Christian's fidelity to God as he continues to walk "in Christ." Paul's strong word for this was "obedience of faith" (Rom. 1:5; 16:26).

DID PAUL CONVERT THE COLOSSIANS?

Although disputed by some, this question was answered affirmatively by Macknight. Here is a summary of his argument:[11]

Verse 1:4 does not mean that Paul did not convert the Colossians; because Paul used this same language when addressing both churches and individuals for whom the apostle was undoubtedly the instrument of their conversion (Phile. 1:5, 19; 1 Thess. 3:6; Ephes. 1:15). Just as emphatically, 1:7 and 2:1 cannot mean that Paul did not convert them. See notes on those verses below.

Positively: (1) Paul stated that on "your account," that is, the account of the Colossians, he had been made a minister; and this implies that when Paul was in Phrygia he preached to them.

(2) Paul's recommendation of Epaphras to them has the ring of coming from one who, in some sense, was responsible both for them and Epaphras.

(3) Paul wrote the salutation with his own hand, as he did to other churches where he was acquainted and they knew his handwriting.

(4) "Even as ye have been taught" (2:6) declares that Paul had the most intimate knowledge of their teaching, and this argues that he himself had done it.

Whether or not one agrees with this reasoning, it seems to be convincing enough.

Verse 5, *Because of the hope which is laid up for you in the heavens, whereof ye heard before in the word of the truth of the gospel.*

---

[10]Ernest G. Ashby, *op. cit.,* p. 483.
[11]James Macknight, *op. cit.,* p. 480-482.

"Because of the hope . . ." This clause makes "hope" the pinnacle and summit of the famed triad of faith, hope and love, just as love is designated in 1 Corinthians 13:13. Of course, such a cavalier treatment of "faith" is deplored by the scholars. As Hendriksen put it:

> Some have experienced difficulty with the fact that Paul here in Colossians 1:4, 5 in which he follows sequence b., seems to be saying that the faith of the Colossians and their love are based on hope. Note the words "by reason of the hope."[12]

It is clear enough that Paul did not here merely "seem to be saying," but that he emphatically affirmed that the Christian's faith and love are derived from and founded upon the hope of the gospel. The NT unequivocally states that we are "saved by hope" (Rom. 8:24, margin); and here the reason for such a truth appears. Both faith and love are "by reason of hope." See more on this in CR 8:24.

"In the heavens . . ." "This appears to be a superlative expression here, including all regions and spheres of the unseen world."[13] The plural "heavens" is a Hebrew conception, probably founded upon such passages as Deuteronomy, 1 Kings 8:27; the rabbis spoke of two heavens; Paul of three (2 Cor. 12:2).

"The truth of the gospel . . ." "This expression (as in Galatians 2:14) is emphatic . . . it refers to a revelation of eternal truth, itself as changeless as the truth revealed."[14] The holy gospel was at that point in time winning its supremacy over all civilized thought and it was particularly needful to warn the Colossians against the sudden growth of wild speculations, as contrasted with the unchanging, eternal truths of the gospel.

Verse 6, *Which is come unto you; even as it is also in all the world bearing fruit and increasing, as it doth in you also, since the day ye heard and knew the grace of God in truth.*

"In all the world . . ." "is not to be understood as hyperbole."[15] Hendriksen supplied the following quotations:

---

[12]William Hendriksen, *op. cit.,* p. 49.
[13]David Lipscomb, *A Commentary on the NT Epistles,* Vol. IV (Nashville: The Gospel Advocate Company, 1964), p. 251.
[14]Alfred Barry, *op. cit.,* p. 96.
[15]Ernest G. Ashby, *op. cit.,* p. 484.

Justin Martyr: There is no people, Greek or barbarians, or of any other race . . . however ignorant . . . whether they dwell in tents or wander about in covered wagons, among whom prayers and thanksgivings are not offered in the name of the crucified Jesus to the Father and Creator of all things.

Tertullian: We are but of yesterday, and yet we already fill your cities, islands, camps, your palace, senate, forum. We have left you only your temples.[16]

There are likewise numerous hints in the NT of the widespread acceptance of Christianity. "All those of Asia heard the word of the Lord, both Jews and Greeks" (Acts 19:10); "The word of the Lord grew and increased mightily" (Acts 19:20); "In every place your faith in God has gone forth" (1 Thess. 1:8); "The gospel has become clear throughout the whole praetorian guard and to all the rest" (Phil. 1:12f).

Verse 7, *Even as ye learned of Epaphras our beloved fellowservant, who is a faithful minister of Christ on our behalf.*

It was Macknight's opinion that the word "also" in verse 8 properly modifies "from Epaphras" and that this verse becomes a denial of what it is usually quoted as affirming, i.e., that Paul did not convert the Colossians. He said:

The Colossians had learned the true doctrine of the gospel, not from the apostle alone, but they had learned it from Epaphras also.[17]

The sequential arrangement of clauses and phrases has a tremendous bearing upon their meaning; and as long as the learned dispute about the proper arrangement in a given verse, all options as to the meaning of it should remain open.

Verse 8, *Who also declared unto us your love in the Spirit.*

"This is the only explicit reference to the Holy Spirit in the letter to the Colossians."[18] Paul declared that "love" was the first fruit of the Holy Spirit; and thus this verse is a testimony to the Spirit's work in the hearts of the Colossians (Gal. 5:22).

Verse 9, *For this cause we also, since the day we heard it, do not cease to pray and make request for you, that ye may be filled with the knowledge of his will in all spiritual wisdom and understanding.*

---

[16]William Hendriksen, *op. cit.,* p. 51.

[17]James Macknight, *op. cit.,* p. 480.

[18]Ernest G. Ashby, *op. cit.,* p. 484.

In this and verses following the limitless aspirations of Paul's prayers for fellow-Christians is observable. Note the unlimited nature of this request:

> He asks that they may be *filled* with the knowledge of God's will in *all* spiritual wisdom . . . unto *all* pleasing, bearing fruit in *every good work*, and *increasing* in the knowledge of God![19]

It should be particularly observed that the knowledge here prayed for is the knowledge of *God's will*, as Barry expressed it, "Not speculation as the the nature of God, or emanations from Deity, or even as to reasons of God's mysterious counsels."[20] Above everything else men need to know what the will of God is, and having learned it, to do it to the best of their ability.

Verse 10, *To walk worthily of the Lord unto all pleasing, bearing fruit in every good work, and increasing in the knowledge of God.*

See under verse 9 above for comment on the unlimited nature of this great Pauline prayer.

"In every good work . . ." Nothing could be plainer in the word of God than the fact of good works being required of those who hope to enter heaven. Furthermore, it is absolutely incorrect to seek the elimination of this requirement by declaring that "Paul attaches high value to good works viewed as the fruit, not the root, of grace."[21] Paul himself emphatically made good works a prior condition of eternal redemption, even for those already saved by the blood of Christ, a truth which is clearly visible in this verse. Paul said:

> We must all be made manifest before the judgment seat of Christ; that each one may receive the things done in the body, according to what he hath done, whether it be good or bad (2 Cor. 5:10).

> God will render to every man according to his works: to them that by patience in well-doing seek for glory and honor and incorruption, eternal life; but to them that are factious and obey not the truth, but obey unrighteousness, shall be wrath and indignation, tribulation and anguish, upon every soul of man that worketh evil, of the Jew first, and also of the Greek; but glory and honor and peace to every man that worketh good, to

---

[19]D. A. Hayes, *op. cit.,* p. 358.
[20]Alfred Barry, *op. cit.,* p. 98.
[21]William Hendriksen, *op. cit.,* p. 58.

the Jew first, and also to the Greek: for there is no respect of persons with God (Rom. 2:6-11).

Reference is here made to the discussion of the above scriptures in the notes in this series of commentaries. See CC, 2 Corinthians 5:10, and CR 2:6.

Paul did not teach that men, in any sense, earn salvation, or that perfection in keeping all God's commandments must be attained; but despite this, those who work evil will be lost, regardless of how much they profess to "believe" in the Lord.

Verse 11, *Strengthened with all power, according to the might of his glory, unto all patience and longsuffering with joy.*

"All power . . . all patience . . ." See under verse 9 for comment on the unlimited nature of the apostle's prayers for Christians.

"According to the might of his glory . . ." Hendriksen has a vivid comment on this thus:

When a multimillionaire gives "of" his wealth to some good cause he may be giving very little; but when he donates "in accordance with" his riches, the amount will be substantial.

Thus the strengthening of the Christian "according to" the might of God's glory is beyond all calculation.

Verse 12, *Giving thanks unto the Father, who made us meet to be partakers of the inheritance of the saints in light.*

"Who made us meet . . ." This is rendered "qualified us" in RSV, which is a definite improvement over the rendition in the RV.

How God Qualifies Men To Be Saved

I. Men must hear the truth to be saved; and it is God who sends out preachers to all the world that men may hear it. See Romans 10:14ff.

II. Men's hearts must be open to receive the truth; and that all-important event is produced by the word of God which opens men's hearts. "Lydia . . . heard us, whose heart the Lord opened to give heed to the things which were spoken" (Acts 16:14ff).

III. Belief enters into qualification for salvation; and, as Jesus said, "This is the work of God, that ye believe on him whom he hath sent" (John 6:29).

IV. Repentance also figures in salvation (see Luke 13: 3, 5); but it is God who "grants" repentance. "To the Gentiles also hath God granted repentance unto life" (Acts 11:18).

V. Confession of Christ is one of the prior conditions of salvation (Matt. 10:32, 33); but it is God who reveals the great truth which men confess. Thus when Peter confessed Christ (Matt. 16:16), Jesus responded by telling him and all the apostles that "flesh and blood had not revealed it to him" but that "the Father in heaven" had done so! Thus it is God who does the qualifying when one confesses the Saviour.

VI. One is baptized "into Christ"; and after Pentecost, salvation is not promised in the NT to any unbaptized person whomsoever. Jesus said, "He that believeth and is baptized shall be saved" (Mark 16:16). But, when one is baptized, is he thus attempting to earn his salvation, or does his obedience of this command deny that salvation is of grace? Indeed no! Here again, it is God who does the baptizing! Note this:

> Jesus was making and baptizing more disciples than John (although Jesus himself baptized not, but his disciples) (John 4:1, 2).

It is still like that today. When one accepts the gospel and is baptized by one of of the Lord's disciples, it is still Jesus (God) who is making and baptizing the convert.

Thus God qualifies people to be partakers of the inheritance of eternal life by preaching to them, causing them to hear, opening their hearts, thus causing them to believe, revealing Christ through the sacred word, granting them (along with all other Gentiles) repentance unto life, and by baptizing them *into Christ!* Now, what about that person who simply will not allow God to do all this for him? The simple and obvious answer is that God will *disqualify* him!

"It is God who makes worthy those who in themselves art not worthy, and thus enables them to have a share in the inheritance."[22] God would indeed make all men worthy, if men would permit it; but God having given men the freedom of choice

---

[22]*Ibid.*, p. 60.

and the freedom of their will, the result is that some men "will not believe"; others "will not repent or confess"; and others will not "arise and be baptized."

"Inheritance of the saints in light . . ." Most commentators find in this an allusion to the allotment of the share of the land of Canaan to each of the tribes of Israel in the OT. Thus Hendriksen:

> The Lord provided for Israel an earthly inheritance, which was distributed to the various tribes and smaller units of national life *by lot* (Gen. 31:14; Num. 18:20; Josh. 13:16; 14:2; 16:1, etc.); so he had provided for the Colossians an allotment or share in the better inheritance.[23]

Verse 13, *Who delivered us out of the power of darkness, and translated us into the kingdom of the Son of his love.*

"Out of the power of darkness . . ." This is the power of Satan, the kingdom of evil, or the realm of the lost. Throughout the NT, the unsaved portion of humanity are represented as subjects of an evil ruler, a heartless tyrant who keeps them captive; and the idea of release from captivity is inherent in the words Paul chose here. "The word 'translated' is a word properly applied to the transplanting of races."[24] "Josephus uses it of the deportation of the Israelites by the Assyrian king."[25] By the use of the same word here, Paul declared the defeat of the evil kingdom, the vanquishing of its ruler Satan, the release of his captives and the transplanting of them into a wholly new and marvelously better environment. "Out of the kingdom of darkness into the kingdom of the Son of his love!"

Note the past tense of the verb "translated." This affirms the existence of God's kingdom at the time Paul wrote; indeed, the Colossians had already been translated into it. Throughout the NT, after the day of Pentecost, references to the kingdom of God are consistently in the past tense; whereas, before Pentecost, they are consistently in the future tense, thus indicating Pentecost as the occasion of the establishment of God's kingdom upon the earth. For excursus on this, see CH chapter 12 under "The Church and the Kingdom Began at the Same Time."

---

[23]*Ibid.*

[24]Alfred Barry, *op. cit.,* p. 99.

[25]G. G. Findlay, *Colossians in Pulpit Commentary*, Vol. 19 (Grand Rapids: Wm. B. Eerdmans Publishing Company, 1950), p. 6.

Verse 14, *In whom we have our redemption, the forgiveness of sins.*

"In whom . . ." This is the characteristic Pauline expression focusing all blessing in the Lord Jesus Christ. Out of Christ there is nothing; in him is eternal life. Out of Christ there is condemnation; in him is redemption. Out of Christ there is guilt; in him is forgiveness, pardon and salvation. The holy scriptures repeatedly declare that "we are baptized into Christ" (Rom. 6:3); and this truth is repeated here because so many seem unaware of it.

Findlay quoted Lightfoot as seeing in this passage Paul's refutation of a gnostic claim that "redemption" consisted of being initiated into gnostic "mysteries"; but, as stated in the introduction, this is highly speculative. Findlay went on to point out that one of the most prolific writers of that age, Philo, "who speaks the language of the Jewish philosophic mysticism of the first century, has no such usage"[26] of the word redemption.

Verse 15, *Who is the image of the invisible God, the firstborn of all creation.*

"Image of the invisible God . . ." The first impression of reading this verse is that the terms "image" and "firstborn" accord Jesus Christ a status below that of absolute deity; but the very next verse emphatically forbids any such inadequate interpretation of this verse.

"Image of the invisible God . . ." John B. Nielson is absolutely correct in the declaration that in these words, "Paul is saying that Jesus Christ is none other than God Himself."[27] He even went further and said that " 'firstborn' is equivalent to 'only begotten,' and is a Jewish technical term meaning 'uncreated'."[28] Why, then did Paul use these particular words here?

"Image . . ." God created Adam in his own image (Gen. 1:27); but Adam promptly sinned and fell from that image; but, by these words here, Paul compels us to see in Jesus a second Adam who was indeed God's image. Christ was man as God created him to be in the person of Adam. Christ was (and IS) also God,

---

[26]*Ibid.,* p. 7..

[27]G. Campbell Morgan, *An Exposition of the Whole Bible* (Old Tappan, N. J.: Fleming H. Revell Company, 1959), p. 379.

[28]*Ibid.*

but the emphasis here is upon his perfect manhood. Again, there is in this passage a strong suggestion linking Paul with the authorship of Hebrews where 1:3 corresponds exactly to what is said here. Paul applied the same title to Christ in 2 Corinthians 4:4. Barclay also stressed the connection this passage has with the creation narrative. By using the word "image," which is the same as that in Genesis, Paul in effect says,

> Look at Jesus. He shows you not only what God is; he also shows you what man was meant to be. Here is manhood as God designed it. Jesus is the perfect manifestation of God and the perfect manifestation of man.[29]

"Firstborn of all creation . . ." Of course, this verse was the major platform of Arianism, the great heresy that denied the deity of Christ. From this they alleged that Jesus Christ was only a creature, understanding "firstborn" in the sense of being first in a temporal sequence; but there is overwhelming evidence that Paul did not so use that word in this passage. As Guthrie said, "*Firstborn* must be understood in the sense of *supreme* rather than in the temporal sense of born *before*."[30] Barclay affirmed that the time sense in this world is hardly in the Greek word at all, and that here, "It is not used in a time sense at all, but in the sense of special honor. *Firstborn* is a title of the Messiah."[31] Dummelow pointed out that, just as so frequently in the English, words have different meanings, *firstborn* has *two*, that of *time sequence* and that of *supremacy over*.[32] Obviously it is the latter meaning which Paul meant here. As a matter of fact, the other meaning was by far the most unusual. David Lipscomb interpreted the word to mean in this place "Over all creation, Christ occupies the relation of supremacy such as is accorded the firstborn; and such is preeminently due to the 'firstborn of all creation'."[33] Thus the two words, *image* and *firstborn*, stand for Christ's perfect manhood and perfect deity.

This verse (15) is the beginning of one of the most important paragraphs in the NT; and, as Hendriksen said, "Before

---

[29]William Barclay, *op. cit.*, p. 118.

[30]Donald Gunterie, *op. cit.*, p. 1144.

[31]William Barclay, *op. cit.*, p. 118.

[32]J. R. Dummelow, *Commentary on the Holy Bible* (New York: The Macmillan Company, 1937), p. 981.

[33]David Lipscomb, *op. cit.*, p. 259.

attempting a study of the separate parts, the passage should be seen in its entirety."[34] We are further indebted to Hendriksen for the following parallel arrangement which enables the reader, at a glance to see the correspondence between the two major sections:

The Supremacy of the Lord Jesus Christ

A. In Creation	B. In Redemption
15 Who is the image of the invisible God, The firstborn of every creature.	18 He is the head of the body, the church; Who is the beginning, the firstborn from the dead, That in all things he might have the pre-eminence,
16 For in him were created all things In the heavens and on the earth, The visible and the invisible, Whether thrones or dominions or principalities or authorities, All things through him and with a view to him have been created;	19 For in him he (God) was pleased to have all the fullness dwell, 20 And through him to reconcile all things to himself, Having made peace through the blood of his cross, Through him, whether the things on the earth Or the things in the heavens.
17 And he is before all things, And all things hold together in him.	

Now, admittedly, this is a very carefully thought-out paragraph, or sentence of 137 words, and the organization of it is obvious; but for another Pauline paragraph manifesting these same qualities see Paul's long salutation in Romans and the analysis and discussion of it in CR 1:8ff. We reject out of hand the allegation that this marvelous paragraph is some kind of hymn or liturgical chant used in worship services of the early church. Such a view is not supported by any evidence whatever except in the imagination of scholars; and it is based upon several very tenuous and unsure premises: (1) that Paul would need to reach into the current hymnology of his day for accurate expression of the nature and essence of the being of Christ Jesus; (2) that the great Christology of this passage had "developed" in the early church. On the contrary, far from having developed any such exalted conception of Christ, those early churches were in danger of being carried away into the worship of angels, etc. If the brethren at Colossae were singing these words already when Paul wrote, there would have been no temptation to gnosticism, and no need for Paul to have written them. Of course, what some have in mind, through making a hymn out of this

---

[34]William Hendriksen, *op. cit.,* p. 70.

passage, is to make it easier for them to deny that Paul wrote it, or that it is indeed authoritative scripture.

This remarkable paragraph has every mark of Pauline authorship, being a similar careful work, comparable to Romans 1:1-7. As G. Campbell Morgan expressed it:

> It is here that Paul set forth the glories of the person of the Redeemer in a passage that is unique for its revealing beauty. He summarized the whole truth concerning the glories of the person of Christ in his declaration that "It was the good pleasure of the Father that in him should all the fullness dwell."[35]

Before leaving verse 15, one other expression should be noted:

"Who is . . ." not "who *was*" etc. Three times in these verses (15, 17, and 18), this imperative IS is used with reference to Christ, strongly suggesting the great "I AM's" of the gospels and of Exodus 3:6, 14. See comment in CMK 6:50.

Verse 16, *For in him were all things created, in the heavens and upon the earth, things visible and invisible, whether thrones or dominions or principalities or powers; all things have been created through him and unto him.*

If indeed, as generally supposed, the Colossians were being drawn away into various philosophies and speculations involving the worship of angels, spirits, demons, and the supposition that certain emanations from God were responsible for the creation itself, this verse was the divine thunderbolt that cleared the atmosphere and let the light of God shine in. Hayes' quotation of Farrar regarding what Paul did in this passage is as follows:[36]

To	Paul opposed
A cumbersome ritualism	A spiritual service
Inflating speculations	A sublime reality
Hampering ordinances	A manly self-discipline
Esoteric exclusiveness	A universal gospel
Theological cliques	An equal brotherhood
Barren systems	A new life
All their problems	Christ as the answer

This verse affirms the deity of Christ as effectively as any in the NT. As the Creator of all things, how could he be anything less?

---

[35]G. Campbell Morgan, *An Exposition of the Whole Bible* (Old Tappan, N. J.: Fleming H. Revell Co., 1959), p. 496.
[36]D. A. Hayes, *op. cit.*, p. 358.

By this the apostle declares that the invisible beings of the world above us, however lofty their names or mighty their powers, are *Christ's creatures* as much as the lowliest objects within our sight.[37]

Lightfoot was of the opinion that Paul here made no affirmation regarding the actual existence of such beings as angels; but, whether that is correct or not, Christ taught of their existence; and the Christians who lived contemporaneously with the apostles believed that every Christian had a guardian angel. See discussion of *Angels* in CH 1:14. Charles Hodge declared flatly that "Angels are a distinct creation being neither God, human nor animal";[38] and with this view full agreement is felt. Paul's failure to make this clear in this verse was probably due to the fact that the Colossians believed in a great many other supernatural beings (other than angels) and that their belief in such beings was totally false.

As Lipscomb said, "This certainly means that Christ created the whole universe,"[39] leaving absolutely no room whatever for the worship or adoration of any lesser beings whatever; and, as Hendriksen put it, "That was Paul's main theme over against the teachers of error who were disturbing the church at Colossae."[40]

A. S. Peake stressed the thought that the words Paul used here "denote angels . . . These angels, Paul insists, so far from being superior or equal to Christ, were as inferior to him as the creature is to the Creator."[41] Agreement is felt with this, to the effect that Paul was speaking about angels as actually existing, and that the reference is not to earthly dignitaries, which would be irrelevant to the polemical purpose of this passage.

Verse 17, *And he is before all things, and in him all things consist.*

Again, here is an astounding coincidence of thought with that of the author of Hebrews. See under Hebrews 1:3, in CH. Not only did Jesus Christ create the universe, he sustains, upholds, and supports it!

---

[37]G. G. Findlay, *op. cit.,* p. 9.

[38]Charles B. Hodge, *Angels* (Nashville: The Christian Teacher, Inc., 1977), p. 4.

[39]David Lipscomb, *op. cit.,* p. 259.

[40]William Hendriksen, *op. cit.,* p. 72.

[41]A. S. Peake, *Expositor's Greek Testament* (Grand Rapids: Wm. B. Eerdmans Publishing Company, 1967), p. 504.

"And he is before all things . . ." See under verse 15, above. Findlay was also impressed with the implications "he is" as used here. He said:

In the mouth of a Hebraist like Paul, the coincidence of the doubly emphatic "he is" with the etymological sense of Jehovah, as interpreted in Exodus 3:6, can scarcely be accidental.[42]

There is a glimpse here of the same thought of Hebrews 13:8, regarding him who is the same yesterday, today and forever.

Verse 18, *And he is the head of the body, the church: who is the beginning, the firstborn from the dead; that in all things he might have the preeminence.*

Here begins the second phase of this grand statement of the preeminence of Christ, the first pertaining to all creation, and this pertaining to the new spiritual creation, that is, the church of our Lord Jesus Christ.

"He is . . ." Note the same imperative use of this expression as in verse 15, 17.

"Head of the body, the church . . ." Some expositors like to take the view that Paul's idea of the corporate Christ, the spiritual body of believers with Christ as its head, was a late blooming idea with the apostle; but such is totally incorrect. As Hendriksen said:

It cannot be truthfully maintained that the proposition, "Christ is the head of the church," was absolutely foreign to Paul's thinking prior to the time of the Prison Epistles.[43]

Paul wrote to the Corinthians that there is "one body" (12:20), and is not a body supposed to have a head? Furthermore, when Paul wrote that the head of "every man" is Christ (1 Cor. 11:3), is this not absolutely equivalent to saying that Christ is the head of the church? As a matter of fact, the expression "in Christ" used so extensively in Paul's writings is the embodiment of that entire corpus of truth which surfaces in this verse regarding "the body of Christ." We dare to offer the challenge that in every one of the 169 times where Paul used "in Christ" or the equivalent "in him," "in whom," etc., it is proper to read it "in the spiritual body of Christ," that being the only way that any man on earth was ever *in Christ* at all. Thus the conceit of the

---

[42]G. G. Findlay, *op. cit.,* p. 10.
[43]William Hendriksen, *op. cit.,* p. 76.

spiritual body with Christ as its head being in any sense a late or "developed idea" for Paul is totally refuted by the magnificent Pauline expression "in Christ."

"The beginning . . ." Christ as the "beginning" actually begins. He brings into being a new creation, the church, his body. "His body, the church, begins in him, dating and deriving from him its all in all."[44]

"Firstborn from the dead . . ." "The word *firstborn* brings over with it into the verse the glory which surrounds it in verse 15," as Findlay said, "The divine Firstborn, who is before and over all things, wins his title a second time for his earthly brethren's sake (Heb. 2:10-15)."[45]

Verse 19, *For it was the good pleasure of the Father that in him should all the fullness dwell.*

"This verse should be understood in the light of 2:9. It is the fullness of Deity, the 'fullness of the godhead bodily' that is pleased to dwell in the Son."[46]

Ashby also agreed with this analysis of the verse, adding that by thus stressing Christ's deity, Paul effectively undermined the whole argument of the gnostics. He said, "It is peculiarly fitting that Paul should thus describe the Saviour. It is God's pleasure that all fullness, the full essence of deity, should reside in Christ."[47]

Verse 20, *And through him to reconcile all things unto himself, having made peace through the blood of his cross: through him, I say, whether things upon the earth, or things in the heavens.*

Hendriksen suggested the probable meaning of this verse to be:

> Sin ruined the universe. It destroyed the harmony between one creature and another, also between all creatures and their God. Through the blood of the cross, however, sin in principle has been conquered . . . the law satisfied . . . the curse borne . . . harmony restored . . . peace made.[48]

---

[44]G. G. Findlay, *op. cit.,* p. 11.
[45]*Ibid.*
[46]John B. Nielson, *op. cit.,* p. 382.
[47]Ernest G. Ashby, *op. cit.,* p. 485.
[48]William Hendriksen, *op. cit.,* p. 82.

Agreement is felt with this paraphrase, except in the matter of its application to the lower creation. While admitting that something like this may indeed be true, this student of the scriptures has never been able to find such premises firmly established in the sacred word. See in CR 8:19ff.

"Things upon the earth . . ." This we interpret to mean human beings, leaving the animal creation out of sight altogether.

"Things in the heavens . . ." The only things in heaven which may be said to be out of harmony with God are "Satan's angels"; and yet they have already been cast down and reserved in chains of darkness. Any further speculation on this would appear to be futile.

"Heavens . . ." See under verse 5, above, for the use of the plural "heavens."

Verse 21, *And you, being in time past alienated and enemies in your mind in your evil works.*

In one of the most perceptive statements read in many a day, Hendriksen observed that:

> This state of estrangement, moreover, was not due to ignorance or innocence. *There are no innocent heathen!* On the contrary, they were estranged and hostile in disposition. It was their own fault that they had been and had remained for so long a time "far off," for they had actually *hated God!*[49]

This is the truth that was hidden from Jean-Jacques Rousseau, the philosophical father of the Romantic movement in literature and thought. It was he, according to Will and Ariel Durant, "who had more effect upon posterity than any other writer or thinker of the eighteenth century."[50] And it was he who filled the men's minds with the garbage relative to "natural man," "the noble savage," and the totally uninhibited human animal. Here in the sparkling words of an apostle is revealed the truth about natural man" or the "noble pagan." Paul described him as the end-result of devolution downward from a prior state of having known God and then having fallen away from it.

---

[49]*Ibid.,* p. 83.
[50]Will and Ariel Durant, *Rousseau and Revolution* (New York: Simon and Schuster, 1967), p. 3.

Verse 22, *Yet now hath he reconciled in the body of his flesh through death, to present you holy and without blemish and unreprovable before him.*

The thought of this is similar to that of verse 28, which see; but here the emphasis is upon the body of his flesh, that is, Jesus' physical body and the death upon Calvary. In verse 28, below, the emphasis is upon the spiritual body, the corporate Jesus, which is the church. Both are absolutely necessary, because the spiritual body could never have existed without the actual death of Christ on the cross.

The second half of this verse refers to judgment and the appearance at that time of all the redeemed before the Lord.

Verse 23, *If so be that ye continue in the faith, grounded and stedfast, and not moved away from the hope of the gospel which ye heard, which was preached in all creation under heaven; whereof I Paul was made a minister.*

"If so be that ye continue . . ." This is another of innumerable denials in the NT of the monstrous proposition euphemistically described as the "final perseverance of the saints." Salvation is conditional, both for the alien sinner and for the sanctified Christian. God has written that chilling word "IF" over against every name inscribed in the Lamb's Book of Life. If men truly hope to receive eternal life, let them behold the condition stated here: "If so be that ye continue in the faith." In short, that means *if they do not quit the church!* "Faith" in this passage is not subjective, but objective, meaning "the Christian religion."

"Which was preached in all creation . . ." The same thought is expressed in verse 6, above. See notes under that reference. "Creation," as used here, is suggestive of Mark 16:15 and Romans 8:22, which see with the comments. Paul loved to speak of Christians as "the new creation"; and thus, by contrast, "creation," as used here, meant the unregenerated part of humanity.

On this verse, David Lipscomb wrote:

It seems strange that the gospel had been preached among all the nations; but, if we consider the earnest character of the Christians, who gloried in persecutions and death for Christ's sake, it will not seem so strange. The greatest hindrance to the gospel in our day is the lukewarm and indifferent character of professed Christians.[51]

"Paul . . . a minister . . ." Hendriksen defined a minister thus:

A minister of the gospel is one who knows the gospel, has been saved by the Christ of the gospel, and with joy of heart proclaims the gospel to others. Thus he serves the cause of the gospel.[52]

Verse 24, *Now I rejoice in my sufferings for your sake, and fill up on my part that which is lacking of the afflictions of Christ in my flesh for his body's sake, which is the church.*

In this verse Paul, dwelling upon the metaphor of the "body of Christ," thinks of it as being actually Christ, and therefore, like Christ, called to suffer tribulations, hardship and persecutions, thus viewing it as a necessity that just as Christ suffered, so also should Christians (see Rom. 8:17; 2 Tim. 2:11, 12). Ellis reasoned from this that "Union with Christ involves *ipso facto* union with Christ's sufferings," but also pointed out that "The sole redemptive sufficiency is in Christ and his atonement."[53] God's imperial "must" is written upon the sufferings of Christians: "Through many tribulations, we must enter into the kingdom of God" (Acts 14:21).

Verse 25, *Whereof I was made a minister, according to the dispensation of God which was given me to you-ward, to fulfil the word of God.*

Macknight understood this verse as saying that Paul had been made a minister on behalf of the Colossians, which presupposes that Paul had surely preached to them.

"Minister . . ." See under verse 23, above.

Verse 26, *Even the mystery which hath been hid for ages and generations: but now hath it been manifested to his saints.*

"The mystery . . ." This word occurs 21 times in Paul's letters, three times in the gospels and four times in Revelation.[54] A mystery in the NT frame of reference is not something hidden, but something which was *once hidden* but now revealed. The conviction of this writer is also to the effect that there are

[51]David Lipscomb, *op. cit.,* p. 265.

[52]William Hendriksen, *op. cit.,* p. 85.

[53]E. Earle Ellis, *Wycliffe NT Commentary* (Chicago: Moody Press, 1971), p. 789.

[54]William Hendriksen, *op. cit.,* p. 88 footnote.

elements of amazement and awe in the scriptural mystery which can never be removed, and that, in some unknown sense, the mystery of God is not even finished yet (see Rev. 10:7). For those interested in an extended discussion of "The Mystery of Redemption," see entire book under that title.[55]

Verse 27, *To whom God was pleased to make known what is the riches of the glory of this mystery among the Gentiles, which is Christ in you, the hope of the glory.*

We heartily agree with Ashby that "There is no need to suppose that Paul borrows this term from the Greek-mystery religions, but rather from the OT (Dan. 2:18)."[56] Also Christ used it himself (see Matt. 13:11).

"Christ in you . . ." This is the essence of the "mystery" as Paul expounded it here; but a comparison with other Pauline writings on the subject reveals the mystery to be somewhat complex. There are eight expressions in the NT, all eight of which refer to a single state, namely, the saved state; and these are: (1) Christ is in you; (2) you are in Christ; (3) God is in you; (4) you are in God; (5) the Holy Spirit is in you; (6) you are in the Holy Spirit; (7) the mind of Christ is in you; (8) the word of Christ is in you. For scriptural references and discussion of all these see Galatians 5:23, this volume. It is mandatory, of course, to see all of these various designations as reference to one condition only, that of the redeemed in Christ. The fact that all such references are indeed synonymous is evident from Paul's usage in this and the following verse. Here he spoke of "Christ in you"; in the very next verse, and speaking of the same thing, he referred to it as presenting every man "in Christ," thus quite obviously using "in Christ" and "Christ in you" interchangeably.

Verse 28, *Whom we proclaim, admonishing every man and teaching every man in all wisdom, that we may present every man perfect in Christ.*

The great goal of Christianity shines in this, namely, that of presenting every man "perfect in Christ." This writer has no patience with the translations and "authorities" that scale down

---

[55]James Burton Coffman, *The Mystery of Redemption* (Austin: Firm Foundation Publishing House, 1976).

[56]Ernest G. Ashby, *op. cit.,* p. 486.

the meaning of "perfect" in this passage, equating it with "completeness" or "maturity." Christ used this word of God himself (Matt. 5:48), and one would hardly speak of God's being *mature!* NO! This verse is the quintessence of the entire system of Christianity. See article on "The Perfection of Christians" under Ephesians 1:4, this volume.

Verse 29, *Whereunto I labor also, striving according to his working, which worketh in me mightily.*

The statement here is that Paul was striving and laboring with all of his strength to unite men in Christ, that being the only possible means of their salvation, and also that the working of Christ himself was present in Paul mightily during those labors. In this significant verse, Paul acknowledged that the overwhelming success of his remarkable life was due not to himself alone, but to the mighty power of Christ Jesus.

CHAPTER 2

This division of the Colossian letter is, of course, quite arbitrary; as someone said, Paul did not write four chapters, but wrote one letter! Nevertheless, the game-plan in this series calls for going with the traditional divisions. After all, those divisions are already known to millions, and any new division would probably be just as inadequate and arbitrary as the old ones.

This chapter deals with Paul's refutation of false doctrine, in which the emphasis by the apostle lies squarely upon the eternal power and godhead of the Lord Jesus Christ. Morgan said, "The central declaration of the epistle is found in this chapter (9-10)."[1] This chapter also exposes to some degree the nature of the false teachings Paul was refuting. True, he does not explain the error, but the refutation may be taken, at least partially, as the opposite of the error; and from this, a fairly accurate idea of it is derived. It is perfectly clear that a strong Judaistic character marked the Colossian errors; but they were colored by pagan misconceptions also. That there may have been traces of incipient gnosticism at Colossae is likely; but the notion that Colossians is principally a response to gnosticism should be rejected. The peculiar characteristics of the Colossians' error most visible in the epistle are Jewish, not gnostic.

Verse 1, *For I would have you know how greatly I strive for you, and for them at Laodicea, and for as many as have not seen my face in the flesh.*

This verse is usually cited as meaning that Paul had never seen any of the Christians at Laodicea and Colossae; but since Hierapolis is the only one of the tri-cities not mentioned here, it is more logical to assume that Hierapolis might have been the location of those addressed in the last clause. As Peake declared, "So far as the words themselves go, they may mean that the Colossians and Laodiceans did belong to the number of those who had not seen him or that they did not."[2] The ambiguity of this

[1]G. Campbell Morgan, *An Exposition of the Whole Bible* (Old Tappan, N. J.: Fleming H. Revell Company, 1959), p. 497.

[2]A. S. Peake, *Expositor's Greek Testament* (Grand Rapids: Wm. B. Eerdmans Publishing Company, 1967), p. 518.

verse is insufficent foundation for the postulations about Paul's never having seen the Christians addressed in this letter.

"As many as have not seen my face . . ." Barry referred to this thus: "This description doubtless indicates Hierapolis";[3] but despite this, he accepted on other grounds the thesis that Paul had not seen the Colossians. To this writer, however, there are certain circumstances in this reference that almost demand a differentiation between the status of Colossae and Laodicea on the one hand, and Hierapolis on the other. Those towns were all three sister cities, tri-cities as they would be called today. It is inconceivable that Paul would have named two of them, omitting the other, without some good reason for the distinction.

Very well. What was that distinction? There existed churches at all three places (4:13); Paul addressed letters to Colossae and Laodicea (4:16) but apparently did not address a letter to Hierapolis. This can be logically explained only on the premise that Paul was well acquainted in two of these cities and unacquainted in Hierapolis. Added to this, there is the omission of the name of Hierapolis in 2:1. Nielson concurred in this explanation, as follows:

> The strife in which Paul finds himself involved concerns both those whom he knows at Colossae and Laodicea, the neighboring town, and those whom he does not know.[4]

Macknight identified those who had not seen Paul's face as "all the believing Gentiles everywhere to the end of the world."[5] If Paul did not know the Colossians, why would he have been writing them a letter? The impossibility of answering this while denying that Paul was acquainted at Colossae has led some of the commentators to add another theory, to the effect that although Paul had not been to the tri-cities, many from the tri-cities had visited Paul in Ephesus or other places![6] This is perfectly possible, of course; but the simple answer is usually the

---

[3]Alfred Barry, *Ellicott's Commentary on the Whole Bible,* Vol. III, *Philippians* (Grand Rapids: Zondervan Publishing House, 1959), p. 105.

[4]John B. Nielson, *Colossians in Beacon Bible Commentary*, Vol. IX (Kansas City: Beacon Hill Press, 1965), p. 394.

[5]James Macknight, *Apostolical Epistles with Commentary,* Vol. III (Grand Rapids: Baker Book House, 1969), p. 521.

[6]William Hendriksen, *Colossians and Philemon* (Grand Rapids: Baker Book House, 1964), p. 102.

best; and the simple explanation is that like most people in all ages, Paul wrote to people whom he knew and loved.

There is something sad about those tri-cities. The only mention of any of them in scripture outside this letter is in Revelation 3:14-22, where Laodicea stands in perpetual infamy as the Church of the Lukewarm. Today there is no trace of Colossae, not even any ruins, with its very location unknown. The other two cities, according to Barry, "played an important part in the subsequent history of Christianity in Asia Minor . . . leaving behind magnificent ruins."[7]

Verses 2-3, *That their hearts may be comforted, they being knit together in love, and unto all riches of the full assurance of understanding that they may know the mystery of God, even Christ, in whom are all the treasures of wisdom and knowledge hidden.*

An unusually incisive and penetrating analysis of the whole paragraph which began at 1:24 and ends with these verses was written by Morgan thus:

> We find reference to a threefold mystery: (1) the church which is the body of Christ; (2) the secret of life in the individual believer, "Christ in you, the hope of glory"; and (3) the deepest mystery of all, "the mystery of God even Christ."[8]

As frequently pointed out, the "mystery" of the NT is exceedingly large and extensive, no less than three facets of it appearing in the single paragraph before us; and yet, strangely enough, all parts of this mystery are wrapped, entwined and fitted together in the most amazing unity.

"In whom are all the treasures of wisdom and knowledge hidden . . ."

Nielson read the meaning of this to be: "In Jesus Christ are hid all the attributes of Deity."[9] The word "hidden" he construed as meaning "Contained, waiting to be revealed in their time."[10] George A. Buttrick wrote extensively on "Jesus Christ as the Truth" (John 14:6), declaring that "The ultimate wisdom for mankind is not another formula, another gadget or a new discovery . . . Every door man opens discloses not the answer, but

[7]Alfred Barry, *op. cit.,* p. 105.
[8]G. Campbell Morgan, *op. cit.,* p. 496.
[9]John B. Nielson, *op. cit.,* p. 396.
[10]*Ibid.*

another corridor with other doors opening into still other corridors, etc."[11] Buttrick illustrated this by pointing out the Copernican discovery. He concluded with a grand proposition that for mankind the ultimate answer is not a mathematical formula, an intricate scientific gadget, nor some startling new discovery — it is a Person; that Person is Christ! Paul discovered this long ago and thundered the message in this verse.

Verse 4, *This I say, that no one may delude you with persuasiveness of speech.*

"Delude . . . persuasiveness . . ." These are two of the 34 words peculiar to Colossians, as mentioned in the introduction; several others appear in this chapter. These new words are just as Pauline as all the rest of his writings, being required by the special circumstances addressed by Paul in this epistle.

The scholars usually understand this as directed against the advocates of gnostic speculations, as follows:

> To beguile (delude) here is "to reason into error"; enticing words are "words of persuasion" rather than reason or revelation. It would be difficult to describe more accurately the marvelous fabrics of Gnostic speculation, each step claiming to be based on some fancied probability or metaphysical propriety, but the whole as artificial as the cycles and epicycles of the old Ptolemaic astronomy.[12]

While such observations appear to be true enough, it cannot be denied that the same words are applicable to the insistent claims of aggressive Judaism.

"No one . . ." This is the springboard from which some speculators identify the Colossian heresy as advocated by one man, called "the false teacher" by many writers; but as Guthrie said, "It is more likely that Paul is using the term generally in the sense of *anyone*."[13]

It is of significance that in this verse it appears that the error at Colossae arose from false speech, rather than from immoral or false practice.

---

[11]George A. Buttrick, *Christ and Man's Dilemma* (New York: Abingdon-Cokesbury, 1950), pp. 29ff.

[12]Alfred Barry, *op. cit.*, p. 105.

[13]Donald Guthrie, *New Bible Commentary, Revised* (Grand Rapids: Wm. B. Eerdmans Publishing Company, 1970), p. 1146.

Verse 5, *For though I am absent in the flesh, yet am I with you in the spirit, joying and beholding your order, and the stedfastness of your faith in Christ.*

"In the spirit . . ." By not capitalizing spirit, the translators indicate that the "Holy Spirit" is not referred to here. Again, this verse is the language of a man who knows the people whom he is addressing. "I am absent in the flesh . . ." Is it necessary to write this to people one does not even know?

"Order . . . stedfastness . . ." Here are two more of the unusual words of Paul used in Colossians; and most scholars declare them to be military words. Barclay, for example, said, "These two words present a vivid picture, for they are both military words."[14] If such is the truth, then it is easy to suppose that Paul's close association with the military in Rome during his imprisonment might have led to his use of these terms here. "Order . . ." means soldier discipline; and a church should stand against all enemies with the solidity of a military phalanx. However, a word of caution is proper concerning the military background of the words Paul chose in this verse. "Meyer and Abbot deny the military reference altogether."[15] Abbot admitted that the words can be used in a military sense, provided that the context indicates it; but here, he said, "The context suggests nothing of the kind."[16]

The ideas of order, or discipline and stedfastness, however, are vital to all spiritual development. Paul's statement here that he was "beholding" such qualities among the Colossians appears to be a reference to the good report of them which Paul had received from Epaphras (1:7).

"Your faith in Christ . . ." Again, it is evident in context that Paul has no reference here to the merely subjective act of "believing," in the manner of current usage of the term "faith." It is the sphere in which that faith is working which lends importance to it, that being "in Christ," as attested in the next verse, as well as being implicit in this one.

---

[14]William Barclay, *The Letters to the Philippians, Colossians and Thessalonians* (Philadelphia: The Westminster Press, 1975), p. 131.

[15]A. S. Peake, *op. cit.,* p. 520.

[16]*Ibid.*

Verse 6, 7, *As therefore ye received Christ Jesus the Lord, so walk in him, rooted and builded up in him, and established in your faith, even as ye were taught, abounding in thanksgiving.*

"In him . . . in him . . . in your faith . . ." These are all references to the Christian's fidelity "in Christ Jesus," that is, as bona fide members of his church, fully identified as followers of the Lord Jesus Christ.

"Rooted and builded up . . ." Barry pointed out a significant change of tense: "*Having been rooted* in him once for all, and *being built* up continually on that foundation."[17] Guthrie's significant analysis of these two verses is:

To receive Christ is but the beginning. The following is to *live in him*, which is described as involving four aspects, the first three very similar: (1) rooted, (2) built up, and (3) established . . . from a building metaphor . . . The fourth aspect is *abounding in thanksgiving*, which echoes the apostle's own enthusiasm to give thanks.[18]

"Abounding . . ." This was one of Paul's favorite words. As Hendriksen said:

Paul does not pray that the Colossians may begin to be thankful, but rather that the ocean of their gratitude may constantly overflow its perimeter. Paul is never satisfied with anything short of perfection. Hence, he loves to use this word *overflow* or *abound*.[19]

Verse 8, *Take heed lest there be anyone that makes spoil of you through his philosophy and vain deceit, after the traditions of men, after the rudiments of the world, and not after Christ.*

"Through his philosophy and vain deceit . . ." It appears that the translators have softened Paul's words in this verse by the insertion of the pronoun "his," thus avoiding a blanket condemnation of philosophy and limiting the warning to the particular philosophy advocated at Colossae. Interlinear Greek Testaments have the following:

Take care that no one make a prey of you through philosophy and empty deceit.[20]

---

[17]Alfred Barry, *op. cit.,* p. 106.
[18]Donald Guthrie, *op. cit.,* p. 1146.
[19]William Hendriksen, *op. cit.,* p. 108.
[20]*Emphatic Diaglott* (Brooklyn: Watchtower Bible and Tract Society), p. 677.

Beware lest any man spoil you through philosophy and vain deceit.[21]

In keeping with the evident intention of watering down Paul's denunciation here, the following comments are typical of hundreds that are made in this context:

The apostle does not condemn sound philosophy.[22]
Paul is not condemning philosophy properly so-called.[23]
Clearly the apostle condemns *false* philosophy.[24]
Empty deceit stands in qualifying apposition with *philosophy.*[25]
Such philosophies as the Jewish and Gentile teachers used.[26]

Isn't it too bad that the apostle just did not know how to make it clear? Despite the temptation to do so, however, this writer does not wish to get on that bandwagon. An incredibly large amount of destructive influences are operative in this very generation, influences which are grounded in human philosophy; and there is no way to deny the gentle words of the immortal Lipscomb, who said:

All the philosophies of men, all the deceits of human wisdom, and all the rudiments of the world discovered by human reason spoil men, ruin their souls, and lead them to everlasting death by leading them away from God and his salvation.[27]

If it be objected that Lipscomb's analysis is harsh or unkind, such an allegation is refuted by the far different tone of what even the most noted philosophers say of each other. Only one of these will be quoted, Jean-Jacques Rousseau, referred to by Will Durant as the most influential of the 18th century philosophers, and one eminently qualified to give an objective and unbiased appraisal of philosophers and philosophy as it existed seventeen centuries after Paul's appraisal. It reads as follows:

---

[21]Alfred Marshall, *The Interlinear Greek-English Testament, The Nestle Greek Text* (Grand Rapids: Zondervan Publishing House, 1958), p. 794.

[22]James Macknight, *op. cit.,* p. 526.

[23]J. R. Dummelow, *Commentary on the Holy Bible* (New York: The Macmillan Company, 1937), p. 983.

[24]Ernest G. Ashby, *A NT Commentary* (Grand Rapids: Zondervan Publishing House, 1969), p. 486.

[25]G. G. Findlay, *Colossians* in *Pulpit Commentary*, Vol. 19 (Grand Rapids: Wm. B. Eerdmans Publishing House, 1950), p. 85.

[26]Adam Clarke, *Commentary on the Whole Bible* (London: Carlton and Porter, 1929), Vol. VI, p. 522.

[27]Foy E. Wallace, Jr., *A Review of the New Versions* (Fort Worth: The Foy E. Wallace, Jr., Publications, 1973), p. 448.

> I consulted the philosophers . . . I found them all alike proud,
> assertive, dogmatic; professing — even in their so-called skep-
> ticism — to know everything; proving nothing, scoffing at one
> another. This last trait . . . struck me as the only point in which
> they were right. Braggarts in attack, they are weaklings in
> defense. Weigh their arguments, they are all destructive; count
> their voices, each speaks for himself alone . . . There is not one
> of them who, if he chanced to discover the difference between
> falsehood and truth, would not prefer his own lie to the truth
> which another had discovered. Where is the philosopher who
> would not deceive the whole world for his own glory?[28]

With deep and poignant sorrow, this student of many modern critics and commentators on the NT finds *some of them* to
be like the philosophers consulted by Rousseau. One false
premise being exposed, they immediately take refuge in another,
exposing themselves as enemies of truth and righteousness.
Christianity Today some time ago had an editorial on this which
is reproduced in this series of writings see CL 21:20.

"After the tradition of men . . ." In this, Paul is in perfect consonance with the repeated denunciations of the Lord Jesus
Christ against the Pharisaical keepers of tradition during his
ministry. A vast portion of present-day Christianity is not based
upon the NT at all, but upon human tradition, supported, of
course, by vain and empty speculations exactly like that Paul
condemned here. See discussion of "Traditions" in CM 15:5ff.

"After the rudiments of the world . . ." The RSV translation
of this as "elemental spirits of the universe" simply cannot be
correct. As Foy E. Wallace, Jr., pointed out:

> The same terminology in Galatians 4:3 refers to the
> rudiments of Judaism, as the connection of chapter 3:24-29 very
> clearly shows . . . so here "after the rudiments of the world"
> refers to the rudiments of heathenism.[29]

See Galatians 3:24-29, 4:3, this volume.

"And not after Christ . . ." This is the summary of all Paul
was saying against the evil teachings and evil teachers of that
generation. Whatever human system of thought, religion,
politics, or anything else that is not held in reference to the
teachings of the Lord Jesus Christ and in full conformity to his

---

[28]Will and Ariel Durant, *Rousseau and Revolution* (New York: Simon and
Schuster, 1967), p. 183.

[29]Foy E. Wallace, Jr., *A Review of the New Versions* (Fort Worth: The Foy
E. Wallace, Jr., Publications, 1973), p. 448.

revealed will, must be classified as secondary in the affections of Christians. It is freely admitted that this is not the way it is among countless Christians of this generation; but it is still affirmed that this is the way it should be.

Verse 9, *For in him dwelleth all the fullness of the Godhead bodily.*

This is an unequivocal declaration of the deity of the Son of God, a thesis repeated at least a dozen times in the Greek NT, and reinforced by literally hundreds of other intimations and mandatory deductions throughout the entire NT. See CH 1:8.

"Godhead . . ." Ellis noted that "The Greek word for *Godhead* or *deity* is the abstract noun for *God* and includes not only the divine attributes, but also the divine nature."[30] Barry declared that "almost every word of this verse is emphatic."[31] Thus the meaning is intense, thus:

All the fullness of the Godhead . . . not a mere emanation from the Supreme Being . . .
Dwells and remains forever . . . not descending on him for a time and then leaving again . . .
Bodily . . . that is, as incarnate in his humanity.[32]

Guthrie stated that "The word *deity (theotetos)* occurs only here in the NT and denotes the divine essence."[33] However the Greek language had other words for God, and one of them is used of Jesus Christ in Titus 2:13, "Our great God and Saviour Jesus Christ."

"Bodily . . ." This is viewed as a reference to the incarnation of our Lord, his becoming a man and dwelling on earth as a human being. The Gospel of John (1:1, 14) is parallel with what is said here; also see in CH under 10:5 and under 2:16. Hendriksen objected to this interpretation on the grounds of the "present tense";[34] but the ordinary significance of verb tenses disappears when applied to him who is the same "yesterday, today, yea and forever."

Verse 10, *And in him ye are made full, who is the head of all principality and power.*

---

[30]E. Earle Ellis, *Wycliffe NT Commentary* (Chicago: Moody Press, 1971), p. 791.
[31]Alfred Barry, *op. cit.,* p. 106.
[32]*Ibid.*
[33]Donald Guthrie, *op. cit.,* p. 1147.
[34]William Hendriksen, *op. cit.,* p. 111.

This is further elaboration of the power and godhead of Jesus Christ. The Greek philosophers, or gnostics, who might have been speculating on emanations from God, or beings operating independently of God, or as the Jewish errorists might have been advocating the worship of angels, or whatever — Paul unequivocally presented Christ as "the head of all principality and power," with the words of Matthew's Great Commission in the background of his thought, namely, "That all authority in heaven and upon earth" was in the hands of Jesus Christ. The angels are all servants of Christ, doing service for the followers of Christ (Heb. 1:1-14); and angels, like Christians, worship him.

"In him ye are made full . . ." Peake has a most interesting observation on this clause. Quoting Oltramare, he translated this verse, "In him ye are made perfect,"[35] which in the light of 1:28 is probably the correct rendition. As is well known, the Greek text in this part of Colossians is somewhat difficult.

Verse 11, *In whom ye were also circumcised with a circumcision not made with hands, in the putting off of the body of flesh, in the circumcision of Christ.*

"Circumcision not made with hands . . ." The reference to baptism in the next verse has sent some of the commentators into orbit, alleging all kinds of wild speculations designed to eliminate Christian baptism as the gateway to all "spiritual blessings in Christ." It is refreshing to find Ellis cutting the bud out of such notions with the following:

> There is no direct analogy between Christian baptism and the "old age" rite of circumcision. Circumcision here is the death of Christ (clearly a metaphorical reference — JBC), by which he wrought severance from the old age, cleansing from sin, and reconciliation to God.[36]

If circumcision should be made a type of baptism, then only men could be baptized; it would have to take place on the eighth day of their lives; there could be no prior conditions such as faith, repentance or confession; and it could be received only by those already in covenant relationship with the Lord; and how could that be applied to an eight-day-old infant?

---

[35]A. S. Peake, *op. cit.,* p. 524.
[36]E. Earle Ellis, *op. cit.,* p. 792.

The obvious reference to the death of Christ (which was the metaphorical circumcision referred to) in this verse naturally raised the question in Paul's thought of just how men are enabled to participate in the death of Christ, share its benefits, and receive its blessings. *That* prompted the immediate reference to baptism. (Compare with Romans 6:3-5).

The Circumcision in Christ

Verse 11 is more easily understood if the intermediate phrases are omitted from the principal statement in the passage which is:

"In whom (Christ) we were also circumcised . . . in the circumcision of Christ."

The Christian is dead "in Christ." "If one died for all, then all died" (2 Cor. 5:14). This means that the penalty of death (due to all sin) was paid by Christ who died for all. As members of his "spiritual body," Christians are, in a genuine sense "in him," identified with him, and *as Christ* they are dead, having been crucified with him, a status they received when they were baptized into his death."

Christians are also "perfect" in Christ (Colossians 1:28, 29). This perfection, like his death, belongs to Christians, not through achievement by themselves, but through their status "in Christ."

Exactly the same is true of the circumcision mentioned here. "In Christ," Christians were not merely "circumcised"; but they also kept perfectly the entire Law of Moses, not by actually observing all those regulations, but by being "in Christ," totally identified with him, being actually his "spiritual body." All of this is plainly said when verse 11 is read without the descriptive phrases. Our circumcision is "in the circumcision of Christ."

See CR 4:11 for more on circumcision.

Verse 12, *Having been buried with him in baptism, wherein ye were also raised with him through faith in the working of God, who raised him from the dead.*

"Buried with him in baptism . . ." Note that nothing is said here of baptism being accomplished without human hands, the same being an obvious impossibility. Note too that there is here the plainest reference to immersion as the action recognized by the apostles as being required in the baptism commanded by Christ. One may read bales of sophistry on this subject, but the simple truth is easy to see. See the parallel Pauline reference in Romans 6:3-5, together with comments in CR.

Verse 13, *And you, being dead through your trespasses and the uncircumcision of your flesh, you, I say, did he make alive together with him, having forgiven us all our trespasses.*

"Trespasses and the uncircumcision of your flesh . . ." The deadness indicated by this denotes the preconversion, or unregenerated state of Christians before they became followers of Christ. Such deadness was often spoken of by the apostles in reference to the unbaptized. Such deadness, however, upon their conversion, was followed by the new life in Christ.

"You did he make alive . . ." When does the new life come to the Christian? Fortunately, we do not need to rely upon human opinion regarding so important a question as this. Note the following:

> We were buried therefore with him through baptism into death that like as Christ was raised from the dead through the glory of the Father, so we also might walk in newness of life (Rom. 6:4).

> Wherefore if any man be in Christ, he is a new creature; the old things are passed away (2 Cor. 5:17).

Even in the sequence of verses before us, baptism is mentioned in verse 12, above, and the being made alive in the next verse, where it logically belongs.

Before leaving these three verses, it is proper to note certain widespread, persistent and stridently vocal errors regarding what the NT says concerning Christian baptism, or rather, *what it does not say!* Nowhere in the NT is it declared that:

> Baptism is a symbol
> Baptism is a token
> Baptism is a type
> Baptism is a figure
> Baptism is a sign
> Baptism is an outward sign
> Baptism is optional
> Baptism is unessential
> Baptism is unnecessary
> Baptism is a physical action alone.

In these studies, the old cliche that "Baptism is the outward sign of an inward grace," if encountered once, has been encountered a hundred times; but it is not, in any sense, true. In the NT, baptism is said to be the reality of which even the salvation of Noah and his family was only "the figure" (1 Peter 3:21).

Furthermore, it is a gross error to suppose that baptism in any true sense whatever is accomplished without the existence of the prior conditions of faith, repentance and confession. One is surprised that even Lipscomb would declare that "Baptism avails nothing without faith."[37] Without faith, no one was ever baptized, although of course he might have been wet. Although it is correct to say that "Immersion avails nothing without faith," which is presumably what Lipscomb meant, the distinction should be made clear to all. It is feared that many have misunderstood the true teaching on this question, which in no sense whatever would substitute immersion for faith as a prior condition of membership in Christ's kingdom, but which requires of all who would be saved that they "believe, repent and be baptized" in order to be saved. This is what Christ commanded when he said, "He that believeth and is baptized shall be saved." This distinction between "immersed" and "baptized" may appear too finely drawn to some; and it is freely admitted that there is a sense in which the words mean *exactly the same thing;* but baptism as compliance with the prior conditions of redemption "in Christ" is never accomplished except with the prior conditions of faith and repentance having already appeared in the candidate's heart *before* he is immersed, that is, before he *can* be baptized.

"Having forgiven us all our trespasses . . ." This is, of course, a reference to the forgiveness of all the old sins of which the believer was guilty at the time of his conversion. The apostle Peter mentioned this "cleansing from his old sins" in 2 Peter 1:9. Sins committed after one has become a Christian are forgiven upon the conditions of repentance and prayer of the Christian.

Verse 14, *Having blotted out the bond written in ordinances that was against us, which was contrary to us: and he hath taken it out of the way, nailing it to the cross.*

---

[37]David Lipscomb, *op. cit.,* p. 280.

"Bond written in ordinances . . ." This is a reference to the Decalogue and to the entire Law of Moses. Widespread denial of this is ill-founded and inaccurate. Peake's skilled exegesis on this question is pertinent:

> Distinction between moral and ceremonial Law has no meaning in Paul. The Law is a unity and is done away as a whole. For Paul, the hostile character of the Law is peculiarly associated with the moral side of it. The Law which slew him is represented by the 10th Commandment, and the ministry of death was engraved on tables of stone.[38]

"Written in ordinances . . ." as in this verse, signifies the tables of stone inscribed by the finger of God. As Wallace pointed out, it is deplorable that "By omission of 'handwriting of ordinances' the revisionists break this connection."[39] The words certainly belong as a sure testimony that the Decalogue is here indicated.

"Taken it out of the way . . . nailing it to the cross . . ." These terms indicate the absolute cancellation and abrogation of the Law of Moses. Also, the fact should not be lost sight of that the heresy at Colossae was deeply involved with the Law of Moses, practically all of this chapter being particularly applicable to it.

The special application of this verse, as inclusive of the moral part of the Law of Moses, was discussed thus by Macknight:

> The moral precepts of the Law of Moses are called the Chirograph, or handwriting of ordinances, because the most essential of these precepts were written by the hand of God on two tables of stone; and the rest Moses was directed to write in a book.[40]

Sabbatarians make two profound mistakes: (1) in their understanding of the sabbath day commandment as in any sense a part of the moral law, and (2) in their insistence that the moral portion of the Law of Moses is still in effect; whereas nothing could be more emphatic than the NT declarations that the Law, not part of it, but all of it, has been changed, abrogated, taken away, nailed to the cross, etc.

Verse 15, *Having despoiled the principalities and the powers, he made a show of them openly, triumphing over them in it.*

---

[38]A. S. Peake, *op. cit.,* p. 527.
[39]Foy E. Wallace, Jr., *op. cit.,* p. 449.
[40]James Macknight, *op. cit.,* p. 534.

"The principalities and the powers . . ." These are understood to be the ranking members of the Jewish hierarchy in Jerusalem, and also inclusive perhaps of the Roman procurator who in Paul's time had already come to receive the eternal infamy of the lines, "Suffered under Pontius Pilate."

Of course, this view is disputed. Peake noted that "almost every word in this verse" is disputed by scholars.[41] On the identification of "principalities and powers," Nielson thought they were "demonic forces";[42] Dummelow was sure that "they were the angels who gave the Law";[43] and Guthrie thought they "were spiritual enemies."[44]

"In it . . ." is also disputed, some thinking it means "in him"; but we shall offer the exegesis on the basis of the translation before us. Here, too, if this is allowed, the antecedent of "it" becomes a factor in the interpretation. Since the overall subject of this whole section is the Law of Moses, we shall take the Law itself as the antecedent of "it," making the passage read that Jesus triumphed "over them in it." The *them*, of course, as already noted, is seen as reference to the religious and political rulers before whom the ministry and Passion of Jesus were enacted. This interpretation has the great advantage of being backed up by the entire Sermon on the Mount, and by all of those astounding events that frustrated and defeated the hierarchy of Israel.

Jesus Christ took up the great moral commandments of the Decalogue, one at a time, quoted each one, opposed his own authority against it, showing that one could indeed keep every command in the Decalogue and yet remain a scoundrel and a rogue; if there were ever a case of Jesus triumphing over the Pharisees in the Law of Moses, that has to be the time. Furthermore, he triumphed over them in the Law on another salient front. They repeatedly accused him of sabbath-breaking; but Jesus destroyed their sabbath regulations by showing that they were of men and not of the Father; and by the time of the confrontation before Pilate, the Pharisees no longer even alleged that Jesus broke the sabbath. (It is still alleged by some, quite

---

[41]A. S. Peake, *op. cit.,* p. 528.
[42]John B. Nielson, *op. cit.,* p. 404.
[43]J. R. Dummelow, *op. cit.,* p. 983.
[44]Donald Guthrie, *op. cit.,* p. 1147.

erroneously, that Jesus broke the sabbath "for sufficient cause.")
For a full discussion of *Jesus' Triumphing Over the Hierarchy
in the Law of Moses,* see CM under that title. It is the opinion
of this writer that this interpretation removes all difficulties of
understanding this admittedly difficult passage, and avoids the
near-impossible task of showing how Jesus triumphed "openly"
over either angels or devils.

Verse 16, *Let no man therefore judge you in meat, or in drink,
or in respect of a feast day or a new moon or a sabbath day.*

So Paul continues to speak of Jewish things. Gnosticism is
not in a hundred miles of this passage. We deplore a statement
like this:

> The church at Colossae was no exception. Instead of its mem-
> bers being harassed by Judaizers, as were the Corinthians, they
> were in danger of being corrupted by the Gnostics. False
> teachers were seeking to deprive the Colossians of that simplic-
> ity which is in Christ.[45]

While there evidently were traces of incipient gnosticism, it
was the Judaizers who were refuted in these verses. As Dummelow said, "The Jewish character of the false teachers comes
very plainly into view here."[46]

"Meat . . . drink . . . feast day . . . new moon . . . sabbath
day . . ." All of these refer to Jewish observances; as Macknight
said, "Some of these were enjoined in the Law, and others by
private authority."[47] Of particular importance is the appearance
of the sabbath commandment in this list. "Although the article
the is not in the Greek, it clarifies the meaning; Paul was
resisting the Judaizers who insisted on legalistic sabbath
observance."[48] As F. F. Bruce expressed it, "It is as plain as may
well be that Paul is warning his readers against those who were
trying to impose the observance of the Jewish sabbath upon
them."[49] The sabbath observance is here placed upon the same
footing as the other things abolished, and "Thus Paul commits

---

[45]Arthur W. Pink, *Gleanings From Paul* (Chicago: Moody Press, 1967), p. 222.

[46]J. R. Dummelow, *op. cit.,* p. 983.

[47]James Macknight, *op. cit.,* p. 538.

[48]John B. Nielson, *op. cit.,* p. 405.

[49]F. F. Bruce, *Answers to Questions* (Grand Rapids: Zondervan Publishing
House, 1972), p. 109.

himself to the principle that a Christian is not to be censured for its non-observance."[50]

SABBATH ABOLISHED

There is no sabbath commandment in Genesis; there is not even an indication that Adam knew anything about God resting on the sabbath day (Gen. 3:2). In Genesis, Moses was merely stating, generations and millenniums after the fact, what God had done in the remote ages long before Moses wrote Genesis. Historically, the very first revelation of any such thing as the sabbath came not to Adam, but to Moses. Note:

> Thou camest down also upon mount Sinai, and spakest with them from heaven, and gavest them right judgments, true laws, good statutes and commandments: And madest known unto them thy holy sabbath . . . by the hand of Moses thy servant" (Neh. 9:13-14).

Conclusion: The sabbath observance did not antedate the Law of Moses; the sabbath was unknown prior to Moses, else God could not have revealed it to him.

Significantly, the reason God assigned for requiring Israel to keep the sabbath was not prior existence of the institution but their deliverance from bondage.

> Thou wast a servant in the land of Egypt, and that the Lord thy God brought thee thence through a mighty hand and by a stretched out arm: therefore, the Lord thy God commandeth thee to keep the sabbath day (Deut. 5:15).

The sabbath is said to be a sign, not between God and all men, but between God and the Jews. "It is a sign between me (God) and the children of Israel" (Ex. 31:17).

"Took it out of the way, nailing it to the cross . . ." In what sense did God nail the sabbath to the cross of Christ? The words of course are highly figurative and symbolical. A day could not actually be nailed to anything. Still, there is a marvelous connection. Many centuries before Christ, some tradesmen who resented keeping the sabbath day came to Amos and demanded to know:

> When will the new moon be gone, that we may sell corn? and the sabbath that we may set forth wheat, making the ephah small and the shekel great, and falsifying the balances of deceit? (Amos 8:5).

---

[50]A. S. Peake, *op. cit.,* p. 531.

The prophet answered this question with words which to the prophet might have seemed to say that the sabbath would never be removed; but here is the word that God actually put into the mouth of Amos:

And it shall come to pass in that day, saith the Lord God, that I will cause the sun to go down at noon, and I will darken the earth in a clear day (Amos 8:9).

Very well; these scriptures teach that the sabbath day was to be abolished when God darkened the earth in a clear day and the sun went down at noon. This of course happened when Jesus was crucified; thus the sabbath day was nailed to his cross. See more on this in Matthew, CM 27:51ff, where significant additional detail is provided. Also see CD, for the entire chapter on the Fourth Commandment.

Verse 17, *Which are a shadow of the things to come, but the body is Christ's.*

"A shadow of things to come . . ." Again we are confronted with an amazing coincidence of thought with that of the author of Hebrews who devoted two entire chapters (9 and 10) to many things in the institution of Moses which were designed to foretell and illuminate the realities in the new covenant.

"The body is Christ's . . ." means that the substance, as contrasted with the shadows, pertains to the institution of Christ and the church.

Verses 18-19, *Let no man rob you of your prize by a voluntary humility and worshipping of the angels, dwelling in the things which he hath seen, vainly puffed up in his fleshly mind, and not holding fast the Head, from whom all the body, being supplied and knit together through the joints and bands, increaseth with the increase of God.*

This passage is another admittedly difficult one, the rendition of various words and clauses being variously advocated; but such technical disputations lie without the perimeter of this work; and we shall content ourselves by undertaking an exegesis of the text as it stands in this version. We rely in part upon the affirmation of F. F. Bruce to the effect that the most accurate of the versions is the ASV.

"Rob you of your prize . . ." The prize is eternal life; and the promise of it is jeopardized for everyone who turns from the worship of the one and only Saviour to worship angels, or any other creatures.

"Voluntary humility and worshiping of angels . . ." As Peake said:

> Their humility found expression in angel worship. It is therefore that lowliness that causes a man to think himself unworthy to come into fellowship with God, and therefore prompts the worship of angels. Such humility was perverted.[51]

"Dwelling in things which he hath seen . . ." Paul made a sharp distinction between the things "that are seen" and things "that are unseen," that is, between the visible and the invisible, the latter being permanent, the other transient, mortal and ephemeral. See full treatment of this in CC under "Seeing the Invisible." The error at Colossae was founded upon the visible, as contrasted with the invisible. This of course resulted in their being vainly puffed up in the fleshly mind.

"Not holding fast the Head . . ." The Head is Christ; and any consideration, of any kind whatsoever, that results in the severance of the Christian from his perfect union with Christ, the same results immediately in his spiritual death. "Severance from the Head cuts off the supply of spiritual life."[52]

Verse 20, *If ye died with Christ from the rudiments of the world, why, as though living in the world, do ye subject yourselves to ordinances?*

"The rudiments of the world . . ." has reference to the forms, shadows and ceremonial ordinances of Judaism. See comment on this under verse 14.

"As though living in the world . . ." A Christian is committed to a different life-style, in which the value-judgments of the world are rejected; and for a Christian to undertake all the ceremonies of Judaism, such would be diametrically opposed to his new life in Christ.

"Why . . . subject . . . to ordinances . . . ?" The ordinances here have no reference whatever to the great ordinances of the Christian religion, such as baptism and the Lord's Supper, the

---

[51]*Ibid.*, p. 532.
[52]J. R. Dummelow, *op. cit.*, p. 983.

obligation to keep which lies squarely upon all who ever hope to be saved. The ordinances which the Colossians were admonished to leave off were the Jewish ordinances like those mentioned in verse 16. The blindness, or perversity, or both which leads some commentators to read this verse as applicable to the Christian ordinances is most deplorable, and traceable, as to its cause, to the great Reformation heresy of salvation by faith alone. May God open the eyes of Bible students. An example of the kind of ordinances Paul meant was immediately given in the next verse.

Verses 21-22, *Handle not, nor taste, nor touch (all which things are to perish with the using), after the precepts and doctrines of men?*

Again reference is made to the great Magna Carta of the Christian religion in the Gospel of Matthew, where the Saviour equated human traditions with the precepts of men, saying, "In vain do they worship me, teaching as their doctrines the precepts of men" (Matt. 15:9). Paul was confronted at Colossae with some of the same punctilious attention to human traditions as that which marked the conduct of the Pharisees and drew from the Saviour himself the denunication just quoted. See Matthew 15:9 with comments in this series. It is futile to inquire just what traditions Paul referred to. We do not know. His words apply to *all* "precepts and doctrines of men," including those which are being received, preached and practiced in our times. All alike are condemned. Worshipers indulging such things are worshiping "in vain," according to the Lord himself.

Verse 23, *Which things have indeed a shadow of wisdom in will-worship, and humility, and severity to the body, but are not of any value against the indulgence of the flesh.*

Some things are startlingly clear in this passage so often disputed. Note these conclusions:

Whatever human precepts and ordinances may exhibit as to their "wisdom," it is a delusion, for "they are not of any value."

Will-worship means the kind of actions engaged in because they please the worshiper, and not because they were commanded by the Lord.

Humility is a fine thing, if it is true humility; but a false humility pretending to be too God-fearing to approach God as God has directed, and then seeking to approach through some angel, or human mediator, or through some deceased saint, such *so-called* humility is actually spiritual arrogance.

THE WORSHIPING OF ANGELS

Of course this is condemned in the NT, not merely in this chapter, but throughout. Even the apostle John "fell down before the feet of an angel to worship him" (Rev. 19:10), but was forbidden to do so. Then, later, the apostle made a distinction between "falling down *to worship the angel*" and falling down in the presence of the angel *to worship God,* only to be ordered not to do either one! (Rev. 22:8, 9). Thus is established the principle that a Christian may neither worship such a being as an angel, and certainly not any such thing as an image, and that it is also sinful to bow down before either on the pretext that we are not worshiping the angel (or the image) but are worshiping God!

The angel worship Paul was combating in this chapter was the Jewish apostasy from the worship of God supported by the same specious reasoning by which the medieval church sought to justify the adoration of images in Christian worship. Barry has an illuminating paragraph on this:

This (the worship of angels) is closely connected with the voluntary humility Paul mentioned. The link is supplied by the notice in the ancient interpreters, of the early growth of that unhappy idea, which has always lain at the root of saint-worship and angel worship in the church . . . "That we must be brought near by angels, and not by Christ, for that were too high a thing for us" (Chrysostom).

Since the Law had been given through the ministration of angels, it was held that angels might be worshiped, probably with the same subtle distinction with which we are familiar in the ordinary pleas for the veneration of saints.[53]

---

[53]Alfred Barry, *op. cit.,* p. 111.

CHAPTER 3

Findlay's outline of this section of the epistle is:

a. The Colossians urged to maintain a lofty spiritual life (3:1-4).
b. They were to put off old vices (3:5-8).
c. They were to put on new Christian virtues (3:9-14).
d. The sovereignty of Christ was to rule them (3:15-17).
e. Instructions regarding reciprocal relationships (3:18-4:1).
   1. As wives and husbands (3:18-20).
   2. As parents and children (3:21).
   3. As servants amd masters (3:22-4:1).[1]

The hortatory section, or "practical teachings," as usual in Paul's letters, comes *after* the doctrinal part of the letter; a number of deductions from this fact are important:

(1) It is not ethics which produces doctrine, but the doctrine which produces ethics, as Peake said: "The ethical exhortation has its basis in the dogmatic exposition already given."[2] All Christian morality, ethics and philosophy are grounded in the historical fact of the death, burial and resurrection of the Lord Jesus Christ.

(2) In putting the doctrine first, Paul followed the usual pattern visible in the NT.

> The NT everywhere insists upon true doctrine ... the whole tendency (today) is to discourage talk about doctrine and to urge that we work together, etc. ... but the fact is that there is no unity apart from truth and doctrine; and it is departure from this that causes division and breaks unity.[3]

From this, the deduction follows that all of the sacred writers stressed doctrine, and on doctrine built the appeal for better conduct.

> The apostle now develops his ethical teaching, erecting, as is his custom, his moral superstructure upon a solid doctrinal foundation.[4]

---

[1]G. G. Findlay, *Colossians in Pulpit Commentary*, Vol. 19 (Grand Rapids: Wm. B. Eerdmans Publishing Company, 1950), p. 147.

[2]A. S. Peake, *Expositor's Greek Testament* (Grand Rapids: Wm. B. Eerdmans Publishing Company, 1967), p. 536.

[3]D. Martyn Lloyd Jones, *The Basis of Christian Unity* (Grand Rapids: Wm. B. Eerdmans Publishing Company, 1962), p. 50.

[4]Ernest G. Ashby, *A NT Commentary* (Grand Rapids: Zondervan Publishing House, 1969), p. 488.

(3) Then, should not doctrine be re-emphasized today? It may be well to note the words of Wagner and Johnson who developed an analysis of why some churches grow and others do not; and they determined that:

> What really determines growth is the intensity of belief that any group has in the particular doctrine it holds ... What we have seen occurring from the time of Constantine in the fourth century has been a general watering down of our belief in our views of salvation and of the church.[5]

Christ strongly emphasized the true doctrine, declaring that those who taught "as their doctrines the precepts of men" were worshiping God in vain (Matt. 15:9). Of course, Paul was one with the Holy Saviour in the strong and emphatic teaching regarding the doctrine.

PAUL'S TEACHING ON DOCTRINE

The trouble Paul sought to correct with this very letter was that of the Colossians following human doctrine (2:22). The unstable and ineffective Christians at Ephesus Paul identified as those "carried about with every wind of doctrine" (Eph. 4:14). Paul classified everything that was "contrary to sound doctrine" as being sinful in the same degree as fornication, falsehood and murder (1 Tim. 1:10). "The words of faith and of good doctrine" were to be proclaimed by Timothy in order for him to be "a good minister of Christ Jesus" (1 Tim. 4:6). Paul commanded him to give heed and attendance to "doctrine" (1 Tim. 4:13, 16), and ordered him to hold in "double honor" those who were laboring "in the word and in the teaching (doctrine)" (1 Tim. 5:17).

Furthermore, the apostasy itself was to come about through the sins of the churches that "could not endure the sound doctrine," but who would cater to their "itching ears" by supplying false teachers (2 Tim. 4:3). All these instructions to Timothy were, in essence, repeated to Titus, where Paul commanded him to "speak the things which befit the sound doctrine," and where all faith and honesty were seen primarily as an "adornment of the doctrine of God" (Titus 2:1, 10).

Therefore, either churches or ministers who neglect to teach the "sound doctrine" of the word of God, or seek to downgrade

---

[5] C. Peter Wagner and Arthur Johnston, "A Pragmatic Concern for Church Growth," in *Christianity Today*, Vol. 21, No. 7 (January 7, 1977), p. 14 (382).

it in any way, are guilty of forsaking the "faith once for all delivered to the saints."

Verse 1, *If then ye were raised together with Christ, seek the things that are above, where Christ is, seated at the right hand of God.*

As Neilson said, *"If then ye were raised* parallels *if ye died with Christ* in verse 2:22.[6] Both of course, refer to Christian baptism.

Macknight affirmed that the meaning here is, "Since then ye have been raised with Christ in baptism."[7] Barclay also elaborated it thus:

> The point Paul is making here is this. In baptism the Christian dies and rises again. As the waters close over him, it is as if he was buried in death; as he emerges from the waters, it is like being resurrected to a new life.[8] . . . We have seen repeatedly that the early Christians regarded baptism as a dying and rising again. When a man was buried, the Greeks commonly spoke of him as being *hidden in the earth;* but the Christian had died a spiritual death in baptism, and he is not hidden in the earth but *hidden in Christ* (verse 3).[9]

How One Dies With Christ in Baptism

There are two different aspects of one's death with Christ in baptism, these being (1) the firm and irrevocable resolution and intention of renouncing sin forever (this is the spiritual aspect of it), very appropriately referred to as dying with Christ, since *as far as the Christian is concerned*, his body (in his intention) is no more to be given over to the indulgence of fleshly lusts and sins, any more than if he had physically died, and (2) the legal aspect of dying in the person of Christ. Christ died on Calvary; therefore, all who are in Christ are also said to have died "in him." Every Christian can say, "I have already paid the penalty of sin, which is death; for I died on the cross in the Person of my Redeemer," this being exactly parallel to Paul's statement that we are "dead to the Law by the body of Christ" (Rom. 7:4).

[6]John B. Nielson, *Colossians in Beacon Bible Commentary*, Vol. IX (Kansas City: Beacon Hill Press, 1965), p. 410.

[7]James Macknight, *Apostolical Epistles with Commentary*, Vol. III (Grand Rapids: Baker Book House, 1969), p. 549.

[8]William Barclay, *The Letters to the Philippians, Colossians and Thessalonians* (Philadelphia: The Westminster Press, 1975), p. 147.

[9]*Ibid.*, p. 148.

It should be observed in this connection that one's having died with Christ unto sin has reference only to the imperative and all-important *change of the will* (repentance) when one becomes a Christian. There is nothing here of God's taking away all temptations. Even Christ was tempted in all points like as we are tempted. This death to sin is suggested by the burial of the convert in the act of baptism. Despite the fact of baptism's nowhere being called a "figure" or "outward sign" of anything in the NT, it is called "that form of doctrine" which must be obeyed by those seeking eternal life. In that frame of reference, it is to be understood, therefore, as a form of death, burial and resurrection of Christ (that is, of the gospel), and also of the convert's death to sin, burial in baptism, and being raised to walk in the newness of life in Christ.

But is not "the form" as applied to baptism in Romans 6:17 the same as "figure," etc.? No indeed; it is an expression which is used of Christ being "in the form of God" (Phil. 2:6), and that usage of it denotes the utmost reality and substance, making baptism to be a reality of the gospel, in fact, the gospel itself that must be obeyed by men seeking salvation. See more on this in CR 6:17ff. The truth is that "obeying the gospel," as used in the NT, invariably means believing and being baptized, there being no other way whatever in which the "good news" could be *obeyed.*

"If ye then were raised together with Christ . . ." Barry said the reference here is "evidently to baptism."[10] Findlay likewise referred it to "the gate of baptism";[11] and Guthrie agreed that here there is an allusion "to baptism."[12]

"Seek ye the things that are above . . ."

"Seek . . ." is stressed by many as a word indicating the most careful and persistent pursuit of the goal indicated.

"The things that are above . . ." The thought of Christ and heaven being above and the sinful things of earth being below is misleading when understood merely in the sense of altitude. "The things above" are rather the things of higher importance,

[10]Alfred Barry, *Ellicott's Commentary on the Whole Bible,* Vol. III, *Philippians* (Grand Rapids: Zondervan Publishing House, 1959), p. 111.

[11]G. G. Findlay, *op. cit.,* p. 147.

[12]Donald Guthrie, *New Bible Commentary, Revised* (Grand Rapids: Wm. B. Eerdmans Publishing Company, 1970), p. 1148.

more exalted principles, and *spiritual* rather than carnal. As
Ellis reminded us, "The words *above* and *below* in the writings
of Paul and of John do not primarily indicate spatial contrasts."[13]

There is a dramatic fourfold reference to "Christ" in these
first four verses; and Barry stated that "The name, four times
repeated, has in all cases the article prefixed to it. Evidently it
is used emphatically to refer to our Lord as our Mediator — our
Prophet, Priest and King."[14]

Verse 2, *Set your mind on the things that are above, not on
the things that are upon the earth.*

See preceding verse.

Verses 3-4, *For ye died, and your life is hid with Christ in God.
When Christ, who is our life shall be manifested, then shall ye
also with him be manifested in glory.*

"Ye died . . . your life is hid . . ." See Barclay's comment on
this under verse 1, above. Also see comment by Bruce, below.

"When Christ . . . shall be manifested . . ." Each of the significant clauses in this verse is actually related to the thought
of the Christian's life being "hid with Christ." True it is hidden
now, but at the Second Advent, when the heavens shall be ablaze
with the glory of Christ, lo, all of his saints shall likewise appear
"with him" in the glory of eternal life which shall be given to
them "at that time."

"Christ, who is our life . . ." The thought here is parallel to
that of Galatians 2:20. Significantly, the consummation of all
the Christian's hope shall be achieved "at the coming of Christ,
which will be a personal and visible appearing of himself."[15]

Another wonderful thought on being "hid with Christ" was
also given by Bruce in reply to a question, "How is our life hid
with Christ in God?" He wrote:

Here is J. B. Lightfoot's answer: "The apostle's argument
is this: 'When you sank under the baptismal water, you disappeared forever to the world. You rose again, it is true, but you
rose only to God. The world henceforth knows nothing of your
life, and (as a consequence) your new life must know nothing
of the world'." Since Christians live "in Christ," and Christ

---

[13]E. Earle Ellis, *Wycliffe NT Commentary* (Chicago: Moody Press, 1971), p. 795.
[14]Alfred Barry, *op. cit.*, p. 112.
[15]Arthur W. Pink, *Gleanings From Paul* (Chicago: Moody Press, 1967), p. 334.

indeed is their true life, it is inevitable that their life should be securely preserved where he is.[16]

"Manifested . . ." The Greek word here is *phaneroo*.[17] Other NT passages where it is used of the Second Advent are: 2 Thessalonians 2:8; 2 Corinthians 5:10; 1 Timothy 6:14; 2 Timothy 4:1, 8; 1 Peter 5:4; 1 John 2:28, 3:2. One of the major NT doctrines is that of the Second Advent of Christ. It is usually understood as the occasion when the dead shall all be raised, the general judgment of all men shall occur, and every person shall be assigned his eternal reward.

Verse 5, *Put to death therefore your members which are upon the earth: fornication, uncleanness, passion, evil desire, and covetousness, which is idolatry.*

"Put to death . . ." Here is a paradox. As Hendrikesen noted:

"You died" (verse 3) . . . "Put to death therefore your members" (verse 5) . . . On the one hand Paul is saying that the Colossians have already died; yet, on the other hand, he is telling them that they must put themselves to death. How can both be true?[18]

Hendriksen answered by pointing out that the *state* and the *condition* of Christians do not wholly coincide; but the answer presented here is to the effect that it is not "themselves" which the Christians are to "put to death," but that they are to put to death those evil propensities *within themselves*, belonging to their carnal nature.

A number of very interesting comments on this place are:

Members is perhaps suggested by our Lord's command to "cut off" right hand or "pluck out" right eye, if they cause offense (Matt. 5:29, 30).[19]
These members are indeed those of the actual body.[20]

Different from the views above is that of Ashby who said: "This is internal, not external, and means renunciation of propensities that belong to the old life."[21] Of course, it is believed

---

[16]F. F. Bruce, *Answers to Questions* (Grand Rapids: Zondervan Publishing House, 1972), p. 109.
[17]E. Earle Ellis, *op. cit.,* p. 796.
[18]William Hendriksen, *Colossians and Philemon* (Grand Rapids: Baker Book House, 1964), p. 143.
[19]Alfred Barry, *op. cit.,* p. 113.
[20]G. G. Findlay, *op. cit.,* p. 149.
[21]Ernest G. Ashby, *op. cit.,* p. 488.

that this accurately interprets, not only what Paul said here, but that it is also, in light of the apostle's inspiration, a divine comment upon what Jesus meant in Matthew 5:29, 30, regarding "the right hand" and "the right eye."

Macknight elaborated this interpretation thus:

> The apostle having represented the vicious appetites and passions of the human heart, under the idea of a body (2:17), because they have their seat in the body, he, in this passage, calls the sinful actions to which these bad affections prompt men, the *members of that body* or the *old man*.[22]

A little different statement of what is meant here is that of Barclay, who said, "What Paul is saying is, 'Put to death every part of yourself which is against God and keeps you from fulfilling his will'."[23]

"Mortify . . ." as used here in the AV has been used by ascetics and others as justification for self-torture; but we may be certain that nothing like that is intended.

"Fornication, uncleanness, passion, evil desire, and covetousness, which is idolatry . . ." In this series, Paul's various lists of sins have been repeatedly examined. Here, all five of these things are sexually oriented, and "covetousness" would seem to apply to all of them, covetousness being "the desire for more."

"Which is idolatry . . ." The pagan temples throughout the world of that era were a constant temptation to Christians to indulge in the impure and unmentionable rites suggested by this word-list. Frequently an idol's temple was a short-cut to indulgence in all of the things mentioned here.

"Covetousness . . . " One is a little surprised to find this word included along with others in this list, thus identifying the love of money and the inordinate desire for it as being on a parity with the grossest of sins. The Christian should especially heed this in the question of determining how much money or income he should devote to the purpose of advancing Christianity in the world.

Verse 6, *For which things' sake cometh the wrath of God upon the sons of disobedience.*

"Wrath of God . . ." At a time in history when the most extravagant claims are being made with regard to God's love,

---

[22]James Macknight, *op. cit.,* p. 549.
[23]William Barclay, *op. cit.,* p. 150.

it is wise to take into account scriptures such as this where the other side of the divine nature is in view. As Ellis put it, "Far from negating God's love, his wrath confirms it. For without justice, mercy loses its meaning."[24] A God in whom no settled wrath against wickedness resided would be like an executive without any authority. The NT is full of teaching to the effect that God has a score to settle with evil and that one day he will settle it.

"Upon the sons of disobedience . . ." Special attention should be focused upon the object of God's wrath. Both here and in 2 Thessalonians 1:8, it is the "disobedient" who shall bear the full weight of the wrath of God. Theologies which seek to eliminate "obedience" as being in any way connected with salvation should be rejected. Regardless of how vigorously one may protest that he has "faith in Christ," unless there is on his part at least some movement to obey the teaching of the NT, his doom is certain. Until he has, in his Christian baptism, been buried with Christ and raised to walk in newness of life, as had these Colossians, he cannot even belong to the company recognized in the NT as the family of God.

> Wrath must not be confused with a vindictive reaction. It is rather the negative side of holiness, the revulsion of righteousness toward all unrighteousness.[25]

"Disobedience . . ." is eliminated in some versions. "But the phrase logically fits here, for it stands in the parallel in Ephesians 5:6."[26]

Verses 7-8, *Wherein ye also once walked, when ye lived in these things; but now do ye also put them all away: anger, wrath, malice, railing, shameful speaking out of your mouth.*

Whereas the list of sins in verse 5 concerned sexual wickedness, the list here pertains to "tongue-wickedness," both lying in the center of man's body, as well as in the center of his nature. As Ellis said, "The words 'out of your mouth' may refer to all the sins listed,"[27] the view here being that they do.

"Shameful speaking . . ." These come from a Greek word meaning "to speak against" either God or man; but

---

[24]E. Earle Ellis, *op. cit.*, p. 797.
[25]Donald Guthrie, *op. cit.*, p. 1149.
[26]John B. Nielson, *op. cit.*, p. 413.
[27]E. Earle Ellis, *op. cit.*, p. 797.

"blasphemy" in English refers to speaking against God. As Hendriksen said, "In the present instance, as the context indicates, 'speaking against man' is meant . . . slander, defamation, detraction."[28] See article *Slander* at the end of the chapter.

Verse 9, *Lie not one to another; seeing that ye have put off the old man with his doings.*

"Lie not one to another . . ." This is added to the list mentioned in the previous two verses. Nielson writes that this is, "Literally, 'lie not to yourself,' and suggests that one who lies may come to believe his own falsehoods."[29]

"Ye have put off the old man . . ." As frequently in Paul's writings, he here dramatically switched metaphors. He had been speaking of "putting to death," but here he changed to "put off," the new figure being that of stripping off old clothes, a metaphor that often occurs in the NT. In Galatians 3:27, Paul wrote, "For as many of you as were baptized into Christ did put on Christ"; and here a little later, beginning in verse 12, Paul will outline what is meant, partially, by putting on Christ. Also in Revelation, the clothing metaphor prevails in 3:4, 5.

Verse 10, *And have put on the new man, that is being renewed unto knowledge after the image of him that created him.*

"Have put on the new man . . ." Macknight referred this to "the very temper and virtues of Christ";[30] but, of course, more than this is meant. The Christian puts on the name of Christ, clothes himself in the spiritual body of Christ, and will appear in glory clothed with the total righteousness of the Lord himself. That is exactly what Jesus meant by the admonition: "I counsel thee to buy of me . . . white garments, that thou mayest clothe thyself, and that the shame of thy nakedness be not made manifest" (Rev. 3:18).

Verse 11, *Where there cannot be Greek and Jew, circumcision and uncircumcision, barbarian, Scythian, bondman, freeman; but Christ is all, and in all.*

All the distinctions stressed by such divisions as these are transcended; and, as Ellis put it, "At the foot of the cross, the

---

[28]William Hendriksen, *op. cit.,* p. 148.
[29]John B. Nielson, *op. cit.,* p. 414.
[30]James Macknight, *op. cit.,* p. 552.

ground is level . . . not a uniformity of status in the present world order, but a change in attitude by which the stigma of being different is loved away."[31]

See Galatians 3:28 for another exhortation similar to this one, the principal difference here being the inclusion of "Scythian," which inclusion, according to Barry, was "clearly intended to rebuke that pride of intellect, contemptuous of the unlearned, which lay at the root of Gnosticism."[32] The word "Scythian" hardly means anything at all to modern readers; but as Hendriksen pointed out:

> In the seventh century before Christ, these Scythians, savage and warlike nomads from the northern steppes, had deluged the countries of the Fertile Crescent, including Palestine, and, having subsequently been repulsed, had left a memory of dread and horror.[33]

Summarizing the barriers that were removed in Christ, they were (and are): barriers that come of birth and nationality, those derived from the ceremonial and rituals observed, the barriers of race, training, experience, social status, or anything else that tends to divide men and lead some to look down upon others as inferior to themselves.

"Christ is all and in all . . ." Here again the absolute supremacy of Christ is affirmed and extolled. Note that Christ is "in" all Christians. See comment on this under 1:27.

Verse 12, *Put on therefore, as God's elect, holy and beloved, a heart of compassion, kindness, lowliness, meekness, long-suffering.*

"Elect . . . holy . . . beloved . . ." Ellis pointed out that these titles belonged in the OT to the physical Israel of God, but that here they are applied "to the church, the true Israel."[34] This writer also believes that "beloved," as in so many of Paul's letters, has reference to the love which the apostle himself had for the addressees, and that this is an incidental indication that Paul was indeed acquainted at Colossae.

"Heart of compassion, kindness, etc. . . ." These indeed are the very virtues and attitudes of the Christ himself, showing that

---

[31]E. Earle Ellis, *op. cit.,* p. 797.
[32]Alfred Barry, *op. cit.,* p. 113.
[33]William Hendriksen, *op. cit.,* p. 153.
[34]E. Earle Ellis, *op. cit.,* p. 552.

true Christ-likeness is the goal of every Christian. Note too, that in all of these admonitions, Paul does not allow for one moment that anyone might attain to the full stature of Christ in a single act, but that the development of the soul into that which pleases God is a growth process. See more on this principle under Romans 6:5, in CR. This is why Paul here admonishes Christians who had already "put on Christ" to put on kindness, etc., and to put on anything else that might be lacking.

Verse 13, *Forbearing one another, and forgiving each other, if any man have a complaint against any; even as the Lord forgave you, so also do ye.*

It is unpardonable that the translators in this place ignored the "many ancient authorities" which read "Christ" in this place (RV margin), rendering it, "As the Lord forgave you"; for, as Guthrie pointed out, "There is an echo here of the Lord's Prayer in the close link between God's forgiveness of us and our forgiveness of others."[35] Thus Paul most assuredly had "Christ" in mind here; but the tenderness of some translators to the implications of this doubtless influenced some of them. The Jews believed, and the Pharisees stated it bluntly to Jesus, that "Who can forgive sins but one, even God?" (Mark 2:7), receiving no contradiction at all from the Christ. Thus Paul's statement here to the effect that Christ forgave us is fully equivalent to an affirmation of his deity.

Roy F. Osborne stated in a sermon that there are only three possible reasons for forgiveness: (1) the person forgiven deserves it, (2) the holiness of the person forgiving is sufficent to guarantee it, or (3) Christ also forgave us! It is not hard to locate the *true* reason.

Verse 14, *And above all these things put on love, which is the bond of perfectness.*

"Above all these things . . ." Barry characterized this verse as "remarkable," saying that it was apparently "suggested by the Gnostic teachers."[36] While it may be true that gnosticism offered a so-called perfection by some device or another, it seems more logical to refer this reference to "the bond of perfectness" to what Paul had already declared in 1:28. See notes there.

---

[35]Donald Guthrie, *op. cit.,* p. 1150.
[36]Alfred Barry, *op. cit.,* p. 114.

"Above all . . ." The thought here appears to be not that of adding love as an additional Christian grace, but rather that of making love the cement that holds everything else in place, or as Nielson put it:

> (The love) is viewed as the *bond of perfectness*, or girdle that bonds together the "clothing" that has just been put on. Both the graces and the Christian persons are bound together by love (*agape*, divine love).[37]

Verse 15, *And let the peace of Christ rule in your hearts, to the which also ye were called in one body; and be ye thankful.*

"The peace of Christ . . ." according to Peake means the subjective peace within the Christian which has been bestowed upon him through his relationship with Chirst. "It is the peace which Christ gives."[38] Ashby noted that it is "peace" in this passage that has the function of the "girdle," a function regarded as belonging to "love" in the parallel place in Ephesians. Paul's mind was not in a straitjacket, and his use of words in slightly different senses "reveals not a different writer but the working of the apostle's mind along similar but not identical lines."[39]

"And be ye thankful . . ." It is strange, in a way, that Paul was so insistent upon thanksgiving as a grace enthusiastically and constantly exhibited by the Christian. The Lord's Prayer does not contain a single note of thanksgiving, except in the comprehensive word "Hallowed be thy name"; but Paul made thanksgiving the ever-present mark of Christian living. This does not mean that there was a difference in the teachings of Christ and Paul, but that "The Lord's Prayer" belonged to that period before the kingdom of Christ was established, and that the teachings of Paul belong to the joyful era of the kingdom itself.

Verse 16, *Let the word of Christ dwell in you richly; in all wisdom teaching and admonishing one another with psalms and hymns and spiritual songs, singing with grace in your hearts unto God.*

"Let the word of Christ dwell in you . . ." The significance of this has already been noted under 1:27, above and under

---

[37]John B. Nielson, *op. cit.,* p. 416.
[38]A. S. Peake, *op. cit.,* p. 541.
[39]Ernest G. Ashby, *op. cit.,* p. 488.

Galatians 5:23, this volume. Briefly, the word of Christ dwelling in a person is equivalent in every way to the Spirit of God dwelling in him. If it be objected that the Spirit is a living Person, then let it be remembered also that the word of God is spoken of as "living and active" (Heb. 4:12f).

"Admonishing one another . . ." The parallel between this verse and similar teaching in Ephesians 5:19, 20, was set forth as follows by Barry:

> Here again we have general identity and special distinction between the two passages. There as here we have "the speaking to one another in psalms and hymns and spiritual songs," the "singing in the hearts to the Lord," and the spirit of "thankfulness." But there the whole is described as being the consequence of "being filled with the Spirit" . . . whereas here, it (all) comes from "the word of Christ" in the soul.[40]

Thus, as Barry pointed out, exactly the same thing is attributed to the agency of the Holy Spirit in the Ephesian passage which here is attributed to the indwelling "word of Christ," lending the strongest possible corroboration to the view maintained in this series to the effect that the "word of Christ," "the mind of Christ," "God," "Christ," and "Holy Spirit" are all spoken of in the NT as "dwelling in" members of the body of Christ, and that all three members of the Godhead are likewise "dwelt in" by Christians, thus giving scriptural designations of one and the same phenomenon. There does not live a person, nor has there ever lived a person, who could make these scriptural expressions to be designations of eight different conditions. On the contrary, they all designate one condition, the saved condition, of the believer baptized into Christ.

"Psalms, hymns and spiritual songs . . ." It would appear that "spiritual" in this verse is the modifier of all that may be properly used in Christian assemblies. By their nature of being in the OT, psalms are surely spiritual, and "hymns" are so by definition; but, as for *any song* so used, it must likewise be spiritual. Significantly not even *all singing* is permissible in Christian worship.

What is the bearing of this passage on the use of instrumental music in Christian worship? The answer is this: By the apostolical injunction "to sing," thus commanding a *special kind*

---

[40]Alfred Barry, *op. cit.,* p. 115.

of music, all other kinds are eliminated. It is contrary to the injunction here for congregations to "whistle" or to play mechanical instruments, the latter having been associated throughout history with pagan worship (Dan. 3:4-7). Historically, no mechanical instruments of music were used in Christian worship till the seventh century, despite the fact of such instruments having been known and used throughout the whole world at the time of the beginning of Christianity and for centuries prior to that time. There is no refutation of the fact that the founder of Christianity, namely, the Christ and the blessed apostles simply left them out. See more on this under Ephesians 5:20, this volume.

Arguments from the word *psallo* to the effect that it refers to playing a harp fail in the light of the truth that the instrument of God's praise appears in the passage, not as anything mechanical, but as the human heart itself.

"With grace in your hearts . . ." This was interpreted by Peake to mean "with thankfulness."[41]

"The word of Christ . . ." Guthrie interpreted this to mean "the teaching Christ brought to men,"[42] and as preserved and communicated to us through the holy apostles. This is one of the most definite passages in the NT, which nails down the identification of Christian doctrine as including the message delivered by Christ, thus making even the OT, valuable as it is, outside the perimeter of Christian authority in all things pertaining to the church of which Christ is the head. See elaboration of this in CM under "The Great Commission."

Verse 17, *And whatsoever ye do, in word or deed, do all in the name of the Lord, giving thanks to God the Father through him.*

"Do all in the name of the Lord . . ." This means to respect the authority of the Lord Jesus Christ in everything. The sectors in which this applies are (1) that of personal morality and conduct, (2) the province of things done in public εssemblies of Christians, (3) in the whole area of thought and action (word or deed), and (4) even in the secret purposes of the soul. In short, *"do all"* in the name of the Lord.

Verse 18, *Wives be in subjection to your husbands, as is fitting in the Lord.*

---

[41]A. S. Peake, *op. cit.,* p. 541.
[42]Donald Guthrie, *op. cit.,* p. 1150.

This begins Paul's instructions on certain reciprocal relationships, that of wives and husbands being treated first. See extensive teaching on this in Ephesians 5:22-33, where Paul elaborated it. The glorious difference between the Christian conception of duty and that prevalent in the world of Paul's day lies in the fact that obligations, even the sacred obligations in marriage, are "reciprocal" obligations. The duty is never all on one side. In the Roman Empire of Paul's day, there were no recognized rights of women, children or slaves, who were all expected to obey husbands, parents and masters upon penalty of death. Christianity changed all that. As observed in the parallel place in Ephesians, here Paul enunciated the great ethic of mutual respect and obligation in these sectors; and this ethic destroyed slavery and other abuses, although, of course, not immediately.

"As is fitting in the Lord . . ." As Guthrie said, "This would at once transform current ideas and invest the wife's position with an adequate safeguard."[43] As spelled out fully in Ephesians, husbands were to love their wives, a command to regard the wife as an extension of the husband's own self, having every true claim against him that ever pertained to himself.

Verse 19, *Husbands love your wives, and be not bitter against them.*

This must be understood in the light of Ephesians 5:28-33. Paul did not need to spell everything out in each of the epistles, because he specifically instructed that his writings should be passed around and made available to others, beyond those addressed in the salutation (4:16).

Verse 20, *Children obey your parents in all things, for this is well-pleasing in the Lord.*

"Well-pleasing in the Lord . . . fitting in the Lord (4:18) . . . fearing the Lord (v. 22) . . . as unto the Lord (v. 23) . . . ye serve the Lord Jesus Christ (v. 24) . . ." Notice that all of the persons addressed regarding their personal and domestic duties were continually reminded of being "in the Lord," and therefore as having "put on" the graces and virtues commanded earlier in this chapter. The whole teaching is that a Christian must not get "out of character" in dealing with everyday relationships

---

[43]*Ibid.,* p. 1151.

and duties. Kindness, meekness, love, gentleness . . . name them all; such virtues must mark the Christian's life *at all times.*

Verse 21, *Fathers, provoke not your children that they be not discouraged.*

This should be read against the stern and tyrannical background of the father's absolute control over his children, as in the Roman Empire when these words were written. As Barclay said:

> A parent could do anything he liked with his child. He could sell him into slavery, . . . he even had the right to condemn his child to death and carry out the execution himself.[44]

In current times, the pendulum has swung the other way; and it is the duty of children to obey their parents that needs emphasis (Eph. 6:1-3).

Verse 22, *Servants, obey in all things them that are your masters according to the flesh; not with eye-service, as men-pleasers, but in singleness of heart, fearing the Lord.*

Some commentators have supposed that, as Onesimus, a runaway slave, was bearer of this letter, Paul made the slave-master relationship the more elaborate part of these reciprocal institutions in this epistle.

There are a number of exceedingly important deductions to be made from Paul's handling of the slave problem in the NT. Two of these are:

(1) True Christianity does not consist of any kind of attack upon social institutions, even so vicious and deplorable a system as that of slavery. Christ and the apostles were not revolutionaries in the modern sense of that word. See article, "Christ and the State" in CR. There were practical reasons for Paul's words here, as noted by McGarvey (see CC, 1 Corinthians 7:20-21); but over and beyond the practical need of refraining from an assault upon society, it was inherently *unchristian* to do so. It is as leaven and not as dynamite that the religion of Christ works. See more on this in CC.

(2) Ancient slavery no longer exists in the civilized part of the world, but there still exists the relationship between employers and employees; and Nielson was correct in suggesting that these

---

[44]William Barclay, *op. cit.,* p. 161.

words of Paul are applicable to that relationship, no less than to ancient slavery. "The master must give a fair and just wage, and the laborer must give a fair and full day's labor."[45] If an ancient slave was commanded to work vigorously and enthusiastically, how much more is it mandatory for every employee to give his best to the job?

"Eye-service . . . men-pleasers . . ." This is a reference to working only when the master is observing. The employee who is careful to appear busy when the boss is looking is guilty of the same attitude here condemned.

Verse 23, *Whatsoever ye do, work heartily, as unto the Lord, and not unto men.*

God has his own way of rewarding honorable and faithful work, regardless of the failure of human authorities to do so; and the difference is brought out in the very next verse.

Verse 24, *Knowing that from the Lord ye shall receive the recompense of the inheritance: ye serve the Lord Christ.*

As Barry pointed out, "The only peculiarity in this passage (as compared with the parallel in Ephesians) regards the strong emphasis on 'the reward of the inheritance'."[46] The inheritance is exactly the thing which no slave could receive; only a son could be an heir of God (Gal. 4:7). Thus the slave on earth is recognized as a son in heaven.

Verse 25, *For he that doeth wrong shall receive again for the wrong that he hath done: and there is no respect of persons.*

Some understand this as a warning to slaves not to do wrong; but since the admonition stands as another reason, along with the one in verse 24, directed to the proper motivation of the slave, it is understood here as a reference to God's judgment of slave-masters if they do wrong. "No respect of persons" favors this view; because it is not likely that the hope of a slave to avoid punishment could be based on any supposed "respect of persons." On the other hand, masters might think that because of their position God might overlook their sins.

Perhaps it is wrong to restrict the meaning of "he that doeth wrong" to either class. Will not God judge and punish all wrong-

---

[45]John B. Nielson, *op. cit.,* p. 420.
[46]Alfred Barry, *op. cit.,* p. 115.

doers whomsoever? Commentators have long struggled with this question, arriving at different conclusions, thus:

> This has reference solely to the master of the slave (Ridderbos).
> This refers to the slave (Lenski).
> It seems best to suppose that both are included (Lightfoot).[47]

Peake summarized such opinions thus:

> To include both is highly questionable, not only because a double reference is on principle to be avoided in exegesis, but because the connexion implies that only one side of the relationship is being dealt with. It is commonly thought that the verse is an encouragement to the slave, based on the assurance that the master who ill treats him will receive his recompense in due course.[48]

The reliance of the Christian, in whatever state of life, upon the eternal justice of God's universe is the great stablizer of the human heart. Without this reliance, life becomes an idiot's dream where injustice, misery, caprice, chance and luck are supreme. On the other hand, one who learns to trust in the assurance Paul here extended to the slaves of the ancient Roman Empire, perhaps the most unfortunate class ever to live on earth, — one who learns to trust that assurance has already won rest for his soul. No matter what inequalities, no matter what injustice, no matter how much unfairness, partiality and wickedness may torture one's earthly existence, the eternal reward is absolutely sure. God will make all things right. Now men may view this as "pie in the sky" if they wish, but it is surely better than any five-year plan advocated by Marx. Without the divine assurance in view here, there can be no true stability of heart, no genuine serenity of the soul, in fact, no real sanity on earth!

SLANDER AND GOSSIP

Singled out by the apostle in verse 8 for one of his apostolical prohibitions was the vice of slander, or "shameful speaking" as our translators have rendered the word, the same being a vice which is universally detested. Something of the pioneer attitude toward this sin is apparent in a story told with reference to the famed Cowboy Evangelist B. B. (Cowboy) Crimm of San

---

[47]William Hendriksen, *op. cit.,* p. 175.
[48]A. S. Peake, *op. cit.,* p. 543.

Augustine and East Texas. Crimm (1886-1950) preached extensively in East Texas and Oklahoma in the first half of the current century and became famous for the sensational and outlandish things said in the pulpit.

One night, in a meeting attended by more than a thousand people, a woman came forward saying,

"Oh, Brother Crimm, I have come to lay my tongue on the altar." The woman was a noted gossip in that community.

Crimm replied:

"I'm sorry, Ma'am, our altar is only eight feet long, but go ahead and put whatever part of it you are able to get on it!"

GOSSIP TOWN

Have you ever heard of Gossip Town
    On the shores of Falsehood Bay,
Where old Dame Rumor in rustling gown
    Is going the livelong day?

The principal street is called 'They Say.'
    'I've Heard' is the public well;
And the breezes that blow from Falsehood Bay
    Are laden with 'Don't you tell.'

Just back of the park in 'Slander's Row';
    'Twas there that Good Name died,
Pierced by a shaft from Jealousy's bow
    In the hands of Envious Pride.

It isn't far to Gossip Town
    For the people who want to go;
The Idleness Train will take you down
    In just an hour or so.

But the people who go to Gossip Town
    All reap of the seed they sow;
And this you will find as they have found
    If ever you chance to go.

— Anon.

CHAPTER 4

The epistle moves quickly to its conclusion in these 18 verses. First, there is the conclusion of the instruction on reciprocal relationships (1), followed by a brief paragraph on prayer and Christian conduct (2-6); next, Paul mentions affairs pertaining to himself and his imprisonment (7-9); then comes the paragraph regarding greetings from and greetings to various persons (10-17); and finally there stands the apostolical autograph, salutation and benediction (18).

Verse 1, *Masters, render unto your servants that which is just and equal; knowing that ye also have a master in heaven.*

Paul had just concluded (3:22-25) a far longer instruction on the duties of slaves, an emphasis which was probably due to the fact of Onesimus, along with both the letter to Colossians and Philemon, being returned to his master in Colossae. The success of both Paul's letters, as well as the successful reestablishment of Onesimus in his former home, is strongly indicated by the historical preservation of these two sacred letters.

Paul did not here dwell very long on the duties of masters, because at the same time he was sending Philemon a personal letter devoted to reconciling the situation with his erstwhile runaway slave, now returned. Nielson stated that "To give their slaves that which is just and equal is really advice to the master to free his slaves."[1] It may be doubted, however, that either Paul or Philemon understood those words in exactly that sense. To have established a rule of freeing all slaves who became Christians would have precipitated a rush of thousands of slaves into the church, resulting in the degeneration of the whole Christian religion into a political party dedicated to social change; and such a thing as *that*, true Christianity never was, or never could be.

Despite this, however, these very letters planted the seeds of love, kindness and justice in men's hearts, leading eventually to the total destruction of the whole institution of slavery.

---

[1]John B. Nielson, *Colossians in Beacon Bible Commentary*, Vol. IX (Kansas City: Beacon Hill Press, 1965), p. 421.

"Just and equal . . ." "The substantive here translated *equal* has the sense either of *equity* or *equality*."[2] Some have therefore believed it should be rendered "equality" in this place; but Peake indicated that even if translated "equality," it would not have the same meaning of the equality conferred by emancipation, giving the true meaning as, "The master should regulate the treatment of his slave, not by caprice, but by equity."[3]

Verse 2, *Continue steadfastly in prayer, watching therein with thanksgiving.*

"Continue in prayer . . ." The meaning here is that the Christian should never stop praying, and not that his prayers should be interminable. Importunity in prayer was taught by Christ in two of his most beautiful parables, namely, those of the friend at midnight, and of the unjust judge (Luke 11:5ff; 18:1ff).

"Watching thereunto . . ." Findlay assures us that the meaning of "watching" here is that of "wakefulness," affirming that,

> To be awake is to be alive in the fullest sense, to have all the powers of perception and action in readiness. The activity of the soul in prayer is to be both energetic and incessant.[4]

"With thanksgiving . . ." Paul, more than any other, stressed the need of thankfulness "in all things." See further comment on this above, under Philippians 4:6.

Verse 3, *Withal praying for us also, that God may open unto us a door for the word, to speak the mystery of Christ, for which I am also in bonds.*

"Praying for us . . ." Much as Paul prayed for others, he himself felt the need of the supporting prayers of brethren in Christ.

"That God may open . . ." As Nielson reminded us, "This reminds us that even though the spread of the gospel is under divine direction (Acts 16:7), it is also subject to satanic hindrances (1 Thess. 2:18)."[5]

"The mystery of Christ . . ." See other Pauline references to "the mystery" (Eph. 1:9; 3:3, 9; Col. 1:26, 27; 1 Tim. 3:9, 16, etc.).

---

[2]Alfred Barry, *Ellicott's Commentary on the Whole Bible,* Vol. III, *Philippians* (Grand Rapids: Zondervan Publishing House, 1959), p. 116.

[3]A. S. Peake, *Expositor's Greek Testament* (Grand Rapids: Wm. B. Eerdmans Publishing Company, 1967), pp. 543, 544.

[4]G. G. Findlay, *Colossians in Pulpit Commentary*, Vol. 19 (Grand Rapids: Wm. B. Eerdmans Publishing Company, 1950), p. 209.

[5]John B. Nielson, *op. cit.,* p. 422.

"For which I also am in bonds . . ." One of the salient features of the mystery stressed so often by Paul was that of God's purpose of inclusion of the Gentiles in one body with the Jews as children of God; and specifically, it was for that very conviction that Israel hated Paul and created the mob scene which led directly to his imprisonment (Acts 22:2ff).

Verse 4, *That I may make it manifest, as I ought to speak.*

Paul was deeply concerned that his speech should always be effective in making known the mystery of Christ; and, if a preacher of Paul's eloquence and power solicited prayers regarding the manner of his speaking, how much more should every preacher in all ages be mightily concerned about "how" he ought to speak? While dwelling upon this thought, it occurred to the great apostle that the manner of every Christian's speaking "to those without" is also a matter of the most urgent concern; and, in keeping with that consideration, he added the next two verses.

Verses 5-6, *Walk in wisdom toward them that are without, redeeming the time. Let your speech be always with grace, seasoned with salt, that ye may know how ye ought to answer each one.*

"Them that are without . . ." The reference here is "to non-Christians, those without the church."[6]

"Redeeming the time . . ." is somewhat of an idiomatic expression, meaning "buying up the opportunities," "taking advantage of all occasions for doing good," etc. Here again, in this passage, is encountered the startling likeness and subtle differences in this passage and the parallel in Ephesians 5:15. As Barry said:

There the "strictness" and "wisdom" are to guard against excess or recklessness within; here the "wisdom" is to watch against external dangers and make full use of external opportunities.[7]

"Speech . . . with grace . . ." Some think this means divine grace, but Peake is confident that the Greek text denies this, affirming that the meaning is "speech that is pleasant, marked by sweetness and courtesy, that their conversation may impress favorably the heathen."[8]

---

[6]A. S. Peake, *op. cit.,* p. 544.
[7]Alfred Barry, *op. cit.,* p. 116.
[8]A. S. Peake, *op. cit.,* p. 544.

"Seasoned with salt . . ." Despite the fact of most commentators denying it, there is perhaps included here some reference to the judicious use of humor, or wit, in the Christian's speech. Among the Greek classical writers, "*Salt* expressed the wit with which conversation was flavored";[9] and this student has encountered no compelling reason why the same meaning should not be understood here.

"How ye ought to answer . . ." The admonition here is most similar to that given by the apostle Peter who commanded:

> Sanctify in your hearts Christ as Lord: being ready always to give an answer to every man that asketh you a reason concerning the hope that is in you, yet with meekness and fear (1 Peter 3:15).

Verses 7-8, *All my affairs shall Tychicus make known unto you, the beloved brother and faithful minister and fellow-servant of the Lord: whom I have sent unto you for this very purpose, that ye may know our state, and that he may comfort your hearts.*

"All my affairs . . ." Here, through verse 9, Paul added some very personal words, explaining how the messengers with whom he was sending the epistle would be able to fill in all details regarding how things were going with Paul and to comfort the Christians at Colossae.

"Tychicus . . ." The high praise for this companion of Paul justifies a little further attention to this beloved NT character, thus:

TYCHICUS

Tychicus was an Asian, perhaps an Ephesian, who went with Paul to Jerusalem with the collection (Acts 22:4 ff; 1 Cor. 16:1-4), and was possibly one of those appointed by the various churches to convey the money to the Christians in Jerusalem. He carried the epistle to the Colossians and that of the Ephesians to their destinations, and if, as is often thought, Ephesians was a circular letter, he carried it to other churches as well.[10] Lockyear also pointed out that "Tychicus also had a mission to fulfill in Crete

---

[9]*Ibid.*, p. 545.
[10]*The New Bible Dictionary* (Grand Rapids: Wm. B. Eerdmans Publishing Company, 1962), p. 1302.

(2 Tim. 4:12; Titus 3:12)."[11] Paul spoke of this brother in the very highest terms of praise and appreciation.

"Whom I have sent unto you . . ." "This is epistolary aorist,"[12] meaning that at the time when the Colossians would be reading this, it would be true that Paul had already sent him; thus, the actual meaning of this clause is that "I am sending Tychicus unto you."

Verse 9, *Together with Onesimus, the faithful and beloved brother, who is one of you. They shall make known unto you all things that are done here.*

"Onesimus . . ." This man was the slave of Philemon. He had gone AWOL from his master Philemon's home in Colossae, but some circumstance had thrown him into association with Paul in Rome, where he became a Christian. It comes to view here that Paul was sending him back, but with a marvelous new status. Now, he is:

"The faithful and beloved brother . . ." Furthermore, he enjoys an equal status with Tychicus, both of whom are commissioned to tell the Colossians all of the news regarding the apostle. For further teaching of the NT regarding Onesimus and Philemon, see Paul's letter, *Philemon.* As Peake said, "Paul's word here that Onesimus 'is one of you' enables us to infer that Colossae was the home of Philemon."[13]

Verses 10-11, *Aristarchus my fellow-prisoner saluteth you, and Mark, the cousin of Barnabas (touching whom ye received commandments; if he come unto you, receive him), and Jesus that is called Justus, who are of the circumcision: these only are my fellow-workers unto the kingdom of God, men that have been a comfort unto me.*

"Aristarchus my fellow-prisoner . . ."

ARISTARCHUS

This man, a Jew of Thessalonica, is first mentioned in the NT in Acts 19:22, where it is reported that, along with Gaius, he was dragged into the theater at Ephesus. When the riot was over and

---

[11]Herbert Lockyear, *All the Men of the Bible* (Grand Rapids: Zondervan Publishing House, 1958), p. 332.
[12]A. S. Peake, *op. cit.,* p. 545.
[13]*Ibid.*

Paul left Ephesus, Aristarchus went with him (Acts 20:4), appearing again as one of the committee in charge of Paul's collection for Jerusalem. Presumably, Aristarchus remained with Paul continuously; because, after the two-year imprisonment at Caesarea, Luke reveals that Aristarchus was "with us" in the long voyage to Rome (Acts 27:2). The deduction has been made, "Whether voluntarily or involuntarily, Aristarchus really shared Paul's imprisonment,"[14] a deduction that is suggested, or demanded, by the words "my fellow-prisoner." He is mentioned again in Philemon 24.

"Mark, the cousin of Barnabas . . ." For a somewhat extensive discussion of this character, author of the gospel that bears his name, and a principal in the dispute between Paul and Barnabas (Acts 15:37ff) due to his having deserted the missionaries in Perga of Pamphylia (Acts 13:3), please see (in this series of commentaries) the introduction to the Gospel of Mark.

"Touching whom ye received commandments . . ." This, according to Dummelow, refers "to commands they must have received at an earlier time."[15]

"If he come unto you, receive him . . ." As Lipscomb said, "This recommendation is somewhat of a church letter,"[16] showing that the old breach between Paul and Barnabas regarding Mark had long been healed, Mark appearing in this passage as a definite comfort to the apostle.

"Jesus that is called Justus . . ." It is very curious that so soon after our Lord's ascension there should have been a Christian named "Jesus" whose surname, "The Just One," is one of the titles of our Lord.[17] Nothing at all is known of this man, except what is stated here, there being no other reference to him in the NT.

"Who are of the circumcision . . ." This means that Aristarchus, Mark and Justus were "of the circumcision," that is, Jews, with the undeniable implication that Luke, mentioned a moment later in verse 14, was not a Jew, the same being the strongest evidence that Luke was a Gentile.

---

[14]Alfred Barry, *op. cit.*, p. 116.

[15]J. R. Dummelow, *Commentary on the Holy Bible* (New York: The Macmillan Company, 1937), p. 984.

[16]David Lipscomb, *A Commentary on the NT Epistles*, Vol. IV (Nashville: The Gospel Advocate Company, 1964), p. 312.

[17]Alfred Barry, *op. cit.*, p. 117.

"These only are my fellow-workers unto the kingdom of God
. . ." The words "are my" are italicized, meaning they are not
in the Greek; so it is proper to read this sentence without them.
"These only . . ." There is infinite pathos in these tragic words.
Paul's concern for the salvation of many Jews in the great
Roman capital had been frustrated and defeated. Of all the Jews
in Rome, "these three . . .!" As Hendriksen expressed it:

It must not escape our attention that the apostle's statement
with reference to these three men as the *only* Jewish-Christian
fellow-workers who had been a comfort to him implies deep disappointment with other people of his own race.[18]

"Men that have been a comfort unto me . . ." We are indebted
to Findlay for the amazing fact that the word here rendered
"comfort" comes from a Greek word meaning "soothing relief,"
the same Greek word chosen as the name of a widely used medi-
cine for children, "paregoric."[19] This is a medical term, and one
of those "peculiar" words found only in this epistle. Perhaps Paul
had been extending his vocabulary somewhat through his association with the "beloved physician, Luke."

Verses 12-13, *Epaphras, who is one of you, a servant of Christ
Jesus, saluteth you, always striving for you in his prayers, that
ye may stand perfect and fully assured in all the will of God. For
I bear him witness that he hath much labor for you, and for them
in Laodicea, and for them in Hierapolis.*

EPAPHRAS

All of the comment on these two verses, almost, pertains to
this distinguished worker who appears to have been a preacher
and teacher for all three towns in the tri-cities mentioned here.
Lockyear called him "a giant of prayer," saying that:

It is in his prayer ministry that Epaphras is conspicuous; he
knew how to lay all before the Lord . . . that the saints might
be perfect and complete. He "strove earnestly in his prayers."
He brought to Paul in Rome the report on conditions at Colossae that prompted this epistle. Like Epaphras, all of us should
be concerned with the spiritual welfare of others.[20]

---

[18]William Hendriksen, *Colossians and Philemon* (Grand Rapids: Baker Book
House, 1964), p. 190.
[19]G. G. Findlay, *Colossians in Pulpit Commentary*, Vol. 19 (Grand Rapids: Wm.
B. Eerdmans Publishing Company, 1950), p. 213.
[20]Herbert Lockyear, *op. cit.*, p. 110.

Certainly, there must have been something extraordinary about the prayers of Epaphras, because, as Guthrie noted, "The word used is *agonize*, which may be some kind of allusion to the prayers of our Lord in Gethsemane. That kind of praying ranks a man high in spiritual nature."[21]

"Servant of Christ . . ." Paul must have meant something very high and holy by this.

> It is a title used by James and Jude (in their epistles), as well as by Paul himself, but given by him only to Timothy (Phil. 1:1), and to Epaphras here.[22]

Verse 14, *Luke, beloved physician, and Demas salute you.*

For a brief biographical sketch of Luke, see CL Introduction. Only in this place in the NT is Luke referred to as a doctor, or physician. Nevertheless, the undeniably medical cast of his vocabulary is a total corroboration of what is stated here.

"And Demas salute you . . ." As Peake said:

> Demas' being mentioned here without commendation is commonly explained as due to a foreboding of Paul that he would turn out badly, suggested by the reference in 2 Timothy 4:10.[23]

Harry Emerson Fosdick preached a sermon on the three NT references to Demas, calling them three points that enable the plotting of the parabola of Demas' life. The sermon is interesting enough but founded on a misconception. Philemon and Colossians were written at the same time and carried by the same messenger; and in the letter to Philemon, Demas is mentioned as a "fellow-laborer," and even before Luke! Still, it is tragic truth that Demas fell from whatever eminence he enjoyed in these passages, the reference in Timothy revealing that he forsook the apostle, "having loved this present age." There is an old tradition to the effect that he became the owner of a brothel in Dalmatia.

Verse 15, *Salute the brethren that are in Laodicea, and Nymphas, and the church that is in their house.*

This reveals, of course, the existence of a church in Laodicea; but it is not known why Paul singled out Nymphas, the name

---

[21]Donald Guthrie, *New Bible Commentary, Revised* (Grand Rapids: Wm. B. Eerdmans Publishing Company, 1970), p. 1153.

[22]Alfred Barry, *op. cit.,* p. 117.

[23]A. S. Peake, *op. cit.,* p. 546.

of whom might be feminine (Greek margin in RV), thus justifying the rendition in some translations as "the church that is in her house." It is not wise to make anything out of this because, as Peake said, "The word may be either masculine or feminine."[24]

Verse 16, *And when this epistle hath been read among you, cause that it be read also in the church of the Laodiceans; and that ye also read the epistle from Laodicea.*

One of the important revelations from this is that Paul's letters, and presumably those of other sacred writers, were widely circulated and passed among the churches; nor can there be any confidence that any more than a fraction of Paul's letters were preserved. It was God's providence alone that preserved for us the writings which make up the sacred canon of the NT; and we should believe that the overruling of an all-wise providence entered into which letters were lost and which were preserved.

Dummelow and others believe that the epistle to the Laodiceans mentioned here might be our canonical epistle to the Ephesians. It is impossible to settle the question, but these two comments are added because they represent learned and consecrated opinion on it.

Wiess argues that (the epistle to the Laodiceans) cannot be the epistle to the Ephesians, for that was sent at the same time as this, and therefore Paul could not have sent salutations to Laodicea in this epistle. But this is natural if Ephesians was a circular letter (and the absence of salutations is difficult to explain otherwise), and if this letter was to be passed on to Laodicea.[25]

The epistle to the Laodiceans is perhaps our Epistle to the Ephesians.[26]

Verse 17, *And say to Archippus, Take heed to the ministry which thou hast received in the Lord, that thou fulfil it.*

Archippus may have been at Laodicea, but, as Peake said, "probably not," as otherwise he would have been mentioned along with Nymphas in verse 15.[27]

---

[24]*Ibid.*
[25]*Ibid.*, p. 547.
[26]J. R. Dummelow, *op. cit.*, p. 984.
[27]A. S. Peake, *op. cit.*, p. 547.

This verse establishes the principle that a church is responsible for admonishing and encouraging ministers, nor is it evident here that Archippus was in any way standing in special need of encouragement.

From Philemon 2, where Archippus is mentioned along with Philemon and Apphia in a manner suggesting that he may have been their son, it is also concluded that Archippus had had previous service together with Paul.[28]

Several interesting speculations have risen around the name of Archippus, but they are of no value.

Verse 18, *The salutation of me Paul with mine own hand. Remember my bonds. Grace be with you.*

This apostolical autograph and salutation served to authenticate the epistle. From this, Macknight reasoned that Paul knew the Colossians and that they knew him and his handwriting, else this autograph would not have meant anything.

The brevity of this salutation was probably due to the fact that with a chain on his hand Paul might have found the writing of even these few words a painful and difficult task. The placement of the utterance, "Remember my bonds," seems even to suggest this thought. How much the Gentiles owe to the patient zeal and labors of this beloved apostle can never be known until the redeemed of all ages shall greet him around the throne of God and of the Lamb.

---

[28]*The New Bible Dictionary, op. cit.,* p. 77.

BIBLIOGRAPHY . . . COLOSSIANS

The following authors and sources were quoted in the text of the commentary on Colossians:

Ashby, Ernest G., *A NT Commentary* (Grand Rapids: Zondervan Publishing House, 1969).

Barclay, William, *The Letters to the Philippians, Colossians and Thessalonians* (Philadelphia: The Westminster Press, 1975).

Barry, Alfred, *Ellicott's Commentary on the Whole Bible,* Vol. III, *Philippians* (Grand Rapids: Zondervan Publishing House, 1959).

Bruce, F. F., *Answers to Questions* (Grand Rapids: Zondervan Publishing House, 1972).

Buttrick, George A., *Christ and Man's Dilemma* (New York: Abingdon-Cokesbury, 1950).

Clarke, Adam, *Commentary on the Whole Bible,* Vol. VI (London: Carlton and Porter, 1829).

Dummelow, J. R., *Commentary on the Holy Bible* (New York: The Macmillan Company, 1937).

Durant, Will and Ariel, *Rousseau and Revolution* (New York: Simon and Schuster, 1967).

Ellis, E. Earle, *Wycliffe NT Commentary* (Chicago: Moody Press, 1971).

Emphatic Diaglott (Brooklyn: Watchtower Bible and Tract Society).

Findlay, G. G., *Colossians in Pulpit Commentary*, Vol. 19 (Grand Rapids: Wm. B. Eerdmans Publishing Company, 1950).

Guthrie, Donald, *New Bible Commentary, Revised* (Grand Rapids: Wm. B. Eerdmans Publishing Company, 1970).

Hayes, D. A., *Paul and His Epistles* (Grand Rapids: Baker Book House, 1959, Reprint from Copyright Edition, 1915).

Hendriksen, William, *Colossians and Philemon* (Grand Rapids: Baker Book House, 1964).

Hodge, Charles B., *Angels* (Nashville: The Christian Teacher, Inc. 1977).

ISBE (Chicago: The Howard-Severance Company, 1915).

Johnston, Arthur, "A Pragmatic Concern for Church Growth," in *Christianity Today*, January 7, 1977, p. 14 (382).

Lipscomb, David, *A Commentary on the NT Epistles*, Volume IV (Nashville: The Gospel Advocate Company, 1964).

Lloyd Jones, D. Martyn, *The Basis of Christian Unity* (Grand Rapids: Wm. B. Eerdmans Publishing Company, 1962).

Lockyear, Herbert, *All the Men of the Bible* (Grand Rapids: Zondervan Publishing House, 1958).

Macknight, James, *Apostolical Epistles with Commentary*, Volume III (Grand Rapids: Baker Book House, 1969).

Marshall, Alfred, *The Interlinear Greek-English Testament, the Nestle Greek Text* (Grand Rapids: Zondervan Publishing House, 1958).

Morgan, G. Campbell, *An Exposition of the Whole Bible* (Old Tappan, N. J.: Fleming H. Revell Company, 1959).

New Bible Dictionary (Grand Rapids: Wm. B. Eerdmans Publishing Company, 1962).

Nielson, John B., *Colossians in Beacon Bible Commentary*, Vol. IX (Kansas City: Beacon Hill Press, 1965).

Pack, Frank, "The Gospel of John in the Twentieth Century" in *The Restoration Quarterly*, Vol. 7, No. 4 (Abilene: The Restoration Quarterly Corporation, 1963).

Peake, A. S., *Expositor's Greek Testament* (Grand Rapids: Wm. B. Eerdmans Publishing Company, 1967).

Pink, Arthur W., *Gleanings From Paul* (Chicago: Moody Press, 1967).

Wagner, C. Peter, "A Pragmatic Concern for Church Growth," in *Christianity Today*, January 7, 1977, p. 14 (382).

Wallace, Foy E., Jr., *A Review of the New Versions* (Fort Worth: The Foy E. Wallace, Jr., Publications, 1973).

Wesley, John, *Explanatory Notes Upon the New Testament* (Napierville, Ill.: Alec. R. Allenson, Inc., Reprint, 1950).

INDEX

*Articles marked by aterisk are treated more fully.